Praise for

A House in the Sky

"There isn't a superfluous word in the book. I gobbled it as I do thrillers."

—Christie Blatchford, *The Vancouver Sun*

"A poetic, profound, and thrilling exploration of one woman's misadventure set against the backdrop of global terrorism . . . Elegant and evocative . . . The traveling years are a joyous riot of golden empanadas, swishing palm trees, the purpling light of a Caribbean dusk, and the growing confidence of a young woman starting to see herself as a citizen of the world."

—Rebecca Johnson, *Vogue*

"A searingly unsentimental account . . . Ultimately, it is compassion—for her naïve younger self, for her kidnappers—that becomes the key to Lindhout's survival."

—Holly Morris, *O, the Oprah Magazine*

"Exquisitely told . . . Much more than a gonzo adventure tale gone awry—it's a young woman's harrowing coming-of-age story and an extraordinary narrative of forgiveness and spiritual triumph. . . . There's no self-pity or grandiosity in these pages. In the cleanest prose, Lindhout and Corbett allow events both horrific and absurd . . . to unfold on their own. Lindhout's resilience transforms the story from a litany of horrors into a humbling encounter with the human spirit."

—Eliza Griswold, *The New York Times Book Review*

"Riveting."

—*Good Housekeeping*

"A great book . . . The lesson [Amanda Lindhout] taught me and others who know this remarkable young woman is: What matters is not how you got there, but what you do once you've arrived."

—Robert Draper, *ELLE*

"[A] harrowing, beautifully written memoir . . . The wide-eyed optimism and unflappable determination that led [Amanda Lindhout] to danger also kept her alive. . . . A brave, compassionate, and inspiring triumph."

—Korina Lopez, *USA Today* (4-star review)

"An elegant and wrenching memoir."

—*The Daily Beast*

"[Amanda Lindhout's] story matters because she has been an extraordinary survivor from a young age, and not just a survivor, but one whose humanity has been deepened while facing down the worst human behavior."

—Jerry Large, *The Seattle Times*

"Vivid . . . Page-turning drama . . . *A House in the Sky* is about spiritual survival—the title refers to the mental exercise that enables Lindhout to endure her darkest days, building a dwelling, room by room, floor by floor. That imagined refuge, like this clear-eyed book, is a testament to human endurance."

—Tom Beer, *Newsday*

"Keenly observed and sprinkled with arresting details, *A House in the Sky* is more than one woman's heartbreaking tale of captivity. The book sheds light on a conflict area not often painted with nuance. It dares to explore the outer reaches of human empathy. A stunning, haunting, and redemptive read, Lindhout's story is one that stays with you long after the book has been closed."

—Grace Bello, *The Christian Science Monitor*

"A crushing tale, beautifully told."

—Jeff Inglis, *The Portland Phoenix*

"A beautiful memoir . . . A probing look at the nature of survival."

—PureWow.com

"Lindhout is a woman of extraordinary courage and spirit. And this is an extraordinary book. . . . Absorbing, triumphant, and inspiring . . . Unputdownable."

—Linda Wolfe, FaboverFifty.com

"Lindhout's empathy, in the face of those who have done and still do her so wrong, is what is most striking about *A House in the Sky*."

—Caitlin Van Horn, Bustle.com

"A testament to resilience and character in the face of unimaginable trauma . . . Haunting, brave, inspiring, and empowering."

—Ruby Cutolo, *Publishers Weekly*

"Humble, brave, and naïvely optimistic, Lindhout possesses the elements of a classically compelling hero."

—Annie Atherton, *Shelf Awareness*

"[A] remarkably keen-eyed, honest, and radiant memoir . . . Moving and informative reading for everyone."

—Barbara Hoffert, *Library Journal*

"Writing with immediacy and urgency, Lindhout and Corbett recount the horrific ordeal in crisp, frank, evocative prose. But what readers will walk away with is an admiration for Lindhout's deep reserves of courage under unimaginable circumstances."

—Kristine Huntley, *Booklist* (starred review)

"A vivid, gut-wrenching, beautifully written, memorable book."

—*Kirkus Reviews* (starred review)

"A well-honed, harrowing account."

—*Publishers Weekly* (starred review)

A *NEW YORK TIMES* NOTABLE BOOK

NAMED A BEST BOOK OF 2013 BY *VOGUE, KIRKUS REVIEWS, PUBLISHERS WEEKLY, SLATE, THE GLOBE AND MAIL,* AND *OUTSIDE*

"*A House in the Sky* is the riveting story, exquisitely told, of a young woman's passionate quest to create an uncommonly large life, against all odds. With stunning honesty and clarity, Lindhout and Corbett have made certain of two things: No reader will ever forget this book—or be able to put it down."
—SUSAN CASEY, author of *THE WAVE: IN PURSUIT OF THE ROGUES, FREAKS, AND GIANTS OF THE OCEAN*

"This is one of the most powerfully written books I have ever read. Harrowing, hopeful, graceful, redeeming, and true, it tells a story of inhumanity and humanity that somehow feels deeply ancient and completely modern. It is beautiful, devastating, and heroic—both a shout of defiance and a humbling call to prayer." —ELIZABETH GILBERT, author of *EAT, PRAY, LOVE* and *THE SIGNATURE OF ALL THINGS*

"*A House in the Sky* is a stunning story of strength and survival. It is sometimes brutal, but always beautiful, as Amanda Lindhout discovers that in a fight for her life, her most powerful weapons are hope and compassion."
—JEANNETTE WALLS, author of *THE GLASS CASTLE* and *THE SILVER STAR*

"An amazing, mesmerizing tale that shows international terrorism at a shockingly personal level. Lindhout's strength of character shines through on every page." —JANE MAYER, author of *THE DARK SIDE*

"A vivid and moving account of how Amanda kept alive the inner light and the spirit of forgiveness even as she found herself in the heart of darkness."
—ECKHART TOLLE, author of *THE POWER OF NOW* and *A NEW EARTH*

"If you have ever wondered how extraordinary people overcome physical and mental anguish, you must read *A House in the Sky*. Amanda Lindhout's riveting account of strength and survival will inspire and leave a lasting impression."
—JARED COHEN, author of *THE NEW DIGITAL AGE*

A House in the Sky

A MEMOIR

Amanda Lindhout
and
Sara Corbett

SCRIBNER

New York London Toronto Sydney New Delhi

Scribner
A Division of Simon & Schuster, Inc.
1230 Avenue of the Americas
New York, NY 10020

This is a work of nonfiction. We have drawn from a number of sources—
including journals, correspondences, media reports, interviews, and
transcripts of recorded conversations and other communications with
investigators, negotiators, and kidnappers. It is also a memoir, which is to say
that the story reflects Amanda's recollections and interpretations of events.
Dialogue has been re-created from memory. We have changed the names
of a few characters and compressed timelines or omitted details in places.
The English passages from the Koran are taken from translations by H.M.
Shakir and Abdullah Ali Yusuf. Any dollar amounts are referring
to U.S. currency, unless otherwise noted.

First Scribner paperback edition June 2014

SCRIBNER and design are registered trademarks of The Gale Group, Inc.,
used under license by Simon & Schuster, Inc., the publisher of this work.

For information about special discounts for bulk purchases,
please contact Simon & Schuster Special Sales at 1-866-506-1949 or
business@simonandschuster.com.

The Simon & Schuster Speakers Bureau can bring authors to your live event.
For more information or to book an event, contact the Simon & Schuster
Speakers Bureau at 1-866-248-3049 or visit our website at
www.simonspeakers.com.

Manufactured in the United States of America

11   12   13   14   15   16   17   18   19   20

Library of Congress Control Number: 2013016015

ISBN 978-1-4516-4560-6
ISBN 978-1-4516-4561-3 (pbk)
ISBN 978-1-4516-4562-0 (ebook)

For my mom and two dads

&

Katherine Porterfield

In the burned house I am eating breakfast.
You understand: there is no house, there is no breakfast,
yet here I am.

—*Margaret Atwood,*
  from "Morning in the Burned House"

A House in the Sky

Prologue

We named the houses they put us in. We stayed in some for months at a time; other places, it was a few days or a few hours. There was the Bomb-Making House, then the Electric House. After that came the Escape House, a squat concrete building where we'd sometimes hear gunfire outside our windows and sometimes a mother singing nearby to her child, her voice low and sweet. After we escaped the Escape House, we were moved, somewhat frantically, to the Tacky House, into a bedroom with a flowery bedspread and a wooden dresser that held hair sprays and gels laid out in perfect rows, a place where, it was clear from the sound of the angry, put-upon woman jabbering in the kitchen, we were not supposed to be.

When they took us from house to house, it was anxiously and silently and usually in the quietest hours of night. Riding in the backseat of a Suzuki station wagon, we sped over paved roads and swerved onto soft sandy tracks through the desert, past lonely-looking acacia trees and dark villages, never knowing where we were. We passed mosques and night markets strung with lights and men leading camels and groups of boisterous boys, some of them holding machine guns, clustered around bonfires along the side of the road. If anyone had tried to see us, we wouldn't have registered: We'd been made to wear scarves wrapped around our heads, cloaking our faces the same way our captors cloaked theirs—making it impossible to know who or what any of us were.

The houses they picked for us were mostly deserted buildings in tucked-away villages, where all of us—Nigel, me, plus the eight young men and one middle-aged captain who guarded us—would remain invisible. All of these places were set behind locked gates and surrounded by high walls made of concrete or corrugated metal. When we arrived at a new house, the captain fumbled with his set of keys. The boys, as we called them, rushed in with their guns and found rooms to shut us inside. Then they staked out their places to rest, to pray, to pee, to eat. Sometimes they went outside and wrestled with one another in the yard.

There was Hassam, who was one of the market boys, and Jamal, who doused himself in cologne and mooned over the girl he planned to marry, and Abdullah, who just wanted to blow himself up. There was Yusuf and Yahya and Young Mohammed. There was Adam, who made calls to my mother in Canada, scaring her with his threats, and Old Mohammed, who handled the money, whom we nicknamed Donald Trump. There was the man we called Skids, who drove me out into the desert one night and watched impassively as another man held a serrated knife to my throat. And finally, there was Romeo, who'd been accepted into graduate school in New York City but first was trying to make me his wife.

Five times a day, we all folded ourselves over the floor to pray, each holding on to some secret ideal, some vision of paradise that seemed beyond our reach. I wondered sometimes whether it would have been easier if Nigel and I had not been in love once, if instead we'd been two strangers on a job. I knew the house he lived in, the bed he'd slept in, the face of his sister, his friends back home. I had a sense of what he longed for, which made me feel everything doubly.

When the gunfire and grenade blasts between warring militias around us grew too thunderous, too close by, the boys loaded us back into the station wagon, made a few phone calls, and found another house.

Some houses held ghost remnants of whatever family had occupied them—a child's toy left in a corner, an old cooking pot, a rolled-up musty carpet. There was the Dark House, where the most terrible things happened, and the Bush House, which seemed to be way out in the countryside, and the Positive House, almost like a mansion, where just briefly things felt like they were getting better.

At one point, we were moved to a second-floor apartment in the heart of a southern city, where we could hear cars honking and the muezzins calling people to prayer. We could smell goat meat roasting on a street vendor's spit. We listened to women chattering as they came and went from the shop right below us. Nigel, who had become bearded and gaunt, could look out the window of his room and see a sliver of the Indian Ocean, a faraway ribbon of aquamarine. The water's proximity, like that of the shoppers and the cars, both comforted and taunted. If we somehow managed to get away, it was unclear whether we'd find any help or simply get kidnapped all over again by someone who saw us the same way our captors did—not just as enemies but enemies worth money.

We were part of a desperate, wheedling multinational transaction. We were part of a holy war. We were part of a larger problem. I made promises to myself about what I'd do if I got out. *Take Mom on a trip. Do something good for other people. Make apologies. Find love.*

We were close and also out of reach, thicketed away from the world. It was here, finally, that I started to believe this story would be one I'd never get to tell, that I would become an erasure, an eddy in a river pulled suddenly flat. I began to feel certain that, hidden inside Somalia, inside this unknowable and stricken place, we would never be found.

1

My World

When I was a girl, I trusted what I knew about the world. It wasn't ugly or dangerous. It was strange and absorbing and so pretty that you'd want to frame it. It came to me in photographs and under gold covers, in a pile of magazines, back-issue *National Geographics* bought for twenty-five cents apiece at a thrift store down the road. I kept them stacked on a nightstand next to my bunk bed. I reached for them when I needed them, when the apartment where we lived got too noisy. The world arrived in waves and flashes, as a silvery tide sweeping over a promenade in Havana or the glinting snowfields of Annapurna. The world was a tribe of pygmy archers in the Congo and the green geometry of Kyoto's tea gardens. It was a yellow-sailed catamaran in a choppy Arctic Sea.

I was nine years old and living in a town called Sylvan Lake. The lake was six miles long, a Pleistocene gash in the vast brown prairie of Alberta, Canada—well north of the Calgary skyline, well south of the oil rigs scattered around Edmonton, a hundred or so miles east of the Rocky Mountains, a solidly in-between place. In July and August, tourists came to float on the lake's calm surface and toss fishing lines from the docks of their cottages. There was a downtown marina next to a red-topped lighthouse and a small amusement park where vacationers bought tickets to ride down a giant spiraling water slide or run through a play maze made from brightly painted plywood. All summer long, the sounds of laughing kids and the buzz of motorboats floated through town.

We were new to Sylvan Lake. My mother, having split from my father a few years earlier, had moved my two brothers and me there from Red Deer, the small city where we'd always lived, fifteen minutes down the road. Russell, her boyfriend, had come with us, and so had his younger brother, Stevie. His uncles and cousins and other brothers and second cousins often dropped in on us for payday parties and ended up in our apartment for days, camped out in our living room. I remember their faces hoisted in sleep, their slim brown arms hanging from the sides of our chairs. My mother referred to Russell and his family as "Native," but around town, people called them Indians.

Our building was a white stucco fourplex with a pitched roof and dark wood balconies. The recessed windows of our basement apartment were small and narrow and let in next to no daylight. A green municipal Dumpster sat in the gravel parking lot outside. My mother, a fan of all things bright and tropical, hung a teal shower curtain in our new bathroom and draped a brightly patterned spread over her bed. Out in the living room, she parked her exercise bike next to our old brown sofa.

People always looked at my mother. She was tall and lean, with dramatic cheekbones and dark permed hair she kept fluffed up around the ears. She had limpid brown eyes that suggested a kind of vulnerability, the possibility that she might be easily talked in and out of things. Five days a week, she put on a white dress with red piping and drove back to Red Deer to work a cash register at Food City. She returned with whole flats of generic-brand juice boxes, bought with her discount, which we stashed in the freezer and ate after school using spoons. Sometimes she came home with a plastic tray of bakery leftovers, Danishes and éclairs gone sticky after a day under glass. Other times she brought video rentals that we never returned.

Russell worked only sometimes, signing on for a few weeks or occasionally a few months of contract work as a tree trimmer with an arbor company called High Tree, cutting limbs away from power lines along narrow roads. He was thin as a whippet and wore his dark hair long around his shoulders and feathered on the sides. When he wasn't working, he dressed in thin silk shirts in colors like purple and turquoise. Etched on his left forearm was a homemade tattoo, a blue-lined bird with broad wings, an eagle or a phoenix, maybe. Its outline had begun to fade, the bird's details washed into a pale blur on his skin, like something belonging on the body of a much older man. He was twenty-one to my mother's thirty-two.

We'd known Russell for years before he became my mom's boy-friend, since the time he was thirteen, our families knit together by some combination of bad luck and Christian largesse. He had been raised on the Sunchild First Nation Reserve. His father had disap-peared early; his mother died in a car accident. My mother's parents, who lived about an hour's drive from the reserve, ran a Pentecostal summer camp for First Nations kids and ended up taking in Russell and his four younger brothers as foster children. My mother and her siblings were long gone at that point, and the Native kids offered my grandparents a kind of second go-round at parenting.

My grandfather was a welder, and my grandmother sold Tupper-ware—more Tupperware, in fact, than anybody in central Alberta, with regional sales records and a company minivan to prove it. For many years, they hauled Russell and the other boys along to church and prodded them through high school. They drove them to track meets and hockey games and to weaving classes at the Native Friend-ship Center.

When the boys brawled, my grandmother sighed and told them to go on outside and get it all out. She forgave them when they stole money from her. She forgave them when they cussed her out. The boys grew into teenagers and then into young men. One made it to college; the rest ended up somewhere between the reserve and Red Deer. What nobody banked on, what Jesus himself might never have foretold, is that somewhere along the way, coming home to her par-ents' farmhouse for visits and holiday meals, my mother—with her three little kids and imploding marriage to my father—would fall for Russell.

*

She called him Russ. She did his laundry for him. She liked to kiss him in public. Every so often he bought her roses. Early in my childhood, I'd thought of him like a sideways cousin, but now Russell—having moved directly from my grandparents' house into mine—was something different, a hybrid of kid and grown-up, of kin and interloper. He did kickboxing moves in our living room and ate potato chips on the couch. Once in a while, he bought stuffed animals for me and my little brother, Nathaniel.

"A funny little family" was what my grandmother called us. My older brother, Mark, put it differently. "A fucked-up little family" was what he said.

I'd been to the Sunchild reserve a couple of times to visit Russell's relatives, always over the protests of my father, who thought the place was dangerous but no longer had any say. Russell's cousins lived in low-slung tract homes built along dirt roads. During our visits we ate bannock, a sweet, chewy fry bread, and ran around with kids who never went to school and drank cans of beer out of brown paper bags. Every house, as I remember it, had walls cratered with fist holes. I recognized the shape because Russell sometimes did it to the drywall at our house.

My mother's life with Russell might have been viewed as a kind of screw-you directed at all the white kids she went to high school with in Red Deer, most of whom still lived around town. My mother had left home at sixteen and gotten pregnant with Mark at twenty. Russell gave her an odd new cachet. He was young and mildly handsome and came from a place that people considered wild and unusual, if also dirty and poor. My mother wore beaded earrings and drove around town in a little white hatchback car, a feathered dream catcher fluttering from her rearview mirror.

There was also the fact that my father, her early-twenties sweetheart, the man holding her babies in the delivery room photos, had recently announced that he was gay. A fit young guy with a big smile and a neatly trimmed beard named Perry had moved into my dad's house. When we visited, Perry took us swimming at the rec-center pool, while my father, who had never cooked in his life, made us bachelor-style dinners. He rolled lunch-meat ham into cylinders speared with toothpicks and surrounded them with a few slices of cheese and some celery, adding a piece of bread on the side. He laid our plates on the table—all four food groups duly represented.

My father had begun building his new life. He hosted dinner parties with Perry and enrolled in college to become a rehab practitioner and assist mentally disabled people. My mother, meanwhile, worked on her own resurrection. She read self-help books and watched *Oprah* on her off days.

In the evenings, Russell poured rye whiskey from a big bottle into a tall plastic cup. My mother sat with her feet resting in his lap on our sofa in front of the TV. More than once, he pointed at the screen, at the moment's hot cop or tidy-haired young dad. He'd say, "You think that guy's good-looking, don't you, Lori?"

It was a flicker we all recognized.

"I'll bet," Russell would continue, his eyes on my mother, "you wish you were with someone like that."

A pause. The TV man's face would seem, in an instant, to melt and reshape itself into something more aggressive and leering.

"Right, Lori? That's what you're thinking?"

My mother responded gently. He'd broken some of her bones before. He'd hurt her badly enough to keep her in the hospital for days. As the rest of us stared hard at the television and the air in the room grew electric, she'd reach for Russell's arm and squeeze.

"No, baby," she'd say, "Not even a little."

*

Mark was thirteen and on the brink of a lot of things. He had a scraggly mullet, blue eyes, and a washed-out denim jacket he rarely removed. He was a solitary kid, given to roaming, the devoted owner of a sling-shot made of hard plastic. Nathaniel, meanwhile, was six years old and had a cyst on his lower-right eyelid, giving him a baleful look. My mom and Russell doted on him, calling him "Bud" and "Little Buddy." At night he slept in the bunk beneath mine, clutching a stuffed rabbit.

It was Mark I followed around, trailing him like a dinghy behind a boat.

"Check this out," he said one day after school as we stood in front of the green Dumpster outside our apartment building. This was several weeks after we'd moved to Sylvan Lake, a warm afternoon in early fall. I was in fourth grade, and Mark had just started middle school. Neither one of us had many friends. The kids in our new town instantly had read us as poor and uninteresting. Mark planted his hands on the lip of the bin and boosted himself upward, slinging a leg over and dropping inside. Seconds later, his head bobbed up again, his face flushed, his hand wrapped around an empty Labatt bottle. He waved it at me. "Come on, Amanda," he said, "there's money in here."

Our Dumpster served as an openmouthed repository for the whole neighborhood's trash, collected by a town truck every Wednesday. It became my brother's version of a country club swimming pool. The interior, even on the crispest days of October, was soft and damp like an old leaf pile, smelling like sour milk. The two of us slid between mounded bags, their skins greased by leaked liquids and loose trash, our voices ringing tightly off the walls. Mark ripped into sealed garbage bags, pitching cans and bottles out onto the grassy strip in front of the apartment, rooting up lost quarters, old lipsticks, pill bottles, and Magic Markers, most of which he stuffed into his back pocket or tossed in my direction. Once he held up a fuzzy pink sweater, just my size, and gave a little shrug of outrage. "Jeez, what's wrong with people?"

We loaded the empties into plastic shopping bags and, smelling like old food and malt, carried them to the bottle depot in town. Twenty cans equaled a dollar. One Food City bag usually held fifteen cans. One bag x fifteen cans x five cents = seventy-five cents. A dollar-fifty for two bags; three bucks for four. And then the sum total divided in two—half for Mark and half for me. No fourth-grade math lesson could compare. The real money lay in what we called sixties or sixty-pounders—terms gleaned from Russell—the hefty sixty-ounce liquor bottles that got us an easy two dollars from the bottle depot man. These were our gold.

Over time, Mark and I began to travel, a few blocks north and south of our street, over to the cul-de-sacs where single families lived in bungalows instead of apartments, visiting five or six garbage bins regularly. Better real estate, for the most part, meant better garbage.

You'd be surprised at what people throw away, even poor people. You might find a doll with a missing arm or a perfectly good videotape of a perfectly good movie. I remember finding an emptied-out wallet, brown leather, with a delicate gold clasp. Another time I found a pristine white handkerchief with smiling cartoon characters embroidered on it. I kept them both for years, the handkerchief folded up neatly inside the wallet, a reminder of all that was pretty and still to be found.

*

I almost always blew my bottle money in one place, at a thrift store by the lake. The store was underlit and arranged like a rabbit's warren, selling old clothes, porcelain knickknacks, and the literary detritus of summertime tourists—fat Tom Clancy thrillers and everything by Danielle Steel. The *National Geographics* were kept on a shelf in a far corner, their yellow spines facing outward and neatly aligned.

Lured by what I saw on the covers, I took home whatever I could afford. I snapped up the mossy temples at Angkor and skeletons brushed free of volcano ash on Vesuvius. When the magazine asked ARE THE SWISS FORESTS IN PERIL?, I was pretty sure I needed to know. This is not to say that I didn't, in equal measure, rummage through the Archie comics sold new in a different corner of the store, studying Veronica's clingy clothes and Betty's pert ponytail, the sultry millionaire's daughter versus the sweet, earnest go-getter. Theirs was a language I was only just starting to understand.

I kept the Archies in a drawer but put the *National Geographics* on a table in my bedroom. By Thanksgiving, I had accumulated probably two dozen. Sometimes I would fan them out like I'd seen on the coffee tables at the homes of some of the fancier kids from my old school. My uncle Tony—my father's brother and the richest person in our family—was a subscriber. At night, in my top bunk in Sylvan Lake, I went through the magazines page by page, feeling awe for what they suggested about the world. There were Hungarian cowboys and Austrian nuns and Parisian women spraying their hair before going out for the night. In China, a nomad woman churned yak yogurt into yak butter. In Jordan, Palestinian kids lived in tents the color of potatoes. And somewhere in the Balkan Mountains, there was a bear who danced with a gypsy.

The world sucked the dankness out of the carpet in our basement apartment. It de-iced the walkway outside, lifted the lead out of the sky over the plains. When at school a girl named Erica called across the hallway that I was a dirty kid, I shrugged like it didn't matter. My plan was to move on, far away from my school and street and from girls named Erica.

*

One evening just before I started fifth grade, Carrie Crowfoot and I went walking around town. Carrie was a beautiful Blackfoot girl, a year older than I was, and one of my few friends. She had long black hair and almond-shaped eyes and eyelashes that stuck straight out. She was related to Russell somehow and had moved with her mother and brothers from the Sunchild reservation to Sylvan Lake. She lived in a house a few doors down from the thrift store and never went to school.

At ten years old and with no money, Carrie still managed to work a brassy kind of glamour. She sassed the patronizing shopkeeper who sold us five-cent pieces of gum and bragged to me about various kids she'd beaten up when she lived at the reserve. When she came to my house, she never looked twice at our ratty furniture or Russell's stray cousins lounging boozily in our chairs. I liked that she'd pronounced the dinner of crushed dry Ichiban noodles I'd served her "amazing," that she'd recently enlightened me about what a blow job was.

We wandered along Lakeshore Drive, heading toward the amusement park. A cool wind had picked up over the water. It was early September. Tourist season was pretty well over. The sidewalks were empty; a few cars hurtled past. Carrie complained often about how dull Sylvan Lake was, saying she wanted to move back to Sunchild. She was jealous that I got to stay with my dad in Red Deer on weekends. I might have told her it was nothing to envy, but the truth was, I counted down the days. My father's house had plush carpeting and thick walls. I had my own bedroom with a brown ruffled bedspread and a cassette player with New Kids on the Block tapes and a collection of new paperbacks, entire sets of the Baby-sitters Club and Sweet Valley Twins series. I said nothing about any of it to Carrie.

At the marina, rows of powerboats floated in their dock slips. The amusement park lay dormant. The fiberglass waterslide stood drained for the night, skeletal against a pink sky.

"You ever seen what's in there?" Carrie asked, kicking a foot against a shuttered ticket kiosk. I shook my head.

Before long, she'd found a way to pull herself up from the top of a garbage bin to straddle the high wall of the Crazy Maze, which zigzagged like a cattle fence around one edge of the park. Abruptly, she disappeared behind it. I heard sneakers hit pavement and then a laugh.

I was a frightened kid, almost all the time. I was scared of the dark and I was scared of strangers and I was scared of breaking bones and also of going to doctors. I was scared of the police, who sometimes came to our house when Russell's crew got noisy in our living room. I was afraid of heights. I was afraid of making decisions. I didn't like dogs. I was supremely afraid of being laughed at. And in this moment, I had a sure feeling about what would happen next: Not wanting Carrie to make fun of me, I would scramble up the wall, get dizzy, fall down, break some bones. The police would come—strangers, all of them—and they would bring their dogs. Naturally, this would all happen in the dark, and then I'd have to go to the doctor.

Which was why I almost turned on my heel and ran. But the way home was dark now, too, and I could hear Carrie calling from inside the maze. I heaved myself up onto the garbage can and boosted myself to the top of the wall. Then I jumped.

As I landed, Carrie took off running. In the dim light, her hair seemed to glint blue. The interior walls had been painted with bright amateur renderings of clowns and cowboys and silly monsters—whatever would amp up the joy and light terror of summertime kids running free.

Carrie Crowfoot and I would be friends only another six months. Her mother would move the family back to the Sunchild reserve sometime that spring. Before that, I'd start to get more interested in the kids I met at school and in school itself, getting chosen for an enrichment group for advanced students. Carrie would remain an outlier, uninterested in school and seemingly not required to go. A few years later, when I was finishing middle school, I would hear from my grandmother that Carrie had a baby. I wouldn't know much more about how things went for her, because eventually, my family would purge all of them from our lives, Russell and Carrie and most everyone we knew during this time.

Inside the maze that night, though, she was impossible not to follow. We were fast, corkscrewing around corners, screeching to a stop when we hit an abrupt dead end. When I think back on it, I imagine we might have squealed as we ran, heady with the moment's disorientation. The truth is, we were serious and silent but for the sound of our thwupping sneakers and the rustling of our jackets. Carrie's hair floated behind her as she charged ahead, sidewinding through the alleyways, caught up in the split-second decision-making about which way to go next. Finally, though, we allowed ourselves to relax and feel giddy, forgetting that it was dark and we were trespassing, forgetting everything that scared or haunted us, lost in the playland we'd never before seen.

*

High Tree, Russell's arbor company, was having a big holiday party at a restaurant in Red Deer. My mother had been thinking about it for weeks. After her shifts at the supermarket, she'd go looking at dresses in the Parkland Mall, flicking through the sale racks. At home, she announced she was on a diet.

We put up a Christmas tree in one corner of the living room, a raggedy pine that my mother had picked from the parking lot sale at Food City. She went to the Christmas Bureau in Red Deer, signed a paper attesting to the fact she had three kids and made seven dollars per hour, and picked up gifts for free. They'd been collected and wrapped by volunteers, embellished with colorful curling ribbons. I knew which two of the presents beneath the tree were for me because they were both labeled GIRL, AGE 9.

A few days before the party, my mother got a new perm. She'd found a dress, which was hanging in her bedroom closet. It was black and shimmery, and already I'd spent a lot of time touching it.

Now it was Friday night. Russell had showered and put on a pair of black pants and a collared shirt buttoned neatly up to his neck. He poured some rye and sat on the couch, pulling a squirming Nathaniel onto his lap. Stevie, Russell's seventeen-year-old brother, was babysitting. We were waiting for my mother.

The blow dryer hummed from the bedroom. Mark and Stevie clicked cassettes in and out of our boom box, fast-forwarding to the songs they liked, while I did math homework on the floor. Nathaniel, holding his stuffed bear, had drifted over to the TV and pressed his face close against the screen, trying to hear over the noise.

Russell poured a second drink and then a third. He hooked one leg over the other and began good-naturedly to sing: "Loooori LoooooRIIII."

When she walked down the hallway, we all turned to look. Her black dress was short in the front and long in the back, cascading in a pile of ruffles that brushed the floor. Her thin legs flashed as she walked. She wore new shoes.

As if following a script, Russell rose to his feet. My mother's cheeks looked flushed, her eyes bright, her lips painted red. Her pale skin looked creamy against the black dress, which was so tight and shiny it seemed shellacked onto her body. We kids held our breath, waiting to hear what Russell would say.

"Fucking A" was what he said. "You look awesome."

True enough, my mother looked like a movie star. She smiled and held out a hand to Russell. She kissed our cheeks to say good night. We were cheering, as I remember it, literally shouting with excitement about the grand time they would have.

Russell put down his cup, found my mother's dress-up coat, an ill-fitting mink number she'd inherited from my great-grandmother, and then he whirled her out the door.

*

That night we watched movies from our video collection. We watched *Three Men and a Baby* and then the new *Batman*. I made popcorn in the popper and passed it out in bowls. Somewhere in Red Deer, my mother was dancing with Russell. I imagined a ballroom scene with glittering pendant lights and wide-mouthed glasses of champagne. I dipped in and out of sleep until it was late and I woke up with a jolt. The TV screen was dark, the apartment silent. I pulled Nathaniel from his spot on the floor and guided him to the room we shared, nudging his sleepy body onto the bed. I climbed up into my bunk, a trace of holiday sparkle still lit in my head, and went to sleep for real.

There was a surreal quality to what came next. There always was, if only because these things—when they happened—almost always happened in the middle of the night. My mother's shouting would tunnel into my sleeping mind, gradually stripping the scenery out of my dreams, until there was no more clinging to unconsciousness and I was fully awake.

Something crashed in our living room. There was a shriek. Then a grunt. I knew these sounds. She was fighting back. Sometimes I'd see scratch marks on his neck in the morning. The words were streaming out of Russell, high-pitched, hysterical, something about cutting out her eyeballs, something about blood on the floor, so much of it that nobody would know who she was. "You cunt," I heard him say. Then a big thud, also recognizable: the sofa being flipped.

I heard her run from the kitchen to the living room and down the hallway. I heard her panting outside our door before he caught her and threw her against it. I could hear him breathing, too, both of them seeming to gasp. In the bunk below me, Nathaniel started to cry.

"Are you scared?" I whispered, staring at the dark ceiling.

It was an unfair question. He was six years old.

We had tried before to stop it. We had dashed out of our rooms and started yelling only to have the two of them, their eyes dark and wild, run to their bedroom and slam the door. If my mother wanted our help, she wouldn't show it. Sometimes I'd hear Stevie in the hallway saying "Hey, cool it" to his brother. "C'mon, Russ." But he, too, grew meek in the face of their fury. Eventually, a neighbor would call the police.

A few times my mother had gone to the women's shelter in Red Deer. She'd made promises to my grandmother and grandfather that she'd leave Russell, but before long they'd be back together. At the women's shelter, there were shiny linoleum floors, lots of kids, and heaps of good toys to play with. I remember my father looking crushed when he came there to pick us up.

The holiday-party fight wound down pretty quickly, my mother and Russell stalking back into each other's arms, my popcorn strewn across the living room, the couch frame broken, a fresh hole in the wall. I knew how these things went. The next morning Russell would weep and apologize to all of us. For a few weeks, he'd be repentant. He'd sit in the living room with his head down and talk to God, looping through the language we knew from our grandparents' church—*dear Lord our savior in your name blessed be your son please save me from Satan yours is the way and in Jesus Christ thank you and amen.* In the evenings, he'd make a big show of going to A.A. meetings. My mother, for those weeks, would have more power. She'd order Russell around, telling him to pick up his clothes and run the vacuum cleaner.

But the needle on some unseen inner gauge would start to quiver and creep back toward red. The contrition would slip away. My mother would blithely go out one afternoon to get her hair cut and come back, by Russell's estimation, late. He'd be waiting on the couch, his voice a flipped blade. "What took you so long, Lori?" And "Who were you meeting, all whored up like that?" I'd watch my mother blanch as it dawned on her that the jig was up, that before long—maybe tonight, maybe three weeks from now—he'd go nuts on her again.

I couldn't profess to understand it. I never would. I just tried to move past it. By the time the lights were off and all the bodies had settled, I was gone, launched. My mind swept from beneath the bedsheets, up the stairs, and far away, out over the silky deserts and foaming seawaters of my *National Geographic* collection, through forests full of green-eyed night creatures and temples high on hills. I was picturing orchids, urchins, manatees, chimps. I saw Saudi girls on a swing set and cells bubbling under a microscope, each one its own waiting miracle. I saw pandas, lemurs, loons. I saw Sistine angels and Masai warriors. My world, I was pretty certain, was elsewhere.

2

The Drink

When I was nineteen years old, I moved to Calgary. For any kid from central Alberta, Calgary is the big city, a beacon of possibility, ringed by busy highways, its glass towers rising up from the plains like a forest. It's also an oil town, a boom-and-bust headquarters for stock traders and energy executives working to extract and sell the huge reserves of oil sitting beneath the soil. I arrived in 2000, when times were especially good. Oil prices were on their way to doubling, and before the year was out, they'd triple. Calgary was flush with wealth and new construction. Glitzy restaurants and shops were opening at a frenetic pace.

My boyfriend, Jamie, moved with me. He was a year older than I was and had grown up on a farm south of Red Deer. We'd been dating for about eight months. Dark-eyed and brown-haired, he was handsome in a Johnny Depp way, with narrow shoulders and strong hands that helped make him an excellent carpenter. The two of us liked to trawl through thrift shops, putting together outfits we thought of as edgy. Jamie dressed in cowboy shirts with cloudy mother of pearl buttons. I wore anything that was sequined, along with the biggest earrings I could find. He could play any instrument, from the harmonica to the bongos to the violin. He strummed love songs on his guitar. He worked construction jobs when he needed money but otherwise spent whole days drawing pictures or playing music. I was totally smitten.

I thought that in Calgary, Jamie could record a CD, maybe get some sort of deal. For me, too, the city would be a new platform—though for what, I wasn't exactly sure. We found a one-bedroom apartment in a dirty downtown high-rise. Our bed was a mattress on the floor. Jamie painted the bathroom walls yellow. I hung pictures and set houseplants on the windowsill. My life felt instantly urban, adult. But the city was expensive. I got a job at a clothing store, a different branch of a national chain I'd worked for in Red Deer during high school. Jamie found work washing dishes at Joey Tomato's, a trendy restaurant in the Eau Claire Market, while looking for a job in construction. Between the two of us, we could barely make rent.

On a bitingly cold afternoon not long after we arrived in Calgary, I put on my winter coat, a vintage brown leather jacket with an enormous fur collar, and went out walking with a pile of résumés tucked in a manila folder. I wanted to try my luck as a waitress. I had never worked in a restaurant, but when I saw the girls who worked at Joey Tomato's, I was both jealous and awed. They glided around in high heels. Jamie told me they made a lot of money.

*

The first place I walked into, mostly because I was cold, was a nice-looking Japanese restaurant with a glossy black sushi bar and hanging lamps styled to look like lanterns. It was the post-lunch lull. Techno music pulsed quietly over the stereo, while a couple of strikingly beautiful waitresses set tables for dinner. In a far corner, about six men were having some sort of lunch meeting, papers spread out in front of them on the table. I sheepishly handed my résumé to the willowy Japanese hostess and stammered a few words about having just moved to the city. I thanked her and turned toward the door. It was clear I would not fit in.

"Hey, wait a second," somebody called.

One of the men from the corner table followed me to the entry. He looked to be in his late twenties, with dark hair, chiseled cheekbones and a sharp jawline, not unlike a comic-book superhero. "Are you looking for a job?" he said.

"Uh, yes," I said.

"Done," he said. "You got one."

This was Rob Swiderski, the manager of a nightclub called the Drink, located a few blocks from the Japanese place and owned by the same restaurateur. He was offering me a job as a cocktail waitress.

I felt vaguely conflicted. I was flattered. I had heard about the Drink from friends in Red Deer who sometimes came to the city to party and had said it was trendy and expensive. But I wanted to serve meals, not drinks. Somehow that seemed more respectable.

When I said no, Rob laughed. "If you're looking for a job, you're looking to make money, right?" he said. "Just give it one week—one shift, even. If you hate it, you quit."

I walked back into the cold, having agreed to show up the following evening. He had never even asked for my résumé.

*

The Drink took up the corner of a city block, with a restaurant and five separate bar areas, offering forty different kinds of martinis. Chandeliers hung, lit like constellations, from the high ceilings. A hardwood dance floor occupied the center of the space, with a short stairway leading to a velvet-roped VIP area. About twenty waitresses worked at a time, all of them pretty. They wore high heels and designer dresses and carried little round drink trays coated with rubber to avoid spills. A few introduced themselves, but most hardly looked in my direction. I'd soon learn that new girls came and went all the time, some too flaky to keep drink orders straight and others not managing to pull off the right image for the club, which—as Rob reminded everyone at weekly staff meetings—was "classy-sexy." If you looked cheap, you got sent home.

Under Rob's management, the Drink had become the hottest club in town—hosting an after-work happy hour for corporate Calgary, which morphed into a more glamorous and freewheeling late-night pickup scene. This was where NHL players gathered after their games, touring rock stars came after their concerts, and oil barons showed off their money. On weekends, the line to get in was five people wide and stretched around the block.

Working from ten P.M. to two A.M. on my first night, wearing high heels, dangly gold earrings, and the nicest dress I owned, I was given a tray and some instructions on taking drink orders and printing up bills. I was then assigned a quiet section at the back of the club. For the next few hours, I shuttled chilled martinis and tumblers of rye between the bar and four or five tables, where the customers—most of them businessmen—thanked me politely and handed me their credit cards. At the end of the evening, a waitress named Kate showed me how to use the computer to cash out my tips. I had made fifty dollars in four hours, in addition to my wages, and was overjoyed. Though Jamie, who had no interest in bars, had been angry when I told him I'd taken a job as a cocktail waitress, I thought now he might at least recognize that money was money, and this money was good.

"How'd you do?" said Kate, looking over my shoulder. Catching sight of my total, she winced. "Oh," she said, "that's brutal."

I had no idea what she was talking about.

*

By my standards, I got rich working at the Drink. Showing up for my second shift, I was again handed a dead section at the back of the club, but before long, a group of garrulous stockbrokers showed up and started ordering three-hundred-dollar bottles of Cristal. I went home a few hours later with five hundred dollars in tips. Over the course of several months, I worked my way up to handling bigger sections and busier nights. I bought nice shoes and elegant cocktail dresses. On a good night I could make seven hundred dollars. On an exceptional night, I made a thousand. I kept rolls of cash stuffed in a jar in our kitchen cupboard, until there was so much of it that I started stashing the bills in the freezer. When another waitress told me that freezers were the first place burglars looked for cash, I got better about making deposits in the bank.

I became friends with the other girls, learning how to deftly dodge drunken propositions, how to milk a good tip with some attentiveness and a smile. I was drawn to Priscilla, a legendary high earner at the Drink, who used her tip money to take long, exotic vacations. When I first met her, she'd just returned from Thailand, which seemed to me unimaginably far away. Priscilla showed me how to maintain a pack of regulars—good customers who would be sure to buy their drinks from you—by giving them VIP treatment, plopping "reserved" signs on their tables, and serving their drinks not in the usual plastic cups but in heavy glasses fetched from the bar upstairs.

For a while, I just enjoyed the freedom that came with having money. I quit my retail job. Jamie had been picking up day labor on the city's many construction sites, though more and more, he stayed home to be with me during my off hours. Sometimes he played a short set at an open-mike night in a café near our apartment, always to enthusiastic applause.

He'd stopped minding that I worked at the Drink, but he never came to see me there. I'd cook us an early dinner and spend almost an hour in front of the mirror while Jamie sat in the other room reading a book or playing music. For me, getting ready for work was like getting ready to go onstage. I had a closet full of black dresses, a bucket's worth of makeup. The whole act was easy by now: You put on your highest heels, trussed up your hair, painted your eyes and lips. Your job was not to be pretty but to be stunning, and in a way that made men want you and other women jealous, even if was just flirty playacting. Some of the girls at the Drink had cashed in a few months' worth of tips and gotten boob jobs as a professional investment. I opted for an old waitress trick I'd learned in the changing room at the Drink, layering a push-up bra over a padded bra, which made me feel a little like I had an iron bar strapped to my chest but nonetheless served its purpose.

After work, while some of my friends from the Drink were going to after-hours clubs, I was heading home to curl myself around Jamie as he slept. He and I had settled into a quiet routine. In the mornings we went for meandering walks along the Bow River. When he wasn't working, we went out for expensive lunches. I found a used bookstore called the Wee Book Inn near our apartment and bought piles of paperbacks to read. For the first time in my life, I had real money in the bank, enough to fund a year at university. I'd just turned nineteen. I knew I was supposed to want a stack of textbooks and some sort of high-minded career plan, but that didn't interest me. I figured going to university would only put me in lockstep with all the twentysomethings in suits who coursed down our street in the mornings headed to their skyscraper jobs, resurfacing at the Drink ten hours later, acting as if they were fifty years old, flopping into the leather barrel chairs, saying, "Jesus, what a shitty day. I'll have a gimlet, straight up."

*

Back at home, my mother's latest boyfriend—a cruel man named Eddie with whom she'd been living in Red Deer—had been sent to jail for racketeering. My brothers and I agreed this was a relief. She had dumped Russell back when I was twelve, but still she gravitated toward unstable men. As a result, I'd spent most of my high school years living with my dad and Perry in a house they'd bought in Sylvan Lake. Mark had moved in with friends, while Nathaniel had stayed on with our mother. We all loved her, but we worried anytime a man got close.

My mother was in her early forties, her dark hair not yet showing any gray. After Eddie left, I took the bus from Calgary every few weeks to have dinner with her. She'd moved into a sweet little house in Red Deer and found a good job with a Catholic social services agency as an aide in a group home for troubled teens. She'd been reading self-help books, trying to teach herself to meditate. She spoke about saving her money to travel. Her talk was filled with the language of fresh starts.

I used to joke with Jamie that my childhood seemed tailor-made for *The Jerry Springer Show*—not just an episode, more like a whole season. My mom had a thing for bad men. My dad was one of the few openly gay people in town. My grandparents prayed fervently to Jesus, speaking in tongues when the occasion called for it. My brothers struggled with drugs. I, too, had issues. I often starved myself to stay thin, obsessively counting calories. I cut my food into halves and quarters and then ate half of that. After going days without a real meal, I'd snap and binge, eating everything in sight before forcing myself to vomit. This, too, was right out of the dysfunctional-family handbook.

Still, we tried. The year Eddie was sent to jail, my father called my mother and tentatively invited her to come to Christmas. They'd softened toward each other, my parents, over years of forced communication about school schedules and which child needed new shoes. Also, Perry and my father were as settled and married-like as the next couple, more so than my mother had ever been with any of her men. Slowly, she'd come to appreciate this.

Christmas morning, Mom walked through Dad and Perry's door, with its tinseled wreath and velvety red bow, smiling at me and my brothers, apologizing all over the place that she hadn't been able to afford gifts. What she'd brought was a painstakingly written batch of letters, printed on pages of computer stationery with colorful Christmas lights around the borders. One for each of us in the room, including Dad and Perry. I opened my letter and read it slowly. In it, she described a few of her best memories, clear and happy moments like the two of us horsing around in front of the mirror in that basement apartment in Sylvan Lake, fluffing up our hair. She spelled out her love for me, and her hopes that I would always have good luck and great adventures. I don't know what she put in the other letters. All I know is that every one of us was silent and a little teary.

After that, we spent every Christmas together. We would never be a close family, exactly, but we loved one another in a certain fierce way.

3

Going Somewhere

J amie," I said, "let's go somewhere." We'd brought a blanket down
to the river one late-summer evening about nine months after
moving to Calgary. I was tired and antsy. I had been studying the travel
ads in the Sunday paper—the eight-hundred-dollar round-the-world
flights, the grainy pictures of palm trees in faraway places, the package
deals and flights to cities whose names I'd never heard.

Jamie was on his back, watching the summer clouds slide through
the sky. I admired the simple arc of his nose, the smoothness of his skin,
the honey brown of his eyes. He was imperturbable, a puzzle to me. His
ability to loiter in record stores and thrift shops, to pass time without
purpose or go weeks without working, sometimes made me impatient.

"Where do you want to go?" he said.

"Anywhere," I told him. "I mean it, anywhere. Let's just plan something, go somewhere."

Here was what I loved about Jamie: the slow-breaking smile, the
long-fingered hand that clamped affectionately onto my shoulder.
"Let's do it," he said. "Anywhere's good."

★

The next day, I was at the Wee Book Inn, digging through old issues of
National Geographic. Where I wanted to go, really, was Africa, but that
hardly felt like a beginner trip. The only place I'd ever been outside of
Canada was Disneyland as a kid, once with my dad and once with my

mom, after her divorce settlement came through. Jamie had never left Canada. I tugged out a thick plank of magazines, slid to the floor, and started shopping for a destination.

Jerusalem? Tibet? Berlin? The funny thing about *National Geographic* was that it told the same sort of elemental story every time—featuring whatever was lost or unexplored, mystical or wild. *You're here,* the magazine seemed to say, *and we're there.* It was not meant to be a taunt, more like a small flag planted on behalf of the stay-at-homers. Having the magazine was a gesture of respect for the world's outer limits, its predators and prey. *I see that it's all there,* it enabled you to say, *and now, thank you, I'll stay put.*

For me, it was also a provocation. There was a cover article on Bolivia and the Madidi, a small national park in the upper basin of the Amazon, where parrots flashed through mahogany trees. In another story, I found photos of white-mist waterfalls slicing into the forests of Paraguay. I unearthed an old issue I'd had as a kid, with a story about a slablike magical plateau somewhere in Venezuela called Roraima, covered in quartz crystals and drifting above the clouds. The names alone seemed delicious and made up. They ran through my mind like poetry as I walked home, erasing the blunt syllables of the place I lived, the places I came from. *Madidi. Venezuela. Paraguay.* The decision about where to go seemed straightforward. No city, no country, no coast in particular. Just a continent: South America.

*

There was a place called the Adventure Travel Company a few blocks from the Drink, where two women sat behind computers, encircled by a mini-coliseum of glossy resort brochures in racks. The cheapest plane tickets we could get from Calgary were to Caracas, the capital of Venezuela. It was now early September 2001. I reserved two seats for a trip in January, with return flights six months later, paid in cash.

It was done, happening. The trip became our organizing principle. This was how Jamie and I started our sentences: "When we go on our trip," or "When the trip gets closer . . ." At the secondhand bookstore, I bought a Lonely Planet guide to South America, thick as a Bible, five years old, and already thumbed-over. Jamie and I went through it page by page. We imagined ourselves pushing through tangled jungles, communing with the Quechua on our way to summiting snowy peaks beneath a blinding sun.

We read the guidebook's section on insects and snakes and flesh-eating flies that tunnel into your legs and pythons that dangle from trees, and we let that unsettle us. We read the section called "Dangers and Annoyances" that said we could be pickpocketed or mugged or conned into handing over all our money to an orphanage that wasn't really an orphanage. We read the warnings about malaria and flim-flam artists and highway bandits. We allowed our parents to heap on their concerns about car accidents and fatal fevers. We imagined the worst—or what, in our innocence, we thought of as the worst—because that seemed to be some necessary part of our preparation, owning up to the inherent gamble.

*

By the time Jamie and I left for South America on a frigid morning in January 2002, the world's dangers were more overtly on display. Thousands of people had died on September 11. There had been anthrax scares and false alarms and people talking on television about a jihadist underworld and an axis of evil. Just before Christmas, a terrorist had boarded a plane in Paris and tried unsuccessfully to ignite his shoe. In Pakistan a few weeks later, a *Wall Street Journal* reporter named Daniel Pearl set off to do an interview connected to the shoe bomber's financing. He was kidnapped and later beheaded. When it came to danger, the totally unreal had, in the span of a few months, become entirely feasible.

Despite it all, we were going. Our plan was to drift from Venezuela into Brazil and then to Paraguay. Sitting on the tarmac in Calgary as our plane was de-iced, I tried to push away any thoughts of death and disaster. South America was not the Middle East, I told myself. It was not America, even. We'd compressed and rolled and shoved our belongings until they were dense as bricks, making room for what we saw as necessities—extra bottles of mosquito spray and sunblock, laundry soap, antifungal spray for our shoes, plus a giant squeeze bottle of ketchup and the salt and pepper packages we'd been collecting from fast-food restaurants for months.

When I visited my grandmother before leaving, she donated a hefty jug of antibacterial gel and some Tupperware, all of which I improbably managed to fit into my pack. By way of goodbye, she offered a cheery and quick double disapproval of my travel plans and my everyday fondness for short skirts and high heels. "I hope you know you won't be able to go down there and wear those, you know, *model* clothes you like to wear," she said as I planted a kiss on her cheek.

From his recliner in their living room, with its old piano and Grandma Jean's collection of ceramic purple roses, my grandfather added, "I hope you know if you get yourself into trouble, we won't have any money to get you out."

I let this comment float right past.

4

A Small Truth Affirmed

Caracas late at night looked only a little like the jungle city I'd been imagining. Our cabdriver spoke English and pointed out landmarks. Most of the buildings were shuttered for the night. I could see big palm trees, their fronds pinwheeling heavily over the broad boulevards. The city looked sedate, leafy, exotic.

This might have been a moment to tuck myself under the crook of Jamie's arm or kiss his palm and say something about how alive I felt, having traversed this impossible-seeming curve of the earth with him in one day, beginning in the numbing cold of Canada and ending in the drippy heat of another hemisphere. But I didn't do any of that. It wasn't that sort of moment. Some part of me was scared by what we'd done.

The next morning, we woke in a three-star hotel room, which our travel agent had booked in advance and was more expensive than any other place we'd stay. I drew back the curtains and got my first glimpse of the waking city. A massive Pepsi billboard sat outside our window. There were skyscrapers in the distance and jets flying overhead. On the street several floors below, people sat in their cars, staring blankly ahead as they waited for the stoplight to turn. It was oddly, depressingly familiar. There were no donkey carts, no parrots, no panpipers or charming old women wearing ruffled blouses and lace on their heads. Only the air felt foreign—thick and a little mossy.

I pushed open the window and peered down. On the sidewalk, several brown-faced men in baseball caps were selling fruit out of wooden crates: piles of oranges, peaches, papayas, and several things I didn't recognize. "Jamie, come see this," I said.

Looking over my shoulder, he said, "Should we go buy some?" Jamie was always hungry.

I was remembering what the guidebook said about fruit and vegetables, how everything had to be scrubbed and peeled. I was afraid of bacteria at that point, the same way I was afraid of terrorists and bandits and being alone. I was planning to eat nothing but thoroughly cooked rice and beans all the way through South America, and to do a lot of hand-washing. Beyond that, we had our ketchup.

"Let's not," I said.

*

Here's a lesson we learned quickly: Your guidebook—especially when it is five years old—is at some point going to fail you. While the world's Hiltons and Sheratons, with their breakfast buffets and Friday-night poolside mariachi bands, will probably be there for eternity, places like the Hostel Hermano and the Posada Guamanchi, in the strata where rooms rent for eight dollars a night, come and go. The *doña* who once fixed morning *churros* with sliced mango and hot coffee for guests leaves for an indefinite visit with her grandchildren. The elderly man who runs an "immaculate and friendly" guesthouse near the bus station hands it off to his son, who worries less about the spiders and roaches and the creeping shower mold and focuses on making late-night passes at all the tanned lady backpackers who, without an update in the guidebook, have yet to be directed elsewhere.

In our first weeks in Venezuela, Jamie and I walked miles, strapped sweatily into our backpacks, looking for low-interest money changers and two-star posadas that had morphed abruptly into massage parlors or motorcycle repair shops. We waited at a roadside bus stop in the withering heat only to learn hours later, bickering and thoroughly sunburned, that the Tuesday-afternoon bus to Caripe was now a Friday-morning bus.

After a time, we figured out that the most accurate information could be milked from our fellow travelers, the Brits and Germans and Danes with their own tuberous luggage and varying tales of inconvenience and whimsy, which they were happy to narrate over rounds of cold beer. We swatted mosquitoes and traded bits of highly subjective data. Ana from Portugal knew a good place to get laundry done. An Aussie named Brad had just come back from a mind-blowing trip to Angel Falls and said that everyone should hire his guide.

Worrying became too much effort. When the bus didn't come or the ceiling fan didn't work, or when a Swedish girl talked us into joining her and nine other backpackers as they hitchhiked a nighttime ride with a sea captain bound for Trinidad and we ended up seasick and miserable on his treacherously seesawing boat deck, I realized, in the end, there wasn't much I could do about it. Travel was good for my anxious soul. Which is not to say that I relaxed completely. When we made land in Port of Spain, Trinidad, in the deep black of early morning, spattered in vomit and haunted by the ocean's violence, the port authorities handcuffed our boat captain right on the dock and marched the rest of us off to a detention center for not having visas. I did, in that moment, start to sob.

But being in motion made me easygoing in a way I hadn't felt before. I relaxed my stance on fruit-eating, for starters. The offerings were too rich and could be found on practically every corner. We ate meaty bananas and sweet green guavas. We pushed the Swiss Army knife into the thick rinds of fresh melon and used it to scoop the candy-like pulp out of yellow soursop fruit, landing it directly in our mouths. We'd also started to shed bulk and weight from our packs. We handed off our Tupperware to villagers, left Grandma Jean's jug of hand sanitizer in a filthy hostel, and gave away a pile of clothes.

Jamie's dark hair grew coppery and sun-streaked, his skin brown and sleek from days spent outside. I, too, felt tanned and lithe, as if I'd been born for warm air. The sun brought back the freckles I'd had as a kid. Jamie and I picked out the most captivating postcards we could find and sent them home with messages trumpeting the general magnificence of everything. On Margarita Island, off the north coast of Venezuela, we found wide, soft beaches and leggy palm trees that swished in the sea breeze. We pitched our yellow two-person tent in the backyard of a budget hotel for a week, striking a deal with the manager to use the bathrooms, paying under half the regular room rate. With the money we saved, we ate shark sandwiches and drank cheap rum at lunchtime.

We became friendly with the local girl at the front desk who collected our rent money every afternoon, stashed our passports in the hotel safe, and sold us bottles of water and golden empanadas filled with tangy cheese that she'd brought in a paper sack from her village. She was about twenty, like me. Peggy was her name. She had round cheeks and a shy smile and stuffed herself into low-cut tops and long skirts. She spoke a stunted but versatile English. Her village was about ten kilometers away. "Why don't you come there?" Peggy said one evening as I was trekking through the lobby with my toothbrush and contact lens case. "You can meet my family. We'll cook you food."

In retrospect, it was a small thing to do—taking a taxi to Peggy's town, meeting her vast family of *tíos* and *tías* and little barefoot brothers and cousins, allowing her to show us to a nearby beach, a five-minute walk along a brushy path, where we could pitch our tent for free. At the time, though, it felt large. The beach was a stunning half-moon of white sand rimmed by arching palm trees at the mouth of a sheltered cove. There were no signs of human trespass—no bottlecaps shipwrecked in the sand, no yachts drifting offshore. Peggy brought us a batch of doughy empanadas and sliced pineapple at dinnertime, and with the sky starting to go purple and the evening breeze lifting, she left us. Our isolation was freakish and exciting. Jamie and I waded around in the warm water, watching schools of small bluish fish flick through the shallows. If we'd zoomed upward and looked back down, we'd have been half recognizable to ourselves—a young woman, a young man, caught in a textbook paradise, aimless and happy and utterly alone.

It occurred to me that we were also unfindable, that without giving it a thought, we'd stepped off the travelers' grid. Peggy's village wasn't listed in the guidebook. We'd told no one where we were going. My joy dissolved quickly, my mind tracking through our inevitable disappearance. The police would find their way to the hotel we'd left and to our taxi driver. The taxi driver would lead them to the village. The villagers would point them to Peggy, and she would walk them to the beach. And there they'd discover us splayed and long-dead in the sand, our tent in weathered tatters, Jamie and I having been struck by lightning simultaneously, or drowned in the strong undertow and washed back ashore. Probably, though, it would be bandits, and the bandits would have been smart enough to march us off the beach before robbing us and killing us and burying our bodies where they'd never be found.

I fell asleep that night petrified and uncertain, clinging to Jamie's back as he dozed in the tent, bolting upright every time the wind luffed the trees or a frog urped from the woods. This, I supposed, was what a frontier felt like, a knifepoint between elation and terror.

We woke to the early sun blasting through our tent, the air inside steamy and suffocating. Jamie kissed my forehead.

We'd survived. Of course.

★

Something was unfolding for me, especially as one long bus ride led to a second and a third and we floated ever deeper into Venezuela, following a loose plan but not a schedule. The effect was narcotic. I watched the countryside stream by in tangles of brush and dense cloud forest, punctuated every so often by the sight of a scarlet macaw or a small village built near a cacao plantation.

The last bus dropped us at a town called Santa Elena de Uairén, near the border of Brazil. We found a hostel and slept under a tent of mosquito netting in a room painted a jarring shade of turquoise. The next morning, after some haggling, we hired a Pemon Indian guide and hiked off into the foothills.

It was two full days of walking almost straight uphill along a switch-backing trail before I saw what I'd come for: the view from the top of Mount Roraima, which was less a mountain and more a mystifyingly huge plateau, a nine-mile-long windswept slab of sandstone, so wide and high that it created its own weather. Its sheer walls dropped several thousand feet to the grasslands below; white waterfalls threaded down its sides. For five months, we'd sat with Roraima on our coffee table in our little apartment in Calgary, its pie-wedge shape occupying the pages of our most treasured issue of *National Geographic*. And now the looking glass had flipped. We were like fantasy characters climbing around a picture that had gone three-dimensional. Here were the pinkish quartz crystals spilled by the thousands across the slopes of a valley; here were the jewel-colored hummingbirds and the tiny prehistoric-looking black frogs we'd marveled at in the photographs.

"Can you believe it?" I heard myself saying to Jamie over and over. "Can you? I can't."

The two of us sat on the rocky rim of the mesa, our feet dangling over the abyss, saying nothing. Below, clouds spiraled into tufts and pompadours, forming an eery white fence line that cut us off from everything that lay beneath. It was as if we were poised at the edge of a witch's cauldron or sat at the prow of a great ship in the center of an otherworldly ocean. I had seen this place in the magazine, and now we were here, lost in it. It was a small truth affirmed. And it was all I needed to keep going.

5

A Haircut on a Lake

On our way down Mount Roraima, Jamie stumbled and broke his foot, causing us to cut short the rest of our grand South American tour. There was no talk of my continuing on without him. We were two rural kids on a limb, each afraid to make a move alone. We flew back to Canada, both of us tired. Somehow, even as we drifted through another year together and managed another backpacking trip, this one through Southeast Asia, the end of our relationship already felt prewritten. We were both restless, realizing we'd gotten serious too young. The breakup was painful and slow. When Jamie finally stormed out of our place one spring evening in 2003, saying he was leaving for good, what I felt was mostly relief.

I tried to keep myself busy. I got a new restaurant job, working at a place called Ceili's, an upscale corporate hangout styled to look like an Irish pub, with planked wooden floors and piped-in jigs and shanties. The money there was better than at the Drink. I took as many double shifts as I could, intent on saving for more travel.

For the first time in my life, I was living alone, renting a tiny barebones apartment in downtown Calgary. Between restaurant shifts, I dipped in and out of the Wee Book Inn, buying travel narratives and old magazines and stoking a new set of plans. I got a Lonely Planet guide for Central America—a brand-new, updated one—and started bringing it to the restaurant to read on my breaks.

At work, I'd become friendly with a girl from Vancouver Island named Kelly Barker. She was petite and pert-nosed, with electric green eyes that made people on the streets stop and stare. She had a long, trilling laugh, black hair that tumbled like a Breck Girl's past her shoulders, and she never seemed to get tired. She did better in tips than just about anybody in the restaurant. One summer Friday, Kelly and I went for a late lunch at a restaurant called Earls. Our restaurant had been quiet, and so was Earls. We ordered artichoke dip and a round of high teas—a slushy, tall-glassed rendition of the Long Island iced tea. I pulled the Lonely Planet out of my bag to show her pictures of Costa Rica, my destination of choice. Kelly had traveled around Europe with her family and done a student exchange program in Mexico, but she'd never backpacked.

"I think I should come with you," she said.

"Of course you should!" I said.

We calculated how much tip money we'd need to finance ourselves and how much time it would take us to earn it. We started by planning a three-week trip, but three cocktails in, we decided we needed at least six weeks. I moved on to reading descriptions of Guatemala. Kelly removed her shoes and listened to me read as she fiddled with her straw. "There are swing bridges over a waterfall," I was saying, flipping pages. "Butterfly garden, coffee plantation . . . Oh, it looks like there's a spiritual retreat where you can learn how to meditate and stuff."

"Yes," Kelly said, to all of it. "Uh-huh, yep, and I bet there will be boys in Guatemala."

By the time our lunch check arrived, we'd scrapped putting an end date on the trip and were now thinking we'd fly to Costa Rica, backpack through Guatemala and Nicaragua, and hop a flight to St. Thomas, where Kelly was positive we could get resort jobs that would have us waitressing right on the beach. From there, who knew?

We blew through the door of the Adventure Travel Company just before it closed, jovial and fully drunk and driven to make it all real before we thought better of the idea. Composing a serious face, I planted my elbows on the counter. "We'd like two tickets to Costa Rica for six weeks from now," I announced. Kelly stood next to me with a lopsided smile. The travel agent was only a few years older than we were but wore a blazer and had a sensible haircut. She looked from me to Kelly and back, as if attempting to channel our mothers.

"Please," I said. "We're one hundred percent serious."

*

Kelly was right. There were boys in Guatemala. About five weeks into our trip, having already traversed Panama, Costa Rica, Nicaragua, and Honduras, we rode several hours out of Guatemala City on a chicken bus, one of the old American school buses that totter around Central America, repainted in carnival colors, bearing rooftop racks mounded precariously with luggage and stray farm goods. We got off in a chilly Mayan town called Todos Santos, and there, in a damp little low-ceilinged restaurant with yellow walls, we happened upon Dan Hanmer and Richie Butterwick.

Yes, those were their names, like two characters out of my old Archie and Veronica comic books, like two boys in varsity letter sweaters. Only they were British. Dan Hanmer was sandy-haired and blue-eyed and went to the University of Exeter. Richie Butterwick was a law student. Both had the ruddy glow of travelers, minus the backpacker grizzle—the unkempt, unshaved, beaded-bracelet look that caused a lot of men, Kelly and I had decided, to start looking like trolls. They spoke in arch upper-class accents. They laughed and peppered us with questions as we unloaded our travel stories with the appropriate riotousness and charm—how we'd qualified for our scuba licenses in Honduras, been eaten by sandflies on the beach in Panama, and gotten caught in a nasty storm on top of a volcano in Nicaragua.

For the next couple of days, the four of us went everywhere together, hitching rides in the pickup truck beds of Mayan farmers, watching horse races at the annual All Saints' Day festival, hiking to some hot springs set on a hillside between pink-flowering hibiscus. Richie Butterwick and Dan Hanmer were big laughers. They extended courtly hands to pull us into the back of the trucks.

At night, lying on our beds back at the guesthouse, Kelly and I had fits of laughter over the scenario. We said the boys' names in British accents, adding, "Well then!" and "Cheerio!" The truth is, they were nice guys with interesting things to say. Also, something exciting was happening. As the four of us caught another chicken bus and relocated ourselves down the road to Lake Atitlán, as we piled onto the overgrown patio of a little vegetarian café and ordered bowls of black bean soup with mounds of salty guacamole, as Richie and I continued to swill beer like old buddies, Kelly and Dan Hanmer had begun to stare meaningfully into each other's eyes.

"Are you falling for Dan Hanmer?" I asked her as we lay in the hammocks outside our room one evening. Both Kelly and I had been living chastely as we traveled, flirting with male travelers but always stopping short of an actual hookup. I was teasing her, and his name was just so fun to say. We would talk about Dan Hanmer for years to come, and he would always be Dan Hanmer—never Dan, never that guy we met in Guatemala.

"I am *so not* falling for Dan Hanmer," Kelly said in a way that was completely unconvincing. "No more questions."

Lake Atitlán was a hypnotically glimmering blue-black pool of water cupped between three green volcanic mountains, with reedy shores and drifting fog and all sorts of honeymooners and hippies camped out in pretty little guesthouses along the shoreline. The village we were staying in was a new age enclave, with a meditation center where you could take classes in water massage and metaphysics. There were posters advertising sunrise Ashtanga and cheap Indian head massage, and used bookstores carrying dog-eared copies of Kerouac and *The Kama Sutra*.

Everyone we met announced the same thing: They'd planned to stay three days or ten days but were heading into their third week. It was a badge you wore: The more time you logged on the banks of Lake Atitlán, the more everyday obligations—the plane tickets home, leases on faraway apartments, relationships with faraway people—you allowed to slip away. Which, as the meditation people would say, left you in the moment you were in: not thinking backward, not thinking forward. Just being peaceful, being present. Which was a pretty good excuse to do whatever you felt like doing.

Dan Hanmer was now holding Kelly's hand everywhere we went.

Meanwhile, Richie Butterwick and I drank a lot of beer and had a few make-out sessions, both of us knowing it would go no further, that we were just killing time. His flight was leaving in another few days to take him back to England, to whatever lawyerly life he would go on to lead. After we all said goodbye to him at the bus depot in San Pedro, I left Kelly and Dan Hanmer to their own private period of no backward/no forward, while I went to a different lakeshore village to reconnect with an American girl we'd met earlier. There were only forty-eight hours before Dan Hanmer, too, had to leave for home.

*

One of the best things you can believe about the world is that there is always, no matter what, someone worth longing for. Two days later, when I took a water taxi back to San Pedro to retrieve Kelly, I found her sobbing on the stone steps that led from the waterfront up into town. She had indeed, at least for a moment, fallen for Dan Hanmer. And now Dan Hanmer was gone.

"Oh, come on," I said, wrapping my arms around her, offering what at that point had become our all-purpose panacea, "we'll go have some beers."

She pouted for the twenty-minute boat ride back to the village and cried off and on as we sat eating a late lunch at the patio restaurant of our lakefront hotel with my American friend, a freckled yoga devotee named Sarah. Sarah and I fed Kelly another brown bottle of Gallo beer whenever she started to get misty. We avoided bringing up Dan Hanmer's name, but then we'd be talking about him again. "He played Bob Marley on his Discman," Kelly said wistfully, as if this were the single most romantic thing that ever happened in her whole entire life. She would cry and then start giggling. Or she'd giggle and then start crying. Then all three of us would sigh. Dan Hanmer—for everything he was and came to stand for—was already a legend.

Late in the afternoon, we wandered down to the rickety wooden dock that belonged to our guesthouse and sat listening to the licking water and the quiet buzz of fishermen's boats heading home for the day. Kelly's pretty face was bloated from all the crying, but she seemed done with it at last. Sarah and I were lying on the dock, chatting about whether we should stay in town longer and take a three-day course in "lucid dreaming" at the meditation center, when Kelly's voice broke abruptly into our conversation: "I want you to cut my hair."

Sarah and I turned to look at her. "What?"

Kelly raked a hand upward through her hair and then let it fall— as if it weren't the down-to-the-butt envy of every woman she'd ever met, the glossy cornerstone of her beauty, but rather some sort of tiresome dishrag. "I want this gone," she said. "All of it."

"No way," I said. "You're talking crazy."

The idea of it was making her smile. I recognized the ignition point, a new flame running up some edge of Kelly. We eyed each other sternly for a good thirty seconds before I shrugged. "Just don't hold it against me when you hate it."

This would become the thing I remembered, a memory I'd lunge for in my mind five years later, when I was locked up and kept alone in a rat-infested room in Somalia, when I was suffering and half starved and my earlier life seemed like a made-up story. This warm early evening on a shimmering satin lake in Guatemala would feel like a fever dream. I would reach back for it, trying to lasso the small details and rope myself closer: Kelly and Sarah with their legs kicked out on the dock, their faces lit orange in the sunset. The way I ran barefoot up to the guesthouse lobby, borrowed a wooden chair and a pair of blunt-edged office scissors from a drawer in the front desk, and asked Kelly one last time if she was sure. There was the fact—refreshingly unimaginable, given that one of my kidnappers had hit me so hard, he'd broken several of my teeth—that the stakes of a haircut ever could have seemed so high. There was the specter of Dan Hanmer and the half-bloomed, eternally perfect love affair, and the first loops of Kelly's dark hair dropping heavily to the dock. There was the way the mountains angled like green drapery behind the sparkling eye of the lake. We were laughing at this point, harder than I think we'd laughed all those three months we'd spent traveling, as Kelly sat in the chair and I struggled to hold the scissors steady, hacking off one thick tendril and then another, as Sarah—whom we'd never see again after that week—streamed tears of hilarity and clutched at her belly, and as Kelly, no longer heartbroken and still lovely with a shingled, jaggedy bob, reached down and swept the remnants of her hair into the big lake.

6

Hello, Madame

As I calculated it, three or four months of serving martinis to nightclubbers in Calgary could buy me a plane ticket and four or five months of travel—six, if I kept the budget extra-tight.

"What do you do?" people would ask me casually, the way people do—new friends, the dentist, the woman seated next to me at a wedding. Or "What do you *want* to do?" was what people who came into the bar more often asked, presuming correctly that nearly everyone working there had other aspirations.

"I'm a traveler" was what I'd say back. "I want to see the world." It felt exactly that simple.

I'd made two trips to Latin America and one to Southeast Asia, and I was fully obsessed with doing more. Travel gave me something to talk about, something to be. That I'd just been to Nicaragua or was thinking about going to Ethiopia seemed, in the eyes of the people I encountered at work, to override the fact I hadn't been to college or that I was late in getting a round of dirty mojitos to table nine. It helped erase the past, too, allowing me to duck questions about where I'd grown up or who my parents were. Among travelers, talking about the past usually meant talking about the just passed. The expiration date on old experiences came quickly. What mattered most was where you were going next.

In the late fall of 2004, when I was twenty-three, I spent a month traveling in Thailand with my mother. We wandered beaches and Buddhist temples, ate curry and mangoes, and slept in three-star hotels rather than my usual budget backpacker places. My mother was a surprisingly mellow traveler. For the first time, she and I were learning to really laugh together, to excise some of the ugliness of the past. When she flew home, I continued on to Burma, where—still nervous as a solo traveler—I immediately grafted myself to a group of traveling geologists who were doing field research in the jungles. From there, I went to Bangladesh, in part because the flight was cheap and in part because it was on the way to India, where I wanted to go next. I had an idea that I needed to get better at being independent. I didn't know anybody in Bangladesh. I didn't know anybody who'd ever even *been* to Bangladesh. It felt like the right next place.

*

Bangladesh is one of the most densely populated countries on earth, and Dhaka, where I landed in January 2005, is the country's most densely populated city. Walking from the airport arrival hall and into the swelter of the afternoon, I saw nothing but people, a few hundred of them pressed up against the black iron gates separating the airport from the parking lot—taxi drivers, rickshaw drivers, unofficial baggage porters, women in bright saris clutching the hands of little children, vast families waiting for a relative to turn up.

"Hello, madame!" a man shouted, a hopeful taxi driver, it seemed. And then another—"Hello! Hello, madame?"—and then more— "U.S.A.? Den-a-mark? Where from? Hotel? Hotel?"

On the plane I'd met a man named Martin, a middle-aged German guy roughly my father's age who worked for an electronics company and did business in Dhaka all the time. "You're traveling alone?" he said, lifting his eyebrows. "That's going to be interesting."

Martin had insisted that a taxi ride to the Old City and the twelve-dollar-a-night hotel I'd picked out of Lonely Planet would take three hours and the driver would overcharge me by virtue of my white skin and my gender. "They never take you to where you want to go, anyway," he said. "You'll end up at their cousin's hotel."

He had a driver waiting behind the fence with an air-conditioned white minivan parked nearby. Walking out of baggage claim, I took one look at the taxi drivers scrumming madly for our attention and decided it was okay—a minor infraction of my mandate to be self-reliant in Bangladesh—to accept a ride in Martin's car.

It took us two hours to crawl through Dhaka's traffic to the old part of the city, along the north bank of the Buriganga River, which was full of slow-drifting freight barges and ferrymen rowing blade-thin canoes over the mud-brown water. The sun was going down. The streets narrowed, and the intersections between them were an unpatrolled bedlam of thousands of swarming bicycle rickshaws, honking vehicles, and wandering pedestrians. When Martin's driver found a way to ease the minivan over to a corner near my chosen hotel, I climbed out, hefted my backpack, and cheerily shook both men's hands.

The noise around us was deafening, a cacophony of bike bells and blaring car horns, people yelling at one another, and some sort of shrill siren cutting through it all. Martin was sweating through his nicely pressed shirt. He had to shout so I could hear him. "Are you sure," he was saying, "you don't want to just stay at the Sheraton?"

I waved a hand as if I'd stood on this corner a hundred times before. "No, no, this is good!"

Martin pressed his business card into my hand. "All right, then, call if you need anything."

With that, they drove off. And I was alone.

Only I wasn't at all alone. Every head on the street seemed suddenly to swivel in my direction. As I walked the fifteen feet toward the sign marking my hotel, pedestrians stopped and stared. A round-bellied man was trotting behind me, calling, "English? Hello? Hello, hello, hello?"

I ducked inside the hotel and climbed a narrow flight of stairs leading to a small second-floor lobby. Two men in white Muslim prayer caps sat behind a Formica desk, watching a soccer game on a small television in the corner. The guidebook had identified this as a cheap English-speaking place with clean Western toilets.

"Hello," I said. "I'd like a single room, please." I pulled out my wallet and passport.

The older of the two men took a long look at me. He had deep brown eyes behind a pair of rimless spectacles and a sparse gray beard. "For you?" he said.

"For me."

"Where is your husband?"

"I don't have a husband."

The man tilted his head. "Then where is your father?"

I'd met young women travelers who wore fake wedding rings and pretended to have husbands stashed elsewhere, in an attempt to ward off men who believed that an unmarried woman who wasn't staying virtuously at home while her father negotiated her bride-price had somehow been disgraced and therefore was either a prostitute or a witch. I had always been irritated by this, thinking that the male attitude toward women like me was bullshit and that the fake-ring solution was not helping the cause. I was wearing a couple of rings on my right hand—cheap, chunky silver and rhinestone things I'd bought on the beach in Thailand—but I wasn't going to pretend they meant anything.

"My father's home in Canada," I told the man a little hotly, "and I need a room, please."

By now, the second guy had taken his eyes off the soccer game and was shaking his head slowly and silently, as if the very thought were preposterous. The older man leaned back in his chair. "What are you doing here?" he said. "I cannot understand it. Does your father know you are here?" He lifted his hands in the air with feigned helplessness, as if to say it was not his fault that my father had let me out of his sight. I did not mention that my father was home with his gay lover and that I was in Bangladesh on vacation from my job serving alcohol to unmarried young people who went out at night, largely looking to get laid.

Instead, I continued to angle for a room. "I won't bother anybody. My money is no different than a man's money. What is the problem here?" At the same time, I was examining the hotel map in my Lonely Planet, relieved to see another recommended hotel a couple of blocks away. Giving in to what seemed like inevitable defeat, I descended the stairs in search of another place.

Old Dhaka smelled of diesel fuel and fish paste. Horns blasted and rickshaw bells jingled as I left the first hotel. It was early evening now. The round-bellied man materialized almost instantly, taking up his chant of "Hello? Hello? How are you? Madame?" Within minutes, I was caught inside a swirl of inquisitive onlookers, a rapidly dividing cell of mostly men.

A man with a neatly trimmed mustache and short-cropped hair had pushed his way into the patch of space where I was standing, the eye of our human hurricane. He wore a white prayer cap, but where the men at the hotel had worn loose-fitting Arab-style shirts and Asian-style *lungi* wrapped around their waists, he was dressed in jeans and a short-sleeved shirt.

"Excuse me, excuse me," he said officiously, "what is your good name?" The crowd leaned in close to listen.

"Well, my good name is Amanda!" I said back, finding it funny, raising my voice over the noise. "I am from Canada!"

"Can I help you?"

I pointed at the map, turning the guidebook so he could see it. "I think it's just up here, right?"

"Ah," said the man, taking the book and examining it. Someone from the crowd offered what sounded like advice in Bengali. More people chimed in. The Lonely Planet was passed around enthusiastically until a consensus appeared to have been reached, and the whole knotty mass of us started moving down the block.

The friendly man with the mustache introduced himself as Mr. Sen and trailed me inside the hotel. Another narrow flight of stairs, another tiny lobby with a Formica desk, though this time there was a sofa, and on it, three dark-haired young men who looked like they'd been dozing. A fourth sat behind the desk.

I asked for a room.

The deskman pointed to my new friend. "This is your husband?"

I sighed. "No, I need a room just for me."

Mr. Sen jumped in, speaking a fast Bengali as the guy behind the desk waved his hands to indicate he was not in any way interested in renting me a room. Mr. Sen turned to me. "He is saying that if you have a husband here, then it is no problem." He gave a flustered smile. "Do you have a brother with you?"

I could feel a small kernel of fear beginning to form. "No, no brother. It is just me, and I need a place to stay."

Mr. Sen smiled again. "No problem, no problem," he said. He added, "You can come to my home. My mother, she will welcome you."

"No, I can't go home with you. I need a hotel." I smiled, hoping not to offend him. "Please," I said, "I am tired."

We walked several blocks to the next hotel listed in the guide-book—me and an entourage of what had to be forty Bangladeshi men, led by Mr. Sen, most everyone in the group seeming to be jabbering to somebody else about my predicament, calling out to others we passed in the dusk. A woman was frying chili peppers over an open fire and selling them in bags to people headed home for evening curry. The scent nagged at me. I hadn't eaten since morning.

At the third hotel, the older man behind the desk looked me up and down and then asked about my husband. I started to quietly panic. This was no lark. These people really were looking at me—with my harmless ponytail and jeans and battered blue backpack, with my hoop earrings and eager-beaver smile—and seeing some sort of threat.

I was not totally naive. I understood the intricacies here, at least a little. I understood that it was a culture built on modesty and strict adherence to Islam. Most of the women on the street wore head scarves. Some kept their faces covered completely. I had read about *purdah*, the practice of shielding women's faces and bodies from public view. I was aware of how completely foreign I appeared.

"Na, na, na!" the latest deskman was saying, waggling a finger emphatically, as Mr. Sen mounted some sort of argument in Bengali.

Their words hummed indistinguishably past me, a telegraph-wire blur, until my self-appointed protector turned back to me.

"You see," he said calmly, "it is simply not possible for you to stay." He added with a note of defeat, "I am sorry."

Not knowing what else to do, I dragged my pack over to the black vinyl couch along the lobby wall and plunked myself down on it. "I'll sleep right here, then," I heard myself saying, surprised by the forcefulness of my voice. I fixed the white-haired hotel man with a stare. He looked away. I fought back tears. I crossed my arms over my chest, trying to appear formidable. "I'm not leaving," I said.

The hotel man looked uncertainly to Mr. Sen for a translation.

A quiet conversation ensued. The man behind the desk appeared to be weighing his options. After a few minutes, he signaled grudgingly for me to step forward and hand over my passport. His eyes stayed down. A rushed notation was made in the guest register. A small brass key was produced and passed to a skinny young boy in an embroidered skullcap who stood waiting by the stairs leading up, apparently with fresh orders to guide me to a room.

The truce was awkward. The enemy was inside the gate. I thanked Mr. Sen warmly, taking care not to further damage his reputation by shaking his hand. I made an awkward bow in the direction of the deskman and then wordlessly and gratefully followed the boy with the key upstairs.

*

Once I got used to it, Dhaka excited me. I bought a sheer black head scarf and draped it loosely over my hair, like many Bangladeshi women did. I grew used to being the only Westerner on the sidewalk, the only woman in a restaurant. I strolled the Hindu market street, where clouds of incense wafted and jewelers in little stalls pounded silver. I stepped into one of the city's high-domed mosques where, beneath an eggshell mosaic ceiling, rows of kneeling, murmuring men touched their foreheads intently to the floor.

Islam was everywhere in Dhaka. On the mirror in my room was a small arrow-shaped sticker helpfully pointing the way toward Mecca. Five times a day, the muezzins chanted and the prayers began. These moments were strangely private and public at the same time. The men in my hotel lobby, guests and employees, arranged themselves into lines and bowed in unison, unaware of or unruffled by my presence. People, mostly men, were praying in the streets, outside of the mosques, which were often too small to hold everyone, especially on Friday, the Islamic holy day. I thought it was beautiful. The repeated bowing, the rows and rows of people humbled before God. After the bowing, they sat with their hands cupped in front of their faces in supplication, whispering a finish to their prayers. It was so foreign to me, a religion that required so much from its believers, this display of devotion every few hours.

As a traveler, I was formulating an edge that would help me in years to come—finding and holding the line between the pleased-to-meet-you openness that both served backpackers and made them easy prey, and a more aggressive way of using my own power. Without the language or a way to pick up cultural cues, it could be hard to parse opportunity from danger. Your mind always had to be thinking a move or two ahead. I believe I was good at this, for the most part. I'd spent enough of my childhood trying to read cues and navigate uncertainty. Uncertainty was what I knew.

Back in my hotel room one evening, I heard a rustling in the hall and some raggedy masculine breathing. When I got up to investigate, I realized with horror that a man was lying in the hallway, his cheek pressed against the floor as he tried to see through the half inch of space beneath my door. My first instinct was to scream, but I quickly thought better of it. The blame for any disturbance, I was sure, would fall on me. Any problem and I'd be kicked out, forced to make another humiliating quest for a hotel.

I did what I always did when I was scared. I reminded myself to breathe, to ignore the prick of anxiety, to settle back into my body. *Calm, calm, calm,* I thought. I then checked the lock on my door, dragged my chair out of sight of the doorway, and sat waiting for him to get bored and go away.

A couple of days later, having wandered my way to the outskirts of the city, I flagged an auto rickshaw and asked the driver to take me back to old Dhaka, to my hotel. "No problem!" he said as I climbed in. He was young, close to my age, I guessed, and I was tired enough that it took me fifteen minutes to realize that instead of steering us into the dense city, he'd driven us into an outer ring of Dhaka, and the two of us were now, as night began to fall, traveling what was almost a country road, the city high-rises having given way to ramshackle huts and roadside food stands.

I said, "Wait, excuse me, where are you taking me?"

The driver didn't look back. He waved a hand. "No problem," he said. "There is no problem, madame."

In Bangladesh there never seemed to be a problem. Or that was what everyone said, anyway.

I spoke a little louder. "I think you are going the wrong way. Please take me to the hotel. In the city. The *city*."

"No problem, no problem," the driver said. He seemed to be driving faster.

We rode on another few minutes as my neck began to tingle. Was this some sort of shortcut? Was I being abducted? Would I be killed and sold off organ by organ on the medical black market, as per the most popular backpacker horror scenario of the day? What was I supposed to do?

What happened next surprised even me.

From my spot in the backseat, I yelled, "You need to turn around!"

For good measure, I leaned forward and slammed a fist into the side of the driver's head as hard as I could, the rhinestones of my cheap Thai rings slicing thickly into his temple.

I had never in my life hit anyone.

Stunned, the driver slowed the rickshaw, reaching a hand up to feel the blood. I watched him examining it in the dark.

My knuckles throbbed. A new paranoia buzzed. I had obviously crossed a line. Now, surely, this man was going to hurt me.

But I was wrong. Without a word, the driver made a slow, arcing U-turn and we began the long, silent ride back to old Dhaka, where

the streetlights and frenzied sidewalks gave me an odd kind of relative comfort. Reaching the corner where my hotel was, I climbed out,
flooded with a mix of anger and relief. The young guy looked at me
sheepishly. He had a deep cut above his right cheekbone. It was unclear
what his plan had been, where he had been taking me, and for what
reason. Whatever it was, he'd been shamed.

"I am sorry," he said twice. He bowed his head and I turned away. I
didn't give him any money and he didn't ask for it.

7

The Rule of Proximity

I had momentum now, for real.

After three months in Asia, I was learning to navigate the backpacker ghettos—the chaotic crossroads for the world's wanderers that are found in nearly every big city, the streets stuffed with hotels that are cheap but not too dirty, with street vendors selling bootlegged DVDs, used novels and guidebooks, flip-flops, luggage, fake Gucci sunglasses, and the billowy cotton harem pants that travelers buy to stay comfortable on overnight train rides but lapse into wearing everywhere. For the broke, there are Western Union offices. For the ill and anxious, there are pharmacies selling antibiotics and blister packs of generic Valium. For the planless, there are travel agents working out of kiosks, their sandwich-board signs reminding you that with two hundred dollars, you can get yourself to Phuket or Angkor Wat or Mysore.

I tacked my way from Bangladesh into India by bus and train, arriving in Calcutta sometime in February and finding a room at the Salvation Army guesthouse, in the heart of the backpacker ghetto. After Bangladesh, India seemed more user-friendly but no less crowded. Children tailed me down the street, calling "Aunty, Aunty!," their palms held open for change. Men brushed up close, muttering "Ganja? Ganja? Hashish? Smoke?" I spent about two weeks there, volunteering at one of Mother Teresa's charities, working the morning shift in the women's wing of the Kalighat Home for the Sick and

Dying Destitutes, delivering tea and giving sponge baths to patients
with tuberculosis, malaria, dysentery, AIDS, and cancer, sometimes
in combination. The frankness of it was galling, even nauseating at
first, but slowly I relaxed. I would never be saintly like the nurses who
staffed the place, but I tried at least to be helpful.

I was also getting used to being alone. What once might have overwhelmed me no longer did. I could read bus schedules, figure out the
various classes of train tickets, ask for help when I needed it, sit in a
restaurant and eat a meal alone without feeling self-conscious. I was
learning to seize my opportunities.

*

My mother was not a worrier, exactly, but she did want to have a sense
of where I was. As I moved around India, she sent me encouraging
e-mails. She expressed her love. I wrote similar things back, often copying my dad and Perry. I sprinkled my e-mails with descriptions of what
amazed me most—the honey-colored camels ambling around Agra
or the snake charmers plying their trade on the Varanasi ghats, the
flower-garden brightness of Indian women in their saris. I used a lot
of exclamation points to illustrate how great it all was. "Tomorrow,"
I wrote to my parents from an Internet café in Agra, "I am going to
a different city called Jodhpur. It is a city in the desert, called the Blue
City, as all the buildings are painted blue! I am having the BEST TIME
EVER!"

And I was. I was meeting people from all over the world—some
nurses from Australia, a couple of Israeli teenagers on leave from the
army—traveling with them for a few days or a week before parachut-
ing off again on my own. Riding the bus one day in Calcutta, I struck
up a conversation with a fellow Canadian—a blond guy in his early
thirties with arresting blue surfer-boy eyes—and ended up having a
several-month mini–love affair with him. His name was Jonathan. He
carried a black canvas backpack and a guitar.

I was a sucker for guitar strummers. Since my breakup with Jamie,
I'd been guarded around men, unwilling to jump into the ongoing
carnival of traveler romances. Sex on the road seemed, for a lot of

long-haul travelers, like a given. The pints of beer in warm air, the months passed without a haircut or a good shave, the boastful chitchat and dazed hours spent at bus windows all lent themselves to a certain sexual ease. The options were almost too exotic to be ignored. I'd seen Chileans wander off with Danes, old men and young women, older women with younger men, men with men, and women with women, and every once in a while a boozy international threesome tiptoeing back through the tamarinds to somebody's room.

I wasn't against any of it. I had just never been all that self-assured. If I got involved with a man, even briefly, I usually ended up feeling overattached and extra-vulnerable. I wanted to be more like other girls my age, able to have fun and move on, but it didn't happen easily. With Jonathan, who was extroverted and not serious about anything, I did learn to lighten up a bit. I had fun and never once asked myself if I was falling in love. We were both so devoted to solo travel that we saw each other only every few weeks, arranging by e-mail to meet up for a few days in one city or another before moving on alone.

People would say to me all the time, "It must be so hard to travel by yourself as a woman." But I was finding that it was easier. I was sure about it. If you smiled, if you showed people that you were happy to be there, you were met most often with warmth. The swindlers backed off easily. The tuk-tuk drivers and beggars eased up and became more human, maybe even a bit protective.

Nothing slowed me down. I took a train to Varanasi, a holy city for Hindus, thought to be a direct portal to heaven. There, pilgrims sat half-sunk in the gray-green water of the Ganges, washing their bodies, washing laundry and dishes, washing cows, while dead bodies burned on the ghats above. I went to Delhi, Mysore, Pushkar. I learned to sleep on trains, to not think twice while using the toilet holes that emptied directly onto the tracks rushing below. I tried the southern beaches of Kerala, where the lip of the Indian Ocean foamed over long stretches of white sand.

Here is the rule of proximity: You get to one place, and it becomes impossible, basically, not to start looking at whatever else is nearby. Climb to the top of one mountain, and you see the whole range. If you make it as far as Cambodia, what's keeping you from Malaysia? From Malaysia, it's just a little hop to Indonesia, and onward from there. For a while, the world for me was like a set of monkey bars. I swung from one place to the next, sometimes backward, sometimes forward, capitalizing on my own momentum, knowing that at some point my arms—or, more accurately, my quivering bank balance, accessed through foreign ATMs—would give out, and I'd fall to the ground.

Pakistan was next to India. Unignorably so.

There were plenty of reasons to avoid Pakistan. If you read the news or listened to people sermonizing about the state of the world, Pakistan was a big fat problem. There were bombs on buses, headless bodies turning up in ditches, land mines, kidnappings. Al Qaeda was in Pakistan, bin Laden was in Pakistan, the Taliban was in Pakistan. Nobody there, it seemed, was to be trusted.

Still, people went. I'd met a couple of travelers in India who'd been. And I'd met people who knew people who said they'd met a guy a week earlier who'd just come over the border from Lahore or had a friend who'd gone six months ago. The word on Pakistan in this context was always positive, an interesting bass line playing beneath a more familiar song. The place was amazing, untouched. The food was awesome, the people friendly and welcoming. The headlines were the headlines, as ugly and frightening as they were anywhere. The country itself was supposedly something very different.

I sent my mother an e-mail, telling her I was planning to head into Pakistan to travel around. While in Delhi, I'd gotten a visa. I was now in the far northern Indian city of Amritsar, seventeen miles from the Pakistani border.

Her response was swift and emotional, announcing that she did not want me to go. She garnished the request with a thick wedge of guilt. "I would never want to change you, Amanda, nor would anyone else in your family," she wrote. "But I want to ask you to put the shoe on the other foot and consider us and our feelings before you go . . . I can't help but feel physically ill to think of the danger you'd be in." She went on to compare my travel plans to having sex without a condom. Reckless, in other words.

I read her e-mail and thought about it. I tried to put the shoe on the other foot. But it didn't work. My mother and I were closer than we'd ever been, and yet images of Russell, of his leering relatives, his piled-up liquor bottles reeled through my mind, the uncertainty of the place hanging like a vapor in the air. We weren't safe then. What right did she have, I was thinking, to worry about it now?

*

In Pakistan, I felt like a bird on a limb—perched and ridiculously light. Lahore, where the bus from northern India deposited me, was a booming, modern city. With a Dunkin' Donuts and KFC near my cheap hotel, it was more familiar, less exotic, than most of the cities I'd visited in India. Immediately, I started to erase any fears, chalking up all the warnings to Western paranoia. I kept the argument going with my mother silently for days. What was reckless, I decided, was the way people were writing off huge swaths of the world as unsafe, unstable, unfriendly, when all they needed to do was go and see for themselves.

It was "Sufi night" at my three-dollar-a-night hotel in Lahore. The hotel manager corralled a bunch of us travelers into a van and took us to a mosque where, in a buggy outdoor courtyard, men pounded barrel-sized drums while others shook their bodies, whipping themselves into a state of spiritual ecstasy. The drummers chanted: *La Ilaha Illa Allah!* The hotel manager translated: *There is no god but Allah.*

Meanwhile, I deliberately ignored my mother's e-mails. Rightly or wrongly, I was punishing her for trying to put limits on me. I let her marinate in her worries as I took a two-day bus ride from Lahore to Gilgit, in the Hunza Valley of northern Pakistan, where I met up with Jonathan so we could travel up the Karakoram Highway, a slim ribbon of pavement cut between some of the highest mountains in the world, connecting Pakistan to China.

As instructed by Lonely Planet, we flagged down a northbound truck on the highway, a jingle truck—one of the ornamented trans-port rigs common in central Asia, with chains and bells dangling nois-ily from the bumpers to help shoo away animals in the road. The driver slowed and halted. He climbed out, a smiling, mustachioed man dressed in a sand-colored vest over a white *shalwar kameez*, and gestured for us to climb the metal ladder that led to an open-roofed cargo space above the cab.

It was another daydream actualized—pages from my guidebook, from the magazines, opening into something real.

For the next week, Jonathan and I caught rides on different jingle trucks, roller-coastering through the mountains toward the Chinese border, climbing off at little villages to eat and rest. There were so many trucks, and so many drivers happy for the novelty of loading foreign hitchhikers into their rooftop holds, that we started to be choosy, waving down only the flashiest, most overdone vehicles. The trucks had quilted, sequined interiors and were hand-painted in carnival shades of orange, blue, green, and red. The larger panels held vividly detailed murals of hopeful things—peaceful landscapes, pretty women, verses of the Koran, and bold, lidless eyes meant to ward off evil.

The drivers, usually two to a truck, tended to their vehicles as if they were children. They passed pillows up to us in the cargo hold to make sure we were comfortable. They passed up cigarettes, candies, and lots of apricots. When we offered to pay them, they almost always refused. We communicated in gestures and bits of basic Urdu and English, stopping at roadside stands to buy oily plates of chicken *karai*, so spicy it made my eyes water. In motion, we swerved to avoid herds of yaks and goats, oncoming trucks, and tractor-sized boulders that had tumbled off the steeplelike mountains and slammed into the road. About five months after Jonathan and I rolled up the Karakoram Highway, the biggest earthquake in a century would hit the same part of northern Pakistan, flattening villages and triggering massive landslides, killing some eighty thousand people.

It wasn't that we were unaware of the road's various perils. The reminders were there, from the overturned Suzukis and shattered guardrails to the tiny stone pyramids meant to memorialize a person's death. The possibility of disaster sat at the edges of our days but never moved closer. Children sometimes chased us, throwing rocks in our wake, though it was impossible to know if they were angry or playful.

Jonathan and I were blithe because it was easy to be blithe: One good day reinforced the idea that the next would be good, too.

Already, in my mind, I had half-composed an e-mail home, in which I would narrate the thrill of the adventure, packaging it up for my mother, this little triumph, the one she'd tried to talk me out of. When, maybe a week later, having parted ways with Jonathan, I found myself in the city of Peshawar on the far western edge of Pakistan, at a linoleum-floored restaurant with a dial-up Internet connection and an ancient-looking computer in the corner, I sat down to write it. I was dazzled, still, by the highway and the mountains and the fact that nobody knew where I was.

What I sent off to both my mother and father was a big, overdecorated jingle truck of an e-mail with the subject line "I love Pakistan!!!" In it, I detailed how I was eating heaps of delicious street food and wandering the market alleys on my own, wading among a sea of people—friendly people, I made sure to say, more open and warm than in India. Midway through my note, I announced that I was going the very next day to apply for a visa to visit Afghanistan, another place I'd heard was better and richer than the headlines it earned about troop movements, suicide bombs, and the ongoing search for Osama bin Laden. It was a day's bus ride away. I ended the e-mail by proclaiming myself "the happiest I've been in my entire life."

The jab was intentional. In case anyone missed my point, it was followed by four more exclamation points.

8

Don't F*** with Afghanistan

Right as I was planning to leave for Afghanistan, a woman disappeared in Kabul. She was Italian, thirty-two years old, an aid worker who'd been living there a couple of years. Walking along the pedestrian mall in Peshawar, I'd happened to buy a Pakistani English-language newspaper and read the story. The article was short and not on the front page, but there it was: Her name was Clementina Cantoni. She'd been dragged out of her car in the center of the city one evening by four armed men, put into another vehicle, and driven away. Beyond that, nobody seemed to know a thing.

I went back to the ratty dorm room at my guesthouse, which I was sharing with about ten other travelers, and studied the newest visa pasted into my passport. It had an official stamp in purple ink, blurred slightly at the edges. The particulars—the date, my passport number, my nationality—had been filled out in black pen by a consular employee. "Mrs. Amanda" was granted a month to travel freely in Afghanistan.

Tourists did go to Afghanistan. I'd met an older British couple in a camper van who'd driven through the country without incident. They'd checked in to my guesthouse, plopped themselves on a couch in the common area amid a group of motley backpackers smoking hash, and gushed about the Blue Mosque in Mazar-i-Sharif and the flowering hillsides of Panjshir. It was all I wanted—to see these things, to leap another hurdle—but the kidnapping story stayed with me. It was as if an invisible branch had snagged my collar. I felt fear but also something else, something missing—a sudden absence of conviction. A doubt when I wasn't used to having doubts. My grandmother, I knew, would have labeled it a much-needed attack of *common sense,* but that, to my mind, was code for being afraid of new things.

I spent a week considering my options. I left Peshawar and headed away from Afghanistan, taking a few long bus rides to get myself all the way across Pakistan and into India, figuring I'd try to see the mountains of Ladakh. I was scheduled to fly home from Delhi in a few weeks, to resume my life as a waitress. Already, the prospect seemed dull. On an overnight bus, I found a window seat and proactively piled my belongings high next to me, to discourage potential seatmates. I'd had too many men's fingers creeping toward me as I fell asleep on buses.

For about seven hours, I sat beneath a dome light with a book open on my lap, watching the Indian scenery slip past in the dark. I could make out trucks, trees, the shapes of villages and mountains. I read and dozed. At first light, we pulled over at a roadside complex to use the toilets and have a cup of tea before climbing back on board. Then it was more trucks, trees, villages. My head ached and my stomach churned after so much time sitting still and so little food. Every so often I'd spot a snatch of gray river, a factory twirling smoke into the sky, a farmer using oxen to till a field.

I was chastising myself for not having gone into Afghanistan, for having retreated. A few years earlier, I'd sat on the top of Mount Roraima and quietly vowed that I'd always push forward, no matter what. Each border I'd crossed since then had felt like a revelation. It was better than school. It was better than church.

The book I was reading was called *The Power of Now,* by Eckhart Tolle. I'd lugged it all over India and Pakistan but hadn't cracked it, always choosing to read other books instead. Back in Calgary, the book had been passed around among some of my friends, who were starting to make big decisions about whether or not to marry a guy, buy a house, or take a certain new job. Tolle's point seemed to be that the present moment mattered more than anything. If you could focus fully on the present, things like pain, guilt, and worry all dropped away and you could then listen to your deeper self. And the deeper self would know what to do.

By the time my bus crawled into the Indian city of Jammu, midway through the following day, I had turned the last page. My deeper self was now entirely and exuberantly in command, and it was busy brow-beating my other self for having dashed away from Afghanistan, so full of fear.

I found a station agent, got a refund on the rest of my ticket, and applied it to the cost of a new one—headed right back down the road I'd just traveled, toward Peshawar and the Afghan border. As I waited for the next bus, the Italian woman's fate flashed through my mind. I shuddered on her behalf. But I wasn't her, and she wasn't me. Clementina Cantoni had been unlucky, I decided. I would be okay.

★

I pulled into Kabul on a hot day in early June, having caught a twenty-dollar minibus ride over the Khyber Pass. The city had a distinct smell, not the mix of garbage and sewer and smog that permeated the air of other Asian cities; rather, Kabul seemed to be the site of some massive and unseen incineration, reeking of kerosene and wood smoke with an undernote of something more acrid, like melting plastic. My back-pack and clothing would carry Kabul's scent for weeks, long after I'd left the country and despite multiple passes through the laundry.

It was a beautiful, wrecked city. Armored military vehicles crawled like reptiles through the streets, alongside tottering donkey carts and bicyclists. Amputees from the Russian war in the 1980s begged in the markets. Women walked the streets cloaked in burkas, looking like giant badminton birdies or floating blue ghosts. Men in keffiyeh scarves sold mobile-phone airtime from beneath umbrellas, next to shops selling shoes and Western-style business suits and kiosks full of Chinese electronics. The older neighborhoods built in to the rock-scabbed terra-cotta hills overlooking the city, with their half-rubbled, flat-roofed mudbrick buildings, looked like something out of the Old Testament, while construction cranes hovered over blocks of gray Soviet-style buildings being renovated with a flush of foreign aid.

I'd made the trip with Amanuddin, a friendly, middle-aged rug seller I'd met in Peshawar, and one of his young sons. Amanuddin had emigrated to Pakistan decades earlier but came home to Kabul when he could for visits with his family. In Peshawar, I'd stopped in for tea at his carpet shop almost daily. He'd shown me photo albums from his days fighting the Russians as part of the Afghan mujahideen. He'd described Kabul in detail, from the noisy bird market downtown to the beautiful profusion of his mother's rose gardens.

From the bus station, the three of us took a taxi to a neighborhood on the outskirts of the city and were dropped off when the street narrowed into a lane. Amanuddin had loaned me an abaya from his wife, a draping black robe that was less smothering than a burka and, paired with a head scarf, passed for modest. The abaya was about six inches too short, and I was aware of my jeans sticking out beneath its hem, exposing me for the imposter I was. Carrying our bags, we walked the rest of the way down a rocky path, hopping a trickling brook.

Before we reached the gate to his family's compound, Amanuddin's relatives were streaming toward us, shouting their greetings. Kids, women, men, dozens of them. The women kissed me three times, alternating cheeks. Amanuddin's mother, wearing an indigo burka, took my hand. Everyone swarmed over Amanuddin and his boy. Behind the wall were their three houses, wide and low, made from mud and hay, plus a small outhouse that served the whole family.

After dinner that night, Amanuddin's mother showed me to a room with a mat on the floor and a candle lit on the windowsill. She settled me in wordlessly, her burka removed, her cheeks sunken, her gray hair in two stalklike braids down her back. On the floor she stacked a pile of handwoven wool blankets to protect against the evening chill, each one stitched with colorful yarn embroidery, thicker and heavier than any blanket I'd ever lifted. She disappeared for a few minutes, returning with a pot of tea and a dish of sweets on a silver tray. By then I was standing at the window, looking at the wide sky and the pale moon, thinking, *I can't believe it: I'm really in Afghanistan.* I caught sight of the dense rosebushes growing along the side of the compound walls.

Their flowers lay red, robust, and wide open in the moonlight, exactly as Amanuddin had described them.

*

On my sixth day in Kabul, Clementina Cantoni's kidnappers set her free. Nothing was said publicly about how this came to pass—what deal might have been struck, what concessions had or hadn't been made during the three weeks she'd been held captive. An Afghan minister would insist to the media that no ransom had been paid and no prisoners were released in exchange for her freedom. Outside of Kabul's Italian embassy, Cantoni waved wanly at the television cameras before disappearing inside to spend the night under heavy guard. The next day, she got the hell out, flying back to Italy, saying little about what had happened.

On the day she was released—June 9, 2005—I was oblivious. The truth is, I hadn't thought much about the kidnapped Italian woman since arriving in Kabul. Exploring on my own, I'd taken a taxi that day to a wholesale market area near the center of the city, which sprawled in all directions, straddling the banks of the Kabul River, devolving into a labyrinth of crooked alleys. I bought a plastic cup of raisins and apricots mixed with pistachios and honey-sweetened water and ate them with a spoon. I browsed through little shops. In one, I found a shelf stacked with bars of soap, their wrappers showing a photograph of a smiling woman's face, except that every face had been scribbled over with a marker. This was a fundamentalist Islamic move, something the Taliban once enforced strictly: Any images of things made by Allah weren't to be replicated by a human hand, because it counted as playing god. Amanuddin had explained to me: It was okay to paint or print a photograph of a car or a building but not a person or animal. Idolatry was a sin. It was why, several years earlier, the Taliban had dynamited a pair of ancient grand statues of Buddha in the town of Bamiyan, causing a global outcry. I thought about buying one of the soaps as a souvenir, but staring at the blotted-out face of the Middle Eastern model gave me the creeps.

Back outside, I wandered down tightly packed dirt lanes, weaving between shoppers, browsing the goods laid out on tables and blankets—dried fruits, pyramids of ground spices, mountains of polyester clothing—when I felt something drill into my back, the force of it like voltage from a wire. When I turned, the pressure increased. A young man was at my shoulder. His expression was bug-eyed. I realized then that it was a gun jamming into my ribs, some sort of pistol.

Into my ear, the man said very clearly, "I will kill you. Give me your money."

It was over before I fully understood what was happening. Only after I handed the man my wallet—a change purse I'd bought in Rajasthan with three hundred dollars in it, about half the money I had for the rest of my trip—and after the crowd had swallowed him up again, did my whole body start to shake. Frozen in place in the middle of the market, with men pushing their bicycles past me and women hurrying onward with their covered heads down, I began to cry—months' worth of tears, it seemed, maybe even years. I felt lost and small. Every instinct seemed to have left me. I couldn't think of a thing to do but weep. My head scarf and too-short abaya had done nothing to help me blend in. I felt fully unmasked as a foreigner, sobbing in a way I knew must appear ridiculous and childlike but which I couldn't tamp down. For the first time in ages, I missed home. I missed my mother. I just wanted to be a woman standing on a street that I knew, in a place where I fit in.

A crowd began to gather, men looking quizzical. Eventually, someone located an Afghan soldier who found a sympathetic taxi driver to get me out of there. A few days later, I used most of the rest of my money to buy a bus ticket back to Pakistan. From there, on a more meager budget than ever, I got myself to Delhi to catch my flight home.

For a week, I carried a star-shaped bruise of that pistol in the soft spot below my ribs, on my right side. It ached and changed colors and then very slowly faded away. But its message remained clear to me, like an asterisk added to what had been almost seven months straight of heady travel, as if at last I'd hit some final fence line. *You don't fuck with Afghanistan*, it was saying. Yet even so, there was something still flickering inside me, the pilot light that had fueled me all the way through and was not, even now, extinguished—the thing that said, *Yes, do.*

9

The Start of a New Sentence

*I*t was about eight months later, in the winter of 2006, when I first spotted Nigel Brennan—a thin guy wearing a fleece jacket, cargo shorts, and hiking boots, sitting alone on an empty hotel veranda in Addis Ababa, the capital city of Ethiopia. I'd spent the summer and fall waiting tables in Calgary, stockpiling my money. I was now five weeks into what I figured would be a six-month tour through Africa and the Middle East, so long as I stuck to a careful budget.

This was my dream trip. Seeing Africa had been a goal since I first started traveling. Already, I'd made my way through parts of Uganda and Kenya, taking buses over wide plains, passing long days alone. I felt awestruck and intimidated by what I'd seen, by the sweating city crowds and the thorny flatlands. How different the landscape was from Afghanistan's craggy splendor or the heavy lushness of South Asia. Even the sky looked uniquely African—flatter and wider, like blue chrome layered over the land.

By the time I reached Addis Ababa, I was lonely. It seemed almost like Nigel had been waiting for me, though in reality, he was just a traveler who happened to find a quiet spot to read a book, on a sagging couch on the porch of the one-star Baro Hotel, right about the same time my taxi rattled up on the street out front. I felt an instant pull in his direction.

He was in his mid-thirties, I guessed. I recognized the cover of the book he was reading—a thick paperback travelogue by Paul Theroux called *Dark Star Safari*, which was becoming a cult hit among the back-packer crowd. I had devoured it twice. The first lines went like this: *All news out of Africa is bad. It made me want to go there . . .*

Carrying my bag past Nigel on my way to reception, I said, "Hi, how are you?"

He looked up. He had blue eyes, an aquiline nose, and a handsome, unshaved face. "Oh," he said, as if I'd woken him, "I'm good." He went back to reading.

At the Baro's reception desk, I handed over my passport and got a ten-dollar room. A couple of extra-frugal travelers had pitched sun-beaten tents in front of the reception area. My room had a stained car-pet and was weakly lit, with a twin mattress and a small bathroom. On a tray over the sink lay a packet of African condoms—a customary ges-ture in a country working to lower its HIV rates, at a hotel that some-times doubled as a brothel for locals, and amid intermingling travelers who tended to be young, impulsive, and charged up on adventure.

I moved the condoms to one side, brushed my teeth, fished a pack of cigarettes from my bag, and went back out to find the guy on the porch.

*

Cigarettes, for low-budget travelers, are a universal icebreaker. On the streets of just about any city or town, they can be bartered for direc-tions or the use of a toilet. Among those traveling, they're an excuse to talk and to share.

I flopped myself down on the chair near Nigel and waved my pack of cigarettes. "Okay if I smoke?" I said.

He shrugged. "Sure." At last he set the book down, pulling out a cigarette of his own.

He was an Australian living in London—a photographer, he said, newly arrived in Ethiopia to shoot pictures for the International Res-cue Committee, to help promote some of its aid projects. He was trav-eling alone. He'd be in Africa for the next three months.

The conversation flowed easily. Nigel had a ready smile. We talked for a while about the Theroux book. I quizzed him on how he'd gotten his start in photography. He said he'd realized how much he loved taking photos during a trip to India years earlier, prompting him to go back to school to get a photography degree. It struck me as glamorous, to get paid to travel like that, to capture a foreign landscape or face, to offer it up to all the people who would never have the guts to go see it themselves. Nigel had thin, muscled calves, a quick laugh, and a thick Australian accent. He came across as self-assured, successful. He casually mentioned that he'd had a meeting with someone from the *Times* of London.

I had spent years studying magazines and newspapers and travel books, feeding myself on other people's impressions of the world while gathering my own. That Nigel was not just a photographer but a photographer *who lived in London* felt significant. And he seemed to wear it well, as if inhabiting exactly the life he'd planned for himself.

It was getting late. I stood up and stretched, announcing that after the distance I'd come that day, I had to get some sleep. "I guess I'll see you tomorrow?" I said.

Nigel looked at his watch. "Actually, I'm on the six A.M. bus to Harar." Harar, I knew from my reading, was a walled city in the eastern part of Ethiopia, a historic Islamic trade center about ten hours away. "Anyway, I hope you get some rest," he said. "Good luck with your travels." He reached again for his book.

I masked my disappointment. He hadn't even asked for an e-mail address. Maybe, I thought, this was the dividing line between journalists and backpackers.

Walking back to my sparse room, I felt a ripple of confusion. Something about him had stirred me. He seemed to be resisting it, but I believed I'd stirred him, too.

Around nine the next morning, I woke, showered, and headed back out to the terrace.

I was having a second cup of coffee when Nigel appeared at my table. He was dressed in the same outfit he'd been wearing the night before. In the daylight, he looked a bit older. The skin around his eyes creased when he smiled.

"Hey, doll," he said, using an endearment that only an Australian man can pull off even half-winningly, "looks like I'm back."

His taxi, it turned out, had gotten marooned in the snarl of early-morning traffic. He'd missed his bus to Harar by five minutes. The next one, he told me, wouldn't come for another twenty-four hours. A stroke of luck, it felt like. As Nigel dragged a chair to my table, something inside me clicked on.

★

We liked each other, Nigel and I. We spent his extra day in Addis together, visiting the market, flirting gently. In the evening, we went dancing at a nightclub, drinking *tej*, a sweet, potent honey wine. Nigel was intelligent, interesting. He'd grown up on a middle-of-nowhere farm outside of Goondiwindi, Australia, and knew how to do things like build barns and slaughter sheep. He used the word "piss" more often and more flexibly than anyone I'd ever met—"I'm just pissin' in yer pocket," he'd say, or "I took the piss out of him, didn't I?" or "Let's hit the piss" or "What a piece of piss that was." He assured me that his family back home spoke the same way. London, he claimed, had buffed some of his rough edges.

Back at the hotel, we went to his room. It seemed we might be beginning to lean in toward our first kiss. I was ready for it, happy for it, but instead, Nigel blurted out some news: He had a girlfriend back in London.

I pulled back. I didn't kiss other women's boyfriends. It had been a long time since I'd kissed anyone at all.

Suddenly, we were both stammering. "I hadn't realized," I was saying. "I didn't know."

"No," he said. "I'm sorry. My fault." He added, "It's a confusing thing."

We sat back on the bed and passed a long moment staring at the floor.

Nigel then started to talk. His girlfriend's name was Jane. She was also Australian, he said. They'd been together a long time, about ten years, having met when they were quite young. They were in the midst of an agonizing, slow breakup, he said. It was her job that had taken them to London. That they were far from home and living together made it harder for them to extract from the relationship. It was sad, he said, but it was over. The trip to Africa was punctuation on the end of the sentence.

I let it go at that. I wanted to be the start of a new sentence. I was charmed. He was different than the boy backpackers I met on the road, a little cocky but also earnest. I thought it kind of noble, even, that he'd spilled the truth about the soon-to-be-ex-girlfriend. I knew plenty of guys who wouldn't. I was a believer in fate, and something told me that despite our individual plans and our homes on different continents, Nigel and I were fated to be together.

That night, we did a lot of kissing. The next morning, he caught the early bus for Harar. We promised to meet up again as soon as possible.

For the next six weeks, it went like this: Nigel traveled and shot pictures for the aid group while I explored on my own, as I'd planned it. We used e-mail to arrange rendezvous, coming together for a few giddy days in one crossroads town or another before staunchly resuming our travels. I took a punishingly hot two-day bus trip over the border into Sudan, where I spent a week at a backpacker encampment at the Blue Nile Sailing Club in central Khartoum. I befriended a Sudanese businessman named Ayad, who showed up at the club in the late afternoons and took loads of camping foreigners for sunset rides in his powerboat, showing us where the Blue Nile fed into the larger Nile River, its waters flowing north toward Egypt. Despite the fact that alcohol was banned in northern Sudan, he served chilled beer from a cooler in the stern. When I asked how he got it, Ayad, wearing designer shades and driving at full speed, shouted, "Anything is available on the Nile!"

I also at one point got myself all the way to the border between Ethiopia and Somaliland, a breakaway state in the northern part of Somalia that had managed to keep itself out of the nasty civil war going on in the south. I was hoping to spend a few days in the city of Hargeisa, which I'd heard was pretty and welcoming. I had another motive, too: Like a lot of backpackers, I was a country counter. We were always looking to improve our numbers. Listing the number of countries we'd visited gave us a way to measure ourselves. Most country counters kept quiet about their numbers until they got over thirty.

After four years of on-again, off-again travel, I'd been to forty-six coun-tries. A trip over the next border would bring me to forty-seven.

The uniformed border guards—each with a Kalashnikov slung idly over a shoulder—took one look at me and started shaking their heads. "Not now. Too dangerous," I was told.

I'm pretty sure "not now" meant not while Muslims around the world were feeling jittery and provoked. A few months earlier, a news-paper in Denmark had commissioned and published a group of satirical cartoon images of the Prophet Muhammad, setting off a furor among conservative Muslims. There had been riots and protests everywhere from Nigeria to Lebanon, and the controversy seemed to be continuing.

I don't know if some faraway official had issued a dictum regarding foreigners in Muslim Somaliland or if it was a gut decision on the part of the border guards in their squat concrete shack amid the swirling dust of eastern Ethiopia that I was bad news, but before long I was turned around and heading back where I'd come from, my country count stuck on forty-six. There was, I supposed, no upside to letting someone like me in.

*

Nigel, meanwhile, was coming alive in Ethiopia. When we talked on the phone during our stretches apart or I read his e-mails from an Internet café, I could sense him firing on the cylinders of each new day. I recognized the feeling. He sounded exuberant, untethered, even while complaining that he was ground down by the long bus rides and the flies that crawled up his nose and the unending barrage of begging children. When we met up, we feasted on meals of chopped collard greens and dollops of mashed chickpeas spread over pancakey *injera* bread. We tossed our backpacks into the corners of grotty guesthouse rooms and threw ourselves into bed. He was strong and capable, and I loved the golden hair on his arms.

I did my best not to worry about the girlfriend named Jane. When Nigel talked about her, he grew flustered. Sometimes when telling me a story about his past, I could tell he was editing her out of it. But mostly he didn't talk about Jane. He talked about me.

He was soon to return to London. Before he did, we made one long excursion together, into the brown desert of northwestern Ethiopia, across a legendary swatch of land called the Danakil Depression. I'd read about it during my pretravel reading binge at home, in a *National Geographic* story titled "The Cruelest Place on Earth." The Danakil was far from anywhere and scorchingly hot. My Lonely Planet carried a brief mention of the area but didn't provide instructions or encouragement to go. Which somehow made it perfect.

We took buses until we reached a market village on the outskirts of the desert. The town was populated by a tribe called the Afar—Muslim nomads who made their living pickaxing salt from the flats on a distant edge of the Danakil, then loading it onto camels and trekking it many miles through the some of the hottest weather in the world to sell to traders. The Afar women wore loose head scarves, and many had henna tattoos on their faces, three thin lines or a series of droplets on their cheeks. The Afar men were famous, apparently, for castrating their enemies.

We wanted to see the salt mines. Nigel thought maybe he could sell some photographs of the miners to a magazine. I thought I'd try my hand at writing about the experience, possibly for a travel website or my hometown newspaper. After asking around, Nigel and I found a guide—a short, rotund Afar man with a face that was wrinkled like a walnut shell and a long gray beard into which he'd rubbed a rust-colored henna dye. Hereafter known to us as Red Beard, he spoke no English but, in an agreement brokered by a local guy who did, Red Beard said he'd take us out to the salt flats and back, a trek of about ten days. We were joined by a solemn younger man—the Camel Whisperer, we called him—who said nothing in any language but had beautiful bladelike cheekbones and a shy smile and walked devotedly next to the four camels in our little caravan: one for each foreigner, one for Red Beard, and one for the luggage. Each animal also hauled two yellow plastic jerry cans, sloshing with water.

We rode behind Red Beard on a path that took us first across low hills of hard-packed sand and shrub and eventually out onto the flaking gray expanse of the sodium flats. From atop our camels, Nigel and

I sang songs, played Twenty Questions, and shouting over our shoulders at each other, told silly stories from childhood. He had spent his school years at a boarding school for rural kids, where he hated all the rules. He'd been angry at his parents for years afterward, he said, for sending him there. He tutored me on all things Aussie—why they loved Vegemite; how to shout "Why the fuck not, mate?" as a kind of battle cry for life.

We slugged water out of our bottles, let the sun broil our shoulders, behaved like high-schoolers on a rambunctious first date, only our date was taking place in an Ethiopian desert, with Red Beard and the baby-faced Camel Whisperer quietly and inscrutably observing our every move. The unspoken assumption was that Nigel and I were married. Which was why it was okay for me to rest a hand on his cheek or for him to give my butt a playful knock as I pulled myself back into the saddled notch of my camel's back after taking a food break.

I was coming to understand a few things about Nigel. He was less a photographer from London—at least not in the way I first interpreted it—and more a hopeful guy at the start of his career, even at the age of thirty-five. He talked about wanting to do more with his photography, how the idea of being a war correspondent appealed to him. We talked about Afghanistan, Sudan, Iraq, Somalia, all the places in the world where wars raged, all the places where a photojournalist would want to be. I told him about the week or so I'd spent in Kabul, staying with Amanuddin's family. Despite having been robbed there, I thought of it as intriguing and beautiful, a place I wanted to return to. Nigel let me borrow his camera—a black Canon, as heavy as a brick—and play around with it, clicking through its settings and experimenting with what happened when you switched one soup-can lens for another. He showed me how to frame a landscape shot, how to filter the bleach of the high sun.

On our second night, we stayed in a tiny Afar village, a way station for the camel drivers transporting salt. Red Beard had dragged a wide, thin mattress from someone's twig home and put it out in the open air for us. There were zillions of stars blinking infinitely over the blue desert, slinging the occasional meteor, each one hooking through the sky on a quick shimmering tear before flaming out. It was impossible to look away; we watched for what felt like hours. I was just beginning to nod off when Nigel reached over and gave my hand a squeeze. "Know what?" he said. "Right now I can't think of anywhere in the world I'd rather be." He paused a second and added, "Or anyone else I'd rather be here with."

I knew what he was trying to say and I was happy for it.

*

The Danakil Depression is a surreal, sunken basin dozens of miles wide and long, over three hundred feet below sea level in places. It's like a half-picked scab on the earth's surface, with the guts of the planet oozing in its cracks. As we moved deeper into the depression, we saw spitting fissures and bubbling pools of yellow and blue sulfur, which thickened the air with its stink. Nigel and I stared at it all. We took photos we were sure were gorgeous and unforgettable, anything to document that the whole thing was real.

Sometime on the fourth day, I stopped sweating. My thighs ached from all the hours clamped on the camel. My tongue felt heavy. My lips were cracked and sore. Even the desert-bred Afar men were getting fried. During a midday break in our lumbering, I refilled my water, a little woozily. Nigel and the Camel Whisperer walked a short distance away to pee. Red Beard swatted two of the camels until they dropped to a kneel. He slid the heavy saddles from the animals' backs and propped them up on the ground, stringing up a canvas cloth between them. His efforts yielded a low, makeshift tent that created a slim puddle of shade, into which all four of us crawled and quickly, within inches of one another, as if we had absolutely no choice in the matter, fell sound asleep.

By evening, I was shivering and disoriented, feeling ice run up my spine, dehydrated to the point of delirium. After another few hours on the camels, we had bedded down for the night on the salt flat, the crystals like little razors pushing through our straw mat. Nigel dribbled water from a bottle down my throat. I said something to him and watched his brow furrow; I was babbling nonsense, my bearings slipping away. The sky whirled overhead. Later, Nigel would tell me he was sure I would die that night, that they'd have to rope my body onto a camel to get me out, and the whole mess would be his fault.

It didn't go that way, though. Early the next morning, I opened my eyes and sat up. I felt better, with just the slightest hint of a headache. I shook Nigel awake. His eyes went wide.

"Aw, thank *God*," he said, stroking my hair. "You gave us a fucking scare, you know."

His relief seemed huge. I found it touching.

I convinced Nigel there was no reason to turn back, that we should continue. I promised to drink extra water and keep myself fully covered from the sun. He went along with it, reluctantly. "You're pushy," he said, handing my backpack over to the Camel Whisperer to strap on the cargo camel. "Pushy, pushy, pushy."

That day we followed Red Beard over the last miles to the salt mine— a dirty, grim outpost, the extreme reaches of an already extreme place, where maybe two hundred painfully skinny Afar men dressed in shorts and T-shirts were using long sticks to pry up giant cementlike slabs of heavy gray salt, then chipping them into square tiles that could be bundled and loaded onto waiting camels. Upon arrival, Nigel and I disembarked from our animals, grinning with relief, stretching our backs and shaking out our sore legs as if finishing up a pilgrimage, as if we'd come to some end-of-the-road auberge and were about to have ourselves a soapy shower and a three-course meal. Because that's the thing about the exact moment when you get somewhere that has required effort: There's a freeze-frame instant of total fulfillment, when every expectation has been met and the world is perfect.

We weren't thinking about the long trek back, or the fact that Nigel was still entangled with Jane, or even that the salt miners were staring at us with unbridled hostility. No, this was the moment *before* the moment when reality reasserted itself, which it promptly did, as one of the Afar miners spotted the camera in my hands and, pegging me for the invading alien that I was, scooped up a heavy chunk of salt and hurled it right at me.

10

A Camera and a Plan

From Ethiopia, I went on to Cairo, following my original plan. Nigel flew to London, where he said he was going to break up with Jane once and for all. He would then move back to Australia. I'd get a work visa and join him there. I bought a cell phone so he could call me as I continued traveling, which he did almost every day. Our phone calls were quick—we were on tight budgets—but loving. The longer we were apart, the more perfect he became. I'd never in my life imagined I'd follow some guy to Australia, but it seemed like precisely what was supposed to happen.

Then one afternoon he called me and, in short order, started to cry. The truth followed quickly, propelled by a rush of fully uncorked guilt. As it turned out, Nigel did not have a girlfriend in London named Jane. The woman in London named Jane was his wife.

They'd been together about ten years, like he'd told me in Ethiopia. What he'd left out was the part where they'd spent the last year of it married. They still were married, though it had been rocky, he said. He had gotten himself—with her, with me—into the ugliest sort of jam and was confessing all around. On the phone, I could hear his breath catching as he spoke, his tone pleading. He was calling the marriage a mistake, and lying to me about it had been another mistake. For a few minutes, we were both sobbing until, without another word, I hung up on him and stared at the yellowish high-rises outside my Cairo hotel window as both my plans and my heart seemed to burn up on the spot, as I thought,

Did that really just happen? Then came the secondary thought as the recklessness of the last five months replayed in my mind, this time with "Married Man" subbing for "London-based Lover": *How stupid am I?*

I felt adrift, cheated, alone. For the next few months, I traveled numbly—through Egypt, then Jordan, Lebanon, Israel, and Syria. Damascus had a labyrinthine covered souk where men sold things that glittered—glass beads, jeweled slippers, rolls of silk embroidered with gold thread. In the old city, there were cobblestone streets and arched wooden doors and vine-covered buildings built by the Ottomans some five hundred years earlier. There were shops selling flaky pieces of baklava dripping with honey and tiny cups of strong Turkish coffee. Rows of dark-suited old men sitting on benches in the shade. I met people, I saw things. My cell phone buzzed with calls from Nigel, but I ignored them. In my weaker moments, I clicked back through my photos of Ethiopia, studying his face, looking for signs of guilt and fakery. Sitting at an Internet café one day, I Googled Jane's name, wondering what she made of the whole mess, trying to guess at what kind of person she might be. I put labels on all of us—her, me, Nigel—good, bad, villainous; innocent, dumb, guilty. Or maybe it was just victim, victim, victim. I wasn't sure.

*

I got past my heartbreak the only way I knew how—by making more plans, bigger plans. I bought myself a new camera, a fancy professional one, an upgraded version of what Nigel had carried with him in Ethiopia. In some ways, given my finances, it was an absurd purchase, but I saw it as an investment in my future. I'd watched Nigel use his photography to sponsor several months on the road. It didn't seem illogical to think I could teach myself to do something similar. I was a traveler, after all, and the world was full of travel magazines. Who was to say I couldn't try to sell photos of the places I went? I wasn't thinking about a career, just a little income here and there. The goal was to keep myself moving.

The camera became a salve, a new repository for my hope. I went back to Canada and spent the rest of 2006 waitressing to recharge my bank account. Meanwhile, Nigel never stopped calling. He was back in

Australia, in the middle of divorce proceedings. His family and all his
friends were mad at him, he said. Though the whole thing was uncomfortable and weird, I'd started picking up the phone when he called,
feeling somewhere between still pissed and totally lonely.

I was twenty-five years old, fully accustomed to the cycle of making
money fast in a Canadian bar and then spending it slowly, as far out in
the world as I could get. I could travel on fifteen dollars a day without
feeling hungry or uncomfortable. I still felt a knock of fresh happiness
every time I reached a new place. I was also getting older, slowly out-
growing the flightiness of the people around me, both the waitresses
back home and the travelers I met on the road. I didn't want a desk
job, but I did want to be something more than a waitress. I went back
to Calgary and took a photography class between waitressing shifts. I
started to nurse a larger purpose, thinking that if I declared myself a
photographer, something good would come of it.

All the while, I continued to talk to Nigel, laughing a little bit more,
wondering whether we really were fated to be together. Maybe it was
his other relationship that had been the fluke and ours that had value.
He lived in a house he'd built with his own two hands. He had a job
he liked, working as a photographer for a newspaper in a small city
called Bundaberg. It all seemed very stable and grown-up. About ten
months after he broke the news about Jane, while I planned another
trip through Asia for the winter of 2007, Nigel talked me into stopping
for a layover in Australia.

*

It wasn't instantaneous, the rebuilding of our romance, but it wasn't
slow. I landed in Sydney on a February morning, and after fighting off
a full-blown panic attack in the airport bathroom, I walked into the
arrivals hall, where I watched Nigel turn and catch sight of me with a
slow smile spreading upward. The beard he'd sported in Ethiopia was
gone. He looked to be a paler, more neatly trimmed version of the
person I'd known, dressed in new jeans and a pressed shirt. When he
hugged me, it was firmly, as if placing me with a prolonged squeeze
in his world.

This kicked off a honeymoonish tour of eastern Australia. We had two weeks before I was to continue on to Bangkok and then Delhi, where I had plans to meet Kelly Barker, my favorite travel companion from home. Kelly had shifted from waitressing into working as a flight attendant, which had perks for both of us: She'd given me a "buddy pass" for a discounted flight to Asia and was flying for next to nothing herself.

In the meantime, Nigel and I climbed the Harbour Bridge, picnicked in a lush green park, and took a ferry to Manly Beach to play in the waves. We flew up the coast and booked a cabin on a small charter boat headed to the Great Barrier Reef, where we scuba-dived on psychedelic-looking blue and yellow coral and swam silently among flapping rays and gliding turtles. At night, we drank a lot. We picked apart grilled pink prawns and mud crab, dipping the sweet meat into melted butter. We sat up late, talking in the balmy sea air beneath an unreal pantheon of stars before taking ourselves happily to bed.

Still, I had flashes of paranoia. Was the man I'd met traveling, with whom I was now traveling again, the more authentic rendition of the guy who not too long ago had a wife, a flat in London, and an entirely different future? Had I rearranged that, or was I merely an excuse for the rearrangement? I tried to shove off the doubts, but we were operating under some pressure: The wreckage of Nigel's marriage became less horrid when repurposed as a true-love story, a meant-to-be affair so predestined that it couldn't have been helped, in fact, *shouldn't have gone any other way*, for if it had, we wouldn't be narrating it to nine grandkids someday from our rockers on the porch, having long ago made one painful correction for the sake of a full, happy life.

The whole premise worked if we ended up together, if I loved him and he loved me. We said these words to each other, but this time I made no promises to move to Australia. I tried to be bold in order to feel less weak. When I left Nigel, I did so on my terms. I told him I was going to end this next trip through Asia with a longer stay in Afghanistan, having banked some extra money during my last stint at home. Once there, I thought I'd try to get some paid work as a photographer. If he wanted to be with me, he could save his money and join me there. The next step belonged to him. Our lives, I said, could be fantastic.

11

Press Pass

That spring, I made it to Afghanistan as planned, moving into the Mustafa Hotel in downtown Kabul, negotiating a monthly rate and landing myself a small room with dark carpeting and a twin bed covered by a soft pink blanket. The window overlooked a busy square.

The Mustafa was famous, the place most journalists had bunked at the outset of the American invasion of Afghanistan, when foreign correspondents first poured into the city. It had been one of the first places in post-Taliban Kabul to start serving alcohol. The era when the hotel teemed with journalists, though, had passed. As the war in Afghanistan dragged on, some of the press had moved into fortified compounds or guesthouses that had been converted into news bureaus. Other media organizations didn't bother to keep a regular correspondent in Afghanistan, funneling their resources toward the other dragging-on war in Iraq. As a result, I'd heard that Afghanistan was a freelancer's paradise—rich in conflict but not overly populated with media. The barriers for people just starting out were far lower than they were at home.

Kabul, in May of 2007, resembled a stripped-down rock garden, with whole blocks of half-destroyed Soviet-style buildings followed by blocks of sprouting commerce. The dust off the plateau sat like a second skin on the faces of the raggedy kids who sold chewing gum and old maps on the street corners, the crispness of the high-altitude air

lacquered by the motor buzz and stink of hundreds of diesel genera-
tors attempting to make up for missing infrastructure.

I had business cards that read "Amanda Lindhout, Freelance
Photographer," and listed my e-mail address and new Afghan mobile
phone number, with the same words written on the back in Dari, the
most common language spoken in Afghanistan. I pressed them into
the hands of everyone I encountered. At the Mustafa, I met a friendly
photojournalist from England named Jason Howe, who'd charted his
own way through the guerrilla war in Colombia, through the Israel-
Hezbollah war in Lebanon in 2006, followed by a stint in Iraq. He was
now en route to Helmand Province to embed with British troops.

He explained the tenets of freelancing. You planned for yourself,
paid for yourself, and assumed your own risk. You rode out the bumps,
went without health insurance and long-term plans of any sort, and
grew accustomed to being broke. When it came to assignments, you
created your own, getting yourself to the most opportune spot.

Nothing about this intimidated me. It did not, in fact, sound a whole
lot different than the tenets of low-budget backpacking.

I took pictures of everything I could, though I found it hard to photograph Afghans. Even women fully shielded behind burkas turned
away from my lens. Men glared openly at me through my viewfinder.
I had reconnected with Amanuddin, the rug seller I'd met a couple
of years earlier. He'd relocated permanently from Peshawar to Kabul,
where he'd opened another store. Thinking he might be able to help
me, I asked whether he'd take me out to see the Kuchis, the nomadic
people who camped in makeshift villages in the bald brown hills
behind his extended family's house on Kabul's southern fringe, where
I'd stayed during my first visit.

There were Kuchis all over Afghanistan. Most were of Pashtun
heritage; some were more nomadic than others, moving across the
highlands over seasons. You'd see the Kuchis walking the sides of otherwise remote roads with their sheep, the women wearing bright wool
dresses with beaded bodices and wide sleeves, the men wrapped in
scarves and topped by mushroom-shaped Pakol hats. The few hundred
living in the furrowed valleys beyond Amanuddin's house slept under

a patchwork of woolen tents. The locals—the Afghans with land and homes—tolerated them, but mostly with distaste. The Kuchis reminded me a little bit of the First Nations people back in Canada, independent and unintegrated and pretty much worse off for it.

Having packed all my camera gear and all my ambitions as a newly minted, not-exactly-making-it professional photographer, I proposed to Amanuddin that we spend the night at the Kuchi camp.

His response was sharp: "Why do you need this?" Amanuddin's idea of a good time was listening to Bollywood music or bringing a picnic of lamb kebabs wrapped in newspaper and eating them on the shady banks of Qargha Lake. It was clear there were limits to what he would do in the name of tour guiding.

He did agree to walk me out to where the Kuchis were staying and make an introduction. The sun was beginning to dunk behind the hills as we approached, softening everything to a dusty plum. People were driving their herds of sheep and goats in toward camp for the evening. The scene had looked pretty and pastoral from a distance, but now I could smell the shit stink of hundreds of animals as they rivered closer. A turbaned man dressed in loose white clothing and a brown vest was moving toward us from the tents—the headman of the group, who introduced himself as Matin.

After some conversation in Pashto with Amanuddin, Matin took me to the tent belonging to his sister, saying I could sleep there. Amanuddin continued to insist it was not a good idea to stay—not safe, he said—but I was set on it. Giving me a suit-yourself shrug, he said he'd return for me in the morning and then loped back over the hills just ahead of the darkness.

The headman's sister was in her forties, with a sun-weathered face and her hair in two matted braids. She wore a red dress patched with pieces of green wool. Matin loudly pronounced her name for me. *Maryam.* He then pronounced mine for her. *Almond-a.* By way of bidding me good night, Matin touched his hand to his heart. I touched my hand to my heart in return.

Maryam lifted the flap to her tent and waved me in. A small fire burned inside. Her two children wrestled on a carpet laid over the gravelly ground. Their possessions were stacked neatly in canvas bags against the tent's far wall. Maryam set about making us a dinner of rice and thick yogurt and naan, which we ate right out of the cooking pots, washed down with sweet, warm tea.

After the meal, she swept the dirt floor and hauled several thick woolen blankets from the back of the tent. She took me outside so we could pee, side by side, on the hillside. Then the two of us lay awake, lit by the orange embers of the cooking fire, each propped on an elbow, talking in our respective languages, aided by hand gestures, somehow never tiring of the effort. We discussed our families and the war, converting a thumbnail's worth of actual comprehension into something that, in the moment, anyway, felt significant. When she couldn't make herself clear, Maryam laughed and reached for my hand, as if to say, *Whatever. We are having ourselves a little bit of fun.* From time to time, she leaned over and pulled the blankets higher over my shoulders.

In the morning, stepping out of the dark tent into the white blare of sunlight, I was rewarded for having spent the night. Maryam and her Kuchi sisters-in-law—older women who clucked their approval of my presence—stroked my hair and pinned beaded amulets to my shirt. They showed me their own adornments—chunky stone necklaces from Saudi Arabia, bracelets inlaid with bits of lapis lazuli, silver earrings in the shape of crescent moons.

I waited a while to pull out my camera, and when I did, it was not an event. The first time I lifted the viewfinder to my eye and pointed it at the women, nobody flinched. Nobody turned away or hid her children from me or gave me a single hostile look. Any assessment of me had already been done, perhaps the second I'd stepped out of the tent with Maryam and her kids, all of us intact and no worse for the wear. The men drank tea in the shade of a tent. The women lined up goats for milking. A wizened grandmother type squatting outside one of the tents looked at me squarely and frankly with what felt like centuries living in her eyes, and in that split second, I let the shutter close.

That picture—a close portrait of her spiderwebbed wrinkles and gorgeous clear eyes—became my first published image. An editor at a local magazine for expats called *Afghan Scene* accepted it a few weeks later to run as a cover photo. She liked the image so much that she asked if she could print a copy to hang in her living room at home. She then commissioned me to go back and report a full feature-length story on the Kuchis. A three-page, eight-photo spread, written and photographed by me.

By the standards of big-time journalists, it was nothing—a couple of sales to a low-budget magazine, a slim English-language monthly containing restaurant reviews and culture stories set between ads for everything from Visa cards to dog adoptions and armored cars—but for me it was a score. It was an actual assignment, a little bit of money— the reward for going and an excuse to stay.

*

Encouraged now, I studied the websites of newsmagazines and news-papers. I paid attention to what people photographed, how the stories read. I forced myself to be extra-outgoing and introduced myself to pretty much everyone passing through the Mustafa, asking questions about where they'd been and what they'd seen. I e-mailed editors in Toronto and New York, attaching photos I'd taken as I made short trips to different provinces, traveling with aid organizations or other freelancers from the Mustafa. Sometimes I got responses and requests to stay in touch, though never a commitment to publish what I'd sent. Most seemed to want only photographs of the war.

One tactic among enterprising freelancers is to get letters of intent from editors or photo editors—a few short lines written on official let-terhead, or an e-mail with an official-sounding address, saying that he or she is interested in seeing, for example, your story on opium farm-ers who've taken up growing pistachios or images from your trip to the Tajiki border. The letters are vague, with no guarantee of publication, but when they're forwarded to press officers or other gatekeepers, they function as gold.

The only letter ever written on my behalf came to me by way of one of the Mustafa's many strange barflies, a pale Brit with a pronounced

stutter named Anthony Malone, who, like a lot of the buzz-cut men
in desert boots hanging around the downstairs lobby area, referred to
himself obliquely as a "private security contractor." He lived in a ritzy
Kabul neighborhood, in a mansion with a staff. He knew people. He
threw parties. He talked in a low voice into his cell phone.

One night over a beer at the bar, he told me that if I wanted to get
an official military embed, he could help me out. Within a few days,
he'd procured a letter from a buddy of his, an editor at a magazine
called *Combat and Survival*, saying that he'd like to see any photos I
could get of the Canadian troops in the field. The letter did the trick.
Within a week, I was off to Kandahar.

Combat and Survival is a publication geared toward soldiers—current
soldiers, retired soldiers, and people obsessed, for whatever reason,
with war and soldiering. Its pages, when I checked them out, featured
reviews of monstrous-looking patrol vehicles and offered manly-
sounding frontline reports from places like Serbia and Central Africa,
the world's buzzing hot spots. I had no business working for it, but in
truth I was long past worrying about where and how I belonged. After
eight weeks in Afghanistan, I'd convinced myself that all I needed to
do was to maneuver myself into a place where something newsworthy
was going on.

I touched down in Kandahar on a 115-degree afternoon in late June,
lugging my photo equipment and a peacock-blue flak jacket, several
sizes too big, which Abdullah, the friendly manager at the Mustafa,
had dug out of his lost-and-found closet. Showing up at the Canadian
press tent at Kandahar Airfield, I felt my nerves flutter. There was a
team from Global News Television and CanWest Media and another
guy from CTV. Serious reporters, doing serious work, with their Peli-
can cases full of equipment, their satellite phones and ballistic-proof
sunglasses and combat helmets. Shortly after my arrival, a dark-haired
woman in a long white shirt breezed into the tent behind me, looking
freshly showered and very much at home. I recognized her instantly
as Mellissa Fung, a national reporter for the Canadian Broadcast Cor-
poration. I'd seen her on TV plenty of times, but now she was just

ten feet away from me—petite, confident, and not nearly as sweaty
as the rest of us, busily conferring with her cameraman over a tripod-
mounted video monitor.

I felt like a kid standing alone in the school lunchroom. As I filled
out the obligatory military paperwork, including an ominously worded
next-of-kin contact sheet, one of the Global News reporters walked
over to introduce himself. His name was Francis Silvaggio. I did what
I could to sound experienced. I was a photographer based in Kabul, I
said. I had flown down to shoot for *Combat and Survival*. As I was speaking, I saw his gaze settle on my Superman-blue XXL flak jacket, which
sat propped like a deli sandwich board on the ground next to my pack.

"What is that?" he said.

I sheepishly explained that it was body armor, old and too big and
on loan from my hotel in Kabul. He lifted his eyebrows. "I'm a freelancer," I said, as if this weren't obvious. I waited for him to say something condescending or find a quick way out of the conversation, but
he didn't. "You know," Francis said, "I think we've probably got an
extra vest that'll fit you better."

Before long, courtesy of Global News, I'd been outfitted in a snug
and comparatively sleek Kevlar vest the color of dry leaves. In it, I felt
less loserish. After being issued a helmet by the military public affairs
officer, I seemed to fully blend in. A handful of us media people were
heading to a forward operating base at a place called Masum Ghar, in
one of those areas that got referred to in the news as a "Taliban stronghold." We would drive an hour and a half in a convoy of light armored
vehicles to get there.

We got a procedure briefing from a commander before continuing.
He reviewed the threat of roadside bombs, his instructions clipped and
shouted. "If we're hit by an IED and there's no damage," he said, "we
move on. If we're hit by an IED and there's a vehicle down, we will
cordon it off and fight our way out if we need to."

Taking advantage of what could be the last strong cell reception,
the other reporters jumped on the phone with their editors, discussing
story angles, arranging deadlines. I stepped out of the tent and called
Nigel in Australia. I was feeling afraid.

We'd grown distant already. Our rekindled relationship seemed to be waning quickly. One phone call between us would be exuberant and loving—full of *aw babe* exclamations and ideas about the future—while the next would be terse and detached. Nigel's divorce had become official, but instead of feeling like he had a new life and a fresh start, he seemed mostly depressed. Though I understood it, I didn't want to understand it.

It was late afternoon in Australia. "I'm going out with the troops," I said to Nigel, launching into a description of my day thus far, explaining about my helmet and flak jacket, about the Taliban stronghold and the IEDs.

Maybe it sounded like a boast. Maybe I knew that. We'd had a phone fight earlier in the week. He'd been saying he was coming to join me in Kabul, but he'd made no move to book flights. He'd accused me of being pushy. I'd accused him of being docile.

"You won't hear from me for probably ten days," I told him now. "But don't worry, okay?"

There was a pause. I pictured Nigel at work at a desk in a clean shirt, editing his photos of whatever had gone on that day in Bundaberg.

"Okay, then," he said coolly. "Just don't get killed."

We hung up without a single endearment.

*

I spent the next eight days in the field with Canadian soldiers, mostly men my age and from rural parts of Canada. It took only a brief dip in to understand that war was not just dangerous but also a grind. The sun over southern Afghanistan roasted everything—the liquid soap in the latrines, the toilet seats—to almost scalding. Gear was heavy, the dust ubiquitous. I met a classical pianist who was worried about hurting his hands. I met a young father who kept laminated pictures of his children strung on a chain next to his dog tags. I met a couple of guys who passed their patrol time trading fantasies about the singer Nelly Furtado.

On my second day at Masum Ghar, word came down that three Canadian soldiers had been killed by a roadside bomb during a patrol southwest of Kandahar. The embedded reporters immediately cranked into gear, waiting out the necessary blackout period while the families were contacted before shooting the news out into the universe.

Soldiers lived inside the wire—within the protected confines of the military camp—but roamed, as needed and as ordered, on the outside. Inside the wire, there was a library, satellite television, and eggs cooked to order at breakfast. Outside the wire, the threats multiplied infinitely. The Taliban operated from the nooks and shadows, from the brown folds in the uptilted mountains, and inside the thick walls of little villages, un-uniformed and therefore indistinguishable from innocent civilians. They attacked with rockets and by laying IEDs along the roads.

The threat was almost always invisible. It could be anything. It defined everything, dogged everyone, caused the adrenal glands to pulse and fritz. The threat was hissing camel spiders the size of tea saucers. It was overhead tracer flare in the night, the bad-news e-mail from home, the eerie stillness on a road. It was anything on either side of the wire that could erupt into disaster.

Going outside the wire felt to me like being shot into space. One morning I followed a group of infantrymen as they stalked their way through fields of tangled grape arbors, holding guns and metal detectors, looking to investigate a suspicious wire spotted at a distance by an earlier patrol. I took photos and tried to keep up as the soldiers in their combat gear hopped over low mud walls dividing the fields, maintaining a twitchy silence as they crept closer to the worrisome spot. I felt scared, useless, enthralled. My nerves pulsed. A few Afghan boys watched us closely from a dry wadi as we moved delicately, not wanting to trip any bit of buried ordinance, wondering what the boys knew or didn't know—were they innocent or not innocent?—until at last we came upon the source of the hubbub, the threat glimpsed earlier, now in focus: a sun-withered scrap of rope lying in a ditch.

12

The Red Zone

*I*t is an obvious fact that you can never look ahead with clarity at your own future or anybody else's. You can't know what will happen until it happens. Or maybe it dawns on you the split second before, when you get a glimpse of your own fate. I think back to the day when I showed up in Kandahar with my camera and dubious *Combat and Survival* press pass. There were three Canadian soldiers who couldn't know then that a roadside bomb was waiting for them and they were soon to die. Back home were three sets of parents or spouses who weren't prepared for the call. Mellissa Fung, the CBC television correspondent who looked so purposeful and confident, couldn't know that sixteen months later, on a return trip to Afghanistan, she would get kidnapped outside of Kabul and spend twenty-eight days as a hostage, kept half-starved in an underground room in the mountains. Anthony Malone, the British security guy who got me the magazine letter, would be thrown into one of Afghanistan's most notorious prisons, charged with fraud and failure to pay debts, and held for two years. Jason Howe, the freelancer I met at the Mustafa, would go on to hit the big time, selling photos to all the major newspapers—*Le Figaro*, the *Times* of London, the *New York Times*.

I, too, was carrying around my own fate. All the things I couldn't know sat somewhere inside, embroidered into me—maybe not quite fixed to the point of inevitability but waiting, in any event, for a chance to unspool.

I left Afghanistan when my money ran out, returning home to Calgary to refill my bank account, work on my photography, and make new plans. My plans no longer included Nigel. He and I had fallen out of touch completely.

I got a job in the lounge of a new restaurant called Seven, a showoffy place that looked better suited to Miami, with white leather couches and white walls. The tips were lavish. The work wasn't hard. Outfitted once again in high heels and grasping a cocktail tray, I kept my Kabul experiences housed in one corner of my mind. I sublet a room in a condo owned by a girl my age who had an office job downtown, and I filled it with trinkets from the Middle East, hanging photos from Pakistan and India on the walls. For a few hours every week, in service to where I'd been and wanted to go, I took lessons with a local photographer, who was teaching me how to work in black and white and how to use Photoshop.

*

Around Christmastime, out of the blue, I was offered a television-journalism job in Baghdad. A real job. A job in Baghdad, with a four-thousand-dollar monthly salary and all my living expenses covered. It seemed unfathomable, but it was true. A guy I'd met months earlier at the Mustafa—an Iranian man named Ehsan who'd been in Kabul briefly, trying to find an NGO job—had sent me an e-mail saying that a television network in his home country was looking for an English-speaking correspondent. When I Googled it, a serious-looking news website came up. Press TV was freshly launched, an international twenty-four-hour English-language network financed by the Iranian government and designed to be similar—in appearance, anyway—to Al Jazeera and CNN International. Just as Al Jazeera had done, Press TV was hiring Westerners to work on camera. There were correspondents already in place in New York, London, Beirut, and Moscow.

I e-mailed back and forth with a female producer for a few weeks and spoke with her several times by phone. I cobbled together an audition tape. At work, I delivered drinks, letting myself imagine what it would be like to fly off to Baghdad. I wasn't sure what to think about who was hiring me. I knew that Iran had an Islamist government and a poor track record on human rights. But I'd also hung out with Ehsan, who was young and intellectual and hopeful about change in his country. He lived with his fiancée in Tehran and told stories about the place that made it sound full of sophisticated, cosmopolitan people who wrote poetry, went to underground nightclubs, and thought broadly about the world. At one point I asked the producer if there was a certain viewpoint represented by the network, whether I should be concerned about censorship. Her reply was no, Press TV was not biased, all stories were done fairly. In the moment, that was enough for me. The idea of having a salary, of being a TV reporter, and living in a place like Iraq was exciting enough to eclipse any doubts.

My mother helped pack my bags and drove me to the airport. She'd long since given up on voicing her worries to me.

*

I landed in Baghdad at the end of January 2008. Press TV had rented me a room at the massive Palestine Hotel, along with an adjacent office suite. The hotel would have been grand back in the 1980s, but now it was outdated and worn. The office suite had a few old couches in the corner, a fridge, a table, and some desks with video monitors and tape players for editing equipment that was old and huge but nonetheless did the job. I met Enas, an Iraqi woman with wide-set brown eyes, a plump body, and red-tinted hair that fell to her shoulders, who would act as my field producer. By phone, I was introduced to Mr. Nadjafi, the news director in Tehran who would be my immediate boss.

Baghdad was not dramatically beautiful the way Kabul, with its lunar brown mountains, had been. It had the same taxis and creeping traffic of other big cities I'd visited, the same oozing smog. It had the same golden light and splaying palm trees I'd seen in Damascus and Beirut and Amman. But with military checkpoints, concrete pylons, and twelve-foot blast walls everywhere, with its characterless square buildings and flat, sand-dusted horizon, whatever inner grace the city held, whatever mythic past it had as a land of milk and honey, was not easily glimpsed. Baghdad seemed harsher, more battle-worn than anyplace I'd been. My room at the Palestine looked out at a traffic circle and a ghostly white bubble-topped mosque. This was Paradise Square, where almost five years earlier an American tank had famously toppled a statue of Saddam Hussein. A block away, the Tigris River slipped past, sluggish and muddy and boatless.

There were not many Westerners staying at the Palestine. There were not many people at all staying at the Palestine. An American-funded television station called Alhurra, which broadcast information about U.S. policies in Arabic, was based out of the hotel, staffed mostly by Iraqis who came and went during work hours. Otherwise, the place seemed largely empty—in part because at eighteen stories, it was one of the tallest buildings in the city, which made it an easy target for insurgents. On my first night in Baghdad, I lay awake listening to the rat-a-tat of gunfire and the blare of sirens outside the window, feeling afraid, understanding that I was officially in over my head.

I had a lot to learn. Somewhere during the rushed move from Calgary to Baghdad, I'd downloaded a manual on broadcast journalism onto my laptop, which I'd gone through start to finish several times. In Damascus, where I spent over a week waiting for my visa to be processed at the Iraqi embassy, I began working my way through Robert Fisk's somber eleven-hundred-page *The Great War for Civilisation: The Conquest of the Middle East,* realizing how little I knew. In the evenings, alone in my room, I worked to drop my register from young-lady soprano to a newscaster's calm, stern alto.

Enas, the Press TV field producer and translator, became my friend. She was about thirty-five and had a bright smile. She carried a purse full of plastic-wrapped candies and could strike up easy banter with just about anyone. When we were not working, she and I went shopping for head scarves and visited the juice bars in Karada Market. Later in the winter, we went for walks along Abu Nawas, the beat-up corniche that runs east along the Tigris, which recently was reopened after being closed off to civilians for several years. According to Enas, Abu Nawas once teemed with bohemian art galleries, strolling couples, and fish restaurants that served cold beer. Now many of the restaurants were closed, their walls pocked with bullet holes. The riverbank park was overgrown with weeds, but in the evenings Iraqi children showed up to climb over freshly erected playground sets donated by European aid agencies.

Enas was Muslim, but she wore a head scarf only when she felt like it, and she didn't pray five times a day. None of the Iraqis I got to know—people on the Alhurra staff, the freelance cameramen I worked with—prayed like that. They were Muslim the way many of my friends at home were Christian: They observed the major holidays, went to a mosque on Fridays, and had worked out their own private arrangements with God. They found strength in the Koran but were not governed by ideas that struck them as ancient or overly restrictive. They were as afraid of radical Islam as the rest of us were. Most seemed to agree that the war was muddled both by religious fighting—the Sunnis, the Shias, the quarreling subgroups within each—and by foreign interest in Iraq's oil.

If working for the Iranians made Enas uncomfortable, she didn't show it. She hummed as she made us strong black tea and ran through the day's schedule with a legal pad on her lap. Iraq had invaded Iran in 1980, when Enas was a child, and the countries then spent eight years at war. Half a million people had died. Neither country had prevailed, but the resentment was still active. Iraqis regarded Iran with generalized suspicion. A few people I tried to interview politely turned away once they learned I was with Iranian television. "I am sorry," one man said to me in a marketplace, declining my request. "I do not want to get you in trouble with your bosses. It is just that Iran has caused so many problems here."

I was a part of the propaganda machine. I realized this right away. As Enas and I drove around with a cameraman, reporting stories on street children, wounded civilians, and cease-fires that didn't cease anything, Mr. Nadjafi collected my footage and edited it in ways that cast American troops and American policy in the worst possible light. He rewrote my scripts so that any mention of the war would be described as "the American-led invasion" or "the American-led occupation." The Koran was "the Holy Koran." Our assignments often took us into Sadr City, a dilapidated and violent Shiite district where the Mahdi Army frequently did battle with U.S. troops. Mr. Nadjafi rejected my requests for more money so that Enas and I could hire a security guard. I began increasingly to feel unsafe and taken advantage of.

In the evenings, from my room, I called my mother on Skype, cling- ing to the sound of her voice any time I was feeling uncertain. Worried about the lack of a security budget, she urged me to find a new job. Hoping to improve my skills, I scoured the Internet, studying the work of some of the big-time correspondents and photographers based in Baghdad, trying to figure out what they covered and how they covered it. I sent inquiries to Canadian newspaper editors and managed to talk an editor at my hometown paper, the *Red Deer Advocate,* into letting me write and shoot photos for a weekly column. I would get thirty-five Canadian dollars for each story and twenty-five for each photo that ran.

Driven by loneliness, I moved myself and the little Press TV bureau to the Hamra Hotel, in a residential neighborhood a couple of miles from the Palestine and more populated by Westerners—a mix of jour- nalists and foreign contractors, some of whom were rotating through Baghdad, many of whom appeared to be there indefinitely. The Hamra was built around a courtyard with balconies that looked over a central glimmering pool surrounded by white plastic loungers. There was a small bar that sold Heineken and Lebanese wine and a restaurant serving Iraqi food. High blast walls had been built around the entire compound, which included a couple of houses, one of which served as the *Washington Post* bureau. The *Los Angeles Times* had staff living at the Hamra, as did NBC News, *USA Today,* and a few others.

At night, people drifted out of their rooms and down to the pool area, bringing with them bottles of Bombay gin bought at the military PX. Hotel staff set up tables and brought glasses and ice for the alco- hol. They delivered beer, wine, and food orders from the restaurant. On one of my first evenings at the Hamra, I got a little dressed up and headed down to the pool, ordering a beer from a waiter and trying to look like I belonged. All around, I could hear journalists chatting about their workdays, describing their meetings or griping about delays. I felt a wave of excitement. Finally, I'd found people I could talk to, who could teach me something.

I walked up to a few guys standing by a table. "Hi!" I said. "I'm Amanda!"

We smiled and shook hands all around, like colleagues, comrades. All three looked to be in their early thirties. For just a second, I felt buoyant. And then one of them asked who I worked for.

"Press TV."

"Who?"

I found myself explaining about the Iranians, making sure to mention that I was planning to quit as soon as I could line up different work.

The silence that followed was long and disdainful. The lights reflecting off the pool threw a wavering green over all of us.

"What about you guys?" I said, trying to shift the focus. "Who are you here with?"

They named their media organizations—all American, all serious. Legit, legit, and legit. We talked another minute before each one managed to excuse himself, drifting off into the shadows, and I was alone again.

During those first weeks at the Hamra, it seemed that I had no good answer for anything anyone asked me. It took nothing to size me up.

Where was I from? A little town in Alberta, Canada. Where had I gone to grad school? Um, I hadn't actually gone to university, let alone grad school. Who did I work for before I came here? Well, nobody.

Theirs was a language I couldn't speak; their world was entirely foreign. I had never been to Washington, D.C. I didn't know New York. Even as I paid attention to the mainstream news via the Internet, I knew little about the American media scene. I'd come to Baghdad by way of all the other places I'd been—Beirut, Aleppo, Khartoum, Kabul—but I hadn't been to Yale or Columbia. I worked long hours

and took every opportunity to ask questions of the established journalists, but almost always I felt awkward and out of place.

Not everybody was standoffish. One evening I struck up a conversation with the NBC reporter Richard Engel. He was handsome and fit
and shorter than I was, with a big-wattage smile and hair that had been
cut high over his ears like a marine's. When we got to the inevitable
moment when I confessed that Press TV was funding my stay in Iraq,
he was sympathetic, telling me he understood the scramble to get by.
He'd first come to Iraq in 2003, crossing the border as an uncredentialed freelance journalist with a handheld video camera. Now, five
years later, he was the big-shot reporter at NBC News. Several weeks
after we met, he'd be promoted into the role of chief foreign correspondent for the network.

"Everyone's got to start somewhere," he told me. "Use it as a stepping stone. But you're going to want to move on quickly."

*

After another month or so, I managed to quit the Press TV job,
supporting myself with freelance assignments from France 24, an
English-language television station out of Paris. I reported a culture
story on Iraq's National Symphony Orchestra. I sold a story on
Iraqi refugees returning to the country and one on the plight of the
Palestinians living in Baghdad. As when I reported for Press TV, I was
often humbled by the Iraqis I encountered—an overburdened doctor
at a local hospital, a teacher in Sadr City sweeping up glass after an
explosion blew out her classroom windows, two orphaned brothers
selling Kleenex on the street. It was impossible not to feel perplexed
and saddened by the war. Bearing witness to it, even in my own small
way, felt like a privilege.

I was making just enough money to get by. For every minute of
my work that aired on the network, France 24 wired fifteen hundred
euros into my bank account, though most of that went toward the
expenses of hiring a driver, translator, cameraman, and editor, on
top of the three thousand dollars I was paying monthly to live at the

Hamra. I continued to write my column for the newspaper back at home. And I'd made a real friend, a shy freelancer named Daniel, who was American and, like me, had been shut out of the mainstream media crowd. He and I sometimes stood on my balcony at the Hamra and watched the swirl of journalists—the Fancy-pants, we'd taken to calling them—laughing, boozing, swimming, and dancing below.

I had another friend, a gentle-voiced American named Julie who was about my age and working for a big news service. Julie was one of the Fancy-pants, but we had a sort of bond.

One night she came by my room. I poured her a glass of wine. "You know," she said, "that everybody's mad at you, right?"

"What?" I said. I'd just returned from a few weeks of vacation time in Portugal, traveling again with Kelly. I looked at Julie in disbelief. How could anybody be mad? What could I have done?

In my absence, it turned out, some of my neighbors at the Hamra had discovered a video on YouTube. Unbeknownst to me, the Press TV anchor had uploaded a live broadcast I'd done with him a couple of months earlier, when I was still living at the Palestine, before I'd had any real contact with foreign reporters.

I hadn't realized that live broadcasts went up on the Internet. As I watched it on my laptop after Julie had gone off to bed, I felt my chest squeezed by a monumental dread. On-screen, the Iranian anchorman was asking me, with no small degree of incredulity, how it was that the mainstream Western media seemed to be supportive of George Bush's troop surge when the death toll among American troops had just ticked up to four thousand.

Standing in the heat of the day on a lower rooftop of the practically empty Palestine Hotel with a placid row of palm trees behind me, having spent a number of weeks driving around Baghdad with Enas and no security guards, I had answered with what I thought was the truth. At that point, I'd seen foreign reporters only in the heavily guarded Green Zone, absorbing the daily briefings given by bland-voiced Coalition Provisional Authority press officers. I'd heard from the Iraqis working for Alhurra that in order to limit their risks, and often governed by media-outlet insurance policies, Western journalists sometimes sent Iraqi reporters—translators and fixers, usually—out into the city to do interviews so they could assemble the reporting and write their stories from the relative safety of their bureaus.

Sitting against a pillow on my bed at the Hamra, I braced myself for what came next. Already, I felt older than the version of myself I saw on the screen. I wished she'd never opened her mouth. I imagined all the Fancy-pants gathered around somebody's computer, scoffing at every word.

"The problem with reporting in Baghdad, for many media outlets," I was saying to the anchorman in the broadcast voice I'd worked so hard to cultivate, "is they don't actually see what's going on. They are living in compounds. They're sequestered inside the Green Zone. And actually, by contract, they're not allowed into the Red Zone, where you see me . . ."

Listening to myself talk, I felt ill. Since moving to the Hamra, I'd lamented that nobody seemed to want to include me. But I had made the mistake long before I met any of the journalists working there. After barely two months in Baghdad, I had awarded myself the upper hand on wisdom and experience, on live television, no less— and worse, immortalized on YouTube. And I'd been wrong. There were plenty of journalists living and working in the Red Zone. But I hadn't been entirely misinformed, either. It was hard for anybody to see what was going on in Baghdad, myself included. It was just too unsafe.

I had no choice but to live with what I'd said. I had been quick-talking and naive, and now I was pretty much screwed. I gave up on making friends or professional connections in Baghdad. I wore my embarrassment like an iron lung. I studied my bank balance and looked for flight deals online, thinking I should find another place to report from temporarily—Africa, maybe. In the past, I'd calmed myself with breathing exercises, or by trying to meditate the way I'd done in back-packer hostels in India, but in this context, it didn't seem to work. I felt stuck and alone and totally depressed.

Then came a surprise e-mail from Nigel, saying what seemed to be a simple hello. He had a new girlfriend and had moved with her to Scotland. He was living on an estate near Glasgow, working as a groundskeeper. He was checking in on me, sending good wishes. He signed off with "Take care, darling, and stay safe over there." Despite the news about the girlfriend, it was a blast of old sweetness right when I needed it.

A few days and a few e-mails later, we arranged to talk on the phone. The sound of his voice caused my eyes to well. I missed what we'd once had. Nigel made jokes about his new job, the Scottish weather. Since we'd spoken last, he'd anchored himself into a whole new life, though he didn't sound all that excited about it. I didn't understand what had led him from his newspaper job in Bundaberg to trimming hedges in Scotland. I knew nothing about how he'd spent the last year. I knew only that he wasn't taking pictures anymore.

I told him a few stories from Baghdad, making it sound as though I were leading a fascinating, exciting life and leaving out the part about how everyone hated me. After about ten minutes, the conversation trailed off. A beat passed.

I heard myself blurting a question I probably should have kept to myself. "What about your photography? What happened? You had such big plans for yourself."

It was a bit of a taunt, but some part of me was genuinely curious— the dim region of my mind trying to understand why, when I was the one who'd pulled off some version of the dream life we'd imagined for ourselves a couple of years ago in Ethiopia, I was the one who was miserable.

"I don't know, really," Nigel said. He sounded flummoxed, thoughtful, maybe a little glum.

I blurted onward. I mentioned that I was thinking about buying a plane ticket to Nairobi and that, from Nairobi, I thought I'd get myself to Somalia sometime in the next month. I had researched possible Somalia story ideas to pitch to the France 24 news director. I'd been thinking all these things, but now I was saying them out loud. And as I did, something old and hopeful snapped on.

"You could come, you know," I said to him. "There's so much going on there. You could shoot pictures for a magazine, and I'll do something for TV."

"Maybe I could," he said.

I hung up feeling pretty certain that he wasn't serious. After all, he hadn't joined me in Kabul when we were involved, and now, nearly a year later, he had a new girlfriend and was no doubt more rooted than ever in the comforts and safety of domestic life.

It didn't matter, though. Over the course of that conversation, I'd quietly made up my mind. I was ready to get myself out of Baghdad.

*

There's a famous old story in the journalism world about the news anchor Dan Rather. He was a young and inexperienced television reporter working for a second-rate TV station in Houston, Texas, in the early 1960s, when a monstrous hurricane barreled through the Gulf of Mexico, headed toward the island of Galveston. All the other reporters, it's said, scrambled for the shelter and safety of their mainland newsrooms. But Dan Rather drove over the bridge and waited for the storm. When it bore down on Galveston, ripping up trees and houses and hurling ocean waves at the shore, he delivered live reports from the windiest and most dangerous heights.

He might have failed that day. He could have been injured or killed, in which case he would have become a footnote, known fleetingly as the guy who inserted himself into a hurricane and died, ruined by his own ambition. Instead, though, the gamble paid off. He survived the storm. Because he was there, because he'd taken the risk, he managed to tell the story in a vivid and meaningful way. His career was made. He was credited for convincing thousands of viewers in the hurricane's path to evacuate their homes and promptly hired by a national network.

After almost seven months in Baghdad, I set my sights on Somalia. The reasons to do it seemed straightforward. Somalia was a mess. There were stories there—a raging war, an impending famine, religious extremists, and a culture that had been largely shut out of sight.

I understood that it was a hostile, dangerous place and few reporters dared go there. The truth was, I was glad for the lack of competition. I figured I could make a short visit and report from the edges of disaster. I'd do stories that mattered, that moved people—stories that would sell to the big networks. Then I'd move on to even bigger things.

Somalia, I thought, could be my hurricane.

13

Doors Wide Open

The idea was to spend four weeks in Africa. That was it. In and out. A photographer I knew from Baghdad—a friendly Frenchman named Jerome—had given me contact information for a fixer working in the Somali capital of Mogadishu. Fixers are hired to serve as on-the-ground planners for traveling journalists, setting up interviews, handling logistics, and often serving as translators. This one, Ajoos Sanura, was the elder statesman of Somali fixers and trusted by Western reporters. Jerome had been to Somalia twice already. He'd recently been offered a newspaper assignment to go a third time but had turned it down, in part because the country had become so dangerous. In his late thirties, married to another journalist and with a teenage son, Jerome had been in lots of war zones and had some scrapes with danger.

He warned me that everybody's luck eventually ran out. There was no upside to moving between the world's wars. "You're still young," he told me. "You should do something else with your life." Yet I couldn't imagine doing anything else. I was twenty-seven years old, and my greatest successes so far—however modest they were—had come to pass in war zones.

The cheapest route to Nairobi from Baghdad was by way of Addis Ababa, the Ethiopian city where I'd met Nigel two years earlier. I went there first, checking in to the Baro Hotel for nostalgia's sake. It was still a dump, still home to enthusiastic, sun-blasted backpackers wafting their traveler pheromones, clustering and pairing and seeking out new things. I remembered the feeling, the allure, but I could no longer pull it up in myself. It was like they were dancing to music I couldn't hear.

I flew from Addis to Nairobi on August 10, 2008, finding a hotel downtown—a two-star place instead of my usual one-star, in deference to my laptop and wad of cash and the need to keep them safe. I didn't plan to stay long. I'd been e-mailing with Ajoos and was encouraged by his responsiveness. For a hundred and eighty dollars per day, he would take care of logistics, including a translator and security. He would arrange a room at a place called the Shamo Hotel, the only lodging he recommended for foreigners, for an additional hundred dollars per night. I sent him a list of things I was interested in doing in Somalia: I wanted to visit a camp for displaced people, interview a female Somali doctor who was renowned for her medical relief work, and film the arrival of a Canadian naval vessel that was escorting a shipment of food aid funded by the World Food Programme to the coast of Somalia. Ajoos seemed to think it all would be possible.

The reality was that I was starting to need Nigel, or somebody, to come with me and share the costs. Ten days in Somalia would decimate my savings if I went alone. Nigel and I had e-mailed a few times. He seemed to be wrestling with himself over what to do, whether to come or not. He missed photography and the thrill of traveling. Some vain part of me hoped that he missed me, too.

On my second day in Kenya, I went to the Somali embassy and paid fifty dollars for a three-month journalist visa, granted overnight. Somalia was supposed to be the most dangerous country on earth, but its doors were wide open.

Another e-mail arrived from Nigel. He was coming. He would fly to Nairobi from London in a few days. He'd bought the ticket, packed his camera, and was on his way.

I was surprised by his decision and confused over what it meant. There was so much unresolved between us. The last time we'd seen each other had been in Australia sixteen months earlier, when we'd clung together in the airport, sure that our relationship was going to work out. Between Afghanistan and Iraq, my life had rearranged itself, and so, too, had Nigel's. We'd given up on each other without any real discussion. If I was honest with myself, I understood that I'd dangled the invitation to join me in Somalia precisely so he could turn it down. To torment him just a little bit about his lost dreams. To give myself the chance to paste up his "no" next to my "yes."

But Nigel had called my bluff. He was saying yes. The prospect of seeing him again, of having him physically next to me, made me nervous. Why was he coming? What would we do? Whatever old affections we had, whatever resentments had gone unexpressed, I wasn't sure I was ready to have them pried up—especially not in a place like Somalia.

*

Somalia is shaped like the number seven. It sits hooked over the top of Ethiopia, with one coastline pointing north toward Yemen and another, longer one facing east, overlooking the vast stretch of ocean that runs to the southern tip of India. Because of its location—wedged between the Middle East and the rest of Africa, with relatively easy sea access to Asia—Somalia has always mattered, especially to traders. The port of Mogadishu was once afloat with ships bringing in loads of spices from India and heading out stuffed with Somali gold, ivory, and beeswax. Much later, having been colonized by the Italians and the British, Somalia became a glamour destination for jet-setting Europeans who came in the 1940s and 1950s to bake themselves on the white sand of Mogadishu's Lido Beach and clink glasses in its nightclubs and cafés.

This, though, was not the Somalia I was reading about in my Internet research. Mogadishu, some 630 miles north and east of Nairobi, was described as hellish—a chaotic, anarchic, staggeringly violent city, the shredded capital of a country that had ejected the colonialists and resisted democracy for the last fifty years. Power had been endlessly, hopelessly parsed between a network of mini-empires run by ancestral clans, warlords, and criminal gangs. A socialist dictator named Siad Barre had ruled unevenly for just over twenty years but had been driven out by rebel groups in 1991. Seventeen years later, those groups—having splintered, morphed, and shifted allegiances repeatedly, in some cases joining forces with Islamic fundamentalists—were still battling one another for control. There had been thirteen different attempts at establishing a central government in Somalia, and all had failed. A fourteenth government was in place, basing itself out of one neighborhood in Mogadishu, though it was, by all accounts, almost completely ineffectual. When diplomats talked about Somalia, they called it a "failed state," as if to suggest there was no possibility of solving its problems, as if it were deeply and permanently ruined.

Beyond that, it had been an especially bad summer. The rainy season that year had brought no rain. Crops had failed. Food prices were high; people were beginning to starve. Rebel militias, understanding that food was power, were hijacking trucks carrying food aid brought in by the United Nations, sometimes shooting the drivers. At least twenty aid workers had been killed that year; a few others had been kidnapped and held for ransom. A number of international organizations had pulled out of Somalia altogether, saying it was too dangerous to work there.

I'd like to say that I hesitated before heading into Somalia, but I didn't. If anything, my experiences had taught me that while terror and strife hogged the international headlines, there was always—really, truly always—something more hopeful and humane running alongside it. What you imagined about a place was always somewhat different from what you discovered once you got there: In every country, in every city, on every block, you'd find parents who loved their kids, neighbors who looked after one another, children ready to play. Surely, I thought, I'd find stories worth telling. Surely there was merit in trying to tell them. I knew that bad stuff happened. I wasn't totally naive. I'd seen plenty of guns and misery by then. But for the most part, I'd always been off to one side, enjoying the good, the harm skipping past me as if I weren't there at all.

14

Crossing

Nigel walked out of customs at the Nairobi International Airport on the afternoon of August 16, carrying the same red backpack he'd had in Ethiopia. He hadn't changed a whole lot. Same bright eyes, same razored dimples in his cheeks.

"Trout, get your ass over here," he said, holding out his arms. Trout was a nickname I'd had in high school, a play on my last name. Nigel had appropriated it in Ethiopia.

We hugged. I said, "It's so good to see you." I meant it. I'd been alone so much in the last year, on edge with just about everyone I'd met. Before leaving Iraq, I'd had a dalliance with one of the American reporters, a bureau chief who lived down the hall from me at the Hamra and who, despite being arrogant, had seemed briefly like a friend, or at least someone to pass time with. Yet even that had felt alienating.

The familiarity I felt with Nigel was instantly calming. He threw an arm affectionately over my shoulders as we walked outside into the warm Kenyan air. I let myself be flattered by his presence, by the fact that he'd gotten on a plane and flown all the way to Africa—to work, yes, but also to see me. We took a taxi to the hotel so he could drop his bags in his room, down the hall from mine, and then went out to do the only thing that would help speed us through the awkwardness of the reunion: We got drunk.

We went to a café for a beer and on to a restaurant for dinner and some wine. From the street, we spotted a second-story bar, its balcony crowded with Kenyans in business suits, and we found our way there for tequila shots and more beer. We were talking more easily, looking at each other frankly, but avoiding any conversation that would qualify as meaty or emotional. We agreed we wanted more from our lives, but we stopped it at that.

By the time we landed at a smoky karaoke place sometime after midnight, by the time we'd downed another drink, climbed onstage, and belted out a George Michael tune at full volume in front of a group of locals who stood up and danced as we sang, I felt like we almost didn't need to discuss our relationship. I felt somewhere between 90 and 95 percent sure that we didn't love each other anymore, that we could be friends. I took one last turn with the microphone—woozily dropping a little New Kids on the Block on the Kenyan crowd—promising myself I'd wake up the next day and get back to thinking about work.

After we'd lurched back to our hotel, Nigel dipped toward me for a kiss, almost as if it were obligatory, and it felt so immediately weird and wrong that I knew for sure, as a couple, we were finished.

*

A few days later, the two of us crossed the tarmac at the Nairobi airport, headed toward a decrepit-looking Daallo Airlines plane. We were both tense, lugging a couple of carry-on bags, a few thousand dollars in American money, the currency of choice in Somalia, and our cameras. We'd each checked a bag. We were not saying a lot. The night before, we'd gone out for a nice dinner at an Italian restaurant called Trattoria, giving ourselves a sort of last hurrah before moving into what we'd figured would be more austere conditions in Mogadishu. Given that Somalia's population was almost entirely Muslim, and Muslims as a rule don't drink, it would probably be our last taste of alcohol, too. Late in the evening, Nigel had made another attempt at a kiss, and this time I'd actively pushed him away. "You have a girlfriend," I scolded.

I was sure that his girlfriend wasn't pleased with him these days, for a lot of reasons.

The airplane was packed with about a hundred Somali men and women, plus a few kids who clambered over the ripped canvas seats. The walk across the hot tarmac, coupled with a sense of foreboding I couldn't quite shake, had combined to make me feel light-headed and a little bit sick. I noticed many of the women wore a conservative form of hijab, heavy dresses with long veils. A number of them were wearing niqabs, their faces fully covered except for the eyes. A few had stuffed their feet into white plastic bags before putting on their sandals, an effort to cover every last millimeter of skin out in public.

Everyone seemed to be chattering loudly while loading what seemed to be an insane amount of carry-on luggage—plastic bags of every color, packed with clothes and books and food, knotted tightly to stay closed. The walls of the plane were streaked with dirt. The door to the bathroom hung partially off its hinges. In the waiting area, I'd exchanged a few words with what appeared to be the only other non-African on the flight, an older Italian man who spoke English. He said he worked for a Christian NGO and was headed for the northern city of Hargeisa, the capital of the independent province of Somaliland, which would be the plane's second stop after Mogadishu.

Hearing that we were disembarking in the south, he raised his eyebrows and made a dramatic poof with his lips, a gesture of disbelief. "Be very careful in Mogadishu," he said. "Your head"—he tapped his own head—"is worth a half million dollars there. And that's just for your head."

I knew what he was saying. Westerners were a useful commodity in Somalia, even dead ones. A body was a trophy; living hostages could be sold back to their home countries. The notorious 1993 "Black Hawk Down" incident, in which a failed raid by American commandos on a Mogadishu warlord had resulted in Somali militiamen proudly dragging the corpses of two American soldiers through the streets. More recently, in the Gulf of Aden to the north, Somali pirates were getting rich, holding foreign ships captive until seven-figure ransoms were paid. I knew exactly what the Italian NGO worker was trying to tell me, but I didn't appreciate hearing it.

Nigel and I were sitting at the back of the plane. Around us, people talked on cell phones, appearing agitated, standing up to shout out what sounded like news to others in neighboring rows. A Somali woman who'd been raised in America and now worked in Hargeisa translated for us. "They're saying the war has broken out at the airport in Mogadishu," she said. "There is fighting on the road. Maybe it will be closed. Maybe we can't fly."

I wasn't sure what that meant, exactly—*the war has broken out*—especially against the backdrop of a war that had been going on for almost two decades, but in the plane, among the Somalis, it appeared to be causing a stir. We waited for some sort of announcement. The blood seemed to be pumping with extra force through my veins. For a second, I allowed myself to feel relieved by the prospect of being ordered off the plane and back into the Nairobi airport, to have the matter taken entirely out of our hands.

But after a few minutes, the plane's engines kicked on. A flight attendant pulled the door shut, vacuum-sealing us off from the morning heat of Nairobi before taking to the loudspeaker to order people off their cell phones. War at the airport be damned, we were flying.

Sitting beside me, Nigel looked almost gray. "I have a bad feeling about this," he said. "I can't help it. I feel like something bad's going to happen."

I reached over and squeezed his arm. In my mind, I ran through the reasons we should be feeling good and not bad. I'd arranged to have us met at the airport. Ajoos had told me that an armed security crew would escort us to the hotel. He'd mentioned other foreign journalists were staying there. How bad could it be? If the fighting around the airport was a problem, I figured the pilot would continue to Hargeisa with us on board. Everything was more or less settled. We'd be okay.

I looked at Nigel. "This is just what it feels like to fly into a war zone," I said, sounding more confident than I felt. "It's totally normal. You'll feel better when we get there."

On cue, the plane began to roll, rattling over the asphalt like an old jalopy, until it picked up speed, tilted, and took off. I felt my stomach press against my spine. Nairobi fell away beneath us, an expanse of glinting shantytowns and flat brown plains. I sat looking numbly out the window as we lifted through the clouds.

The Italian man was sitting just across the aisle. He had removed a Bible and a pair of black-framed eyeglasses from his bag and was reading quietly.

I powered up my laptop, plugged a headset into the jack, and hit play on a meditation audio file I kept stored on my hard drive. It was something I'd listened to in the evenings in Baghdad, in my room at the Hamra as I tried to fall asleep. The recording had been made by a woman I knew from home who ran a meditation group that Jamie and I had gone to when we lived together. On it, in a sonorous maternal voice over a backdrop of piano music, she gave instructions to breathe, long and slow, again and again, adding words to feed through the mind as a mantra: "With this breath, I choose freedom. With this breath, I choose peace."

I sat with my eyes closed and I breathed, the words pattering through my mind, more rhythmic than meaningful. *Freedom, peace, freedom, peace.* I did this for maybe half an hour, cooling my nerves. When I opened my eyes again, I felt better, more even. I stowed my laptop and noticed that the Italian man had shut his Bible and was looking at me. "Were you praying?" he said.

"Sort of," I answered. Then I amended it. "Yes." The man smiled and said nothing. "I was trying to ground myself," I said. I wondered if he was a missionary or a priest.

The man nodded. He was old, maybe the age of my grandfather, his eyebrows overgrown and tufted, his eyes a little watery. He leaned in my direction. "It's good you are going to Mogadishu," he said. "I respect it. I hope you are careful." This was possibly an apology for having scared me earlier, for raising the specter of my head on some warlord's plate. In any event, it was as close as I'd get to a blessing for what we were about to do.

*

Ninety minutes after leaving Nairobi, we began to descend. Out the window, I caught my first glimpse of the Somali coastline—thickets of deep green vegetation hemmed by a highway of white sand, all of it pressed against a foaming mint-colored sea. It had to be one of the most astonishingly beautiful places on earth. There was no sign of roads or beachfront hotels, no sign of humanity whatsoever. There was only land—thick jungle, abundant and unshorn, like a tropical paradise spotted through the spyglass of an old-time explorer. The city of Mogadishu, when it came into view, was also stunning—a hive of whitewashed colonial buildings built around a crescent-shaped harbor.

Everyone on the plane had swiveled toward the sight of it. In front of me, the Somali woman who'd grown up in America had her face pressed against the window. "This is the only beautiful thing about Mogadishu, right here," she said, directing her words back toward me and Nigel.

Nigel, for his part, didn't seem ready to look. He'd gone rigid in his seat, his body a brick fortress inside of which, somewhere, lived the merry guy who'd once taught me Aussie pub songs from the back of a camel. I felt a pang of culpability. I'd asked too much of him, probably. Somalia was hardly a starter war zone.

*

Off the plane, the air was damp and fishy. The landing strip ran right alongside a wide beach with crashing sapphire waves. The terminal at the Aden Abdulle International Airport of Mogadishu was a washed-out aqua-colored building. Nigel and I waited in line to get our passports stamped. Once on the ground, he had come back to life a bit, swinging his red backpack over his shoulder with a faint smile. The airport was poorly lit and teeming with people.

A slim young Somali man standing by the passport booth jumped forward at us. He held a sign that read AMANDA, SHAMO HOTEL.

I felt a wash of relief. We'd been received. I gratefully pumped the man's hand. "Are you Ajoos?"

He wasn't Ajoos. He was the cameraman Ajoos had hired to work with me during my stay. Abdifatah Elmi was his name. He had an arresting, handsome face, the sharp curves of his cheeks set off by a thin goatee. We could call him Abdi, he said. Ajoos would meet us at the hotel. There had been fighting only a couple of hours earlier, but we'd gotten lucky: The road that led to the city center had been reopened. "Come, come with me," he said.

We followed Abdi through the crowd in the arrivals hall. I was wearing jeans and a long shirt. Abdi had brought a thick green and purple scarf for me to wear draped over my head and shoulders, which did little to hide my foreignness. Nigel and I were jostled and shoved. Nobody smiled. The airport crowd seemed to be regarding us with a could-give-a-shit weariness. We pushed our way through a frenzy of touts, taxi drivers, and freelance luggage handlers, seemingly governed by a group of African Union soldiers—Ethiopians and Ugandans—dressed in forest-green camouflage uniforms and bearing Kalashnikovs. I'd landed in plenty of chaotic places before, but this one was different: The chaos here felt edgy, dangerous, as if we couldn't keep ourselves outside of it and were breathing it in, as if it sat already in the lungs of every last person in that airport, the cyanide edge of a nasty war.

Maybe I was just imagining it. I ordered myself to stop freaking out.

A pack of would-be porters surrounded a heap of baggage that had been unloaded from our plane. Many of them were shirtless and bony, their chests shiny with sweat. I handed my claim ticket to the first one to reach me, a young man as tall as a pole.

Something hissed in the air past my head, moving with a crackling speed. I turned to see a portly Ethiopian soldier holding a whip made from a tree switch. Catching my gaze, he smiled and waggled it teasingly at me. With his wrist, he flicked it back and then unleashed it again, over the pile of luggage and the fumbling, over-eager porters. If he were trying to separate legitimate porters from potential thieves, I couldn't see how. *Whiiii-tah*. The soldier brushed aside a man with a humped back. *Whiiii-tah*. He landed a blow on the tall youth who held my ticket, catching his bare shoulder just as, with a look of triumph, he'd hoisted my dirty black backpack over his head.

The idea, in Mogadishu, seemed to be that you never lingered. Safety came from moving quickly, as if every second spent standing in one place compounded the risks. Abdi rushed us toward a waiting Mitsubishi SUV, parked in an area surrounded by more African Union soldiers. Ignoring his brush with the whip, the tall porter quickly loaded my luggage and Nigel's into the back. I hastily handed him a five-dollar bill, a small fortune in a country where the average adult lived on the equivalent of about twenty U.S. dollars per month. I had never seen a human being whip another human being. Already, I felt confounded by Somalia. We peeled out of the airport with me wondering whether I should have given the guy a twenty instead.

Along with Abdi, three men had piled into the car with us—one driver and two grim-faced guys in uniforms riding beneath the back hatch, each carrying a weapon. These were guards from Somalia's Transitional Federal Government, or TFG, as it was known, who would escort us any time we left the hotel. From what I understood, government soldiers—Somalis, all of them—were officially charged with the job of protecting visitors, but they also needed paying off on the side to ensure their loyalty, so they wouldn't sell us out to some money-hungry criminal gang. All this was wrapped into the daily security fee charged by Ajoos.

Seeing Mogadishu from the ground, I realized that it wasn't nearly as quaint as it had appeared from the air. Or that it could be quaint only if you squinted to blur the lines, to notice the bougainvillea blossoms tumbling in bright fuchsia over old whitewashed walls but not the bombed-out buildings or the fact that many of the homes appeared to be vacant, the windows closed up. Bullet holes pocked nearly every structure, walls had been crushed into rubble, rooftops had collapsed as if some apocalypse had come and gone. We drove at high speed, slowing only for split-second stops at a couple of TFG checkpoints.

We passed a pickup truck with four lanky teenage boys riding in its bed, their arms clamped over a mounted machine gun that pointed like a spear out the back.

I leaned forward in my seat and asked Abdi what he knew about the violence that had gone on around the airport earlier in the day, the news that had made the Somalis on our flight so panicky.

Abdi shook his head with the grizzled forbearance of an on-the-ground Somali, not, like the people on the plane, someone coming back for a visit, someone who'd grown accustomed to the comparative safety of Nairobi. "It was just some fighting," he said, adding that militias often exchanged fire with the soldiers guarding the airport road.

"Did anyone die?"

He lifted his shoulders and let them drop. "Every day in Somalia people die," he said, his voice impassive. "Maybe five or six got killed."

★

A number of hours later, Nigel and I stood on the rooftop of the Shamo Hotel, breathing the humid sea air. As the sun set, the view was expansive. Mogadishu lay in front of us like an exotic beach town, bathed in the late-day light. There were endless narrow lanes lined by low buildings painted in pastel shades of pink and blue, seeming almost to glow in the dusk. Great big trees grew between the houses, making the landscape green and lush. In the distance, we could see the rolling blue ocean. The city was beautiful despite itself.

Arriving from the airport, we'd checked in to the hotel and talked briefly with the owner—Mr. Shamo, a round-bellied man, who came from what appeared to be a wealthy family. He had homes in Tanzania and Dubai, where he and his brothers also owned some sort of factory. Mr. Shamo's fortunes as a hotelier had shifted in 1992, when Dan Rather from CBS News—the hurricane hero himself—had shown up in Mogadishu, along with a dozen colleagues, to report on a growing famine and the impending arrival of U.S. troops in Somalia. Someone had called Mr. Shamo, asking if he could make room for them in his modest guesthouse, even if people had to sleep on the floor. The profits from the CBS crew's stay had helped Mr. Shamo convert his residence into a full-fledged five-story hotel with high, fortified walls and armed guards manning its gates.

Although the Shamo once netted a small fortune by Somali standards, now that Mogadishu was tattered by war, unpromising for foreign businesses, and openly hostile to journalists and aid workers, the hotel was faltering. Mr. Shamo said he came and went from Somalia. Two of his children lived in the U.S., one in Atlanta, one in North Carolina. He was friendly and accustomed to foreigners.

He had given us keys to a room with a king bed, a giant wardrobe, and a bathtub. Nigel and I were sharing the room in order to save money, but Ajoos had said we'd have to pretend we were married. "Otherwise, it makes the staff uncomfortable," he'd told me over the phone. "In Islam, something like this is *haram.*"

Haram was the Arabic word used to describe anything that was forbidden. I'd learned that in my travels, but in Mogadishu, where Muslim insurgents had seized control of many neighborhoods and were imposing a strict form of *sharia* law—outlawing music, television, and sports, among other things—the concept of *haram* was more widely applied and severely enforced. I'd read that under the rules of Al-Shabaab, one of the dominant extremist groups, men were required to grow beards and women were forbidden to walk the streets alone.

From the rooftop, Nigel and I watched darkness slowly fall over the city, lost in our own thoughts. In the distance, I saw lights blinking on. This surprised me. Parts of Mogadishu had electricity, which seemed to suggest that it was more stable than Baghdad. Baghdad, at night, went almost entirely black.

"Can you believe," I said to Nigel, "that we're here?"

"Hardly," he said.

I watched him light a cigarette, then tuck the pack in the pocket of his jeans. The moist air made his hair stand up a little higher on his head. He seemed worn out by the journey but no longer fretful. I felt almost tranquilized by fatigue.

"This is so different than Baghdad," I said.

In Baghdad, almost every night, you heard bombs, gunfire, sirens happening at irregular intervals—just loud enough to be jarring, just close enough to feel threatening. When I thought about it, I realized I hadn't slept well in months. By contrast, Mogadishu had gone eerily silent. We couldn't hear a single vehicle on the street. There was no sign of human activity. I could hear tree branches swaying in the sea breeze, with nothing but stillness beneath it.

Mogadishu wasn't Baghdad. It was different. It looked peaceful, not at all like the place so often described in the foreign newspapers as "hell on earth." I was glad we'd come to see it for ourselves. What I didn't realize was that I was mistaking the quiet for something it wasn't.

15

My Hurricane

*I*n all my years of studying *National Geographic*, in all the fantasizing I'd done about making my way in journalism, I'd somehow never managed to imagine, let alone meet, anyone who actually worked for the magazine. Here they were, in Mogadishu—a writer-and-photographer team, two guys, one American, one French—and in addition to me and Nigel, the only other guests occupying the forty-eight-room Shamo Hotel. Robert Draper was an established Washington, D.C.–based reporter. He had a dramatic sweep of blond hair, a slight Texas accent, and a seen-everything confidence. Pascal Maître was a gentlemanly veteran photojournalist who lived in Paris with his family but spent much of his time on the road. He'd covered stories all over Africa and had been to Somalia several times before. The two men had arrived in Mogadishu three days ahead of us, having hired Ajoos in advance as their fixer.

Encountering them in the Shamo dining room, I was both starstruck and a little miffed. Ajoos, it became clear, would be working primarily for the *Geographic* guys, spending his days accompanying them as they did their reporting, leaving Nigel and me with the mild-mannered, not terribly experienced Abdi. It turned out that Ajoos had hired another man to work with Abdi and serve as translator for us, but just hours before our arrival, the guy had quit, saying it was too dangerous to be seen with white people in Mogadishu. Abdi thus had been thrust into the triple role of cameraman, translator, and junior fixer.

When I asked Pascal, the photographer, for a rundown on what they'd done during their time in Somalia, thinking it might give us some ideas, he declined to tell me. He was kind but firm. "I am sorry," he said in a thick French accent. "If I told you where we went and then you went there yourselves, you would be running a huge risk. In Somalia, you can't do the same thing twice. They will catch you." By "you," he meant foreigners. By "they," he meant both Al-Shabaab and the roving, less organized militias, all of whom might want to snatch us.

I liked Pascal for his straightforwardness. He was guarding his own stories, but he seemed sincere in his worries about our safety, too. He and Robert struck me as hardworking journalists intent on doing their jobs and wasting no time. They were in Somalia for ten days. Next to them, I was certain that we appeared inexperienced, underfunded, and a bit directionless. If that was their opinion, though, they kindly kept it to themselves.

"Keep your wits about you," Pascal told us before he headed to bed that first night. "And listen to what Ajoos tells you."

*

Ajoos Sanura had dark skin, rectangular glasses, and a serious manner. He was constantly on his cell phone, seeming to have friends all over the city, people whom he plied continuously for news. Somalis, he explained, loved to talk, to trade gossip. In a city with no infrastructure, where impromptu street battles went on almost daily and allegiances were always shifting, the mobile phone was, for its citizens, something of a lifeline. News spread rapidly and informally, traveling over vast family networks, cousin to cousin to cousin. "Don't go to Bakaara Market today," they'd say. Or "There was gunfire near the K-4 intersection just now. Two women died and one soldier was hurt."

Ajoos made it his business to tap in to as many of these networks as possible. He kept his pockets stuffed with cash, passing out tips, bribes, and favors at will, cultivating contacts among rival militias, inside the government, and outside the city limits. He had friends from every faction. Al-Shabaab friends. Ethiopian military friends. Friends in the transitional government and in various clans. The idea being that when he had journalists in town, he could secure interviews, track down news, or arrange for safe passage over roads patrolled by violent militias. On his left wrist, he wore a heavy gold watch.

Ajoos, who was about forty, had a wife and ten children. He lived with his family in a house in a different part of the city, but when he worked with foreigners, he stayed in a room at the Shamo Hotel. Meeting me and Nigel for breakfast the following morning, he addressed our worries, speaking fluid English, assuring us that he would take good care of us from afar, that he would remain in constant touch with Abdi while he himself went off to work with the *Geographic* guys. All the while his phone rang, his legion of unseen informants checking in one after another, with their morning reports.

Working with white people in Somalia was a risky but profitable undertaking. Nobody took it lightly. Ajoos had gotten his start in 1993, when he was hired to help a visiting BBC cameraman carry his tripod around town. Before that, he'd been eking out a living waiting tables at the restaurant in the Shamo. Since then, he'd done well financially as a fixer, though his business, like that of the hotel, was tailing off drastically due to the rising danger. Two journalists he'd worked with had been killed—both times, he said, because they'd failed to heed his advice. A female producer with the BBC had been shot in 2005 while waiting outside—ill-advisedly, Ajoos said—for her car to pull up in front of the Hotel Sahafi. The second death happened in 2006, when a Swedish cameraman ignored Ajoos's warnings, wandered into a crowd at a political demonstration, and was promptly shot in the back by a teenage boy. The losses seemed to weigh heavily on Ajoos.

True to his word, Ajoos issued strident orders about where we could and couldn't go around Mogadishu, based on his incoming phone calls. On our second morning, when we wanted to visit a camp for internally displaced people (IDP) west of the city, his sources told him it wasn't a good time to travel that particular road. He offered no details on why, but we understood that his judgment was not to be questioned. The city and its roads, after all, were a patchwork of competing fiefdoms.

Moving around with Abdi and our two armed government guards, I felt continually on edge. Shamo guests were transported in the hotel's fleet of gleaming Mitsubishi Pajeros—big, dark-windowed SUVs that sped conspicuously through the streets, hiding our faces but announcing our presence not just to everyone we passed but to every cousin and cousin's cousin who subsequently might get a phone call: *There are foreigners living at the Shamo.*

On the second day, we visited two feeding centers run by the World Food Programme in Mogadishu. Nigel and I both took photographs. Abdi toted a rented video camera and filmed my interviews with Somalis who'd left their homes due to the fighting or the scarcity of food or often a combination of both. This was the first time I'd seen true desperation—people who were not just hungry but starving. Inside the gates of the feeding center, the WFP staff stirred giant vats of steaming lentil soup and a thin millet porridge while about a thousand people waited in disorderly lines outside, the men in one line, the women in another. Each person held an empty tin or plastic pail. I noticed listless, knob-kneed children sitting at the feet of many of the women, their bald heads looking too large for their bodies. A few kids clustered in the shade provided by the wheel well of a rusted-out, stripped-down car body that looked as if it had been marooned in the sand for years. Because of the fighting, because of the pirates on the ocean and the bandits on the roads, food shipments came sporadically. There were days when people turned up only to be sent away.

When the gates opened, those who'd been waiting rushed forward. The noise amplified. Government soldiers used batons and tree switches to hold back the crowd. Children wailed. The men pushed and brawled their way toward the front, while the women in line remained poised in single file.

Once they reached the feeding vats, the men were given three ladlefuls of food; the women got two; the children one. Their pails loaded, many of them dropped to their knees on the spot and started shoveling food into their mouths, fueling themselves for the walk home. Most weren't headed back to their own neighborhoods, explained the WFP staffer who was hosting us, but rather to makeshift squatter settlements that had sprung up along roadsides where the fighting was less intense, where their access to food was better.

I'd say it was like watching a movie, or standing at the side of something so fast-moving and incomprehensible that it didn't seem real. But it wasn't quite that way. It was a toe dipped in the river of other people's misery. It was upsetting, confusing. I was removed from it, but I was also there. I was taking notes, writing a script in my head as Abdi filmed it, thinking—believing—that I could help do something about it.

*

Back in our room at the Shamo, I wrote up my weekly column for the *Red Deer Advocate*. It was not *National Geographic* or even France 24. It was a newspaper with a circulation of about thirteen thousand, read by people on the faraway Canadian flatlands. I don't know if my column meant anything to anyone besides my dad and Perry, who sent me e-mails after each one ran in the Saturday paper, but it meant something to me. I had turned in seven hundred new words and a handful of fresh photos every Friday from March right through August, like clockwork. I'd sent columns from Baghdad, from Addis, and from Nairobi. I loved the discipline imposed by the regular deadline. I loved learning how to write. I was getting better at translating what I saw into words. Going through my notes and the research file on my laptop, I worked up a story that described Mogadishu's beauty and its desolation. I wrote about how a combination of war, lack of rain, and inflation had made food expensive and difficult to come by. I described the crowds lined up outside the feeding center and the danger that families faced just navigating the streets. I described a woman I'd interviewed, named Haliimo, who'd walked with her family to Mogadishu from central Somalia after one of her children died of starvation.

I wrote the story in a frenzy, weaving in the official statistics I'd written down during my interviews with the World Food Programme employees. The magnitude of the numbers was hard to grasp, even as I'd seen some of the living proof. More than three million Somalis going hungry. One in six children malnourished. Sitting on the bed, propped up with pillows, I finished the column, revised it a few times, and then picked a few photos from the feeding center to upload along with it.

The Wi-Fi connection at the Shamo was slow and spotty. About ten minutes into the upload, the signal dropped and I got a failure message. I tried again, then another time, and still again, each time watching the bar on the screen creep upward and abruptly freeze. I heaved a loud sigh. It was now Friday evening. Back in Canada, the newspaper was soon to go to press.

Nigel and I were served a feast for dinner that night. In the hotel restaurant, a handsome young waiter delivered bowls of creamy fish soup, followed by a plate holding a whole grilled fish for us to share, followed by fresh lobster juiced with lime. We ate as much and as long as we could, drinking glasses of mango juice as we went. The waiter brought spaghetti. He brought a plate of goat meat, a bunch of bananas, and a basket of bread rolls. When at last we waved him off, he carried out a last plate of sliced papaya spears and offered to pour tea. Afterward, while Nigel settled in the lounge area and watched the Beijing Olympics on television with some of the hotel staff, I returned to our room and tried another time to send my e-mail and attachments. Another failure message popped up on the screen. I hit the send button again and again. Late that night, knowing the deadline had passed, I made one last effort. This time the connection held. I watched the loading bar on the computer screen tick forward until, after about fifteen minutes, it showed 100 percent transmission—my column and photographs lifted out into the world.

The story would be published a couple of days later, in Monday's *Advocate,* under the headline NOWHERE IS A PERSON SAFE IN SOMALIA. At that point, I myself would be walking proof of this. By Monday, nobody would know where I was.

16

Taken

*L*ater, they would tell me they'd been watching the hotel. They knew we were there. They didn't know who exactly they'd catch, but they were aware there were foreigners at the hotel. What happened was planned, to the extent anything like this can be planned. Guns had been marshaled, men hired, a place to take us afterward had been secured. Knowing we were coming, they'd laid their trap. Maybe it was a cousin's cousin who tipped them off. Maybe it was the sight of our freshly washed SUV ripping around the Old City that caused people to ask questions, to wonder if we could make them rich. Most assuredly, there was cash promised to somebody—a driver, a hotel employee, a guard—in exchange for word of where the foreigners were headed that day. Somebody—we don't know who—sold us out.

Nigel woke up that morning—Saturday, the twenty-third of August—and put on a pink paisley shirt and a pair of designer jeans. We'd been sleeping on the far edges of our king-sized bed at the Shamo. We were both testy. He was sending e-mails to his girlfriend in Scotland. I'd had a call from the American bureau chief in Baghdad with whom I'd had the affair. Though Nigel and I were most definitely not a couple, we hadn't figured out how to be friends, either.

As colleagues, we were at least trying. During our first two and a half days in Somalia, we'd seen only a little of what we'd hoped to, hampered by the safety concerns, waiting for the Canadian Navy to arrive with the food shipment. We'd visited the Old City, one of the few relatively secure parts of Mogadishu, where abandoned Italian colonial villas sat moldering in the heat, their drained swimming pools suggestive of a better past. We'd gone to a hospital whose rooms were crowded with gunshot victims and amputees. Every step we took, any time we got out of the car, our hired guards trailed behind us, Kalashnikovs strapped over their shoulders, not entirely uninterested but not exactly vigilant.

With a strong sun already blasting through the window and roosters crowing from outside, I watched Nigel wind a purple scarf around his neck and reach for his oversized silver aviator-style sunglasses with blue lenses. He was about to head off to meet a Ugandan minesweeping unit with Abdi. I had decided to stay back. Every so often we heard the sizzle and boom of a mortar blast coming from pretty close by.

"You're kidding, right?" I said.

"What's the problem?"

"You can't go out dressed like that, Nige. Not with African soldiers. You just can't."

I once appreciated Nigel's love of bright colors and designer jeans, but what he wore now seemed like a mark of his inexperience. Shooting me a withering look, he took off the scarf and set down the sunglasses but left the rest of his outfit in place.

Downstairs, Ajoos clicked off a phone call and informed us that the mortars were landing near the Ugandan base by the airport. He deemed minesweeping with the Ugandan soldiers "not a good idea" for Nigel that morning, but he promised to make more calls to see if we could visit the IDP camp outside the city, the one where we'd been hoping to go a day earlier. The camp was run by a well-known Somali doctor named Hawa Abdi, a gynecologist in her sixties who had opened a small women's health clinic on her family's farmland back in the 1980s. When the civil war started in 1991, she began allowing people displaced by the fighting to stay on her land and now had something like ninety thousand Somalis living at and around her place. Dr. Hawa was a hero. Despite harassment and threats from Al-Shabaab, she'd expanded her clinic until it was a three-hundred-bed hospital; she also ran health education programs for women. Her two daughters had left Somalia to attend medical school and returned to help her do her work. The prospect of interviewing them excited me.

"I will tell you in thirty minutes whether it's safe to go," Ajoos told us, turning back to his phone. "Please wait."

Dr. Hawa's land lay about twenty kilometers to the west of where we were staying, just outside the city limits, along what was called the Afgoye Road. The first thirteen kilometers of the Afgoye Road sat inside the boundaries of Mogadishu proper and were protected, as much as anything in the city could be protected, by government troops. Neither the Transitional Federal Government nor the African Union peacekeepers had any influence or backup beyond the city. Leaving Mogadishu, we'd be entering the Wild West of militia-controlled Somalia. The two TFG soldiers who'd been acting as our bodyguards for the last few days, Ajoos explained, would be willing to accompany us to the city limits, to the edge of their territory, but no farther. After that, we'd need to hire new guards who weren't affiliated with the government. This would cost us another $150.

A few phone calls later, Ajoos had everything set up. He'd arranged for replacement guards to meet us on the road a few kilometers after the last TFG checkpoint. In addition to Abdi and our driver, we would have an extra escort for the day, he said—the head of security for Dr. Hawa's camp, who was on his way to the Shamo to meet us.

The logistics sounded fine. Besides, what did we have to compare them to? It wasn't like I could say, *Well, last time I drove across the line where the Islamic militias battled the uniformed soldiers, here's how we did it . . .*

I loaded my backpack for the outing. My camera. A wide-angle lens. An extra memory card. My iPod. A small notebook. Two pens. Some lip balm. A hairbrush. A couple bottles of water. I wore a pair of jeans, a green tank top, and some leather sandals I'd bought in Kenya. Over that I layered the heavy Somali-style abaya that Ajoos had borrowed for me from his sister-in-law—polyester and black, like a long choir robe—along with a somber black head scarf to cover my hair, which was what I had worn each day when stepping outside the hotel.

Leaving the lobby about twenty minutes ahead of us, Robert and Pascal from *National Geographic* climbed into a different SUV with their own hired TFG soldiers. As usual, Ajoos was traveling with them. They, too, were headed west on the Afgoye Road, going off on a drive more dangerous than ours—traversing the same road but continuing on through militia-held territory to visit the coastal city of Merka. They'd taken extra precautions, hiring a second security vehicle with additional guards.

I wasn't paying attention when we rolled out of the Shamo gates. I felt that morning almost like I was in a trance. I'd learned this about reporting work: You switched on and off. There were so many hours spent upright and fretful, navigating all the small things, looking for advantageous viewpoints, asking questions, taking notes, trying always to think ahead. By contrast, time spent sitting in cars, for me, was time off.

Our vehicle ferried us through streets that were more familiar, less jarring, than they'd been two days earlier. The guy who'd come to escort us from Dr. Hawa's camp—an older man in a white shirt and a Somali-style sarong who spoke no English—had insisted on driving. Our regular driver sat wedged in the middle up front while Abdi rode shotgun. Nigel and I had the backseat to ourselves, while the two TFG soldiers occupied the rear.

The road heading out of Mogadishu was wide and paved. We bumped over potholes and past shelled-out gray buildings. We passed women selling bananas and mangoes and men dragging carts loaded with cooking oil and firewood. We rounded a traffic circle and cruised through a couple of government checkpoints. The traffic thinned. The sky streamed alongside us. My mind flitted away from where I was. I thought about my mother, who had relocated to British Columbia and found a job in a bakery. She'd sounded happy in our last phone call. It was summertime in Canada. People were grilling hamburgers and swimming in cool lakes. Home was a pleasant thought. In order to get back for a visit, I'd have to sell some stories. I pulled my camera from the backpack, turned it on, and started shuttling through images from the previous days. There were some good shots of the scenery, including some of a stone Catholic cathedral, built by the Italians in the 1920s, more recently gutted by bomb blasts. I'd taken a series of photos from inside one of the African Union tanks, showing both the Ethiopian soldiers and their view of the streets below.

Now approaching the city limits, we were passing refugees loping along the road—families hauling themselves westward, away from the besieged urban streets. I could see sprawling encampments, dwellings made of tarps stretched over tree boughs that had been bent like hoops, looking like a fleet of ragtag, rigged sailboats. Minibuses running between Afgoye and Mogadishu traveled both lanes of the highway. A haze of yellow dust hung in the air. We pulled up at the final government checkpoint, where several dozen uniformed soldiers sat in the shade under a large tent. Someone lifted the hatch on the car. Our TFG guards wordlessly climbed out. Our driver rolled down his window and called out something in Somali to the departing soldiers, and within seconds we were moving again, headed into a short stretch of no-man's-land that separated the government area from the militia area.

The road curved away from the checkpoint. In the front seat, Abdi was talking into his cell phone. I was looking at more photos—a series I'd taken of Nigel, sweetly kicking a ball with some children in the Old City—when I felt the car slow. I assumed we were meeting our new set of guards. I didn't bother to lift my head. Sitting next to me, Nigel was absorbed with his own camera. But the energy inside the car shifted; the air seemed suddenly tinged with electricity. The three Somali men in the front seat were muttering. I looked up and saw a dark blue Suzuki station wagon parked on the opposite side of the road. I then saw someone standing in front of our car, a man with a gun, his head, nose, and mouth swaddled in a red-checkered scarf, the kind favored by mujahideen fighters around the world. His dark eyes bulged. The gun was pointed directly at our windshield.

Abdi switched to English. "This could be a problem," he said.

More bandits appeared from behind the parked Suzuki, circling our car, guns hefted—about twelve of them altogether.

I immediately started hoping for a robbery. Something fast, in which they took everything and then vanished.

Someone tugged open the back door, the heat spilling into the air-conditioned capsule of the car. People were shouting in Somali, male voices. Abdi and the two other men in the front seat were pulled out and thrust into a ditch by the side of the road. I watched Nigel climb out. A man in a scarf yelled in my face. I could see beads of sweat running from his covered forehead down past his nose. He looked young. I raised my arms—like I'd seen done a hundred times in movies—and slid my way out into the blaze of sunlight.

Was this real? How could it be real?

Just then I caught sight of a passerby, a woman, floating like an apparition past us, headed toward a junction in the road. She was looking and not looking, trying to pretend she hadn't seen us, her head scarf streaming behind her as she moved. She walked on without once looking back. I began to understand that what was happening was real. From behind, someone shoved me toward the ditch. I knelt first and then dropped forward into the sand next to where Nigel was already lying facedown beside Abdi and the two others. I spread my arms and legs, as everyone else had done.

It got quiet. Someone seemed to be searching our car. Out of the corner of one eye, I could see the narrow cave of a gun barrel pointed at my head, about twelve inches away. My mind and body felt eerily calm. I thought for sure we were about to be shot.

The bandits were jabbering at us again. We were pulled to our feet. Abdi, Nigel, and I were waved back into the SUV. I was relieved to see one of the gunmen rifling through Nigel's backpack. It was a robbery after all, I thought. They'd take our stuff and then let us go.

Three of the bandits now sat in the front seat. Four of us—Nigel, Abdi, me, and another of the gunmen—occupied the middle. I could hear several more climbing into the hatch. I wasn't sure what had happened to the two other guys—our driver and the security guy who'd come from the IDP camp—but the rest of us were packed in tightly, sucking down what felt like the last available oxygen, smelling like sweat and fear. My own backpack sat at my feet, with the fancy camera inside. When were they going to take it? Why weren't they demanding our wallets? The man in the driver's seat turned the key. The car engine jumped to life. We accelerated, falling into place behind the Suzuki, which had executed a quick U-turn and was now leading us. For another minute or so, we rocketed over the paved road and then made an abrupt right-hand swerve onto an unmarked sandy track.

Shit. Panic was rising in me. We were moving off the grid. We barreled over scrubby, russet-colored hills, shoulders knocking, heads flailing, as we dodged thorn trees and ran right over bushes, not following any sort of path. With every passing minute, I knew, we were rushing farther away from anywhere someone would think to look for us. Beneath my abaya, I was sweating heavily. I could feel my jeans pasted to my legs.

"Abdi," I said, "what's happening?" My voice came out high and quavering.

"NO TALKING!" shouted one of the men in the front seat. I took note that he spoke English.

Desperate for reassurance, I tried again, my pitch continuing to rise. "What's happening, Abdi? Is everything going to be okay? You have to tell me. Is everything all right?"

"Be quiet," Abdi said under his breath, fiercely. There was nothing reassuring about it. He was no less terrified than we were.

I thought about the cell phone in my backpack. I had a phone number for Ajoos written on a page in my notebook, also in the backpack. But how could I get it? And what would I say? Looking over my shoulder, I could see a gun barrel fixed on my head, and behind the gun, a kid holding it. His scarf had come loose from his face. His cheeks were round with baby fat, his eyes lit with terror when he caught my gaze. He held the weapon awkwardly, as if he'd never done this before. He couldn't have been older than fourteen, I guessed.

As we banged on through the desert, an order was called out from the front seat. The man sitting back with us grunted something in Somali and held out a palm. Abdi translated. He wanted our phones. Of course he did. My heart sank like a stone. I handed over my phone, and Abdi did the same. I figured that Nigel's was in his bag, which already had been taken away. I watched as the man powered them down.

We lurched to a stop in a flat, empty area, pulling up next to the Suzuki. A man in civilian clothes got out of the driver's side, walked over, and opened my door. He had a black-and-white scarf draped tidily over his shoulders, but his face was uncovered. He was clean-shaven and in his mid-twenties, with thick eyelashes, an alert expression, and slightly protruding front teeth. When he leaned in to look at us, his eyes landed intently on me.

"Hello," he said in relaxed English, his tone soothing, as if welcoming me into a restaurant. He showed no interest in Nigel. "My name is Ahmed." He pronounced it *Ock-med*. "Please, come with me."

Ahmed waved me out of the SUV—me only. He was separating us. I didn't turn to look at Nigel, for fear I'd betray my panic. Already, I was one woman among about sixteen men. Now they were taking me away from my one sure ally. I had to pretend it didn't matter. Quietly, I followed Ahmed as he led me over to the parked Suzuki and directed me into the backseat. A masked man slid in next to me. Two more of the gunmen sat behind me. Nobody's body was touching mine, but I could feel the humid closeness of them. The car shot forward again, skidding through the sand.

Where is it that we learn the cliché about how talking can help keep you alive? How it's necessary to remind the bad guys that you're a human being? I had an idea about what I should do. I focused on Ahmed, who was up front next to the driver. He had one arm slung over the seat, his neck crooked so he could look in my direction. He was smiling, like a fisherman who'd reeled in something big.

As calmly as I could, I started talking. I told Ahmed my name. I told him I was from Canada, a place where many Somalis had come to live. I said I was a journalist. That we were headed to an IDP camp to help tell the story of Somalia. I said I loved Somalia already, that its beauty was stunning. I tried to sound earnest, girlish even. I cautiously worked a political angle. For the first time ever, I felt grateful that I'd spent those few months working for the Iranians, since old Mr. Nadjafi in Tehran had taught me a thing or two about how to tweak my words in order to sound less Western, more Islamic. "I am saddened," I said to Ahmed, "by the occupation of your country." I was referring to the Ethiopians and the Ugandans, the Christians, the outsiders. I added that I had worked for an Islamic television station in Baghdad.

Sitting next to me in the backseat was a man I would learn later was named Ali. His face was wrapped in a purple scarf, his eyes visible through a narrow slit. If Ahmed seemed friendly, almost a peer, this guy—what little I could see of him—appeared hardened and mean. He was looking at me carefully. "You are a Christian?" he said in stilted English.

This was a loaded question. I knew from my travels that in the eyes of devout Muslims, it was generally better to be a "person of the book"—a Christian or a Jew—than to have no religion at all.

"Yes," I told him. "But I have deep respect for Islam." I paused to see how this would go over.

Ahmed turned back to regard me. He smiled again, in a way that gave me some hope. "Sister," he said, "don't worry, nothing will happen to you. There is no problem here. *Inshallah.*" *God willing*, it meant. He added, "We are soldiers in the Islamic army. Our commander would like to ask you some questions. We are taking you to our base. We think maybe you are spies."

I could feel the fear spike in my throat. Journalists often got accused of being Western spies. I tried to keep talking. I was babbling at this point, listing off every Islamic country I'd been to, as if that made me more of an insider. There was a golden-brown fur rug draped over the middle console in the front seat. "What kind of fur is that?" I said, making a ridiculous attempt to sound casual. "What animal does it come from?"

Ahmed ignored the question. He dialed a number on his cell phone and said a few words. A few minutes later, the car stopped again. The back door opened, the guard to my left climbed out, and Nigel, looking pale, got in, having come from the SUV behind us. He was breathing hard, on the verge of hyperventilating. The guard slid in next to him, sandwiching the two of us together.

"Nigel," I said brightly, gesturing to the front seat as the car began to roll, "this is our brother Ahmed. These men are soldiers. Ahmed has promised that nothing bad will happen to us."

I sounded like some insane schoolteacher, I knew. I was pronouncing my words deliberately, keeping an overcooked smile on my face. Nigel flared his eyes questioningly at me. I flared mine back, unsure what we were communicating but relieved at least that we were together.

Inside my head, a battle raged between rational and irrational. Some part of me believed this was only a misunderstanding, that we were unwelcome in this territory, with our flashy hotel car and our white skin, and we'd get some sort of militiaman reprimand about overstepping our boundaries before being sent back down the road. Then again, I knew enough from my stays in Iraq and Afghanistan, from following the news in those places, to understand that angry extremists liked to behead their enemies. I wasn't sure which thought was the more unreasonable one.

Every time the car went over a bump, a gun barrel hit my skull from behind. I felt certain it would get knocked hard enough to go off. "Brother Ahmed," I said, "could you please ask the soldier to take his gun away from my head? I have no weapon. I'm not a danger to you, and it's scaring me."

Ahmed said something in Somali to the soldier behind me. The gun was repositioned but only slightly. I noticed that Ahmed wore a gold watch. I caught a hint of sweet cologne coming off his extended arm.

I tried to think strategically, imagining some conversation we'd have with this Islamic commander who was waiting for us, wondering what I could say to persuade him we weren't spies—that they should relieve us of our belongings and return us to Mogadishu.

Mogadishu at this point sounded like home to me, like a place worth longing for. I imagined this commander rummaging through our bags, inspecting our stuff. I thought then of our cameras, of the dozens of images we'd shot of African Union troops and TFG guards on patrol in Mogadishu. Their existence could create the impression that we were allied with the infidels, that we were on the wrong side of the holy war. All they'd need to do was turn on the cameras and start pressing buttons.

"Excuse me?" I said to the man sitting next to me. "My lips are dry. Is it okay if I open my bag and take out some cream?"

The man stared at me blankly, then gestured in a vaguely permissive way.

I bent down and began rooting through my backpack with both hands, pretending to look for my lip balm. I felt my cheeks flush with the lie as my fingers found the camera and then located the slot that housed the memory card. Working quickly, I pressed the tiny lever that released the card and then, keeping it trapped between two fingers, I flicked it away from the camera and into the recesses of the backpack. Now, at least, they'd have to make an effort to see my photos. I grabbed the stick of balm and lifted it with a flourish. Ali averted his eyes as I rubbed it over my lips, but I could tell he was watching.

"Sister, why are you not afraid?"

"What?"

Ali had asked the question, not looking directly at me. He seemed provoked by my confidence, false as it was—angered, maybe, that I wasn't weeping or begging.

I thought quickly and spoke loudly. "I'm not afraid because my brother Ahmed has promised that nothing bad will happen."

In the front seat, Ahmed was again talking on his phone. I hoped that he'd caught what I'd said. I could hear Nigel, sitting on the other side of Ali, struggling to calm his breathing. I wondered what had happened to his camera.

Just then we tore past another vehicle, coming in the opposite direction, a truck full of young men with guns. I craned my neck to watch them pass. In twenty minutes of driving, we hadn't seen a single human, animal, or structure. I felt a hard knock on my arm, a smack from Ali. *"Why are you looking?"* he screamed. He seized the loose end of my head scarf, yanking it over my face. There was an odd terror in his voice.

We drove on awhile in silence, before I tried again with Ahmed. "My brother," I said, leaning slightly forward in my seat, trying to sound friendly, directing my words toward the back of his head, "is this about money?"

He turned to look toward me, his face breaking into a wide smile, as if we were alighting on the notion together, as a team.

"Ah yes," he said. "Maybe so. Maybe it is like that."

17

Tuna Fish and Tea

After about forty-five minutes of driving, having briefly rejoined a paved road before pulling off into the desert again, we arrived at a small mazelike village where narrow sand lanes snaked between a jumble of walled-off properties. The car pulled up outside a large rusty gate made of blue metal. Ahmed got out, produced a set of keys, and unlocked it. The gate swung open, and I could see more masked soldiers waiting inside, in a compound surrounded by high walls. The Shamo SUV was no longer with us. Abdi and the two other Somali guys we'd been taken with were gone.

I climbed out, holding my backpack, figuring it would be a matter of minutes before they searched it. I counted nine or ten masked men, all of them staring at us, guns strapped over their shoulders. In addition to scarves, they wore jeans and collared dress shirts. Their bodies looked lean and young, despite the Q-tip-like wrapping over their heads. And they were keyed up, it was easy to see. It seemed they'd been ordered not to speak in front of us. One of the soldiers walked over and shut the gate behind us.

If this were some sort of army base, it was a small and hardscrabble one. There was a long, low, tin-roofed building shaped like a shoe box, with three doors equally spaced on its outside wall. I could see what looked to be a cooking area underneath a lean-to made from hammered-together scrap wood and a thick-trunked acacia whose branches hung heavily over the yard. In front of the house beside the gate was a small shed, which I took to be an outhouse. I turned to Ahmed. "Can I use the bathroom, please?" I said.

He pointed in a solicitous manner toward the shed. "Of course, my sister."

One of the soldiers escorted me. I carried my bag with me, hoping nobody would notice. The bathroom had tall walls and no roof. Inside was a stale-smelling shallow hole cut into the concrete floor. It did not seem to have been used recently. Standing to one side of the hole, I pulled out my camera and switched it on, cringing at the sound of its electronic ping, hoping nobody could see me through the wide cracks on either side of the wooden door. Fishing the memory card from the bag, I reinserted it and quickly hit "delete all" on the stored photos, erasing the evidence of what we'd done thus far in Mogadishu. For good measure, I squatted down and peed into the hole before exiting.

Back outside, the soldier named Ali—the one who'd hit my arm in the car—barked an order to one of the younger-seeming soldiers, who approached me with a plastic bucket of water so I could wash my hands. Ali then marched me toward the low building, to a darkened room on the far left, where I found Nigel sitting on a foul-looking foam mat, his shoulders pressed up against a dirty wall. The air was musty. Along the back was a small window with closed metal shutters. A very long time ago, the room had been painted a pale shade of pink. The floor was strewn with bits of electrical wire. Nigel had lit a cigarette and was looking distraught.

Ali hovered momentarily in the doorway. He pointed at a mat along the opposite wall, indicating that I should sit. Then he disappeared.

Nigel glanced at me. We hadn't had a moment alone since we'd been taken. "What are we going to do?" he said.

"I don't know."

"We've been kidnapped, right?" he said. "Or is this something different?"

I was thinking about the difference between being detained and being kidnapped. I'd been detained once with Enas and an Iraqi cameraman while reporting in Baghdad's Sadr City. A group of armed

men had surrounded our car and then taken us to the Sadr Party headquarters, where we'd been questioned about our political affiliations,
whether we were loyal to the Sunnis. I'd been able to make a phone
call to a Shia contact who'd exerted some pressure, and we'd been let
go within an hour. It had been a hassle, and scary, but it had ended
quickly, over and done. How I wished for something like that now.

Before I could say anything much to Nigel, Ali walked through the
door, this time carrying a piece of newspaper. With a flourish, as if
wanting to be sure he had our attention, he folded the paper in half,
then rolled it into a tight cone, expertly flipping back the tip, his long
fingers working around the rim, pressing it into a thin ledge. He leaned
down and dropped his creation on the floor next to Nigel. An origami
ashtray. Nigel and I stared at it wordlessly.

"Have you seen this before now?" Ali said. His English was accented
but understandable, the product of some sort of schooling, I guessed.

We both shook our heads. Ali was still wearing his warrior scarving,
but it seemed as if, hidden beneath his layers, he might be smiling. He
dropped into a squat not far from where Nigel was sitting, as if settling in. "I used to smoke," he said. "Before the jihad." He looked from
Nigel to me. "But since two years, no smoking."

I took this to mean we were going to have a conversation. I tried not
to feel terrified of him despite the glare in his eyes and the gun in his
hands and the bizarre fact we were sitting, the three of us, in a grubby
room in an off-the-grid Somali village, waiting to see what would happen next. I reminded myself that it could only serve us to build some
rapport with Ali.

Ali, it turned out, had plenty to say about Somali politics and jihad.
His jihad was all about driving the Ethiopian troops out of Somalia,
which was pretty much the same jihad being fought by the armed
groups of teenagers we'd seen charging around Mogadishu in pickup
trucks. Ethiopia's population was predominantly Christian. Somalia
was a Muslim country and needed an Islamic government, one that
enforced Islamic rules, Ali said. He'd been battling the invaders for two
years—ever since 2006, when the Ethiopian government sent troops
over the border and he signed on with the mujahideen. As he saw it,

it was a straight-up case of Christians meddling in Muslim affairs. He hated the Ethiopians. He hated everything about them.

"For two years, my life is only jihad," he said from beneath his scarf. He was sitting against the wall now, knees jutting, gun propped next to him.

Being a holy warrior in Somalia seemed to involve giving up the pleasures of your former life and marrying yourself fully to the cause. It meant adopting and abiding by the most rigid interpretation of Islamic law. It meant no television, no music, no smoking, and—what seemed to pain Ali the most—no sports. Football, he said with no small amount of wistfulness, had been his game of choice. He'd played it, watched it on television, considered himself a loyal fan of some of the African World Cup teams.

We did what we could to work Ali over. We empathized with his struggle. We said "of course" each time he mentioned how hard it was to be battling the infidels all the time. Nigel dropped the names of various soccer stars and team rivalries, which seemed to excite him. But whenever we felt even a loose connection starting to build, we'd hit a wall.

"Your country," Ali said, waving a finger at the two of us, forgetting the chitchat, his voice suddenly spewing rage, "sent the Ethiopians to us."

It didn't matter to him that Nigel was Australian and I was Canadian. The differences were insignificant. An unbelieving white foreigner was an unbelieving white foreigner. The Western world was inscrutable and immodest and ruled over by Satan, or *Shaitan,* in Arabic. When we reiterated to Ali that we'd come to Somalia as journalists trying to tell stories about how the people there were suffering, he was wholly unimpressed—suspicious, even. I knew that the worries about spies weren't entirely unfounded. I'd read that the U.S. had quietly sent Special Forces into Somalia to assist the Ethiopians and the faltering transitional government. I'd heard, too, that every so often, unmanned drones passed over Mogadishu, buzzing the city like steel-gray dragonflies.

When Ali left the room, closing the door behind him, Nigel and I

sat silently in the shadows. What did they want from us? It was hard
to know. We tried to buoy each other by reviewing the circumstances.
Ahmed had seemed so certain that everything would be okay. Ali
brimmed with anger but hadn't done anything to hurt us. Nobody had
asked us for money, even.

Light leaked through the shuttered window. On the sill was a stack
of thick hardcover books—Korans, it looked like, about eight of them.
In the far corner, there was an iron coatrack with some men's clothes
hanging from it. The sun radiated across the tin roof above, heating
the room like an oven. Beneath my head scarf, I could feel the sweat
matting my hair. Outside, men were murmuring. Nigel and I went
round and round over the puzzle of what was happening.

"This is a kidnapping," one of us would say.

"No, it's not. It's just a misunderstanding, a political thing."

Something in the act of debating it made us feel better.

After a time, Ahmed poked his head through the door. "I will be
leaving," he said, as if we were friends parting ways. "Be very careful
with these men. They will kill you if you don't do as they say."

Where was he heading? I was desperate for him to stay. That his
English was so dignified and his face was uncovered felt important,
consoling. He was the one guy here who didn't carry a gun. I'd been
running the words he'd said in the car—*Don't worry, nothing will happen
to you*—again and again through my mind.

"Wait," I said, "what about the commander? I thought he wanted
to meet us."

"Ah," Ahmed said, almost as if he'd forgotten. "*Inshallah.* Tomorrow."

Right away, I started to wonder if he'd been lying to us. Was there
no commander? Was it possible that nobody would come to hear us
out? I'd put all my hopes on this one possibility.

I tried to wring whatever I could out of Ahmed. It felt like a last
chance. "My brother, I need to ask you one thing," I said. "Can we
please call our families? Because if we don't go back to the hotel,
they're going to know something has happened to us. Can we just tell
them that we're okay?"

Ahmed nodded as if this were an excellent suggestion. "Perhaps," he said obliquely. "Perhaps that will be the next program."

I told him that if we could at least make a call to Ajoos from the Shamo Hotel, he might be able to help everyone get what they needed.

This, Ahmed said, with a parting grin, could be another piece of the program. He closed the door gently, leaving us again in darkness. We heard the squeak of the gate and the sound of his car driving away.

★

With Ahmed gone, Ali appeared to be fully in charge and relishing the role. He was worked up. Any eagerness to talk about his life or the jihad had evaporated. His anger now seemed focused and specific, directed entirely at us.

He demanded our money. "Where is it?" he screamed. I fumbled in my bag and produced the $211 in U.S. dollars that I'd brought from the hotel that morning, having left the rest in the Shamo's safe. My hand was shaking as I passed it over. Nigel was carrying a few coins and a folded-up hundred-dollar bill he'd stashed in his front pocket. Ali counted our money with open skepticism. "This is all?"

"Yeah," I said.

"I don't believe," he said. The rage was building in his voice. "I don't believe," he repeated. "How can this be?"

Nigel and I said nothing.

"Where is your money?" Ali said.

"It's at the hotel. We left it there." Somehow I'd become the one who did most of the talking.

"Your passports. Give them to me."

"They're at the hotel, too."

Ali gave me a narrow-eyed, judgmental look, as if silently making up his mind about something. I averted my gaze, not sure whether it was better to project meekness or defiance in return. My looking away caused him to laugh, a nasty chortle. He walked out the door. I could hear him conferring with the soldiers outside in the yard. Within a minute, he was back.

This time Ali grabbed my backpack and dumped out its contents. In the light cast by the open door, he inspected everything carefully, disdainfully. My camera, my notebook, my water bottle. He took the lid off my lip balm. He examined both sides of my hairbrush. He handled each item delicately, as if it might explode. He shook his head, seeming disgusted by the things I'd chosen to carry with me that day.

Each time Ali left the room, he seemed to recharge his fury, as if taking hits off a tank full of hatred somewhere just off the patio. After going through my backpack, he stepped outside and then came back almost immediately. He pointed at me, his eyes bulging. "Get up!" he said. He touched the shoulder strap of his gun as if to remind me it was there. Ali had a thick, stocky body—not fat, exactly, but well fed, solid in a way that few Somalis seemed to be. I glanced at Nigel and then got to my feet, my knees and back stiff after all the sitting. Ali motioned toward the door.

The sunlight outside was blinding. We walked a few steps across the concrete patio. Two stairs led up from the patio to another closed door. Ali pointed at it, signaling that I should go inside. For a split second I hesitated, and his hand thwacked my back, hard. "Do you want me to kill you?" he said. He gave me a shove forward and I stumbled on the stairs.

The room we entered was dark and small, with a metal cot against one wall. The air was an unmoving envelope of heat. Ali closed the door.

"Please," I said, trying to keep my voice even. "Do not do this." I searched for his eyes in the dimness and kept talking. "Please, you are Islamic. The Muslims are the best kind of people. I know this is not good in Islam. Please . . ."

I had been thinking about this on the car ride through the desert, crammed in with all those men, imagining the things that could go wrong on top of everything that already had.

If he heard me talking, Ali gave no indication. He pulled at my head scarf and tossed it to the ground. Then he reached out and grabbed the neckline of my abaya, yanking it down so that the snaps popped open and its two sides fell apart. When I lifted my hands to cover myself, he hit me over the head. I yelped in surprise. "Do you want me to kill you?" he said for the second time, and then he pushed me toward the wall. I could see on the other side of the room, on the windowsill, a stack of heavy-looking books—more copies of the Koran.

I felt Ali's hands slide beneath the fabric of my tank top and into the cups of my bra. He was fumbling, squeezing. His breath came in sharp huffs. I closed my eyes so I wouldn't have to see his face. With his right hand, he found the button on my jeans and then the zipper. A thick finger probed me between the legs, then quickly pulled away. I felt repulsion, nausea climbing my ribs. *Don't worry, nothing will happen to you.* Hadn't Ahmed said that? I was crying, jaggedly, feeling like I had a block of wood stuck in my throat. "This is wrong," I was saying in a croaking voice. "You are not a good Muslim."

He gave me another hard shove, toward the floor. "You think I need this?" he said, almost spitting the words. "I have two wives. You are ugly, a bad woman." He picked up his gun from the floor and made a gesture, indicating that I should dress myself. He acted as if I'd offended him, as if I'd violated his honor instead of the other way around. "I was searching for money. Just money."

"Okay," I said back quietly. With trembling hands, I worked to snap up the abaya, suddenly grateful for the fact that it covered me so entirely. I wrapped the scarf over my head. "No problem, no problem."

I hated the words, but that's what came out of me.

He ordered me not to cry. He marched me back to the other room. Seeing Nigel on the foam mat in the gritty dark, exactly as I'd left him, I felt the tears start to flow again. I squelched a sob. I could see the devastation on Nigel's face, a clear reaction to what he was reading on mine.

Before leaving us, Ali jabbed a finger menacingly in my direction. "You are a problem," he said.

*

Nigel and I were pretty sure there was a school right behind our building. We could hear children's voices floating in the air, lots of them. It sounded as if they were playing in a yard, laughing. The Korans piled on the shelves made us wonder if the compound was part of a madrasa, a Koranic school. But the fact that the floor of every room we'd been in was littered with fuses, old batteries, and bits of wire offered an alternative idea—that this was a place where mujahideen fighters built their bombs.

The truth was, we had no idea where we were. Somewhere west of Mogadishu, we figured. We'd driven a long time at high speed. We'd passed nothing but a few camel herders and that one single truck full of soldiers. Early on, I'd caught glimpses of the bright tarps that made up the IDP camps toward which we'd originally been heading, but then we'd veered off again into the scrub. We could hear no sounds of cars driving by, no planes flying overhead, only the occasional ping and crackle of the building's tin roof, expanding noisily under the pour of hot sun. It felt like we were in a box inside another box, sealed away from everything we knew.

Ali delivered us lunch—a flask of sweet dark tea, some bottled water, and two flimsy blue plastic bags, each containing a glop of cold spaghetti. He also gave us a tin of oily tuna fish. I took a few bites but couldn't eat more. The day's fear had accumulated into an acidic brew that sloshed in my stomach.

For a while in the late afternoon, we were allowed outside. Beneath the boughs of the acacia tree, Nigel and I played a few listless games of tic-tac-toe, drawing crosses and circles in the dust, watching the soldier boys out of the corners of our eyes. They were sprawled in the dirt with their guns, boredom seeming to have set in. Blooming white clouds drifted across a blue sky.

I was looking for diversion. "When you were a kid," I asked Nigel, "did you ever play the game where you called out the shapes you saw in the clouds?"

He looked at me like I was insane.

Back inside our room, he began to cry. I was too afraid to put my arms around him or even to move off my foam mattress and over to where he sat. Earlier, Ahmed had asked if we were married, and after giving myself a split second to make a choice, I'd told him that we weren't. This had been a tactical move, since I'd just finished encouraging him to Google us to prove that we were journalists and not spies. I didn't want to get caught in any sort of lie. Now, though, I couldn't comfort Nigel, for fear of igniting the mercurial Ali. I was already worried that he'd separate us for good. In Islamic tradition, an unmarried woman should not be alone with an unmarried man, let alone touch him. I didn't want to take any risks.

Instead, I spoke softly to Nigel from a distance, saying all the things that I myself wanted to hear. It would be all right, I told him. We'd get out of this place. We had each other. At one point, we'd spotted Abdi and the two other Somali guys being walked at gunpoint across the courtyard. Nigel and I had been wondering whether they'd been in on the kidnapping—whether one or all of them had sold us out—but it looked as if they were being installed in one of the other two rooms in our building, captives like us.

I tried to get Nigel to meditate with me, running through the phrases about freedom and peace that I'd listened to a couple of days earlier on the plane from Nairobi, this time saying them aloud. He whispered the words along with me.

At some point, we both nodded off in the heat. I slept hard—for how long, I have no idea. Waking up, I enjoyed a quick instant of unknowingness before my surroundings reintroduced themselves. The grubby walls. The tattered mat. Nigel staring at the ceiling from his own mat about ten feet away. The sound of men speaking a foreign language outside our door. As my mind locked in on the scene, I felt something internal start to plummet. Now what?

Our door flew open. Ahmed was back, dressed in the clothes he'd worn earlier, accompanied by Ali and two other men. One was tall, wearing Ben Franklin glasses and an orange-striped polo shirt. He held a notepad and pen. He looked to be in his mid-twenties, thin and serene-faced, but unable to mask how pleased he was to see us, two trophy animals in a cage. He introduced himself as Adam.

"I am the commander," he said. He shook Nigel's hand but made no move to shake mine. When he spoke, it was with only a slight accent. "What is your country?" When Nigel answered "Australia," Adam wrote it down in the notepad. "What is your village?" he said next.

The other man was introduced as Yahya. He was older than the others, with a short white beard, and seemed gruff, entirely detached. Something in the way he squared his shoulders made me think he had a military background. I recognized him as the guy who'd driven our car away from the spot where we'd been taken earlier. He was looking with scorn at Nigel's pink paisley shirt.

Adam took down our names and professions and addresses. I gave him my father's phone number in Sylvan Lake, wishing that I had my mother's number in British Columbia. She would hold up better in a crisis, I knew. Nigel gave a number for his sister, Nicky. Adam smiled and closed his notebook. *"Inshallah,* this will be over quickly," he said. "You are my brother and my sister."

A while later, he returned to the room, offering some good news. "We no longer believe you are spies," he said. Before anyone could get too excited, he tacked on another announcement: "Allah," he said, "has put it into my heart to ask for a ransom."

I imagined the calls going through, Adam's voice on my dad's line. I couldn't, for the life of me, imagine what he would say. What words got used? How did arrangements get made? My father had chronic health issues and lived on disability checks. My mother made very little money working at the bakery. My bank account was just about empty. My friends in Calgary were mostly waitresses, none of them wealthy. I'm not sure anybody I knew back home could even find Somalia on a map. In Iraq, kidnapping was enough of a worry that it had been a topic of conversation at the Hamra Hotel. The big-time journalists generally had kidnapping insurance through their news organizations. Usually, it would pay for a crisis response company to help negotiate for a hostage's release. Freelancers most often had none. And it was common knowledge that you couldn't rely on your government to get you out. As a rule, governments won't pay off hostage-takers. It's too expensive and too loaded. No government wants to be found handing money over to terrorists.

It was evening when Nigel and I were allowed out of the room again, to use the bathroom and to get some air. Ali ushered us to a straw mat laid out alongside one of the compound's walls. He handed us two more tins of tuna fish and another flask of tea. It seemed clear we'd be spending the night. Calmly, I let go of the idea that this would be a one-day ordeal. It was like putting down one stone and picking up another. This would be a two-day ordeal, I told myself. I could live with that. As darkness fell, the air cooled off somewhat. The sky became a screen, shot through with pinpricked stars. Beneath it, I felt small and lost.

Over near the lean-to, I could see the soldier boys lolling around. Some sat on the ground; a few had laid themselves out flat. They were listening to a silver battery-operated boom box, having tuned in to the BBC Somali Service. A male newscaster's voice blared in Somali, delivering what I assumed was news of the war. Then, with bizarre clarity, I heard him say the words "Shamo Hotel."

In the lean-to area, the words caused a stir. The soldiers were sitting up and beginning to talk. Ali got to his feet and started waving at us excitedly, pointing toward the radio. The newscaster said "Canadeeeean" and then "Australeeeean." My eyes met Nigel's. The news story was about us, for sure. The feeling was crushing. It was confirmation that our troubles were both real and deep.

18

Ransom

I know now that kidnappings for ransom happen more frequently than most of us would think.

They happen in Mexico, Nigeria, and Iraq. They happen in India, Pakistan, China, Colombia, and plenty of places in between. Sometimes the motivation is political or personal, but most often it's about money, plain and simple. Hostage-taking is a business, a speculative one, fed by people like me—the wandering targets, the fish found out of water, the comparatively rich moving against a backdrop of poor. Oil workers in far-off countries, traveling businesspeople, journalists, and tourists get swiped out of cars, or from meetings, or are deftly escorted at gunpoint from a restaurant. Back home, you wouldn't know how often it happened if you didn't pay attention to it. The news stories pop up and then disappear: An American traveler gets grabbed in Benin. A Dutch consultant gets held for ransom in Johannesburg. A British tourist is dragged from a bus in Turkey.

Families get called; governments are contacted. A certain machinery quietly goes into gear. Nobody would ever call these situations common, but they happen frequently enough that there are procedures in place, a way things go, at least on the home front.

In my case, it was not the kidnappers who alerted my family but a radio producer in Vancouver who had noticed a thinly reported wire story coming out of Somalia not twelve hours after we'd been taken. What it said was that two journalists, one Canadian, one Australian, had gone missing outside of Mogadishu. Only our first names were included, but I'd done some work for that producer earlier in the year, giving live radio updates from Iraq, and I'd let him know I was headed to Somalia. Searching for contact information on the Internet, the producer had called my uncle in Red Deer, who then rang my father. He and Perry had been sitting, until that moment, in the sun on their back porch.

My father called my mother. My mother called my brothers. Nobody was clear on what to do. The radio producer in Vancouver had passed on a number for the government office of Foreign Affairs in Ottawa. When my father called it, a staffer explained that while they were aware of what the news said, nothing was confirmed. She then gave a different number for my family to call if they heard anything. She told my father to sit tight.

One news report begat another. My father's phone rang and rang with calls from reporters, dozens of them. A couple of TV trucks had parked in the street outside the house. Neighbors gathered on the sidewalk. The phone rang, but my father, feeling overwhelmed, stopped answering. Perry opened the door only to close friends and relatives. Otherwise, they stayed locked up, waiting for something to happen.

The first phone call from Somalia came the next morning, a rubbly voice on my father's voicemail, the man who called himself Adam saying, "Hello, we have your daughter." He said he'd call again to talk about money, and then hung up. The call made it official. I hadn't gotten lost or run away. I'd been taken. I had captors, and those captors had demands.

I think now of my mother leaving the small house she'd rented in British Columbia. Too rattled to drive, she enlisted a friend to help her make the ten-hour trip through the Rockies to my father's place in Alberta. I imagine the car climbing the crooked road, surrounded by pine forest, my mother perched stiffly in the passenger seat. It was August. The lupine would have been blooming in the dirt along the road's shoulder. The mountains would have carried white veins of snow. Probably there were hawks in the sky. My mother, I would guess, saw none of it.

By nightfall, three agents from the Royal Canadian Mounted Police (RCMP) had arrived in Sylvan Lake and were sitting around the dining room table at my dad and Perry's house, along with my mother. The agents asked questions and took notes. They listened several times to Adam's voice message. They requested permission to tap my parents' phone lines. They offered talking points for what to say when Adam called again. The idea was to try and have Adam put me on the phone—to prove I was alive, to get a sense of how I was being treated, to listen for clues. When it came to money, they were to tell the truth: They had none, and the government wouldn't pay a ransom, either.

My belongings—my journal, my toothbrush, all my odds and ends left in the Mogadishu hotel room—would soon be shipped to the Canadian embassy in Nairobi. My parents would receive a typed bullet-pointed list of everything I'd been traveling with: one green shawl, one brown T-shirt, one bathing suit, one Apple MacBook laptop, two pairs of black trousers, one head scarf, one bottle Nivea sunscreen, assorted pens and notebooks, assorted airline itineraries and electronic ticket records, assorted currency from Thailand, India, and Pakistan. My mother would later tell me she pored over the list, examining what was left of me, as if it would explain something about why any of this had happened.

When it came to the reporters camped on my father's front lawn, my parents were instructed to say little—not just to the media but to friends and neighbors as well. The hope was that, starved of fresh information, the news story about my kidnapping would die out quickly. It was better, the agents explained, to be a low-profile captive than a high-profile one. Hostage-takers, in general, are plenty savvy. They know how to Google. They read the news. They, too, would be scanning for clues during those early days, trying to assess the value of their catch. Did my family have money? Did I work for a big, wealthy company? Was I important to my government? A simple stressed-out comment from my mother in the news about how desperately she wanted me back could lead to an immediate hike in ransom.

The message from the investigators to my parents was that they were not alone. Teams of trained negotiators would rotate in and out of Sylvan Lake, sleeping on mattresses on the floor, monitoring the phones and coaching my parents twenty-four/seven, until it was done. Together, they would work to wrangle, coddle, apply pressure, and offer vague assurances to our captors—to hit whatever levers it might take to get me sprung from Somalia.

Kidnappings happened, my parents were told, but they also ended.

This was meant as reassurance. So was another point the agents made, offering a first bit of hard comfort in what would turn into months of it: Nigel and I were now commodities. The kidnappers had spent money to catch us and keep us. They'd made an investment, which meant that it was in their best interest to keep us alive. If they killed us, it would be their loss, too.

*

In the tin-roofed house in Somalia, of course, we knew none of this. I spent the first day and night of captivity vacillating between panic and something that amounted to faith, a certainty that our ordeal would end quickly if only we could hit upon the right strategy for talking to the men holding us.

Early on the second morning, Adam came into our room, accompanied by Ali, Yahya, and Ahmed, and announced that they had come up with a plan. He would be calling our families shortly to demand a ransom payment. They would be given one day to pay. If no money came, we'd be killed.

Immediately, I started to argue. I said, "Our families don't have money. They can't pay ransom. And besides that, it's Sunday, and so even if they could, all the banks are closed, anyway."

Adam was unmoved. When Nigel asked why they were holding us, he smiled and said something about our governments being at war with Islam. "You have bad governments," he said, as if suggesting that we shouldn't take anything personally. He added that they didn't want money from our families. "If we are going to kill you in twenty-four hours, your governments will find a way to pay," he said. I could see he was missing one of his top front teeth.

I said, "How much are you asking for?"

"Ah!" said Adam, as if I'd hit upon something he'd forgotten to mention. "We are not yet certain." He eyed us as if trying to evaluate our worth. "Maybe one million dollars," he said, shrugging lightly, "maybe two."

Nigel and I sat in stunned silence while the four men filed back out the door. A few minutes later, we heard a car leaving the compound.

We were starting to understand, somewhat, the power structure in the group holding us hostage. Adam and Ahmed appeared to be the leaders, with Yahya, the older military man, and Ali serving as deputies, overseeing the foot soldiers, the eight or so long-legged young men— the boys, we started calling them—drifting around the courtyard with their guns. The leaders came and went in the Suzuki; it seemed they were staying at a different place, possibly back in Mogadishu. Yahya seemed to be directly in charge of the boys, ordering them around in Somali, sending one or two out to fetch thermoses of sweet tea or bags of cooked spaghetti from some unseen market on the other side of the walls.

Ali appeared to be in charge of us. Without his commanders around, he kicked into high gear, barging in and out of the room with a jumpy sort of ferocity. "If your governments don't pay, you will die," he said at one point, looking down at us from the doorway. He dragged a finger dramatically across his own neck to indicate that we would be beheaded. Clearly enjoying the moment, he leaned in close. His voice was high-pitched for a man's. "How does it feel," he said, "knowing you will soon die?"

The morning passed minute by minute. Every few hours, we could hear a muezzin call from a mosque and then the shuffle and murmur of prayer outside our door. Nigel lay on his mat, crying softly, keeping one elbow crooked over his face as if he couldn't bear to look at his surroundings. On the previous day, Ali had given us each a brand-new piece of fabric, a large square of lightweight cotton. Nigel's was red, and he was wearing it instead of his jeans, wrapped like a skirt around his waist to give his body more air, which was how we'd seen some of our captors dressed. I was sweltering, still in head scarf and abaya with my jeans and tank top beneath, knowing I had no choice but to stay fully cloaked. I'd taken my sheet, which was covered with delicate blue and white flowers, and spread it out to put a layer between me and the moldy floor mat.

I made the calculations. Somalia was in a time zone nine hours ahead of the Canadian Rockies. I wondered, Was my family sleeping? Would the kidnappers call them in the middle of the night? I fought off tears. We were behind high walls, outnumbered by men with guns, and with no sense of where we were on the map. Our helplessness seemed complete.

Ali stuck his head through our door again. "How does it feel," he said, "to know you have twenty hours to live?" He made the beheading motion with his finger, this time adding a sound effect—a swift scraping hiss. Then he left again.

I tried unsuccessfully to barricade myself off from his words, to push what I knew from my mind: Our captors were fundamentalists. And fundamentalists really did behead people. In Iraq, I'd gone out one day to do a TV story and had visited a field at the outskirts of Sadr City. The place had become a dumping ground for the bodies of people killed in the fighting between Shiite and Sunni militias. A man's decomposing corpse, lying on the ground amid piles of garbage, caught my eye. His hair was matted and his eyes were open, brown and blank. It took me a few seconds to assemble the picture, to realize what it was that I was seeing. The man's head had been partially severed from his body, the top vertebrae of his spine flashing white like whalebones in the sun.

It was a lesson the world had already taught me and was teaching me still. You don't know what's possible until you actually see it.

*

With time ticking down, we were novelties, Nigel and I. With a now-or-never bravado, two of the soldier boys entered our room with lunch and lingered awkwardly in the doorway. They were keen to practice their English.

One of them, I would actually come to like. Jamal, his name was. He spoke only a small amount of English but compensated with an eagerness to engage. He sat on the floor cross-legged, in a navy blue T-shirt and a pair of tan dress slacks with cuffs that rode high over his skinny dark ankles, and smiled at us in a genuine way. He was a teenager—eighteen years old, he said—a clear work in progress, with long spindly legs and narrow shoulders that sloped forward, as if he were trying to shed some of his considerable height. He had bright eyes and dark curly hair cut close to his skull. On his chin, he had a few sprouting hairs, the very beginnings of a beard. I could smell his cologne, fruity and cheap. I remembered Jamal from the day before. He'd been the gunman who first appeared at my window. His eyes were unforgettably big and frightened in a way that broadcast his inexperience. Though his face had been wrapped, the scarf had fallen partly open, and I'd seen enough that I could recognize him now.

He came to our room with another boy, Abdullah, who was more heavily built and somber-seeming. Abdullah had carried our meals— two more bags of greasy spaghetti—and dropped them quickly into our hands using only the outer edges of two fingertips, as if we might bite.

Jamal, though, was openly curious, only a little bit bashful, averting his eyes when he asked us questions, smiling at the ground as he heard our answers. Where did we live? Were we married? What did we think of Somalia? Did we own cars? Abdullah sat down as well, but he made me uneasy. In a flat voice, he said that he also was eighteen and fighting the jihad.

"Soldier," he said, touching his chest with evident pride. I could feel him looking at me as he said it, even as I avoided meeting his gaze.

Both Nigel and I left our food untouched. To eat in front of them felt like putting a weakness on display.

Jamal, it turned out, had just gotten engaged to be married.

I said, "Is she a beautiful girl?"

He dipped his head sheepishly, the grin irrepressible. "Yes, beautiful."

"When are you getting married?"

Jamal said, "After now."

"You mean soon?"

"Yes," he said. "*Inshallah.*" Searching for the words, he added, "The married party is . . ." He rubbed two fingers together.

"Expensive? A wedding is expensive?"

"Yes." He seemed to beam relief, having made himself understood.

What he meant by "after now," I realized, was "once this kidnapping is over." It occurred to me that for Jamal, this wasn't so much about jihad. He was waiting for his payout so he could go home, throw a wedding, and marry his girl.

*

"You have seventeen hours until you die," Ali said after we'd made a late-day trip to the outhouse and resettled ourselves on our mats. Nigel was lying on his side, facing the wall. I found myself hoping Ali would leave and Jamal would come back, bringing his comparative cheer. Nigel had closed himself off. He hadn't managed to say one reassuring or hopeful thing all day.

Ali said, sounding angry, "Did you hear me?"

"I heard you."

"You will soon die."

My hips were sore from the pressure of the concrete beneath my thin mat. I was feeling drained by the heat. I was sick of his nastiness. "Well," I said, knowing I was being flippant, "if that's how Allah wants it . . ."

Ali's rage was instantaneous. He took a few steps closer, as if to strike me. "You," he seethed. "You think this is a joke? If you are ready to die, then say so. I will kill you now."

I cowered. "No, no, no, I'm sorry," I said, switching my tone to reflect how I felt. Fear, sustained over a number of hours, feels like something you can drown in. I'd been paddling in it all day.

Nigel had quietly rolled over on his mat and was listening.

I said, "I don't think this is a joke, my brother. I don't want to die." I bowed my head. "But if it's my time, then there is nothing I can do about it. That's all I was trying to say."

When I looked up again, Ali seemed to be regarding me carefully. His anger had subsided a little. I regretted saying it. To mock the Muslim belief in predestiny—the idea that Allah had planned our fates carefully and there was little we could do to swerve from them—was sacrilege, a hot-button move if there ever were one.

An idea came to me then, a possibility. "If I'm going to die," I said to Ali as calmly as I could, "I would like to speak with an imam first."

I saw him cock his head in surprise. "No," he said after a beat. "That is reserved only for the Muslims."

There were a lot of things only for the Muslims in Somalia. Because everybody, more or less, was Muslim.

"Well," I said, thinking maybe it would extend us past twenty-four hours, "maybe I want to become a Muslim before I die."

*

That night they loaded us back into Ahmed's Suzuki. In a repeat of the initial kidnapping, Nigel and I were pushed in with a bunch of masked men, a few of whom we recognized. I could identify Ahmed, Adam, Ali, and Yahya. Their guns clattered, knocking against the rounds of bullets they wore draped over their shoulders. Adam drove the car. Abdullah, Jamal's angry-seeming friend, rode in back with his AK-47 pointed at our heads.

Ahmed, who had come to fetch us from the room an hour earlier, had given his usual sunny smile and spoken with the unflappable politeness of a five-star hospitality professional.

"Is everything okay?" I'd said.

"Oh yeah, very good," he'd replied.

"But what about the twenty-four hours?"

He almost looked surprised. "Oh, we will give you more time. No problem! We will take you to a nicer house. I am sorry for these poor beds that you must sleep on."

It was impossible to know whether we should believe him. The car slid through the village, spraying sand. Nigel and I held hands tightly. Out the window, I could see no clues to where we were, just walls and low bushes. Adam, in his Ben Franklin glasses, spun the wheel back and forth, revving the engine to get traction.

I asked Adam, "Have you spoken to our families?"

"Ah, yes, I have," he said. He looked over his shoulder at Nigel. "I talked with your sister." His face broke into a smile, showing the gap of his missing front tooth. "She is . . . what is the word for it? Panicked."

The thought tightened my throat. "My parents?" I said.

"Your mother, she is good, very good," Adam said nonchalantly. He offered nothing more.

19

Electric House

Our new house was close to the old house. After a ten-minute drive, we were dropped in front of another high-walled compound and escorted through a small metal doorway, the group of us filing in like ducks, the boys angling their AK-47s to fit through the door. On the other side was a sand yard and, across it, a single-story house with a wide patio. Someone had strung a few drooping clotheslines across the porch. Inside, it was not much of an upgrade over where we'd come from, though this place had electric lights and a small indoor bathroom with a bucket-flush toilet. A couple of the boys, wordlessly clutching their guns, led us down a hallway and to a damp-feeling bedroom with two stained mattresses on the floor.

A forest of black crystallized mold branched across the back wall, running the width of the room. Left on our own, Nigel and I silently pulled the mattresses as far away from it as possible, each picking a different side of the room.

Adam carried in several plastic bags, thrusting them in our direction with what I read to be pride, gesturing for us to open them. Nigel was given a couple of new sets of shirts and pants, folded tidily. I got a pair of men's jeans and two men's dress shirts, along with a brown sequined skirt that looked small enough to fit a child. All were brand-new. Adam had bought me a notebook and a pen, a bottle of Head & Shoulders two-in-one shampoo/conditioner, some perfume, a bar of

soap, a toothbrush, and a family-sized toothpaste. He looked pleased
by his own thoughtfulness. When I glanced over at Nigel, I saw that he
was holding an identically huge log of toothpaste.

It seemed they weren't planning to kill us right away. I felt a tide
of relief, followed by instant exhaustion. *Jesus,* I thought, holding my
toothpaste, *how long are they planning to keep us here?* To Adam, I said,
"Wow, this is a lot of stuff."

He seemed flattered. "Oh, well," he said, lifting his hands, "you are
our brother and sister. And you can see that it is the real brand, the
Crest toothpaste . . ."

Dutifully, Nigel and I fawned over his purchases. I assumed that
American toothpaste was neither cheap nor easy to come by in Somalia. Then again, as Adam seemed to be calculating it, he'd soon be on
the receiving end of a seven-figure ransom payment that would render
all expenses trivial.

He smiled and said good night.

*

The next several nights were not in any way restful. We'd hear the evening prayers, and then the house would go quiet. The electricity was
spotty. The lights clicked off abruptly and on no sort of regular schedule. Nigel and I whispered until he drifted off, covering every mean-
ingless or pleasant topic we could think of—our pets, our school days,
our past travels. In the darkness, I could just make out the contours
of his face. Sleep, for him, had become a means of escape. By day, his
anxieties were so stark and so crippling that he almost didn't resemble
himself. Back in the last place, the Bomb-Making House I called it,
he'd combed the room for things he might use to kill himself—the cut
wires, the iron coatrack—thinking it was better to stay one step ahead
of Ali and his drive to have us beheaded.

Lying on my flowered sheet, I listened enviously to Nigel's breathing. Cockroaches skittered in the corners of the room. I wrapped
the two edges of the sheet over me and rolled to make it tight, like a
cocoon, as I lay on my side. In the bathroom at the new house—this
one I thought of as the Electric House—our captors brought us water

in a brown bucket from a pump outside, which we used to wash and to pour down the toilet as a flush. Before going to bed, before the lights went off, I splashed water over as much of my body as I could, too afraid to remove any piece of clothing, exposing my skin only in pieces, unsnapping the abaya to run a hand over my clavicles, pulling up the loose sleeves to get to my arms, keeping my pants down long enough after using the toilet to douse myself quickly between the legs. The water felt like a relief, though I was far from clean. But it was relative. Everything was relative. One day's worries were either greater or lesser than the previous day's worries.

What I lay with at night was the fear of being raped. I was the lone woman in a house that included, by my count, twelve men, in addition to Ahmed and Adam, who continued to sleep elsewhere. Four of them were prisoners. Nigel and I had been relieved to hear Abdi and our driver and security guard—Marwali and Mahad, their names were—moved into a room next to ours, if only because it meant they hadn't been killed. We could see their shoes piled on the floor in the hallway outside their door.

The house hummed with what I can only describe as male energy, a buzzy mix of repression and young strength. I felt it when the boys came to deliver food, when their eyes fell on me and then quickly moved away, as if the sight of me, or whatever thought that followed, was shameful. I felt it in the afternoons when Ali plunked himself down on the floor of our room and went on his long rants about how the Western countries, the Christians, were to blame for the war in Somalia. He seemed to view me with a mixture of intrigue and disgust, much like he viewed the world beyond Somalia. "Your *women* . . ." he said to Nigel one day, scooping his hands so they looked like splayed breasts. Then he trailed off, lacking the words, his lips curled in distaste. Pointedly, he did not look in my direction.

I felt it most, though, in those hours spent in the darkness, my sheet and the polyester abaya making a flimsy barrier between me and them, in the moments when I heard a rustle or a grunt from somewhere in the house. I was an aberration, an enemy to their morals, and also fully powerless. With me, they seemed unsure what to do.

"You see," Ahmed said to me at one point, suggesting that the original plan had been to kidnap the *National Geographic* guys off the road, "we were told it would be two men."

*

Midway through the first week, Ahmed showed up at the house and handed me his cell phone. "Talk to your mother," he said.

I took the phone and held it to my ear. "Mom?" I said.

And there was her voice, her voice saying my name. The line crackled and faded, and for a second she didn't seem real. Ahmed had put the phone on speaker. He gestured for me to hold it away from my head so he could listen. There was a split-second delay between what my mother said and when I heard it, causing our voices to overlap uselessly.

"Are you okay?" I asked.

"Well, no, not really . . . Are . . . are you okay?"

"Yeah, we're okay," I said.

Her voice cut over mine. "Okay."

"We're okay."

It felt as if the two of us were swimming between enormous ocean waves, dropping in and out of each other's sight, shouting into walls of water. She told me that she loved me, that people at home were praying for us. She asked if Nigel was with me. She said they were trying to get some money together. Those were the words she used, "get some money together." What that meant, I couldn't imagine.

I asked what the ransom demand was. My mother hesitated and then replied, "One point five million," she said. My mother and I were silent for a few seconds. The money was an impossibility, we both knew. My mother stuttered. "Amanda," she said, "Is, is, there any . . . sorry . . . is there any, um, ideas that . . . that you can think of?"

I wasn't sure what she was asking. Later, I would learn that she was being coached by a negotiator from the RCMP, one of a number of people listening in on the phone call. My mother was now living in a government-rented home in Sylvan Lake, which doubled as the RCMP's operational center. She and the negotiator were trying to figure out how firm the demands were, whether we were safe, and who was keeping us. Meanwhile, I was sitting in our room in the Electric House, surrounded by my captors—Ahmed and several of the others—as my mother's voice entered the room, their world, sounding tinny and weak. "No . . ." I said, feeling tears begin to brim. I tried to think of something, anything, to tell her. But before I could say more, the line disconnected and she was gone.

*

I began to obsess over the idea that Nigel and I needed to stay together—that we had to do all we could to keep them from separating us. Even as he confused our captors by weeping openly in front of them, Nigel still was more familiar to them. Because he was a man, he was accorded more respect. Because we were together, we were treated more or less the same. I hung on to this, knowing his proximity helped keep me safe.

When the leaders showed up at the house, every other day or so, I did my best to appear composed and businesslike, delivering the same message again and again: Our families had no money. Our governments wouldn't pay. Sometimes Nigel joined me in reinforcing the message. Other times he dripped silent tears, following my instructions not to say anything that sounded desperate or emotional. Having discarded the hope that some easy negotiation could take place, my new hope was that after a few weeks or a month, our captors would get tired and give up. Every day I worked to make myself—to make us—harder to kill, by being friendly and remaining neutral on politics and religion. If we could bore them without frustrating them, I figured, maybe they'd deliver us back to the Shamo, just like two boxes that had spent a month uselessly collecting dust in a warehouse.

"How is your situation?" Ahmed said each time he greeted us, stepping into the dark room, looking every bit the visiting nobleman in a clean shirt and pressed khakis.

There were two answers. There was the one I wanted to scream—that our situation *sucked,* thank you very much—and the one that maintained the status quo, that kept the basic arrangement undisturbed, which, given that we were together, receiving two basic meals a day, and had toothpaste to last an eternity, seemed the better choice.

"Our situation is okay," I'd tell Ahmed, "but we want to go home."

"Ah, yes," he would say. "We are working on that."

When the leaders weren't around, the boys loitered in our room, mostly focused on Nigel. They looked him in the eye. In faltering English, they talked about sports and cars, which seemed to break him out of his depression for short stints. Slowly, we were learning their names. There was Ismael, who was fourteen, and a boy whose name was Yahya, same as the older captain's. There was a Yusuf and two Mohammeds and another soldier who seemed sweet, like Jamal, whose name was Hassam. Each one of them carried a cell phone, an AK-47, and a tiny edition of the Koran, about the size of a deck of cards, tucked into his shirt pocket.

Around me, the boys were more cautious. Most, I assumed, had never spent time close to a woman who wasn't a family member. I worked constantly to demystify myself. I learned there was a benefit to mentioning again and again that I'd lived in Afghanistan and Iraq and had traveled in places like Pakistan, Sudan, and Syria. They felt a kinship with these countries, especially Afghanistan and Iraq, where Islamic soldiers were fighting, as they saw it, infidel invaders. Any time I showed even a vague familiarity with Islamic tradition or culture, acknowledging that Ramadan was soon to start, recalling the beauty of the Al-Aqsa mosque in Jerusalem or the time I'd traveled through Tora Bora, they seemed to become slightly less suspicious of me, more eager to engage.

Jamal, it was clear, had been born almost too happy for his circumstances. Misery didn't suit him. He loped in and out of our room, bringing us flasks of tea or small bunches of green bananas. Almost always, he wore an effervescent smile. There were moments when he burst out laughing, having understood one of Nigel's weak wisecracks, and then clamped a hand over his mouth as if to stuff his delight back inside. After one of his trips to the market, he smuggled in a couple of packs of cigarettes and handed them off to Nigel, looking pleased by his own naughtiness.

When Jamal came for a visit, Abdullah often tagged along, the Hyde to his Jekyll, unwilling to laugh or be casual, but listening with interest to everything we said. Even as most of the other boys had stopped wearing scarves over their faces in our presence, Abdullah kept himself carefully swathed. He sat close to me, his eyes flashing an emotion I couldn't read, his nose and mouth buried beneath folds of checkered cotton. He asked me questions about the mujahideen fighters in Afghanistan—what kind of guns they carried, how they dressed, whether they had cars.

Slowly, we began to extract information. Most of the boys had gone to some form of training camp to learn to be a soldier. Ismael, the fourteen-year-old, had been schooled in insurgent warfare somewhere out in the desert. Jamal had joined the mujahideen out of grief and duty. His father had been killed a couple of years earlier by Ethiopian troops, he told us. His mother was still alive. The memory of losing his father was fresh enough that it caused his eyes to water. "For me, this was start of jihad," he said.

Before jihad, we learned, Ahmed and Adam had both worked as teachers. The older Yahya had been a farmer. Before jihad, some of the younger boys had gone to school. Now they got paid to fight, though it wasn't much. I knew from my research that funding for the insurgency in Somalia flowed in from other countries, raised through radical Islamist networks. Some, it was believed, came from the fat ransoms paid for ships held hostage by pirates in the Gulf of Aden. From where I sat, the group holding us captive looked to be a straight-up hierarchy. The leaders—Ahmed, Adam, and a third tall man we'd come to call Romeo—appeared to be reasonably well-off, with cars and expensive-looking clothes. Captain Yahya and Ali seemed to be middle management, while the boys had been given little more than a weapon, housing, and food, plus the conviction that Allah was behind them.

"Jihad," in Arabic, means "the struggle." There are two types in Islam, the greater and the lesser. Both are seen as noble. The greater jihad is inward, the lifelong striving of any Muslim to be a better person, to ward off temptation and desire, to maintain faith. The lesser jihad is outward and communal and violent when called for—the struggle to defend and assert that faith. For our captors, this jihad involved fighting the Ethiopians, although our kidnapping was wrapped into the cause. Not only did we come from "bad" countries, as Ali put it, but any ransom money they got, he said, would get channeled back into the larger fight.

It seemed that young men were organized into cells, getting called out for combat in the streets of Mogadishu or elsewhere when necessary. From what we could gather, most of the boys had been living at home right up until the day we'd been taken on the road to Afgoye, a task for which their cell had been activated—by whom, we couldn't be sure.

While Jamal brimmed with plans for his life after the kidnapping— he would get married, then study information technology in India, since he'd heard there were many universities there—Abdullah seemed stuck on the war. One day I asked what he was going to do later in life. He gave me a fierce look, mimed the act of putting on a jacket, and made the sound of an explosion.

It took me a second. "Suicide bomber?"

Abdullah nodded. Martyr, was how he saw it. At the gates to paradise, soldiers in God's army got to enter through a special doorway.

Jamal shook his head. He waved his hand back and forth, as if to say, "No, no, no." Like me, he had an idea that life could again be normal, that all of this could be rolled back. "I don't want him to die," he explained. "He is my friend."

20

Amina

W hy are you not Muslim?" Ali wanted to know one morning, having surfaced in our room, seeming a little bored. "Why don't you pray?"

He'd expressed this confusion before, perplexed by the idea that our days could be ungoverned by scheduled prayer, whereas his fell so neatly into five slices, the several hours between each appointment with Allah, from the first one in the early morning to the last in the evening. For our spiritual idleness, Ali was certain that we were going to hell. He'd said this to us previously, too, in angry condemnation of who we were, but today he seemed less spiteful. It was hot already, hotter than usual. The air in our room smelled like a bog.

Ali sat with his back against the wall. He sighed. "It is better to pray," he said.

It occurred to me that were our situations reversed, if Ali were captive and unmoored from everything he knew, he would manage to keep his appointments, to live by the order imposed by his faith. As my own days felt increasingly like a long wait for nothing, I realized there was probably strength in that. During prayer times, we could hear Abdi and the two other Somali captives reciting their Arabic in the room next to ours.

Talking religion with Ali was something we did cautiously and only during his calmer moments, when he was not raging about one thing or another. Nigel at one point attempted to say that he leaned toward Buddhism, but Ali wasn't interested.

"We know how to pray, brother," I said, deliberately not looking at Nigel, who had not been raised with a formal religion and was capable of objecting. "We just have to learn more about the Muslim way." I asked if Ali had an English-language copy of the Koran he could loan us, just to look at.

This appeared to make Ali happy. "I will check in Bakaara Market," he said, looking from me to Nigel. "*Inshallah,* there is one there."

Bakaara Market was a well-known area in central Mogadishu, a place where people sold food and supplies and weapons. Before we were kidnapped, I'd asked Ajoos if we could visit, and he'd just laughed. "Impossible," he'd told me. "Bakaara Market is a base for Al-Shabaab. Very, very dangerous for white people."

"*Inshallah,*" I said back to Ali.

I was floating a balloon of willingness. I knew from my time in Iraq that for at least some Muslims, it was not considered such a leap for someone to move from Christianity to Islam. The two religions worshipped the same god under different names. The Muslim faith acknowledged Moses and Jesus, *Musa* and *Isa,* they were called. It acknowledged the Torah, the Psalms, and the Gospels as revelations from God. To convert, you needed to declare Muhammad the Prophet of record, the one whose path you were ready to follow.

I told Ali I had read the Bible many times. I told him I'd spent my childhood on my knees, that my grandparents were very religious.

He picked up on what I was saying immediately. "Then you are fifty percent Muslim already," he said. He gestured somewhat grandly with one hand. "You only have to say the *shahadah*"—the Islamic declaration of faith—"and you will go to paradise."

Nigel gave me an impatient look. He knew what I was doing and didn't like it. We had talked once or twice about pretending to accept Islam, asking to convert. He was solidly against it, thinking it was too big a risk. If we got caught faking their religion, the thing they took more seriously than anything, he said, we'd surely be killed.

I had argued the other side: Our captors would have to treat us well if we converted. They'd have no choice but to see us as fellow believers. They'd have to be more charitable. For me, it would be a way to distance myself from my Western-woman image. My freedom—my travels and work, my way of dressing and talking, my life unyoked to a husband or a family—was a taunt. The sooner I could reinvent myself, the better I'd do.

Ali stood up, brushed the dirt from the floor off his pants, and left the room.

Nigel glared at me. "No fucking way," he said. "Don't do this." He relocated himself to the far side of the room, carefully keeping his distance from the mold on the wall, but also from me.

On cue, a fuzzy-sounding loudspeaker nearby kicked on. The muezzin—different from the one we'd heard at the last house, this one older-sounding—cleared his throat into the microphone a few times and began to chant the call to prayer.

Nigel exhaled loudly and shook his head. "Look, you can become a Muslim," he said, "but I'm not going to."

We couldn't afford to divide. I knew that much. I sighed, too. "That won't work, Nigel," I said. "If I do it and you don't, then they'll move me out of here for sure. You can't have a Muslim woman living with a non-Muslim man."

"Right," he said.

And that was it. We were in a standoff. Conversion, we both knew, was an all-or-nothing move. I let the subject drop.

*

The window in our room was open to the air but covered by several iron bars. It looked out at another house. Every so often, we could hear the noises of the family living there—kids playing, parents talking, laughter. I caught a glimpse of a woman's back, but I felt too nervous to call out, worried that she'd start yelling. Our only interaction at the window was with a cat, a skinny orange creature that one afternoon leaped from the alleyway onto our sill.

We were allowed to come and go freely from the bathroom attached to the room. There, high in the wall that faced the courtyard, opposite the toilet, was a vent—a one-foot-by-two-foot piece of scrollwork cut into the concrete to let fresh air inside. Nigel and I soon figured out that if we craned our necks while standing on tiptoe, we could see through it to a small wedge of the yard where our captors passed most of their time.

The bathroom vent became our portal, our television set, our news station. It was something to monitor.

We took turns watching one morning as a new guy showed up in the courtyard, carrying a yellow plastic bag. He was fat, middle-aged, and well dressed. He walked hunched over, as if the weight of his belly were too much for him, as if he'd been thin all his life and wasn't used to carrying his bulk. He greeted Ali and Old Yahya in the way that was customary between Somali men—offering a hug on one side and a hug on the other. He took a moment to inspect the courtyard, then pulled from his bag a six-inch-thick wad of Somali shillings, the local currency. He handed it to the captain. They talked for a few minutes before the guy left again.

This was how we knew there was a moneyman—somebody funding the operation or delivering money on behalf of whoever was funding it. From here on out, the man would arrive at least once a week, bringing money and supplies for our captors. Once or twice, we saw him carrying a big pot of home-cooked food and leaving it for the boys. We nicknamed him Donald Trump.

Through our spy hole, we watched the boys doing military drills and fitness routines to pass the time. Following the lead of the heavy-set, dark-skinned boy called Yusuf, they performed marches and squat-thrusts and did bicep curls as if holding invisible dumbbells. Sometimes Captain Yahya would referee wrestling matches, pausing the action every so often to demonstrate a certain kind of hold. We would eventually nickname him Skids, since the boys sometimes complained to us privately that he was too strict with them, that he put the brakes on things, that he always said no.

The vent gave me things to look at, but it didn't give me hope. I stood on my toes until my calves throbbed, trying to spot something that might signal a way out. The idea of escape felt fruitless. There were too many people crammed into too small a space for anything to happen undetected, and there was only a single exit point—the small door in the heavy metal gate at the edge of the yard. The walls of the compound had been topped with razor wire. Somewhere beyond it, the craggy-voiced muezzin cranked up another call to the faithful, signaling to all that it was time to stand up and point themselves the same way.

★

One morning a few days after we'd discussed it, Ali arrived in the room carrying two thick books bound in navy blue leather, the covers adorned with intricate gold embossing and, written in English, the words "The Holy Koran." He handed them to us with apparent pride, one for me and one for Nigel. They were brand-new. The pages inside were tissue-thin, the verses written in tiny print—the original Arabic on one side, an English translation on the other.

The truth is, I would have devoured any book handed to me—anything to feed my gnawing mind—but the Koran, in that particular moment, felt like a gift from heaven. It was like getting the key to an intricate code.

I'd been allowed to speak with my mother twice more in the first seven days we were held hostage. Both calls had lasted under a minute. Neither yielded anything but proof that I was alive. Nigel had been granted a single call with his sister, Nicky, for what seemed to be the same purpose. We agreed that help or release did not seem to be coming soon.

I read the book in hopes of using their religion to talk my way out.

Both Nigel and I read for hours, for several days straight. We said very little to each other during that time, handling the books carefully, storing them on the ledge of the window when we ate or went to the bathroom.

Seeing how intent we were, Ali allowed us out into the yard a couple of times, gesturing for us to sit on a low round wall that encircled a
skinny papaya tree. The yard was dry and hot. The boys lounged with
their guns, ignoring us.

I went page by page through the Koran, trying to ignore the
fear roiling inside me. I looked for strands of logic, for insights into
the minds of my captors. I cross-referenced one bit of information
against another. The Koran was dense, poetic in some places, dicta-
torial in others, its messages often mixed. There were many verses
about jihad and enemies alongside many about kindness and mercy.
Paradise was dangled like a sumptuous fruit. Women were most
often described as wives. The Arabic phrase for captives or slaves
was "those whom your right hand possesses." The book was explicit
about what such possession meant: You were basically owned by
your captors. There were verses instructing that captives be treated
with kindness and granted freedom if they were well behaved. There
were others that made clear that a female captive was fair game sexu-
ally. In a couple of verses where the Koran forbade men to have sex
outside of marriage, there was a worrisome little clause tacked on at
the end: "except with those whom your right hand possesses."

We would have to focus on being well behaved and appeal to their
sense of mercy. The book gave us some power. It gave us language to
use, lines of reasoning to apply. It was like getting a look at the operating system that ran our captors' lives.

I found two notions that seemed like they might make a difference:
A believer is not supposed to kill a fellow believer.
And: *A believing slave is given more lenience than an unbelieving slave.*
"Nigel," I said, "they can't kill us if we convert."

He, too, had found the same verses, but still, he was worried about
the risk. Converting would feel false, he said. It could insult them. It
was too dangerous.

I was remembering the back-of-the-throat ripping sound Ali had
made when dragging a finger across his neck, explaining how we
would be killed. I was willing to be false if it gave us more leverage.

*

I woke up on the eleventh morning of our captivity, knowing it was time. Nothing was changing. It felt like we had to make a move, to force some sort of energy shift. Nigel's spirits seemed dangerously low. He sat on his mattress, sullenly reading the Koran.

When Ali walked into the room and he started talking, as usual, about Allah and Islam, I seized the moment, saying the words before I could think too hard about them. "I think we're ready to say the *sha-hadah*," I told Ali, bowing my head to appear modest and also to avoid looking at Nigel.

Ali was unhesitant in his jubilation, treating it like a personal victory. He dropped to his knees and touched his forehead to the ground. "*Allahu Akbar*," he exclaimed, repeating it three times. *God is great. God is great. God is great.* It was the first time in eleven days when I felt like I'd had any influence.

Getting to his feet again, Ali studied me closely. I was sweating, pointedly not looking in Nigel's direction. Ali seemed to read the disconnect between us. His voice grew stern, the words directed at me. He said, "'This is not a game, you know. It is a serious thing."

I nodded, trying to appear humble and capable of great piety. "Yes, of course, my brother," I said. "We understand."

"It is set then, *inshahallah*," he said. "You can prepare, and then, at eleven o'clock, you will become Muslim." *Moo-slim* was how he said it. He left the room.

Nigel slammed his Koran shut. His look was incredulous. "What the hell was that?" he said. "Aren't we going to discuss this?"

We *had* discussed it, I wanted to say. I said, "Nige, we have to do this. It's crazy, I know, but it's a way to keep ourselves alive."

We were aware of the risks. In my Koran, I'd read the word that would apply to us—that would doom us—if they figured out we were converting without believing. Hypocrites. Enemies from inside. Such enemies were considered far more evil and dangerous than those encountered on the battlefield. The Koran gave specific instructions for all pretenders to be killed. *They are the enemy, so beware of them*, one verse read. *May Allah destroy them.*

Returning to the room, Ali instructed us each to choose a set of clothes from our sparse collection and come with him outside so we could wash in the courtyard. This alone felt like a new freedom, our willingness awarded with soap. The Muslim obsession with bodily cleanliness was only going to improve our situation, I thought.

Nigel gathered up his clothes and followed me as I followed Ali down the narrow hallway, past the room where Abdi and the others were being held, past a small unused kitchen, and out onto the concrete veranda that overlooked the yard. When I turned to look at him, he gave me a quick, surprising smile. "What are you getting us into now, Lindhout?" he said under his breath.

The question was both tender and bitter. It flashed through my mind that our story—what got set into motion that first night Nigel and I spotted each other on the veranda in Addis—had been madness from the start. Mad love, mad confusion, and now maybe mad tragedy. What would have happened if I hadn't introduced myself? What if I'd just walked past him with my backpack and left him as he was?

I was sure that in his mind, he'd rewritten the story and its outcome plenty of times.

Slowly, we scrubbed our clothes in a plastic bucket under the hot sun, filling and refilling it at a tap located beneath a tall tree, leaving them out to dry. My nerves tingled. Despite the heat, my hands and feet felt cold. With Nigel, I'd been putting on bravado about converting, reminding him constantly of how much I knew already about Islamic cultures. I realized now that I knew very little. When it came to Islam, I'd been nothing more than a curious tourist. I felt quietly terrified of the decision I'd made.

Back in the room, we were each given a can of tuna for lunch. We took turns washing in the bathroom. We combed our hair and put on our clean clothes, which had already dried. I wore my abaya over my old tank top and one of the pairs of men's jeans they'd given me. All of it smelled blessedly like detergent.

We were stuck together, Nigel and I. It was as if we were preparing for a bizarre sort of wedding, getting ready to cross a threshold,
to seal our fates. I glanced at him, cleaner than he'd been in days,
his hair wet and neatly parted on one side, looking wide-eyed
and a little somber, and I felt a flare of old emotion. He had the
beginnings of a beard, the scruff along his chin making him look
grizzled, more suited to the drab, dusty purgatory of the house and
walled yard.

When we were a couple, I'd imagined so many possibilities for
the two of us, so many ways our lives might play out separately or
together. This was so far outside anything I might have conjured, ever.

I folded my hijab beneath my chin so that it wrapped tightly
around the perimeter of my face, my hair tucked carefully out of sight
beneath. Nigel put on a black cotton shirt given to him by our captors.
Ali returned to the room, having freshened his cologne and changed
his own shirt.

To become a Muslim, you need only to make one honest declaration of your faith. It does not need to happen in a mosque, nor be
witnessed by an imam. There is little ceremony involved. Converting
is a simple matter of speaking two simple lines in Arabic, though the
point is that you feel the conviction of those words in your heart. The
sincerity is what matters.

Nigel and I stood solemnly in the room with Ali as he recited the
words of the *shahadah* in Arabic and we mimicked them in slightly
uneven unison.

We made vows to accept Allah as our only god and Muhammad as
his messenger.

What I felt in that moment wasn't surrender and it wasn't defiance.
This was simply a chess move, an uncertain knight slid two squares
ahead and one to the side. It was not a betrayal of faith—of mine, or
Nigel's, or theirs. It was a way to feel less foreign, and in feeling less
foreign, we could be less afraid. We were doing what it took to survive.

When it was over, Ali left the room, and all the boys filed in and
jubilantly shook Nigel's hand. *"Mubarak,"* Jamal said to both of us.
Congratulations. Another nodded at me and called me "sister." Young

Yahya said something in Somali, which Abdullah translated. *"Jannah, jannah.* He is saying you will go to paradise."

A door, maybe, had cracked open. In our new lives as Muslims, Ali had told us, we were no longer Nigel and Amanda. They'd given us new names. Nigel was dubbed "Mohammed," and I was to be called "Marium." In a few days, we'd be given new names again; this time, at our request, our captors would match them more closely to our old names. Nigel would be called "Noah." My name would be "Amina." I would live with it for a long time. Much later, I would look up its Arabic meaning: Amina was a girl who, above all, was supposed to be faithful and trustworthy.

21

Paradise

Now we needed to learn how to pray. From here on out, we'd be expected to pray each time our captors prayed. It would be the first thing we did upon waking and the final thing we did before sleep.

The conversion to Islam felt like a crossing. It was as if, for eleven days, Nigel and I had been floating on a ship in a harbor, and now we were coming ashore, with our captors lining the pier. I felt unsteady, disoriented. The boys were almost welcoming, showing us new courtesy. Instead of barging in and out of our room without warning, they stood in the doorway and waited for permission to enter. Abdullah, it seemed, had appointed himself to be my teacher, while Jamal attached himself to Nigel. They doled out assignments, gave us lines to memorize from the Koran. They had us write down the movements of prayer—thumbs by the ears, right arm folded over the left—and the words we were to recite as we went. I got the sense that teaching us was a way to relieve their own boredom. During our lessons, the other boys sometimes hovered in the doorway, listening as we fumbled over the Arabic, unable to hide their bemusement.

Muslim prayers are performed in cycles, called *raka'ah*. Depending on the time of day, you go through the cycle either two, three, or four times—a bit like doing sun salutations in yoga. Each prayer includes motion. You stand, you kneel, you touch your forehead to the floor, and you sit back on your heels in contemplation before starting all over again. You recite Koranic verses from memory, each cycle beginning with the same seven lines from the first chapter, but expanding from there to include other chapters. *Surah,* a chapter is called. The most facile Muslims can draw from the whole of the Koran, having committed every last one of the book's 114 chapters—over 6,200 verses in all—to memory.

I prayed awkwardly. I held my thumbs at the wrong angle next to my ears or forgot to keep my toes tucked beneath me when I touched my forehead to the ground. The Arabic words got tangled in my head, unhitched as they were from any sort of meaning. There were a few phrases I'd picked up during my time in Iraq, but for the most part, we were learning syllables more than sentences, stringing them together like beads, a couple of words at a time. *Bismillahil rahman ar-raheem. Al hamdu lillahi rabb el alameen.*

I recognized how gentle it could sound, the lulling lift and fall of the words, how the lines might flow together like waves. Until one caught in my head and refused to come out. *Ar rah . . . ar-raheem?*

Abdullah caught the question in my tone. He leaned in close for a split second. "No!" he snapped. "Wrong."

He was not a patient teacher.

When it came to spoken Arabic, my copy of the Koran was no help whatsoever, since the Arabic was presented in indecipherable script, with nothing spelled out phonetically. So Abdullah chanted breathlessly, and I scrawled notes in my notebook so I could practice it all later. On the other side of the room, Jamal sat close to Nigel, his knees pulled up to his lanky body, taking him through new verses with painstaking care.

I looked at Abdullah. "Can you do that last part again, please? More slowly?"

He shook his head and got to his feet, seeming to signal that our lesson was over. "You are bad, Amina," he said gravely, chucking his chin toward Nigel—Noah—as if he were the model student, the preferable one. He went on to repeat the verse in a last merciless whoosh of Arabic—*Ar-rahman ar-raheem. Malikee yawm ul deen. Iyyak naabudu wa iyyaka nastaeen. Ihdina assirat al moostaqeem*—and then, relishing his own ability to pronounce English, he said nice and slowly, "You are very stupid woman."

★

One thing about Islam is that paradise always beckons. Life is oriented toward the afterlife. Whatever pleasures you miss out on in this world, whatever comfort or richness or beauty is absent from your days and years, you will find it upon entering paradise, where pain, grit, and war disappear altogether. Paradise is a vast, perfect garden. It's a place where everyone wears pretty robes, where there are lavish banquets and comfortable couches decorated with jewels. There are trees, and musky mountains, and cool valleys lined by rivers. Paradise is so perfect that the fruit there never rots and a person stays thirty-three years old forever. It is the finish line to all earthly misery, an entryway into perpetual bliss. According to the Koran, angels wait at each of its eight gates, congratulating new arrivals. "Peace unto you for that ye persevered in patience," they say. "Now how excellent is the final home!"

The more I read about paradise, the more I understood that this was what the boys waited for, what they worked toward with their prayer, as if they had a giant layaway plan for their dreams, paid forward in daily devotion until it came time to meet the angels.

Helpfully, my Koran came annotated. Different passages were accompanied by long footnotes in English, quoting the Muslim *hadith*, the ancient texts that recorded what the Prophet Muhammad did and said and taught during his life. The *hadith* add context and detail to the word of God as written in the Koran. For me, reading in our concrete room in the Electric House, the footnotes helped answer some of my questions. They told instructive little stories and, together with the Koran, made clear that what a person does in this life matters immensely in the next. Paradise, it is said, has seven levels, with its top level further divided into a hundred degrees, and the highest spots reserved for the most righteous. The boys in our house, with nothing to distract them and no responsibilities beyond guarding me and Nigel, were trying to land themselves a good spot in the afterlife. They had plenty of time to work on their faith, to bank their virtue in anticipation of Judgment Day.

If Abdullah had any suspicion about my sincerity as a Muslim, he didn't show it. Instead, he passed hours sitting across from me, listening to my Arabic with intense, unblinking concentration, his eyes fixed on my face as I took baby steps with my chanting. If I managed to get through a few minutes of recitation without a single stammer or pause, he'd commend me. "You are very smart," he'd say. "This is good." But it was only a matter of minutes, usually, before I'd screw something up. Abdullah's mood would flip instantly. He'd pounce on my failures, seething with new rage. When I looked up at him, trying to understand what I'd done wrong, he'd scream, "Look down!" and often lift a hand, threatening to hit me. His hands, I noticed, were unusually large.

When he was gone, Nigel and I wondered aloud whether he was just power tripping or possibly mentally ill. Either way, he seemed to believe that he owned me.

As the third week of our captivity began, I felt grateful for the challenge of learning both a new language and a new religion. It helped to fill the days. When we were left alone, Nigel and I compared notes on what we were discovering inside the Koran. He was focused on the idea that Allah had a lot of rules regarding promises and oaths. If you swore something on Allah's name, you were obligated to fulfill the promise. His goal was to get one of the leaders to swear on Allah that they'd let us go.

Even in the off hours, I could hear the group of boys continuing to chant from the Koran as they sat outside on the patio, their voices braiding together in a long-lasting hum. How, I wondered, did they stay so focused? Did their beliefs really run that deep?

I would have expected that one of the older guards—the captain or Ali—would lead the prayers, but it was the small, serene Hassam, who, at sixteen, was one of the youngest in the group. Hassam's father, Jamal had explained to us, was an imam at a mosque. As a result, Hassam knew more of the Koran than anybody else in the house and thus was put in the pole position for prayers, standing at the front, facing Mecca, and leading the recitations, while the rest of the household stood in lines behind him. Through our spy hole in the bathroom vent, I watched him inhabit the role of an elder. He sang the prayers in a loud, clear voice, exaggerating his hand motions so that everyone could follow along.

Nigel and I were expected to pray in our room, with Nigel standing ahead of me because he was a man and thus our leader. Every so often, Jamal came and invited Nigel to join the rest of them outside. Nigel understood that he couldn't say no and that it was a chance to get some fresh air. He'd look at me a bit apologetically, knowing that, as a female, I'd probably never be invited to pray outside, and then he'd go.

Left alone, I skipped my prayers altogether. Knowing my captors were occupied and wouldn't bother me, I was happy to stare at a wall.

★

"This isn't good," said Donald Trump one evening after stepping into our room and taking stock of our grungy mattresses, the black mold along the back wall. "You can't keep human beings like this!" Along with an expression of mild outrage, he wore a pink long-sleeved dress shirt and baggy trousers hemmed to the proportions dictated by the *hadith*—one hand span above his ankles, to keep the fabric from brushing the ground. He kicked at a roach crossing the floor.

Despite his feigned disapproval, Donald was one of the leaders of the group holding us. We were sure about that. Donald drove in every five or six days with supplies from the city. Ali, for reasons we'd never know, had disappeared sometime during the third week.

Donald's real name was Mohammed, but we already had one Mohammed in the house, and besides that, he handled the household money and was more Westernized than the others. His English wasn't perfect, but he talked a good worldly game. He aligned himself with me and Nigel, trotting out stories from what apparently had been extensive travels in Europe. He told us he'd spent time living in Germany. He rhapsodized about the olive oil in Italy, how it tastes more amazing than olive oil from anywhere else in the world. He'd seen things. He knew things. He wanted us to know that he knew things. He seemed to think it set him apart. That night he showed up with two cans of warm Coke and handed one to each of us.

He squatted down for a chat, his face lit by the bulb overhead. "These people, you know, they're uneducated," he said. "They just want money."

"We don't have money to give them," I responded. "There is no money."

I sipped my Coke slowly, like a cocktail.

Donald lifted his shoulders and then let them fall. "If it was up to me, you would go in one week." He smiled and tilted his head. "No, you would go in one hour."

Not one part of me believed him.

It was midway through September, approaching the one-month anniversary of our kidnapping. It was also Ramadan, the holy month. Ramadan was meant to reinforce purity and patience. There were extra prayers. Everyone fasted while the sun was up, a condition that made little difference to me and Nigel, since we were eating only twice a day anyway. Each morning before sunup, we were brought a few things by Hassam or Jamal, usually some canned tuna and a plastic bag of what looked to be hot-dog buns, though in a Muslim country, given the Koran's prohibition on pork, surely they were meant to hold something else. We ate without enthusiasm and didn't eat or drink again until nighttime, when a similar meal arrived. My body felt uninterested in the food set before me; my muscles were going slack after weeks of sitting. We drank water and craved the tea, energizing in its sweetness, that came with our meals.

What I most longed for was a single square of chocolate. Sometimes, as Nigel dozed on his mattress, I told him long made-up stories, personal fairy tales, that culminated each time with me happening upon a whole pound of dark chocolate or a big pile of M&M's and eating it all up. Or I posed questions: "Would you rather have a piece of chocolate cake or a hot fudge sundae? A hot fudge sundae or a bag of Hershey's Kisses?" He didn't answer, and I didn't care. I fanned the air with my hand to stay cool.

In my version of paradise, the air was always cold and the rivers ran with candy.

Meanwhile, the sweat pooled inside my bra cups, steaming my breasts until the skin grew spongy and raw. Nigel hadn't worn pants in weeks, having adopted the Somali man-skirt to keep himself cool. I had recently stopped wearing jeans and the black abaya and instead donned a long shapeless dress made of thick red polyester that Donald had brought me during an earlier visit. I couldn't bring myself to remove the bra. It felt like protection.

Before leaving our room after his visits, Donald always asked us what we needed from the market. Anticipating the question, I at one point made a list in my notebook to hand over the next time he surfaced, tossing in a few fantasy items for my own amusement: soap, aspirin, chocolate bars, exercise bike, cotton buds for cleaning the ears, a television.

He studied the page when I passed it to him, looking puzzled. I pointed to each item and pronounced the words slowly. "Ex-cer-size bike."

"Ah yes, yes," he said, not wanting to lose face by admitting that he didn't understand.

"Do you think you could find one of those in the market, Mohammed?"

"Yes, I think so. I think so."

A few days later, he brought us the soap and some acetaminophen tablets—so large they looked like horse pills—plus a packet of Q-tips and a pair of small scissors so that Nigel could trim his facial hair. I asked Donald for a new bra and some books in English for us to read. Nigel and I begged him, actually, for the books. More so than our bodies, our minds were beginning to starve.

There was something else I needed to discuss with Donald. I cringed to even think of it, but it was becoming necessary to address. My period was two weeks late. I'd had my fling with the fickle-hearted bureau chief before leaving Baghdad—that one bit of bodily distraction, the one concession to my neediness in a war zone—and now, in pretty much the worst imaginable circumstances, it was catching up with me. I'd never been pregnant, so I had no idea what it might feel like. Was the aching in my hips some sort of symptom? Did the malaise I felt, sweating through the hot afternoons, have nothing to do with my surroundings and everything to do with a kernel of life, another little hostage, inside me? I wasn't sure what it meant or how to feel about it. I just knew it was a secret I couldn't—or shouldn't—try to keep.

Tactfully, Nigel asked permission to leave the room so I could talk alone with Donald. We'd discussed how I should handle it, thinking it best that Nigel not be present. Donald, I figured, having lived in Germany, was the most likely of our captors to handle the news without invoking all sorts of moralistic disgust. Still, I worried what he'd do. On his forehead, Donald had a prayer mark—a dark, leathery-looking callus caused by the frequency and vigor with which he put his head to the ground. Some devout Muslim men cultivated these as a source of pride, a sign of their steadfastness.

"Mohammed," I said, my voice faltering a little, "I have something to tell you." I watched his expression grow serious, picking up on my tone. There was no turning back. "Before I became a good woman, a Muslim woman, I . . . I had sexual relations out of wedlock, with somebody in Baghdad." I dropped my gaze to the floor before continuing. I explained the situation as if somebody I barely knew—the infidel I'd once been—had borrowed my body and taken it out for a joyride.

"I just need to know," I said, "if there will be a baby." I added *"Inshallah"* for good measure, not sure what the desirable outcome would be. Was I saying *"God willing* I am pregnant" or "Please just let me find out one way or the other"? I was twenty-seven years old. I did not want to have a baby, especially not one fathered by a man into whose bed I'd wandered for the sole reason that I'd been deeply and pathetically lonely. Above all, I did not want to be pregnant in Somalia. Then again, beginning with the moment we were ambushed on the Afgoye Road, all rules had been rewritten, all priorities rearranged. Maybe, I thought, a pregnancy would help get us released. Maybe it would make me into a ticking time bomb. I'd walked my mind around in circles already. I imagined they'd at least need to take me to a doctor, and

I could beg that doctor to call the authorities. When I really thought about it, though, I wasn't sure if there were any authorities in Somalia who were capable of getting us out.

Donald received the news of my predicament calmly. "Okay, okay, okay," he said, seeming inconvenienced but not exactly angry. I felt like a teenager confessing to her dad. "Babies are a blessing from Allah," he added.

A few days later, he returned with a paper bag. Inside the bag was a plastic cup with a lid that could be screwed tightly shut. "For your pee-pee," he said.

Nigel and I snickered about the word "pee-pee" when he left. Where had he learned it? We laughed at absolutely everything we could—any little fart or hiccup we produced, any strange thing one of our captors said. Otherwise, there was nothing at all to laugh about. In addition to the plastic cup, Donald had proudly brought us some English reading material, stuff he'd found in a market stall. There was a college catalog for Malaysian students, printed by the British Education Board in Kuala Lumpur. It was dated 1994 and listed courses of study available for foreign-exchange students at a variety of universities in the United Kingdom. We also were given a couple of grease-stained storybooks for Islamic children and a *Times* of London reader from 1981 that had gone dark with mold. Inexplicably, he'd brought us a watch—a cheap-looking black men's digital watch, made in China. As if knowing the hour of day would make life better. Nigel and I laughed at all of this before falling back into the morose silence that governed so much of our time.

When I was ready, I went into the bathroom, peed in the cup, screwed the lid on, and passed it back to Donald, who got into his car with it and drove off.

That evening, when I prayed, I wasn't sure what to pray for.

22

Today's a Good Day

I watched Nigel's hands. Despite the heat and the grime, they were clean—his fingernails neatly trimmed, the Somali dust scrubbed from the furrows of his knuckles. He was fastidious. He always had been. Visiting him in Australia, I'd watched him wash his face in the mornings, floss his teeth, and carefully unfold his clothes. When we'd gone camping on an island off the Queensland coast, he'd been the one to shake the sand out of our sleeping bags and tidy up our tent, creating order out of my piles. Here, Nigel's hands were the cleanest part of him. This was due to the *wudu,* the ritual washing that went on before each of the five prayer sessions. Jamal had taught us the *wudu* just after we converted. You washed your hands three times, then swished water through your mouth three times, then snorted water through your nostrils, then splashed more of it over your face, arms, head, ears, and finally, your feet.

Nigel and I performed our ablutions in the bathroom separately, using fresh water from the brown bucket, which the boys filled at the tap outside. The boys holding us all washed out in the courtyard or in their own bathroom, in a different part of the house, and so, it seemed, did the three Somali captives, since Nigel and I had this bathroom to ourselves. I always skipped over the nostril washing but took care to make fake snorting sounds in case anyone was listening. The *wudu* was important. It purified you before you talked to God. Judging from the outcome, Nigel took to his *wudu* like a surgeon prepping for the OR.

It was one part of Islam that seemed to agree with him. "Cleanliness is half of faith," the Prophet had told his followers. On this front, Nigel— at least when it came to his hands—was in good shape.

I watched his hands because they were something to watch in a room where there was nothing to watch. Sometimes we tracked insects as they climbed the iron window grate. Once, looking outside, we saw a fat brown snake, maybe eight feet long, rippling through the sand in the alleyway behind the house. Otherwise, there was little to see. I was remembering how, what seemed a long time ago, Nigel's hands had given me both pleasure and comfort. They were capable hands. Hands that had held hammers and squared off timber, staying busy until a whole house, floor and rafters and roof, was built. In the confines of our room, I saw his hands as an extension of our brains and our bodies: desperate for a project, a purpose.

One afternoon during the extra-hot time when our captors usu- ally took a siesta, Nigel went over to the plastic bags where we kept our supplies. He rummaged intently through his bag, driven by some unspoken idea.

Within the hour, we were playing backgammon. Nigel had crafted playing pieces from our Q-tips—one of us using the cotton nubs, the other using pieces of the plastic handles, which he'd clipped with his beard-trimming scissors. On a sheet from his notebook, he'd drawn two rows of razoring triangles and then, using a couple of the acet- aminophen tablets and the scissors, carved a set of working dice, itty- bitty white cubes with tiny numbers written on the sides in pen.

We played for hours. And then we played for days. He won. I won. We played rapid-fire and without much conversation or commentary, like two monkeys in some deprivation-oriented psych experiment. If we heard footsteps in the hallway, we quickly slid everything under my mattress. Games, like so many other things that might divert us, were considered *haram*. We felt sure they'd punish us if they knew.

Donald showed up one day and handed me a slip of paper with the name of a pharmacy on top. I saw my age listed next to the name of a Somali woman, an alias he'd used to submit my urine sample. "No baby," he said.

"*Allahu Akbar,*" I said instantly, though it was clear from the look on Donald's face that this was the wrong thing to say. You didn't thank God for sparing you a baby, because a baby was a blessing, and blessings were things you hung on to, no matter what.

Still, I was not pregnant. It was a false alarm, even though my period hadn't come. It seemed I was just stressed, right down through my hormones.

The news felt like a relief, though a relief with disappointment pinned to its backside. I couldn't help feeling a little more alone. Trailing behind the disappointment, like a buzzing little motorcycle, was the faint and cloying memory of sex—a luxury of sensation that seemed almost unreal.

Ramadan came to an end in early October. Our captors celebrated the breaking of the fast—the holiday of Eid—with a meal of stewed goat. Nigel and I were given a small plate to share, along with a few sticky dates, a plate of cookies covered in a thick sugary glaze, and even some toffees. Between us we had one spoon, which Nigel, in a courtly move, passed to me to use. The goat meat was delicious—boiled and tender and served on a heap of oily rice. Afterward, it cramped our stomachs and pulsed savagely through our intestines. We swapped shifts on the toilet and felt ourselves growing dizzy and dehydrated. Despite ourselves, we ate the toffees instead of saving them for when we were well. They made puddles of sweetness on our tongues.

We tried to ignore the fact that our world had shrunk down to the size of our little pain-reliever dice.

*

Five weeks after being captured, I worked at being cheery. "Today's going to be a good day," I'd say to Nigel when we were awoken by the muezzin's first call. Almost always, he pretended like he didn't hear me.

There was nothing good about our days. We both knew it, but for me, being hopeful felt necessary, like pounding a fist on the wall in case somebody might hear it.

"Look," I said one day. "I can't handle the silence."

We were on our mats. He was facing the wall. He said nothing.

I felt a swell of emotion. "Nige," I said. "We need each other. We have to keep talking. It makes me crazy when you don't say anything."

This prompted him to roll over, looking aggrieved. "You think," he said, "that if I fucking talk it's going to be easier for you?" A second passed. "Do you think I really care about making this easier for *you*?"

We were like an old couple, a very old couple, our lust long extinguished, our affection worn away by constant togetherness. We lived like neighbors stuck for decades on the same cul-de-sac, breathing a resentful familiarity. It wasn't helped by the fact that despite our misery, we were too afraid to touch. We never once hugged or held hands or delivered the other person a reassuring pat on the shoulder. When Nigel was brought outside to pray with the boys, he no longer looked sheepish about it. He didn't get rushed back to the room when prayers were over. One day I heard him laughing on the veranda. I could hear them laughing, all together, as a group.

When he got back, I asked what was funny.

"Oh, nothing," he said, climbing back onto his mattress, tired of me already. I watched him close his eyes.

Nigel had been helping Jamal with his English every day, teaching him vocabulary words. They seemed almost like buddies, while Abdullah—my tutor—only got creepier. During lessons, he'd started brushing a hand, as if by accident, against my knee or shoulder any time he reached over to turn a page or point to something in my Koran.

One day Jamal came in bearing a surprise plate of fried fish, a gift from Donald, who was eating outside on the patio with the boys. As he set the plate down, Jamal attempted a joke. He looked at me, smiled, and puffed his cheeks out comically, as though to indicate that if I ate all of it, I would put on weight.

Nigel instantly roared with laughter. "Amina is *fat*," he said, emphasizing the word in the same exaggerated tone he used when running through vocabulary with Jamal. "Yes, fat."

Jamal started to giggle. Nigel laughed harder.

The cruelty of it rocked me. I went into the bathroom and shut the door. I didn't care what Nigel thought of my body at this point, if that was even the joke. It was the allegiance I didn't like, the possibility that he could switch sides, that I couldn't make him laugh but those boys could.

Returning to my mat, I tallied all the ways Nigel had disappointed me. I made a list of his weaknesses. Then I made a second list, the one with which I defended myself against whatever he was tallying up about me over on his mat, all the things that made me detestable and at fault. In my mind, we had a vicious screaming fight. We yelled *fuck you* and pounded each other's chests until we ran out of steam. Then we sobbed in each other's arms and vowed to do better. All this happened without a word, without anyone getting up from his or her mattress, without an actual tear. But somehow it helped.

*

Over the course of the second month, they moved us multiple times— shifting us in and out of the Electric House, bringing us to a bigger place not far away for a couple of weeks, then back to the Electric House, and then finally, for reasons we didn't know, to the new house again. They moved us at night, crammed into Ahmed's Suzuki, the boys having rewrapped their faces in scarves, with extra rounds of ammo hung over their shoulders, gun barrels filling the air around our heads. They ran a second trip to bring Abdi and the other two Somalis to each location. Coming and going, we never saw another soul on the road.

I had caught glimpses of Abdi and the others in the hallway at Electric House. I could hear them murmuring prayers and sometimes spotted one of them returning from the bathroom. They looked ragged, unhealthy, slumped over with depression. From what I could see, the room they were kept in was completely dark. Abdi sometimes sat in the threshold, reading his Koran in the light from the hall. A few times I peered out and flashed him the hand sign for "okay," as in "You okay?" Each time he shook his head, looking forlorn. He touched his belly to show that he was hungry, that they weren't being fed much.

Several weeks earlier, before we left the Electric House for good, a couple of the boys had marched me and Nigel out into the courtyard, where Ahmed, Romeo, Donald, and Adam stood with a video camera set up on a tripod. The boys had covered themselves with their scarves. Brandishing their guns, they surrounded us while Nigel and I knelt on a mat. With the camera running, they coached us to make positive statements about Islam, to urge our governments to pay the ransom. They didn't have us say the amount they were demanding out loud, but that was all I could think about. I'd heard it from our captors many times now: $1.5 million for one hostage, $3 million for two. Back in my waitressing days, I announced drink specials the same way.

They filmed multiple takes, having us repeat the words over and over. The video, I knew, was bound for television. I tried to picture my family watching it. What would they see? Me and Nigel in a semicircle of menacing soldiers and guns. I was pale but not unhealthy. My eyes watered constantly due to the fact that I wore contact lenses and, without contact solution, had been rinsing them in the unsterilized bucket water. I pictured my parents watching the screen, studying what they saw. I kept my shoulders squared even as Ahmed told me to look at the ground. When I said my lines, I tried to inject some intensity into my voice—a message designed for my parents, to show them I was not crumbling.

"Good, good," said Ahmed finally. He shut off the camera and then let us linger outside in the sun awhile. Much later, I'd learn that the videotape would find its way to Al Jazeera and that the network would release only part of it to the international media—and, at least in Canada, with no audio. A clip played on the news at home not long after it was filmed. My parents saw about nine seconds of me, lips moving, eyes down, fully cloaked in the garb of a modest Muslim woman, my voice lost beneath the newscaster's drone.

On the final drive away from Electric House, one good thing happened: Nigel reached into the dark space between us and, without anyone noticing, spent five minutes holding my hand.

★

The new house was the one we called Escape House, but not until later.

Our room there was huge, the size of a living room rather than a bedroom. There were two brand-new foam mattresses, a few inches thick, still in their plastic packaging, and also some mosquito netting, which hung from nails in the wall on either side of the room, above each of the mattresses. The room had white tiled floors and two windows, both with metal shutters, the open spaces covered by decorative metal grilles. One window opened out toward somebody's yard, which had a small shed made of corrugated tin and was locked with a padlock. The second faced a narrow alleyway with a high whitewashed wall directly across the way.

Every evening, one of the boys came in and pulled the shutters across our windows. In the morning, someone came to open them again. When no one was around, Nigel and I tried shaking the grilles to see if they'd come loose, but they were anchored on four sides by concrete, totally solid. From time to time, I stuck a finger through the grille and into the air outside, to give some part of me a chance to feel the air.

It's true, we might have yelled out those windows. And we might have been heard. But both Ahmed and the man we called Romeo had warned us that we were in a neighborhood full of Al-Shabaab loyalists. In other words, we were surrounded by enemies worse than our captors, since our captors were apparently a renegade group, unaffiliated with the dominant extremists. Al-Shabaab, Romeo suggested, would be happy to take charge of our captivity, to sweep us up if we caught their attention.

It was enough to keep me quiet. My mistrust was wrapped in more mistrust. Standing on the far left side of the window that looked out onto the alley, I could see over a fence and into the yard of another home, where one day I saw a woman pinning laundry to a clothesline. She wore a brightly printed, loose-fitting housedress and had her hair wrapped in a scarf that left her neck exposed. With her back to me, she moved slowly, as if killing time, happy with her solitude. She hung a white shirt, and then another white shirt. She hung some granny-style women's underwear, a pale yellow dress made for a child, a couple of bright floral hijab, some men's trousers, and something that looked like a cotton nightshirt. When she was done, I could see her whole family floating on the line.

It had been about six weeks since I'd been allowed to talk to my mother. I felt like she could hear my thoughts, though, when I directed them to her. I sent her thoughts every day. I told her to stay strong, and I heard her say it back to me. I could only guess at what was going on at home. My parents had so few options. I knew they'd be eyeing their one asset—my dad and Perry's house in its Sylvan Lake subdivision, surrounded by the flower beds my father had spent years slavishly tending—thinking they'd sell it to raise ransom money. The thought of this, the guilt, made me queasy. From the first day, I'd drilled the point with my captors: Our families couldn't pay. If this kidnapping was political, as they kept saying it was, then they were punishing the wrong people. Ahmed had reassured me many times, "Don't worry, don't worry. We are interested only in money from your governments. We do not wish to harm your families."

I believed it because I wanted to believe it, even as Nigel told me I was crazy. His family had more resources than mine. When they retired, his parents had sold their family farm at a profit. He thought they'd have at least enough money to negotiate with. What was left unsaid was that the money might cover his release but not mine.

On that last call with my mother, I'd tried to emphasize the idea that my parents should sit tight and not gamble with what little they had. "I don't know what you guys are doing, trying to get money together, but stop whatever you're doing," I said. "Do not sell anything."

It wasn't that I thought our governments would come up with any money. I was holding on to my one serious hope, the idea that we could exhaust our captors with inaction. Nigel and I were not starving. We had each other. For the most part, we were getting by. I still believed that waiting it out was our best strategy.

*

Hamdi was the name of Jamal's sweetheart. She lived somewhere in Mogadishu. Jamal's mother had picked her out for him. Now that they were engaged, Jamal got to see her every once in a while. Before Ramadan, there had been an engagement party for their two families. Jamal had disappeared from the house for a couple of days, returning with a new haircut and a goofy look in his eyes.

"How is Hamdi?" I asked.

"Ah," he said, trying to swallow his grin. "So beautiful."

When Eid arrived, Jamal had been allowed to send gifts to Hamdi. He bought her a new hijab and some chocolate, which seemed like a grown-up gesture for a teenager who, by his own admission, had never talked to a girl outside his family until two months before. "Women, they are *ex-pen-sive*," he declared. He was proud he could pronounce the word. He knew it would make us laugh.

He seemed dazzled by his own prospects, marking out the time between now and the future. He explained that when it happened, the wedding—the "marriage party"—would be small, since big gatherings in Mogadishu sometimes drew the attention of Ethiopian troops. I got the feeling that Jamal was so excited about his wedding, he'd happily invite the whole city. But the two families didn't want to run the risk. Which was okay with Jamal. He just wanted Hamdi.

Nigel and I looked for excuses to mention Hamdi, if only to watch the emotion play out on Jamal's face. He was desperate to hear her name but shy about saying it himself. Every so often he would go to the market for food but would forget to buy the hot-dog-shaped rolls that accompanied so many of our meals.

"Oh, Hamdi," we'd sigh dramatically when he turned up without the bread. We mocked his daydreaming by raising our hands to our foreheads. Every time it made him laugh.

Sometimes, looking out through the grilles of our windows at what I could see of the outside world, I tried to imagine what Hamdi looked like. Was she tall or thin or heavy? Quiet or bold? Was she afraid of what was coming, or did she long for it? I wondered how much Jamal knew about her, whether his excitement came from love or just the possibility of love. He never said so, but my guess was that thoughts of Hamdi were getting him through the long days in our house.

In the meantime, he had discovered the college catalog Donald Trump had delivered to us as reading material, the one designed for Malaysian students bound for the UK. Each page bore a few pictures of university students dressed in clothing that was now outdated. The students carried books over pathways that butterflied through green quadrangles amid Gothic stone buildings.

Jamal flipped through the pages one morning, studying the photos with fascination. He turned the book toward me so I could see a page that had caught his interest. There was a photo showing a group of students sitting by a small pond with a couple of swans gliding on the surface. "Is this like Canada?" he asked.

"Well, yes, but that book is all British schools." I was sitting on my mattress. Nigel stood at the window, quietly reading the Koran.

Jamal ran a finger over the English text as if reading it. His brow wrinkled. "I heard," he said, "that Canada is more beautiful than British. Because British, London, is more . . ." Searching his mind for the word, he pointed at the walls of the room, the ceiling.

"Concrete?"

"Yes, concrete. London is concrete."

He wanted the world. I understood that. I felt him swaying toward it.

"London is very pretty, Jamal," I said. "You'd like it. The buildings are very old. There are a lot of Muslims there."

He seemed to think about this. "But," he said, lifting a finger professorially, "it is not a Muslim country. And it is better to live in a Muslim country."

I was aware of what I was supposed to say next—that yes, of course, he was right—but because it was Jamal, I didn't.

★

From our exhaustion, Nigel and I built a routine. We lived like a two-person family. We took on responsibilities. I poured the tea, and Nigel washed our clothes. We took turns doing dishes in a bucket. Between us, we had two tin plates and a single spoon. With the food we were given, we made menus, eating our meals on a table-sized square of brown linoleum the boys had tossed in our room. Some days we ate the buns followed by the tuna; other days it was tuna followed by the buns. When we were given more, I'd use the straight edge of the spoon to chop up papaya and onion, and then Nigel—pretending to be a chef on a cooking program—would make an elaborate show of tossing it all together for his world-famous tuna salad. Occasionally, Jamal would bring us some wilted lettuce, and I'd use my waitress voice to crow about today's most elegant special: tuna salad *served on a bed of lettuce.*

In the mornings, we straightened our beds and talked about what we'd dreamed while sleeping. I was having vivid dreams of old friends, people I hadn't thought about in years. Rhianna, my best friend from high school, made frequent appearances, and so did my family—grandparents, cousins, aunts. In my dreams, I was always free, but then, inside the dream, I would realize that none of it was real.

Nigel and I talked in ways we never had. I described my shock and anger over how he'd lied to me in Ethiopia about being married, how crushed I had been. He took me through the months he'd spent in Australia, ending his marriage and feeling ashamed. He talked about his girlfriend in Scotland, Erica, who was Australian but was working as a chef on an estate there. She had a dog. She was a good person. He was missing her, torn up over having done something as stupid as run off to Africa, leaving her behind.

We had honest conversations about money, about the net worth of our families. I thought my family could come up with about fifty thousand dollars. He said his parents had access to more. We had faith that our families were talking to each other. Each night, as we were getting ready to sleep, I would turn and say to Nigel, "Now we are one day closer to being free."

Then one morning during the third week of October, the boys stormed our room. Abdullah, Mohammed, Young Yahya, and Hassam came running in, almost at a sprint, startling us as we ate our breakfast on the floor.

"You have to get up," Hassam said.

I said, "What's happening?"

"Get up," he said again, an edge in his voice.

I noticed he was the only one without a gun. I felt my body start to shake. We were on our feet. Abdullah and Mohammed were tearing angrily through our belongings, as if acting on a tip. They pulled everything out of our bags, overturning our mattresses, looking for something, though I couldn't guess what. We were blameless, I reminded myself. Aside from the backgammon game, which was tucked away in one of the books and which I doubted they'd recognize anyway, we had nothing to hide. But I didn't know. How could I know what was wrong?

The boys said nothing. Hassam stood grimly before us while the other three ripped through what little we had. They threw everything across the floor, and next they started carrying things from the room. My backpack went out. Nigel's camera bag. Our notebooks and pens and the plastic shopping bags with our toiletries and clothes. All of it disappeared. And then Yahya picked up one end of Nigel's mattress and started to drag it toward the door.

It dawned on me then what was happening. Abdullah unhooked the mosquito netting from the wall on Nigel's side of the room and walked out. There was a smaller bedroom right next to the one we'd been staying in. We'd peeked into it plenty of times, coming and going from the bathroom down the hall. Through the wall, I could hear someone hammering—Abdullah, most likely, rehanging the mosquito net in the next room. And then they were back for Nigel, guns leveled at his chest, motioning him toward the door. They were separating us. There was no explanation, no dialogue. I watched the back of his shirt as it moved away from me. There was no goodbye or anything. He was just gone.

23

Blame the Girl

I lay for a long time on my mattress, hoping that something would reverse itself. I waited for one of the boys to come in carrying Nigel's mattress and for someone else to hustle Nigel back through the door, maybe even apologetically, as if taking him away hadn't been the plan. I expected to hear some sort of noise—a shuffle, a creak—that would tell me the change was under way, that we were soon to resume our old spots, with our belongings, our routine. Instead, the house was quiet. The silence sat heavily in my ears. I was alone.

One hour passed and then two. Alone felt like a new country. Alone felt like a new planet—one containing just me and my mattress with the blue-flowered cloth and the room's four walls, which seemed to have shot up like tall trees in a dark forest. Without Nigel, I had nothing to say, no one to look at, nobody stirring the air. Alone in that big room, I was nothing but small.

I couldn't guess why they'd chosen this day to separate us. Perhaps it had something to do with the fact that it had been eight weeks since we'd been taken from the road, and there was no sign of a ransom payment. Frustration seemed to be mounting among our captors. The previous afternoon, there had been a commotion at the front of the house, and one or more of the leaders had shown up. We'd heard a long, intense conversation with Captain Skids on the patio. I wondered now whether the leaders had been instructing him to prepare for a long haul, informing him that we'd be houseguests for longer than anticipated. Skids already seemed to view us as a burden. He expressed no curiosity about me and Nigel. He spoke no English and showed no warmth. I wondered whether it was he who'd insisted that Nigel and I be separated, as an exertion of his control. An I'm-the-boss-of-the-house move.

Later that day, Jamal returned, carrying my backpack and the plastic bags with my toiletries, clothes, and the English books, dropping it all on the floor with a clunk of finality. I stared at the divot in the wall where the nail holding Nigel's mosquito netting had been. Had he been there to hear it, I would have said something encouraging and bright to stop the slide of emotions. I would have said, *Come on now, we just need to get through this morning.* Or *Tell me about the happiest birthday you ever celebrated.* There seemed no point. My throat felt as if it had pinched shut. *Calm down,* I told myself. *Calm down, calm down.*

Sitting up, I took out the spiral notebook they'd given me for my Islamic lessons and opened it to a fresh page. "Breadbeard," I wrote, using a nickname I'd had for Nigel in Ethiopia. "Stay strong. Don't give up. We are going to get out of here and be with our families again. I am just on the other side of the wall and will be sending love your way."

I read the note a couple of times. It was the sort of message I'd been giving him every day in person. Did I believe it? I wasn't sure. But it felt good to write. I added another line in the same crimped handwriting: "Flush this down the toilet as soon as you read it."

I tore the page from the notebook and ripped away the blank edges until it was a tiny scrap containing only the writing. I rolled what was left into a compact white pellet about the size of a pencil eraser, and then, before I could talk myself out of it, I knocked on the door for permission to use the bathroom.

The boys had grown too lazy to escort us to and from the toilet, as they had in the early weeks, in previous houses. When one of us knocked on the metal door, the guard on duty, usually sitting out on the veranda, would quickly lean over and glance in our direction and then snap his fingers a few times loudly to indicate that we had permission. The hallway running through the house was L-shaped, with my room located at the junction. A guard sitting on the veranda might have a view of my doorway but would not be able to see around the corner to the rest of the hall—the stubby part of the L—which led to Nigel's new room and the bathroom beyond it.

When the snap came, I stood, holding the balled-up note loosely in my palm, and started down the hall. Whatever soldier was on duty, whoever had snapped his fingers, was nowhere in sight. The hallway was about fifteen feet long, with thick blue walls and a white tiled floor. Nigel's room was on the right, next to mine.

Passing by his open door, I took a fast look out of the corner of my eye to make sure he was alone, and then, with a flick of the wrist, I sent my little note sailing. As the ball of paper skittered across the floor, I caught a sideways glimpse of Nigel lying on his mattress, faceup, possibly asleep. I continued on to the bathroom, my heart racing, hoping like hell he'd find it before any of the boys did.

It had occurred to me that, due to the way our two rooms were positioned, he had no ability to respond. There was no circumstance under which Nigel would have to pass by my door. Our communications could be only one-way.

Back in my room, I stewed over our new reality. I imagined Nigel on the other side of the wall, lost in his own worries, though I knew instinctively that I was now the more vulnerable one. The wall was green and veined with cracks in the plaster. I guessed it was probably about twelve inches thick. As an experiment, I tried rapping a knuckle against it. The sound was slow, not seeming to travel far, caught in the wall's density.

A moment passed. I sat, paralyzed by the stillness.

Then, from the other side, came two short raps. My spirits jumped. Nigel had heard me. And I could hear him back. I wanted to knock all day. I probably would have, were it not for the fact that every hour or so, one of the boys pulled himself off the patio and came wandering down our hallway, gun in hand. I worried that if they caught us knocking, they'd move us even farther apart. Instead, I answered Nigel with one swift knock, and then both of us, being cautious for good reason, fell silent. We could communicate, sort of, but it didn't mean anything.

Evening came. I lay in the inching darkness, trying to stave off panic. So far, our captors had not touched me. Aside from the first-day grope I'd gotten from Ali, I'd been left alone. Nonetheless, I was aware of being female every second of every hour. I knew what the Koran said about captive women, how they could be treated like wives, but I didn't know how literally that might be taken by the men holding us. The captives described in the Koran were mostly men taken prisoner on the battlefield during the seventh century or war widows swept by force out of their villages and conscripted to do housework. It seemed like ancient history, fallout from very old battles. But then again, it was how the leaders of our group described me and Nigel each time they shrugged and told us not to take our situation personally: We were just pawns in a religious war, an old story being replayed in the modern day.

I passed the night alone in the giant room, sleepless. My mind galloped. I was desperate to talk with Nigel, to have an actual exchange. During my ablutions before evening prayer, I'd studied the bathroom he and I shared. There was a toilet and a dingy-looking plastic vanity mounted to the wall above a porcelain sink, framing a square of reflective foil paper instead of an actual mirror. There was a small window in the room, maybe eight feet off the ground, covered by iron bars and with a wide ledge beneath. After breakfast the next morning, I wrote to Nigel again, flinging another ball of paper into his room to explain a new idea: I'd leave a note in the bathroom, tucked back out of sight on the window ledge, and then knock on the wall to signal that it was there. When he'd read it during his next bathroom trip and flushed it down the toilet, he'd come back to his room and knock to let me know he'd seen it. He could do the same for me.

We did a test run. I left a note and then rapped on the wall. About forty minutes later, Nigel knocked twice in return. It was a small triumph, but it mattered. We began to exchange letters—short, cheery-seeming messages and drawings—once or twice a day. We changed the hiding place from the window ledge to an empty lightbulb socket in the vanity, which seemed a bit less likely to be discovered. I wrote notes to Nigel telling him to look for one beautiful thing, even something little, inside his room. I sketched a tiny picture of the two of us sitting on an airplane, clinking champagne glasses, hightailing it out of Africa in the comfort of first class. I drew a dialogue bubble over Nigel's head and wrote, "Shall we have another?"

Nigel's notes to me were affectionate and funny and most often about the future—what we'd do, what we'd eat, once we got out. He drew a picture of the two of us as smiling tourists, pointing at giraffes at the national park in Nairobi. I memorized the contents of each note before tearing it into pieces and dropping it into the stained toilet, sloshed out of sight with water from a bucket.

From our individual rooms, we knocked on the wall, back and forth, several times a day. *Lub-dub*, like a heartbeat.

You there? I'm here.

*

With our separation, all routine had gone out the window. It was as if our captors were running off a different set of batteries. Jamal no longer loitered in my room. Abdullah stopped overseeing my memorization of the Koran and was replaced by Hassam, who came in the early afternoons, first visiting Nigel and then me. Hassam was small for his age. Under other circumstances, I'd have thought of him as cute. His cheeks were smattered with acne. He had a wide, perfect smile and always seemed eager to engage. The other boys liked to pick him up and throw him over their shoulders for fun.

"Okay, today is lesson," he would say to me. "Today is lesson how to be best Muslim." He spoke of Allah as the protector, and prayer as a way of staying on a straight path to paradise. About our kidnapping, he was almost apologetic. "It is money, not Islam," he told me once. Where Abdullah had been erratic and controlling, Hassam was earnest and patient as I ran through the words of the Koran. He sang verses as if they were music, encouraging me to inflect my voice the same way, rising and dipping with each turn of phrase.

"*Lahu ma fis-samawati wa ma fil-'ard,*" he said, then waited for me to repeat. *His are all things in the heavens and on earth,* it meant.

Nigel and I had spent plenty of time discussing which of our captors we feared most. There was young Mohammed, who had hulking shoulders and eyes set close together like a rat's. Mohammed said very little to us. In the early days, he'd sometimes wag a finger at us and make a clucking sound, as if to say, *You are bad people.* Before we knew his name, Nigel and I referred to him as "Son of Satan," for the hatred we saw in his eyes. Topping our list was Abdullah, with his cold glare and mood swings and oft-repeated fantasy of becoming a suicide bomber and killing lots of people.

Seeing more of Hassam and less of Abdullah might have felt like an improvement, a comfort, even, were I not experiencing the frisson of round-the-clock worry now that Nigel had been removed from the room.

I hated everything about being alone. There were days when nobody spoke to me at all—when Jamal delivered the food without saying a thing, when Hassam didn't bother to stop in. The isolation put me into a cistern, dank and deep. I started to understand the old movie trope, the self-fulfilling prophecy where a perfectly intact person is locked up and isolated in an insane asylum and begins, over time, to actually go mad. My own brain pawed at me. If I shouted, would anybody respond? If I died, would it matter? Everything I'd told Nigel, every chirrup about how this would end and we'd soon be sitting by a pool having sandwiches and beer, now seemed like a farce.

All the bricks of courage I'd stacked up over years of traveling were starting to come down.

With the boys, too, something was slipping. Their civility was beginning to lapse. I was allowed to shower every day before the noon prayer, walking to the tiled area that sat beneath a window at the end of the hallway past the bathroom, separated from the rest of the house only by a thin cotton curtain printed with red hibiscus flowers. There was a showerhead and a spindled knob, which, when cranked, sometimes produced a thin trickle of brown water and sometimes nothing at all. Usually, I washed with a bucket of water delivered by one of the boys from the tap outside. I relished the shower, the coolness of the water, the slick sensation of having wet hair, and the milky scent of the German bar soap Donald had brought. Whereas earlier on I'd bathed cautiously and one limb at a time, now, driven by pure need, I stripped down and went for it. I craved those five minutes or so of private nakedness and the dribble of water, even rusty water, over my body. It was my one shot at something that felt remotely like joy.

The curtain, however, was quite sheer. Both the boys and I seemed to discover this at the same time. With the late-morning light pouring through the window, my silhouette was visible through the cloth. I could see through it in the other direction, catching shadows on the other side. Hassam was the first one I spotted, on his hands and knees, peering around the corner as if trying to see under the curtain. The next time I bathed, I heard a snigger and caught sight of two recognizable figures—Jamal and Abdullah—ghosting the boundaries of the shower.

Too nervous to sleep much at night, I dozed on my mattress through the heat of the late afternoon, cycling in and out of wakefulness, my head throbbing with the constant ache of dehydration as I sweated through my clothes and the sheet on my bed. I woke one day with a start when two boys with guns abruptly charged into the room—Abdullah and Mohammed, looking wild-eyed and wound up. They shut the door behind them.

"Mohammed, Abdullah," I said, sitting up on my mattress, my voice a thin tremolo, "is there a problem?"

I used my captors' names every chance I had. It was intentional, a way of reminding them that I saw them, of pegging them, of making them see me in return. I tried to milk something from even the shortest interactions. The traditional Arabic greeting is *Asalaamu Alikum,* which means "Peace be upon you." I'd first heard it way back in Bangladesh and then through Pakistan, Afghanistan, Egypt, Syria, and Iraq. There was a more casual version of the greeting—a simple *Salaam*—and a more extended version, *Asalaamu Alikum Wa Rahmatulah Wa Barakatuh,* "May the peace and mercy of Allah be upon you." I knew my Koran well enough by now to know that Allah had a rule that went with these things. I'd found it in one of my *surah. When a courte-*

ous greeting is offered to you, meet it with a greeting still more courteous, or at least of equal courtesy. I'd tried it out with the boys and seen that it worked. A long greeting evoked a long greeting. I used it every time. I threw the extra words at anyone who walked into my room, just to force him to linger in my presence—to address me as a human—for those extra three or four seconds that it took.

Today, however, there was no greeting. Abdullah took a step toward me and pointed his gun at my chest. "Other side," he said curtly, indicating that I should turn facedown on the mattress.

My mind went into a free fall, dropping through one trapdoor only to find another one opening beneath it. Slowly, I flipped over, pressed my forehead to the fabric, kept my palms next to my face. The two boys were at my bedside, guns hovering by my head. I could see Abdullah's bare ankle, the color of dark coffee and hairless, maybe six inches away. Down, down, I fell. I heard them breathing. I closed my eyes, waiting for the next thing.

Mohammed said, "You are bad woman."

Abdullah said, "The problem is you."

The steel finger of a gun barrel prodded the back of my neck. I tried not to think. The two of them were talking above me in Somali, as if they hadn't quite planned out their next step, as if debating what they could get away with. There was a pause.

Then Mohammed kicked me in the ribs, hard. The pain ripped through my left side, causing an instant rush of tears. "You are bad," he said again. "We will kill you, *inshallah.*" I saw their feet turn and walk away. The door opened and then clicked shut. The room went quiet. They were gone.

I was still crying twenty minutes later, when Jamal stuck his head through the door. The sight of my tears seemed to make him sheepish. Before he could run away, though, I gave him the full Arabic greeting and then waited for him to say it back to me. Gathering my wits, I said, "Jamal, please tell me what's going on. Please."

I watched some sort of unidentifiable emotion track over his face. He looked almost reluctant to speak. He sighed. "Why," he said, "you tell your mother no pay money?" He shook his head as if he were helpless, as if I'd brought it all on myself. He turned to leave. "We are here long time because she no pay," he said. "The soldiers are very mad."

I could almost hear how this theory was put into place. I could imagine Ahmed's velvety voice, delivering his take on things to Captain Skids. Skids would have repeated it to the boys, stirring in his own bile. *For your frustration and misery, blame the girl. For two months of stasis and boredom and homesickness, blame the girl. For everything you don't have, for everything you haven't done, you can blame the girl. It is she who told her mother not to pay.*

24

Maya

There was a little girl living in the house down the alleyway from my window, the daughter of the woman I'd seen hanging laundry on the clothesline in her yard. In the afternoons, during the hot, lazy hours when my captors snoozed in the shade of the veranda, I listened to the girl playing as her mother washed cooking pots or hung more laundry. She squealed and sassed and occasionally pitched a fit, shrieking *maya*, the Somali word for "no." I could lose a whole afternoon to her tiny voice. Sometimes I angled myself to look sideways through the grate toward them, catching glimpses of the mother's head or clothing, a snatch of yellow or deep indigo, over the fence. Donald had given me a round compact mirror, small enough for me to fit through the window bars. When I held it just so, I could get a wider view of the neighboring yard, though I didn't do it often, for fear the mirror might flash and someone would spot my white hand sticking out. The outside world—the threat of being kidnapped away from my kidnappers and held by another group looking for Western dollars or killed for show—filled me with worry.

The neighbor's little girl was too short for me to see, though judging from her voice, I guessed she was about two years old. She seemed always to be in motion, toddling the perimeter of the yard, bellowing *maya* any time her mother tried to reel her in.

Her mother was trying to teach her to converse.

Iska warran? she would say to the girl. I knew from Jamal that this meant "How are you?"

When she was feeling agreeable, the girl would say it back. *Iska warran?*

Waan fiicanahay. "I am good."

Waan fiicanahay, repeated the girl.

Waan fiicanahay, I whispered along with them.

Much of what they said I couldn't understand, but the tones I recognized. A mother and her child, a mixture of love and exasperation. Once in a while I heard a man's voice and what sounded like a grandmother back there in the yard. Sometimes I could hear a group of female voices—friends of the girl's mother, I guessed—trilling and laughing. The sound made me weak with jealousy. Everybody seemed to dote endlessly on the child. In my mind, I could picture them all. I imagined them warm and open, as people who wouldn't betray me. In my mind, I was going to follow them right through the back door and to their table for dinner, a phantom white lady appearing from nowhere, saying, "How are you?" in perfect Somali. I listened for the child's name but never managed to catch it. I just thought of her as Maya.

In the afternoons, it was Abdullah who most often seemed to have guard duty. He stalked the hallway outside our rooms. Sometimes he opened my door without warning. He would step inside and stare at me, saying nothing, clutching his gun, keeping his gaze on me for full minutes without moving. Or he'd come in and tear through my bags as if searching for something. During the first week after I was separated from Nigel, he did this once, then twice, and then a third time. He tossed my things on the floor with a precise sort of violence. He still covered his face in my presence, even as the rest of them had given up and walked around unmasked.

I greeted Abdullah each time. I watched him move around my room. He was bigger than most of the other boys, with a thick torso and long arms. His eyes were dark and spaced widely on his face. He had a deep, barking voice, muffled slightly by his scarf. I did what I could to force a conversation, trying to trigger his interest in speaking

English. "I wonder what we will eat tonight for the meal," I said loudly and slowly. "I'm getting hungry. Are you hungry, Abdullah?" For the most part, he ignored me.

All the noisy rummaging through my belongings, I would later realize, was a testing of the waters. Abdullah was figuring out how much of a disturbance he could make while the other boys slept through, while Nigel stayed quiet on the other side of the wall. He was calculating just what he could do in those empty hours.

*

With nothing else to distract me, I immersed myself in the reading materials Donald had given us weeks earlier—the moldy, antiquated booklets that had previously caused us to howl with laughter. There was the *Times* of London student reader from the early 1980s, filled with reprinted articles about the House of Lords and a tanking British economy, followed by lists of study questions and writing exercises with blank spaces to do the work. There was an English-language storybook about twin Muslim boys learning to be kind. And then the college catalog meant to entice rich Malaysians to study in the UK, its pages rank-smelling and glopped together by moisture. Ha, ha, ha. Nigel and I had flipped through the books with disdain. We'd torn out some of the cleaner pages and used them as plates for our tuna and onion. We'd mocked Donald for the proud way he'd delivered the books, for having paid money for them, for thinking them relevant. We'd mocked the whole country of Somalia for sucking up what would have been trash and selling it in the marketplace.

I remembered laughing with Nigel with the same distant fondness I felt when recalling eating a spinach salad or a piece of cake at home in Canada.

I now sat on my mattress with those books and read every word on every page. I studied a washed-out editorial cartoon showing Margaret Thatcher dressed in a neat suit and a pillbox hat. As the tin roof over my head moaned and expanded under the afternoon sun, I dutifully answered the reading-comprehension questions at the end of each reprinted article in the student reader. *Was this article written from a point of view that is objective or subjective? Please provide supporting evidence.* When it came to the college catalog, I now saw the allure. The book listed universities in London, Manchester, Oxford, Wales, and many places I'd never heard of. Who knew England was so big? The text wasn't terribly interesting—notes on class size and curriculum— but the photos were in color, stained and faded, though still vivid. The buildings were stony and grand. I looked at the grass and flowers, at the students smiling on the pathways, backpacks hooked over their shoulders, talking about what I imagined were abstract and absorbing things.

Those students were now over ten years out of university, I figured. They lived in houses and had jobs, dogs, babies. I wondered: Why hadn't I wanted that for myself? Why had I funneled my savings into plane tickets and not tuition? For fun, I pictured myself in a lecture hall, a dorm room, a cellar pub late on a Thursday night. It seemed to fit. It felt like a plan. I put myself on a quadrangle with brushed hair and a new laptop.

The door to my room opened and closed. I looked up from the catalog to see Abdullah. He wore a purplish sarong and a singlet that was stretched out and yellowed with sweat. His eyes glowered from the open slit of his face scarf. This time he didn't pretend to search my room. Instead, he leaned his gun against the wall. "Get up," he said.

When I didn't move, he said it again.

It didn't matter that I'd worried about this. That I'd had a sense it might be coming. It changed nothing. There was no preparing.

I slid the book from my lap and slowly got to my feet, feeling my body quake, my throat contracting. "Please," I said, "don't."

Abdullah responded by clamping his right hand onto my neck, shoving me back until I was pressed against the wall. The heel of his hand jammed into my windpipe, lifting my chin. I started to cry while his long fingers climbed my face, covering my mouth, digging into my eye sockets. I felt myself suffocating. "Please don't, please don't," I said into the taut skin of his palm, gasping for air. "Shut up, shut up," he was saying back, tightening his hold on my neck. His sarong was now off. Beneath it, he wore a pair of gym shorts with an elastic waistband, and with his free hand, he was touching himself inside the shorts. My mind felt liquid, spilling out of me, unable to hold a thought. I felt him reaching down for the hem of my Somali dress, tugging it upward. I kept talking, my voice muffled, my arms batting uselessly at him. "Don't do this. Please don't." He slammed a fist into the side of my head, and I felt my whole body go rigid. "Shut up I will kill you," he said. "*ShutupIwillkillyou.*" Then he pushed himself into me and I wanted to die.

In ten seconds it was over. Ten impossibly long seconds. Enough time for the earth to rumble and split, making a gulch between me and the person I'd been.

When he released me, I fell to the floor, collapsing like a rag doll.

Abdullah rewrapped his sarong and picked up his gun. He opened the door and checked the hallway. I kept my head in my hands and didn't look. I asked to go to the bathroom. I was desperate to wash, to cry, to hide myself away. He checked the hallway again. "Go," he said. Before I could leave, he pointed his gun at my chest, close enough so that he was almost touching me again. "If you speak of this, I will kill you," he said. And I felt sure he would.

25

Catch-22

Nothing had changed and so had everything. The sea-foam-green paint on the walls was the same, the windows with their shutters and grates, the dirt coating the floor, the roof overhead. The hockey-puck can of tuna that Jamal brought at dinnertime was the same. The call for prayer from the mosque near our house was the same, and the Koranic drone that drifted down the hallway from the boys outside was the same. What was different was me.

I lay on my mat and hardly moved. I kept my eyes closed, one arm covering my face. My back ached. Between my legs, I was raw and sore. I felt as if I'd been evicted from my body, like I no longer fit in my own skin. What had been outside me was now in, like some vicious flattening force. I was a ghost wandering the ruins of a wrecked city.

I should have hated Abdullah, but I hated myself more. My mind ticked through every mistake I'd ever made, every wrong thing about me. Why had I come to Somalia? What had I done? I'd spent eight weeks telling myself that this was all temporary, but now the reality felt unshakable. It didn't help that every minute was basically the same as the last, every hour like the one just past. Alone with myself, I had nothing. Every fear I'd ever had now came back to me—darkness was scary, noises were scary. I felt like a child. Panic swept over me in waves, giant and forceful. To think even half-rationally was an effort. When I tried to steady myself, all I wanted was to hasten the inevitable. I thought about the blue-flowered sheet I kept on my mattress, trying to figure out whether it was long enough to be twisted into a noose. I thought through the layout in the bathroom, wondering if there was anything sharp or blunt or high enough to launch myself onto or off of, something to hammer me right out of the world. He couldn't kill me, I reasoned, if I got to myself first.

I lay for two days like this, getting up only to use the toilet, mimic the motions of prayer, and drink water, unable to go through with trying to kill myself but with no interest in living, either.

On the third morning, not knowing what else to do, I left Nigel a frivolous note in the bathroom, saying nothing beyond a recognizable, half-sunny hello. If I faked sunshine, maybe sunshine would come. I knocked on the wall to tell him the note was there. Then I lay back down on my mat. Waiting for him to retrieve it and send a knock back, I looked around the room with its grotty floor and straw-colored light threshing through the window grates and tried to force a single positive thought. Was there something? There had to be. It would come. The expectation sat. It shot out roots. It became my stand-in for a positive thought.

*

Later that morning, I stood up and started to walk. I did one lap around the room and then another. The walking felt good. It gave me purpose. I walked calmly, at a steady pace, looping in bare feet, holding the hem of my red dress with one hand to keep from tripping. In motion, I told myself things, the words resonating right down through my legs.

I will get out of here. I will be okay.

There was comfort in it. I repeated the words like a mantra and kept moving. For once, I was grateful that the room I was being held in was so big. Now that I was walking, I couldn't think of any reason to stop. Hassam peeked in at one point as if expecting to guide me in learning a new *surah*. I'd left my Koran sitting on the windowsill and made no move toward it. Hassam looked perplexed but said nothing and left. I was certain that none of them knew what Abdullah had done.

When the afternoon arrived—the hot, quiet hours I now feared—I was still walking, sweating like an Olympian. Jamal brought tea and a bottle of water. Mohammed opened the door a couple of times, scoffed at me, then disappeared again. Meanwhile, I was busy getting ready to be free. I'd wiped any uncertainty out of my plans, and all the desperation and vague, sideways bargaining that went along with it. No longer did I think, *If I get out of here, I will be kinder, more patient, more generous.* I was thinking instead, *When. When I get out of here.* When I got out, I would hug my father all the time. I'd take my mother to India, since she'd always wanted to go. I'd eat better food, look into going to university, find a man who really loved me, do something that mattered. I imagined Somalia as a story I would tell my friends. Not a happy story, clearly, but a story with an ending. Walking circles in my room, I awarded myself a future. *Hold on for it,* I said. *Hold on, hold on.*

It was a few days before Abdullah came again, in the late afternoon, just like the last time, pushing me to the wall, his hand gripping my neck, undoing whatever resolve I'd built. He came again several days later, and again on many other afternoons after that. Each time it felt like being robbed, like he was siphoning something vital out of me. Sometimes he'd just punch me and leave.

Six, seven hours a day I walked. Sometimes fast, sometimes slow. The bottoms of my feet grew thick. A dirty pathway took shape in the room, a trammeled-on oval, a miniature one-lane track. I took breaks for water and for the bathroom. I stopped at prayer times and sat on my mattress, no longer bothering to go through the motions. I reversed direction several times a day to take the pressure off the inside foot. To an observer, I might have looked like a pacing, half-mad zoo animal, but what I felt, what I believed, was that I was getting stronger. *I will get out of here. I will be okay.* I strapped the men's watch Donald had brought us weeks earlier onto my wrist. Suddenly, the time mattered. It allowed me to plan. I'd look at the watch and think, *Oh, it's eight o'clock. I'll walk till noon, and then I'll knock on the door and have my shower.* As I moved, I shed despair. My body became all ropes and cords and knots of hard muscle. Hassam stopped me from time to time to work on my memorizations from the Koran. I took solace in my circles. Anytime little Maya let out a defiant yell outside my window, I silently cheered her on.

★

When Donald came for one of his visits, I begged him to let me spend time with Nigel. I asked why we'd been separated and then watched as he blinked placidly, explaining that unmarried men and women should not consort, according to Islam.

I knew that, of course. It was a familiar catch-22 for me. Now that I'd converted, I was supposed to agree with the rules. Never mind that there were plenty of moderate Muslims in the world who were more likely to see things the way I saw them. My captors were fundamentalists. If I argued with their views, I was exposing myself as an infidel. I still didn't know why they'd allowed us to stay together for so long before imposing their rules.

Donald spoke in a consoling voice. He gestured at the room. "This is a good place," he said. "It is better this way for everyone."

I knew he didn't believe that. It was clear that Donald was generally appalled by the way we lived—not just me and Nigel but everyone in the house. He almost always remarked on the dirt and lack of furniture. When he came, presumably driving from his home in Mogadishu where he had a wife who cooked for him, he often brought plates of fried fish or pots of stew for the boys. With me, he made a show of being accommodating. Each time I asked for the same things—a chance to talk to my mother, a king-sized bar of chocolate, more food of any kind. He always nodded as if taking it all in, then did nothing about it.

"How are you?" he said every time, after we'd finished the Islamic greeting.

"Not good," I'd say. "I need to go home."

His answer since the very start had been the same. "I think it will be soon. *Inshallah.*"

The word "Islam" comes from the Arabic language. It means "to surrender or submit to God." I would time and again see what this looked like among my captors. We were, all of us, meant to wait without complaining and see what would come.

On this day, I decided to take a risk. "It's *not* better that we're separated," I said. "One of the boys has been paying visits to my room." I was careful not to name a name, convinced that Abdullah would find a way to kill me if I made a direct accusation. "He does things that are *haram.*"

Donald understood what I was saying. Sitting on the floor in the middle of my room with one knee pulled up to his chest, he appeared uncomfortable but not taken aback. Feeling the sting of tears, I gave him an imploring look. The leaders of the group had always struck me as more sophisticated than the soldiers. Surely they would disapprove of Abdullah. I didn't know whether Donald would want to investigate or admonish the boys, or whether he'd make some sort of change to better protect me, like putting Nigel back in my room.

"I am your Muslim sister," I continued. "You have to help me. Allah says the Muslims have to help one another. You wouldn't let what is happening to me happen to your daughter or your wife, right? Please, make it stop. I need to go home and live with my family. It's too dangerous to be here with these soldiers."

He cleared his throat a few times. He then lifted a finger and pointed at my Koran, sitting open on the mattress, motioning for me to pass it to him. I handed it over and watched him shift into a cross-legged position, propping the book carefully on his lap. He flipped through the pages, skimming over the Arabic. "Ah," he said after a moment or two. He then looked for the corresponding verse in English. "Here."

He turned the book so I could see where his finger had landed. Chapter 23, Verses 1 through 6. I knew the passage. It was miserably familiar, one of several places in the Koran where female captives— those possessed by the "right hand"—seem to be referenced as the exception to the rigors of practicing good behavior and self-control. I got anxious every time I read them, and now the words hit like a cudgel.

> *Successful indeed are the believers*
> *Who are humble in their prayers*
> *And who keep aloof from what is vain*
> *And who are givers of poor-rate*

And who guard their private parts
Except before their wives or those whom their right hands possess,
for surely they are not blamable.

"You see," Donald said, "what is happening is not obligatory but it is permissible." He steepled his hands like a wise man, as if he'd just taught me something interesting. "It is not forbidden."

I understood that the boys in the house took the Koran's instructions as literal, but I'd figured the leaders—especially Donald, having lived in Europe—would leave some space for interpretation, viewing it through the lens of the centuries that had passed, similar to the way my pious Christian grandparents looked at the New Testament, which had its own provocative lines about slavery and the treatment of women, cherry-picking the good while disregarding the bad. Donald was having none of it, though. His verdict: not blamable.

"But," I said, giving it another try, "I'm being hurt. What's happening is a problem."

He passed me the Koran and stood up to leave. He then said to me what I'd been saying to myself, though coming from him, it felt like a slap. *"Inshallah,* Sister Amina, you will be fine. No problem."

*

November arrived. I kept track of the days obsessively, making note of the friends' birthdays I was missing, imagining the turn of seasons in Alberta. I was aware that Christmas was on the horizon. In my mind, I trusted that I'd be safely home by then. Every Friday the boys in the house washed their clothes and took turns going to a mosque— another way of marking a week gone past. I walked myself to the point of fatigue daily, waiting and hoping for some sort of change. I replayed the last conversation—if it could be called a conversation— I'd had with my mother back in early September, telling her not to sell anything, not to pay.

My mother. I could build her in my imagination, head to toe, from the dark shine of her hair to the worn brown cowboy boots she liked to wear. I could put her in the room with me, practically. The last time

I'd seen her was over the holidays, nearly a year ago, just before I'd gone to Iraq. We'd stayed in together on New Year's Eve at her apartment in Canmore, watching movies—her on the couch and me lying on the floor—both of us long past any interest in crowded parties and drunken countdowns. My mother had recently turned fifty. I was roughly the age she'd been when she'd gotten pregnant with me. She was now the age my grandmother had been back then. We were like clicks on a dial. Young, middle, old.

Every once in a while, one of the leaders came to the house and posed a question to me, a query flung over continents, evoking something both intimate and concrete and sent directly from home.

What award did Dad win recently? *Communities in Bloom, for his gardening.*

Where does Oma keep her candy? *In a pumpkin-shaped jar.*

My answers were proof that I was alive, that my freedom was still worth negotiating for. To me, the questions also felt like gifts, an invitation to conjure my grandmother's tidy house in Red Deer or the quivering dahlias in my father's backyard. They were a reminder that I'd had a life outside.

In my mind, I talked and talked to my mother. I imagined thoughts strung between us, spider threads floating over the ocean. She was sending love, I knew it. I sent messages back. *I love you. I love you.* And *I'm sorry, so truly sorry.* And a reversal of my earlier plea, a thought I needed her to hear more than anything: *Please get me out of here. Find a way to pay. Do everything, sell it all.*

It hurt even to think it, but there it was. Each time Abdullah came to the room, I had to talk myself out of dying.

When I wasn't walking or resting on my mat, I often stood at the window on the far right, next to the wall, where the light pooled on the ledge, making it easier to read the Koran or one of Donald's lame books. Sometimes, especially in the mornings, I could hear the sound of rocket-propelled grenades ripping through the air and slamming into buildings not far from where we were. My guess was that we were being held in some satellite village at the edge of Mogadishu. It was impossible to know who was fighting whom—Al-Shabaab versus the Ethiopians, one militia versus another? All I knew was the sound. The fighting would flare and then, just as abruptly, it would stop. After that, the neighborhood would be quiet for hours, eerily so, as people hid themselves away in their homes, waiting for assurances that things had settled. I remembered Ajoos, our fixer at the Shamo, and his continuously ringing cell phone—friends and relatives with moment-to-moment updates about where the fighting was going on, which streets were safe and not safe, about who had died that morning and who had escaped.

Some days I stood at the window, hoping perversely that a mortar would fall on our house, collapsing the roof, filling the place with smoke, sending us all scampering in shock. I didn't care who it killed. They all deserved it, every one. If I survived, I thought, maybe it would give me a chance to run.

★

One day, through the side window, I caught a glimpse of a man I thought might be a neighbor. He looked to be about my age. He was walking across the scraggly adjoining yard and toward a shed, talking with another man whose face I couldn't see. He looked like a good person. I read something in his loping gait, the way he kept a hand flopped amiably over his friend's shoulder.

My loneliness must have been telegraphing across the ether, because almost as if I'd called out to him, the man turned abruptly and looked over to where I stood half-hidden behind the window grille. We locked eyes, both of us startled. Instantly, I ducked out of sight, my heart beating fast. I worried that if my captors realized I could be seen by neighbors, they'd start keeping the windows in my room shuttered. Then again, the man's look sent a wave through my invisibility. I wondered if he'd find someone to tell about me and whether that would bring about any change.

It didn't. More weeks passed. I stopped looking out the side window altogether.

Standing at the other window, the one overlooking the alley, I could read the Koran and feel the outside air leaking in through the grilles. I delighted in the slightest shifts in air pressure, moments when the humidity rose toward bursting, when I could feel the traces of a gathering wind. I imagined that I could see the curve of the earth, the crescent line between me and my old life. Somewhere far away, a blade of cool air might form over the ocean and start to move in my direction, raking across the palm trees and over the desert. Changes in the weather didn't come often, but when they did, it could feel symbolic, a thing running from there to here.

One afternoon, a light rain began to dapple the concrete wall across the alleyway. I stood at the window, listening to it drum on the roof, my elbows propped on the window ledge. The sky darkened to a powdery gray. The wind gusted, rushing through trees I couldn't see, causing the rain to spray sideways on the wall.

"God, it's beautiful," a voice said, clear as day, articulating my exact thought at the exact moment I had it.

The voice wasn't mine. But it was a voice I knew. "Nige?"

The voice said, "Trout?"

For a shocked second, we were both silent. He was maybe ten feet away from me at the window in his room, standing at the sill. Due to the narrowness of the alleyway and the fact that the tin roof of our house overlapped slightly with the roof of the house behind it, the acoustics were perfect. Our voices carried clearly, sheltered by the rooftops, bouncing off the high wall on the opposite side. When I stood at my window and he stood at his, I could hear him and he could hear me. A little miracle of physics. We'd gone weeks without figuring this out, but now we had.

26

A Feast Is a Feast

What I thought about the future was this: Nigel and I always would be close. Our romantic relationship was over, but it had been replaced by something different. We were friends, true friends, best friends, embedded permanently in each other's lives. How else could it be? Not one other soul we would encounter on earth, as long as either of us lived, would know what it was to listen to the boys chanting Arabic out on that patio, or to have our lives regulated by their disinterested finger snaps. I thought we'd need to remember and discuss these things when we got out. We would build two side-by-side existences and have an abiding everyday love. We'd sit on each other's porches for years to come.

At our respective windows, we managed to talk for hours on end, coming and going from our sills, keeping our voices low and our Korans open in case anyone walked in. I was terrified of being caught, but we were familiar with the routine of our captors, most of all their staggering laziness when it came to getting themselves off the porch. There were long stretches of each day when we were sure nobody would wander back to our part of the house.

My window sat at about shoulder height off the floor, and in order to best hear and be heard by Nigel, I had to lean forward, standing on the balls of my feet with my neck craned toward the window grate. I'd stay there until my feet ached. When it was time to take a break, I'd say things like "Okay, talk to you later" or "I'm going to eat my food now," like an office worker about to wander back to her desk. Often, at the end, I'd also say, "I love you, Nige."

He'd say, "Keep your chin up, Trout" and "Love you, too."

If, before our separation, Nigel and I had taken each other for granted, if we'd been irked and touchy, we now knew enough to be thankful for each other. I hung on to the sound of his voice like a rope.

We ran through old stories, adding new details every time. We played word games and told every tired joke we could think of. We discussed our nighttime dreams, our interactions with the boys, our bowel movements. Nigel liked to think about beautiful women to pass the time. Cate Blanchett was his girl. We made guesses about what was happening with ransom negotiations. We guessed out loud that together our families might manage to come up with half a million dollars in ransom money for our captors—an amount that surely they'd have to accept. We talked about the future as if it were arriving at any minute. Nigel said he wanted to jump back into his photography and that maybe he'd even get himself to Afghanistan. I was fixated on spending time in Canada. When we said these things out loud to each other, they seemed like promises, sure to happen.

Images of home floated continuously through my mind. I hardly knew my brothers anymore. My grandparents were getting old. I had friends I wanted to visit. I daydreamed about cold air and the beauty of a snowy winter. I pictured myself moving to Vancouver, which to me was the most beautiful city on earth. On my walks around my room, I blotted out my surroundings and imagined myself pacing the pathways of Stanley Park, moving through groves of tall cedar and along the curving seawall next to the bay.

Something happens when you are alone most of the time, when there are no distractions. Your mind grows more powerful—muscular, even. It takes over and starts to carry you. In the month or so after Nigel and I were separated, I could feel a new sort of energy making itself known to me. It felt physical and also not physical. I could hold my hand several inches over my leg and feel the internal heat. The energy in my hands felt odd, but it felt like power, like a tool I could use if I learned what to do with it. I couldn't tell whether it was a good thing or a bad thing or even a thing at all—whether it was a survival tool or the first flutter of lunacy. One morning I ate a tin of tuna and then sat for an hour holding the spoon in front of me, trying to see if I could bend it with my mind. I couldn't, not even a little, but still, the idea seemed less crazy, more possible, than it once had. Later, at the window, when I told Nigel about my attempt at a carnival stunt, he'd confessed that he, too, was experimenting with his psychic energy, trying to transmit urgent messages about ransom payments to his parents at home.

*

"Who," Nigel asked me one day, "do you hate most?"

We posed questions of one sort or another all the time. They were the springboard into many of our talks at the window. Conversation, for us, shot cleanly in two directions, backward and forward: We spent our time sunk in either memory or anticipation. *What's the best country you've ever visited? What's the best sex you've ever had? What's the first meal you're going to eat when we get out of here? Which are you more excited about—taking a hot shower or sleeping in fresh, cool sheets?*

Now he was asking about the present moment, about our captors. The answer was easy. It was Abdullah I hated most. I hated everything about him, from his hairless armpits to the foulness of his breath. I hated his cruelty and his violence. I hated facing every afternoon, not knowing whether he was coming to hurt me or not. He came three out of every five days, more or less, and when he didn't show up in my room, I lost those hours awash in adrenaline, worrying that he would. When he did, slipping through the door while the rest of the house napped, I had active fantasies about wrestling the gun out of his hands and shooting him in the head with it—waking every damn soul in the neighborhood to the horror of what he'd been doing. I wanted to kill him. I wanted him to die. Those thoughts got me through moments but not hours. And what I needed was to get through hours, lots of them. My hatred was there, simmering like a lava pit beneath the high-wire act of each day. I saw it, but I didn't want to swim in it. I knew I wouldn't last if I did. I would far prefer to talk about meals and sex and plans.

"I don't think I can play this game," I said to Nigel. "Let's not do it."

For everything we'd discussed, I hadn't told him about Abdullah. I didn't want to poison him with it. There was nothing he could do, though I did wonder if he heard noises through the wall.

His relationship to the boys was different from mine, anyway. For exercise, Nigel had taken to doing yoga in his room. He'd told me that Hassam and Abdullah walked in one day to find him moving through poses, and they'd actually joined in, earnestly trying to mimic his movements. They'd come back a few times after that, asking for instructions as they attempted new things, laughing as they winged their bony legs into tree pose beneath their man-skirts. I took it as a sign that they were bored beyond belief. A sign that my side of the wall would never feel like his side of the wall.

*

As the weeks passed, I wished for things that were large and abstract—freedom, comfort, safety. Beyond that, my most specific longings involved food—plates of medium-rare steak, bags of candy, a cold beer in a frosted mug. I could pass two hours imagining one meal in granular detail, the ecstasy of making an omelet, for example, the chopping of a crisp green pepper, the *sssss* of butter melting in a pan, the lemony yellow of eggs beaten in a bowl. More than anything, I craved a hug, the chance to fall into the arms of someone, anyone, who cared about me.

It never occurred to me to yearn for something more direct from home. But midway through November, Donald Trump walked into the room, carrying a big, sturdy-looking yellow plastic bag along with a smaller black bag.

"A package has come from Canada," he said. Slowly, Donald unloaded the contents onto the linoleum square on my floor. He took out a few packets of pills, each one bearing a typed label and instructions: "Noroxin, 400 mg (bacterial infection—take by mouth twice daily)" and "Roxithromycin, 150 mg, 10 tablets (treatment for mild/moderate ear, nose, throat, respiratory tract, skin, and genital urinary tract infections—1 tablet by mouth every 12 hours)," and so on. There were a few pencils and pens, a composition notebook, a pair of finger-nail clippers, some St. Ives body lotion, a cellophane-wrapped packet containing five pairs of cotton underwear, hair elastics, dental floss, several packages of sanitary pads, a plastic box of Wet Ones, and a package of British digestive cookies. He then passed over a small black case containing a pair of clunky-looking prescription eyeglasses and—oh, how my heart leaped—a few books.

"You are lucky," Donald said before leaving the room.

After he'd left, I sat looking in disbelief at each item, the tears starting to well. I was almost afraid to touch anything. I'd been sent a book of crossword puzzles, a long list of Somali phrases, and Nelson Mandela's autobiography, *Long Walk to Freedom,* volumes one and two, some nine hundred pages in all. I could hear Donald out in the hallway, knocking on Nigel's door. I hoped it meant that Nigel was reaping a similar harvest.

A while later, we convened at our windows, both of us giddy. Nigel, too, had been given medicine, toiletries, and writing materials. He also had a recent issue of *Newsweek,* some Sudoku, two books by Ernest Hemingway —*The Snows of Kilimanjaro* and *Green Hills of Africa* — and Khaled Hosseini's second novel about Afghanistan, *A Thousand Splendid Suns.* Like me, he'd received a five-pack of cotton underwear, but someone—was it Adam? was it Donald?—had cut it open and apparently pinched a pair for himself. We would later learn that our captors had thoroughly picked over the contents of the care packages, removing a number of medical supplies and also some personal letters written by our families.

I read the first volume of Mandela's biography in less than three days and launched right into the second, which covered the twenty-seven years he spent imprisoned in South Africa. I seized on the story, reading it like a message directed specifically at me. Mandela wrote that he and his fellow prisoners taped notes for one another beneath the rims of their shared toilet. His mind played tricks on him. He doubted his own sanity sometimes. "Strong convictions are the secret of surviving deprivation," he wrote. "Your spirit can be full even when your stomach is empty." Early on, Donald Trump had given me a small

flashlight, which I'd been using sparingly in order to preserve the batteries, but now I read late into the night, the words bright in the flashlight's narrow beam.

Using the high ledge in the bathroom as our transfer spot, Nigel
and I swapped books. We read and did puzzles. We laughed over a
thin booklet that had been included in my pile. It was titled *5-Minute
Stress-Busting: Instant Calm for People on the Go* and included lines like
"Our fast pace of life, and the pressure to look good and be successful in everything we do, means stress is more prevalent than ever."
Stress is more prevalent than ever. Oh, indeed it was. Though we mocked
it, we read everything. We held a two-person book club at our windowsills. We discussed every detail of each book, right down to
how we'd felt at the moment when we read the words. *Green Hills
of Africa* was full of descriptions of cooking and eating, which tormented us but nonetheless needed to be revisited endlessly at our
windowsills. *Newsweek* had a cover story about green energy, a
topic upon which we became single-source experts. An old friend of
Nigel's, a photographer pal, had a photo in that issue—a picture of
some soldiers in Afghanistan—which seemed to delight and cheer
him, offering a bridge into something real.

It was like being given not just a meal but a feast. We chewed
on every word, feeling as if each one had been spooned up by the
people who loved us most, even though when I really thought about
it, I was certain the supplies had come from the Canadian embassy
and not from my family. My eyeglasses had been custom-ordered for
my prescription, but the case that held them bore the logo of a shop
in Nairobi. And after all the hours of *Oprah* my mother and I had
watched together, all the dog-eared self-help books we'd exchanged
over the years, I doubted she would have chosen a five-minute stress-
buster manual to get me through. Much later, I would learn that I
was right: The package had been mailed from Nairobi, assembled by
RCMP agents working with the Australian Federal Police and sent to
the Mogadishu International Airport. It had been addressed in care of
Adam Abdule Osman, the name given by the kidnapper who'd been
calling my mother a few times a week, the man with the little Ben

Franklin glasses who'd come to meet us on our second day of captivity
but had rarely shown himself since.

Adam was the communications man. He seemed to conduct his
business mostly from his home in Mogadishu, with his two little children running around in the background. In the transcripts of the calls
with my mother, which I would read much later, he referred to her
often as "Mom" and once or twice asked whether it would be okay if
he married me. When she reminded him that he already had a wife,
he reminded her that it was permissible, in his religion, for a man to
marry more than once.

If Adam was worried about being caught, he didn't seem to show
it. He called my mother, repeating the ransom demands, telling her
that my health was deteriorating. The investigators seemed to agree
that he was using an alias. If there was a conversation about setting up
some sort of sting operation to nab him as he picked up the package at
the airport, I don't know. Chances are, he had paid someone to retrieve
the box, anyway, to avoid exactly that scenario.

*

The downside to receiving a package was that it made clear to me that
nobody—not our families, nor our governments, nor our captors—
thought we'd be free anytime soon. A feast is a feast, I soon recognized,
only if it's short-term. Despite the fact that I was constantly battling
both a headache and diarrhea, I saved the blister packs of medicine,
keeping them lined up along the wall next to my mattress. I began
to ration my reading to a few chapters a day. Nelson Mandela got me
through my mornings, but Hemingway, with his pages of dialogue,
his men and women talking lustily, put me to bed at night. I continued
to think of our situation as temporary, but I also was careful not to
squander what we had, except for the digestive biscuits, which I scarfed
down within a matter of days. The care package had made me jubilant
and then sent me crashing. Everything had two sides. There was a fine
line between holding steady and dipping into despair.

Meanwhile, the skin over my top lip had started to feel rough and
itchy. Looking in my little compact mirror, I could see a white rash

there, some sort of fungus. Each day it seemed to creep a little farther across my face, slowly spreading around my nose and spiraling up one cheek in a way I found mortifying. I tried taking some of the antibiotics from my care package, but nothing changed. Then I tried rubbing the patches with my new skin cream, but that only seemed to make it worse. It felt like Somalia was beginning to eat me alive.

In a weak moment one day, I wrote a note to Nigel and left it in the bathroom. I was feeling low—too low even to talk at the window. In my note, I apologized for my sagging spirits and then added an explanatory line: "Someone has been paying unwanted visits to my room in the afternoons." I knocked on the wall to tell Nigel the note was there. In a short while, he knocked back to say he'd received it.

During our next window conversation, he was quieter than usual. I wonder if he'd suspected it all along.

"Who is it?" he said finally. "It's Abdullah, isn't it?"

"Yes, but I don't want to talk about it."

"What is he doing to you? Is he . . ." Nigel's voice trailed off. "How long has this been going on?" He said the words sadly.

For a split second, I wanted to say everything, to dump the details on him ruthlessly, to hear him cry or explode or risk everything to start fighting the boys. But already I regretted telling him as much as I had. It wasn't fair to Nigel, and it only made things more real for me.

When he started to ask another question, I stopped him midsentence. "Seriously, Nige, just forget about it," I said, knowing that he wouldn't.

I went back to holding steady. Mostly because there was no choice.

On the hundredth day of our captivity—December first—I left Nigel another note in the bathroom. "Congratulations on making it 100 days," I wrote. "We have to stay positive. We have to believe there are many people on the other side of the world doing everything they can to get us out of here and home safely before Christmas." As was always the case with my notes, writing it helped me to believe it. It staked some claim on the truth.

27

The Desert

"G et up, we are going," someone said in the dark. I'd been asleep. It was late. The door to my room was open. One of the boys shone a flashlight in my face. It was Hassam. I could see Captain Skids standing behind him. "We are going," Hassam said a second time. He flared the flashlight to the edge of the mattress where I kept my belongings—my books and toiletries and extra clothes. "Put your clothes on and we go."

I sat up in bed. I could hear other activity in the house, a general shuffling. They were moving us to a new place. It had happened before, always abruptly and at night. "We're leaving?" I said to Hassam, my eyes avoiding Skids, whose coldness unnerved me. "Should I put all my things in a bag?"

Hassam looked impatient. "No, no," he said. "Put clothes on only."

I thought about what that meant. "Oh my goodness, are we being released?"

"Yes, yes, fast, now," Hassam said. He pushed his palm toward the ceiling as if to hurry me along, as if lifting me from the dead.

Fireworks shot off in my head, pops of color and light. Joy, incredulity. I located the pair of men's jeans I kept close to the mattress and pulled them over my hips, beneath the red polyester dress I wore both day and night. I scrambled to my feet and found a head scarf. I followed Skids down the dark hallway, with Hassam and his gun walking behind. I kept one hand on the waist of my jeans so they wouldn't fall off. Noticing that Nigel's door was closed, I turned back to Hassam. I said, just to make sure, "We are getting freedom? Yes?" He said nothing.

In the courtyard, Ahmed's Suzuki was waiting, the engine running. Hassam gestured, and I climbed into the backseat. I could see Abdullah walking out of the house, winding a scarf around his face, having swapped his man-skirt for a pair of trousers, which was what the boys did any time they left the house. Next I saw Ahmed emerge. Never once in my presence had he wrapped his face in a scarf, but this time he, too, was wearing one, every inch of his skin covered. Alone in the car, I could feel the optimism draining out of me.

Then Abdullah pushed into the backseat next to me. Ahmed opened the front door on the driver's side and got in. "Abdullah, Ahmed," I said, "is everything okay?"

Neither man responded. It was as if I weren't there. Beneath the dome light, Ahmed turned the key in the ignition and slid the gear into reverse. Behind us, one of the boys unlocked the gate. The rear door opposite me opened, and Skids, fully wrapped, took a spot next to me in the rear seat.

In my throat, I felt a gurgling panic. I said, "What is happening? Where is Nigel? Is he coming? Where are we going?" My voice seemed to get ahead of my brain in sensing real danger. I heard it come out high and reedy.

With one hand draped over the passenger seat, Ahmed backed the station wagon through the open gate and maneuvered it onto the unpaved road. Nobody answered my questions. Nobody said where Nigel was.

We were driving now, the three of them and I, funneling through heavy sand, weaving among the neighborhood's maze of high walls. Some rational part of me told me to take note of where we were, to figure out which street led to what, in case I had an opportunity to run, now or later or ever. But everything looked the same. Our headlights ranged over blank concrete as we turned corners from one unmarked lane to the next. I watched over the dashboard as some shrubbery came into view and then disappeared. After a couple of minutes, Ahmed stopped the car in front of the entrance to a dark compound, where a man stood waiting. It was Donald Trump, the money guy. I was grateful to see that his face was not wrapped and he wasn't carrying a gun.

Donald opened the rear door of the Suzuki and silently wedged himself in next to Abdullah. There were four of us in the backseat now and only Ahmed in the front.

The car lurched forward. I focused on Donald, still dimly clinging to the idea that maybe I was being released. "What's going on, Mohammed?" I said, using his real name. "Where are we going? What's happening?"

As I spoke, he stared straight ahead. He was acting as if he couldn't hear me. I could see his eyes roving over the dashboard—nervously, it seemed—but he wouldn't turn and look at me. I said, "Where are they taking me, Mohammed? Where's Nigel? Please tell me. I'm your sister, remember?" A new fear went spiraling through my rib cage. Maybe I was being sold. They had threatened it a few times, saying that if ransom money didn't come in, they could always recoup their losses by handing us over to Al-Shabaab. I wondered if that was it. It explained why Nigel wasn't with me: I was on my way to be either killed or sold to new captors. Nigel's family had money and mine didn't. They were holding on to him and letting go of me.

Just then I did something instinctive and un-Islamic. I shot a hand out across Abdullah's lap and gripped Donald's forearm, not letting up with my talking, just wanting to hang on to someone who might listen. Hadn't we once discussed what makes a good olive oil? Hadn't he brought me a can of Coke and a pregnancy test? I was crying now. His arm felt stiff beneath my grasp.

"Please," I said, "don't let them kill me. Please tell me what's going on. Where is Nigel? Can you stop this? Am I being sold? Did they sell me? Are things okay?"

Awkwardly, Donald shook free of my hand. He cleared his throat. "Uhhhh," he said, glancing uneasily at Ahmed in the driver's seat. "I really don't know. *Inshallah*, things are okay, but I really don't know."

With that, he went back to silence.

After another minute, the car stopped moving. This time we'd pulled up in front of a small doorway set between two walls. I thought I recognized it as the door leading to Electric House, the place we'd left about six weeks earlier, where Nigel and I had played backgammon. Two men appeared to be waiting for us. They got into the front seat of the Suzuki, next to Ahmed, both of them wrapped up in scarves. One I recognized as Romeo, with his long torso and yellow-checkered scarf, which he normally kept draped over his neck. The other guy was new to me—broad-shouldered, heavyset, imposing.

As if following a set of instructions laid down in advance, neither of the newcomers looked at me. Nobody greeted anybody. Nobody spoke.

We careened forward into the thick darkness, following a dirt road in the path of our headlights. I leaned forward slightly, in part to avoid feeling too close to Abdullah on one side of me and Captain Skids on the other, keeping a hand on the animal fur draped over the middle console for balance. We seemed to be driving down some sort of market street. I saw what looked to be closed-down kiosks made of banged-together scraps of wood and metal. There were shanties built from tree branches and cardboard boxes, from broken crates and corrugated tin. Every structure, large and small, appeared to be made from sticks and garbage. Plastic water bottles skittered in the road. Bits of stray paper twirled in our lights. Ahead of us was a fire, orange and jutting against the black sky, as tall as a tower, almost like an illusion. As we pulled closer, I saw it was real, an enormous bonfire throwing light, its top lashing and sparking high above the human figures gathered around it.

Ahmed didn't slow down for the fire. He accelerated past it, his shoulders hunched low over the wheel. I looked past Skids and out the window as we went. Young men, maybe fifteen or twenty of them, stood in loose clumps at the edge of the inferno. From what I could see, many carried assault rifles much like the ones my captors had.

About a hundred feet down the road, we passed another fire, this one smaller, with another group of men gathered around it. I could see several more bonfires dotting the distance. I noticed that there

were shadows on the street, people moving about, all of them young
and male and drifting. It was as if we were passing through a flickering
underworld grotto.

Donald saw me looking. Without making eye contact, he said,
"Please, look around. You see this place? You see the gangs?" His voice
blazed with scorn. "Did you think you were in Paris or Toronto? Well,
you are not. This is Somalia."

He pronounced the word the way the rest of them did, with a fear-
some kind of pride, treadling through all four syllables, *SO-mal-eee-ah.*

We drove on toward whatever was going to happen. It felt to me
like I was falling through space, tumbling through a vast textureless
emptiness, with no holds, no chance of self-arrest. After a few minutes,
the human scene outside the car window fell away, the people and
shanties and strewn garbage, and then we were in the countryside, on
a paved road, planing over a lightless, utterly still piece of earth. After a
while, Ahmed turned the wheel and the car veered onto a sandy track.
I didn't know what to tell myself. I couldn't for one second imagine
what was ahead. Would there be a desert exchange with Al-Shabaab—
me for a pile of cash? Was it possible they were going to kill me and
leave me, as a way of pressuring Nigel's family to pay more and pay
quickly? My mind lit fires and then put them out. Ahmed calmly spun
the steering wheel as if he knew precisely where he was headed, dodg-
ing bushes that reared up under our headlights, his tires flinging sand.
In forty-five minutes of driving, he hadn't uttered a word.

Without warning, he hit the brakes and threw the car into park. I
heard him shut off the engine. A single silent beat passed in the car. I
started to cry again. I heard myself talking, filling the space. "What's
happening? Why are we here? What are you doing? Don't hurt me,
please, don't."

Nobody in the car turned to look at me. One by one they pushed
open their doors and climbed out. I sat in the backseat, crumpled over
my knees, feeling like I was going to vomit. Someone's hands pulled at
my arm, tugging me toward the door.

The moon was in the sky, narrow and bluish. The stars made a rich
carpet overhead. I noticed it. I don't know why. The sky was there and

so was I, half in the car and half out. It was Donald who had my arm. "Come," he said. I hung on to the inside handle of the open car door with both hands. He pulled harder, attempting to drag me. "Come, come on," he was saying, sounding surly and fed up. My feet slipped through the sand. I let go of the door.

I was upright. We were moving through spindly desert brush toward a clearing with an acacia tree, a gnarled thing lit up by the moon. The men from the car were there already, all but Donald and Abdullah, who were marching me toward the tree. Clearly, they'd discussed their plan, how to go about it. They had lined up, looking solemn and grim, ceremonial. There were no other cars in sight and no people. I let go of the idea I was being sold to Al-Shabaab, even though that had become the more hopeful option. This was it. I was going to die.

Words streamed out of my mouth. I was talking to myself more than to them. *I miss my mom, I miss my dad. I want to see my family again.* All longings became simple. I remember sobbing and trembling and the constant feeling of falling, end over end, through a void. I remember it in ways I wish I didn't, every step we took toward that clearing. How I clung to Donald when we reached the tree, how he put his hands on my shoulders and turned me—gently, it seemed—so that I was facing away from the line of my captors. How I reached and grabbed on to his shirt as he pushed me down, how I heard the *ffft* of fabric ripping as I went, and how all at once I was on my knees in the dirt with my back to the group. I felt the coarseness of the desert sand through my jeans. I remember how heat radiated from the ground, still trapped from the previous day.

From behind, someone pulled off my head scarf and grabbed a fistful of my hair, snapping my head backward. Something thick and cool pressed against my throat, a knife, long enough that, from the corner of my eye, I could see its rounded tip, the end of the blade. I felt myself gag. Whoever was holding my hair gave my head a fresh yank and angled the knife so that it skimmed the left side of my neck, the soft part, the jugular. I realized the blade was serrated; I felt its teeth holding my skin. I begged them not to do it. I thought of every time Abdullah and Ali had mimicked the motion of beheading with their hands. I thought of the hacked-up Iraqi man I'd seen. I kept talking. I blurted a thought I'd never had, not once in my life, but which felt like a desperate certainty: *You can't do this. I haven't had children. I want to have children.*

Was this really me? It was, it was.

There wasn't a way out. They'd said so many times that they would kill me, and now they were. In my body, some internal fuse box stripped itself right to smoke. My muscles went rigid. I heard myself draw in a breath.

Behind me, the men were talking, saying things in Somali. It was Donald and Skids having some sort of disagreement, with Ahmed weighing in. A sharp word was said. The person holding my hair let go abruptly. I fell forward into the sand.

When I looked back to see what was happening, Donald's voice caught me. He said sternly, "You turn around."

They talked for a few more minutes as I sobbed in the dirt, sounding like an animal, like something wounded and incapable of speech. I remember my own sound acutely, the craziness of it. I don't know how much time passed or what caused me to look back again, but this time I could see that Skids had his phone out and was dialing a number. He was talking into it—to Adam, it would turn out. Donald walked over. He leaned down and looked at me directly for the first time all night. He looked actually scared, afraid for me. "How much money does your family have?" he said.

"I don't know, I don't know," I said, my breath spent from crying. "They'll get anything you want. Please don't kill me. They'll get money for you. They will."

"They want one million dollars," Donald said. "You are lucky I am here. I have asked them to give you one more chance. You have seven days, and if there is not that money, then they will kill you."

A moment later, he handed me the captain's phone, with my mother's voice on the other end.

28

Call Home

ROYAL CANADIAN MOUNTED POLICE
LAWFUL INTERCEPTION OF TELEPHONE NUMBER

Case ID	Lindhout
Line ID	403-887-█
Session Number	1122

Date	Saturday, December 13, 2008
Start Time	12:04:24 MST
Direction	Incoming

From	Adam ABDULE OSMAN
Telephone	2521537█
Location	Unknown

To	Lorinda STEWART
Telephone Number	403-887-█
Location	3939 50 Avenue
	Sylvan Lake, Alberta

(Indiscernible conversation in the background)

ABDULE OSMAN: (Clears throat)

STEWART: Hello?

ABDULE OSMAN: Hello?

STEWART: Hello, Adam.

ABDULE OSMAN: Okay, we want to talk and, Amanda (call cuts out temporarily), and then . . .

(Foreign conversation in the background)
[A second phone is patched in.]

ABDULE OSMAN: And then at that time, it is a little time.

STEWART: Okay.

ABDULE OSMAN: Don't waste our time and don't waste your time. It is a little time, understand?

STEWART: Oh, I understand . . .

(Foreign conversation in the background)

LINDHOUT: (Crying) Momma?

STEWART: Amanda. (Crying) Amanda, I love you. (Crying) Amanda . . . Amanda, how are you?

(In background: Foreign)

LINDHOUT: Mom listen. Listen to me, okay?

STEWART: Okay.

LINDHOUT: . . . closely, okay?

STEWART: Okay, I'm listening, hon.

LINDHOUT: (Crying) If, if you guys don't pay (sobs) one million dollars for me, by one week, they will kill me, okay?

(In background: Foreign)

LINDHOUT: Tonight they have brought me out to kill me (sobs), and, but, but they have, they've given me one more chance, to call you guys. (Crying)

STEWART: Amanda, s-stay strong. Stay strong, hon. We . . .

LINDHOUT: (Crying)

STEWART: . . . we're doing . . .

LINDHOUT: Mom.

STEWART: . . . everything we can

LINDHOUT: Mom, listen to me. We have . . . one week, okay? And I don't . . . I feel so awful. I can't believe they're doing this but (sobs) I'd . . . I hate that I am doing this to you guys. (Crying)

STEWART:	Amanda, Amanda, please do not worry about us. Please don't worry about us.
LINDHOUT:	(Crying)
STEWART:	We love you.
LINDHOUT:	(Crying)
STEWART:	You need to . . .
LINDHOUT:	I know I . . .
STEWART:	. . . stay strong and . . .
LINDHOUT:	(Indiscernible)
STEWART:	. . . stay healthy.
LINDHOUT:	(Crying) Is there, is there any way that you guys will be able to pay them in one week?
STEWART:	Amanda, we are trying to do everything we can, to get money together for you, 'cause the . . .
LINDHOUT:	(Crying)
STEWART:	. . . government won't pay. We've gone back to the bank.

(Call is disconnected)

29

Christmas

*L*ate, very late, that night, they returned me to my room. I crawled onto the mattress and pulled the blue-flowered sheet over me, too exhausted to draw the mosquito netting. The house had gone quiet. I had no energy to wonder what had happened, whether the whole thing had been staged—a mock moonlit execution meant to lead me precisely to the place I'd gone, blubbering and projecting terror across ten thousand miles.

The next morning, after Hassam had come in to open my window shutters for the day, I went to my sill and waited for Nigel to arrive at his. When he was there, I told him about the previous night, crying about it all over again, leaving out the part about the serrated knife held to my throat—in some way, I suppose, to protect him from knowing that the knife existed, and not ready to dredge up the image again. I said only that they'd threatened to kill me. I let him assume it was with one of their guns. Recounting the story to Nigel didn't ease anything. He'd heard them taking me away, he said, and wept for a long time. We both understood we'd entered a new and more dangerous territory with our captors. We were moving toward a conclusion. The whole group had rehearsed a death. My death. I tried not to think about it, but there was no shaking it off. I wept uselessly, reflexively, through much of the morning.

Hassam surfaced at my door later, carrying the afternoon flask of

tea. He paused and studied me with what looked like concern. I was
still on my mattress and still crying—the wild sobbing of the morning
having given way to a seemingly endless dribble of tears. Something
in Hassam's expression told me that although he'd stayed behind, he
knew where I'd gone and what had happened.

"Do you like go outside?" he asked me. At first it seemed like a cruel
joke, a reference to the night before, but then I realized it was, in fact,
an offer.

"Go outside? Today? Now? Yes, please," I said. I fumbled for my
Koran and made like I wanted to pick it up and carry it with me, saying
with a sniffle, "I can study outside."

Hassam nodded. "I ask," he said, before closing the door.

I was hardly hopeful. If you've had occasion to read *5-Minute Stress-
Busting: Instant Calm for People on the Go,* you will know that hope is
a thing that can dry up. "People faced with emotionally demanding
situations over a long period," the book had told me in my weeks of
reading after the care package arrived, "can reach 'burnout'—physical,
mental, and emotional exhaustion. The sufferer experiences feelings
of hopelessness, disillusionment, and cynicism (plus the usual physical, mental, and emotional symptoms of stress)."

Which felt about right to me.

To my surprise, Hassam came for me in ten minutes' time. He
waved for me to pick up my Koran and follow him down the hallway, past Nigel's room, past the bathroom and shower, to a door that
was almost never used. The daylight we stepped into seared my eyeballs, which were accustomed to shadows, causing pools of yellow to
bloom between me and the outside world. Once the pools wore away,
I could see we were in a small courtyard that connected to the driveway, around the corner and out of sight from the veranda where the
boys hung out with the captain, though surrounded by the same set of
walls. The sun blazed through the leaves of a papaya tree growing up
out of the dirt, dangling a few nubs of dark green fruit.

Now that we were outside, Hassam seemed almost shy. He had
brought his gun. He gestured for me to sit in the shade by the tree

on an overturned bucket. He then walked to the far end of the driveway, where a set of padlocked metal gates led to the road. I'd passed
through here the night before, in the darkness, but now it was a different place. Still holding on to his gun, Hassam sat himself against the
wall close to the gates, maybe twenty feet away from me. It was as
much space as I'd been given in four months.

Taking a seat on the bucket, I rested my hands on the cover of my
Koran and stared at them, blue veins under opaque skin. I studied the
papaya tree, with its arching branches and curved leaves. A few clouds
floated like white popcorn against the bright sky. In the daylight, my
polyester dress had gone a psychedelic red. The walls surrounding the
compound were painted white with baby-blue trim running along the
top, beneath a tangle of razor wire. A shredded plastic bag was caught
up in the razor wire. Everything felt sharp, weird, unreal. Down the
driveway, in his spot against the wall, Hassam appeared sunk deep
into thought, his eyes scanning the sky. I hadn't bothered to open my
Koran, and he hadn't bothered to look once in my direction. Before it
was over, we'd stay out there about twenty minutes, me and Hassam,
each of us having something that approximated a private moment.
It was just enough time for the sun to work over my pale cheeks and
nose and even the tops of my fingers, burning every exposed bit of me
to a painful but dimly nostalgic crisped pink.

*

Nigel told me I should get my things in order in case they killed me. He
said I should write down anything I wanted to say to my family, or tell
it to him at the windowsill, and he would—if he were lucky enough to
live through this and get out—deliver it to my family. Final thoughts,
apologies, an agonized declaration of love, a last will, a dispensation of
my worldly belongings, whatever it was. This was my chance. I tried
not to be offended by the idea of it, the idea that I would die and he
would live. He was, he argued, being practical.

"Just think about it and let me know," he said.

"I don't want to," I said back.

I thought of him now mainly as a voice, disembodied and floating, like a field of energy. I imagine I was the same for him. Nearly every interaction between us played out in the soft acoustics of the alleyway behind our house.

Once, when I was coming back from the bathroom, Nigel had opened the door to his room and stood waiting at the threshold for me to pass by. I tried not to look shocked by the change in his appearance in the eight weeks since we'd been separated. He was dressed in a sleeveless white tank top with a sarong wrapped around his waist. He was extremely thin, heavily bearded, his skin sallow. His blue eyes were watery and a little jaundiced, the kind of thing you'd see in a very old man. I was my own horror show. I could read it on Nigel's face. I was rickety and pale, and I'd seen in my compact mirror the white fungus creeping across my face, crusting on my cheeks like ribbons of dried salt. At his door, I mouthed the words "Look at me," as in *Look at what I've become.* I smiled and shrugged, and he did, too. There was no changing it. We were happier, probably, thinking of each other as voices crisscrossing the alleyway.

Taking one more risk before moving away, I reached for Nigel's hand and held it. For a full thirty seconds we stood there, locked on to each other, saying nothing.

Seven days came and went. I waited on edge for Donald or Ahmed or Romeo to show up and take me away. The seventh night passed with excruciating slowness. I awoke on the eighth morning in my room, unable to muster anything but dread. Automatically, I recalculated: When Donald declared that my family had one week to cough up the ransom money, he must have meant that they'd wait seven days and *then* kill me. Which meant now or soon after. The eighth day passed and then the ninth. Something vaguely like hope began to crackle, a single ember in an otherwise extinguished pit. I waited for a sign. None of the leaders had visited our house. The captain's phone never rang. I spied on the boys through the tiny keyhole in my door, which gave me a slot view of their lives on the patio. I watched them praying, sleeping, eating, and drinking tea. In the late afternoons, after teatime, the boys often gathered around Captain Skids, who sat on a low circular wall—probably a garden planter in better times—and delivered lectures on what seemed to be military matters. Sometimes he'd stand up and demonstrate a maneuver with a gun.

I watched the boys try to pass the long hours. When they weren't praying or listening to Skids, I'd seen them meticulously plucking hairs from their own armpits using their fingernails, keeping up with the Prophet's rules about hygiene.

I was growing desperate for some signal that the immediate threat had passed. In my care package, there had been several sheets of Somali phrases with the English translations printed next to them. With phrases like "Does anything make the pain better?" and "Please don't shoot: We are doing everything we can to save lives," it was clear the sheets were meant for foreign doctors and nurses doing medical missionary work in Somalia. I studied them carefully, looking for a way to reach out to Captain Skids, who rarely came to my room but was the only person in the house likely to know what was happening with ransom negotiations. Copying a mishmash of Somali words and phrases onto a piece of notebook paper, I composed a letter meant to ask for news and to assure him that my parents at home were doing all they could to get some money together. The letter said something like: "Peace be upon you. It is one week. What is the situation? Please tell me. We are doing everything we can to save lives." At the bottom, I signed it "Amina."

Later that day, I knocked on my door and signaled for Jamal to come see me. I handed him the letter and asked him please to give it to the captain and please to ask for a response. Jamal studied the piece of paper. I watched him first start to smile and then to giggle.

"Is it okay?" I said.

Jamal composed himself. He folded the note in two, still grinning. "Yes, okay," he said. "I will give."

Within minutes, I could hear them all laughing on the porch. Through my keyhole, I saw my note being passed around, the boys leaning in, sputtering with glee over my chunked-together bits of Somali. Soon they were falling down with laughter, the hilarity growing, their voices elevated as the letter got reread and reinterpreted. It

was the hardest I'd heard them laugh the whole time we'd been prisoners. I caught a glimpse of Captain Skids; even he was swept up in
the guffaws. The boys were talking excitedly, cracking one another up,
creating what I guessed was a whole flow of secondary jokes about me
and my words. It was my gift to them, I suppose, a little diversion on a
hot day. I'd sent the message out, and now I knew that nothing would
come back. I'd get no answer.

You're welcome, I thought from behind my door. *You motherfuckers,
enjoy.*

*

Earlier in December, our captors had celebrated Eid again. The holiday comes twice each year in the Muslim calendar—once to mark the
end of Ramadan, the breaking of the fast; and once two months later,
around the time of the hajj, the annual pilgrimage to Mecca. This one
was the second type of Eid, called Eid al Adha. It was similar to the last
Eid, the boys washing and dressing themselves with extra care, food
and prayers in more abundance. I spied on the festivities through my
keyhole, watching as our captors came and went from services at the
mosque, as Skids went out and returned with a big pot of food. He
came to my room himself and delivered a tin plate with a few pieces
of goat's meat, taking a second plate to Nigel. Jamal brought us each
three foil-wrapped toffees. Later that day, we were summoned to join
the whole group as they prayed in a big empty room at the front of
the house. Because I was a woman, I was expected to perform my
prayers in the back, which was a vast relief. I'd gotten so lazy about my
praying, I worried they'd notice that I'd almost forgotten how to do it
properly. As the straggler, the sole member of the last row, I only had
to follow along.

Returned to our rooms, standing at our respective windowsills,
Nigel and I made a decision—something small and also big—which
was to save our toffees for later, for Christmas. Was it pessimism or
pragmatism that told us we weren't going home before then? I don't
know, but the thought of it was so stark, so totally miserable, I figured
we should at least prepare. I couldn't bear the idea that I'd be apart

from my family for the holiday, stuck in a hot room with nothing but a mattress, a mosquito net, and a piece of brown linoleum, still enduring Abdullah's assaults, still praying for a way out.

Christmas was the one time of year when my brothers surfaced at home, when my grandparents and father and Perry congregated to eat my mother's roast turkey, when we took pictures and felt like a regular, united family. As the day drew closer, it seemed certain that even in the wake of my near execution, there was to be no change in the stalemate between our captors and our governments or our captors and our families. Nigel and I started to make more plans. We had the toffees, to begin with. I had stored mine in the lineup of care-package treasures I kept next to my mattress, right next to my St. Ives body lotion. We agreed to exchange gifts and write stories for each other—stories of the best Christmases we'd ever spent, recorded in exacting, drawn-out detail, especially the parts about food.

I worked hard on my story, pulling up long-past memories of the Christmas my mom had surprised us with a trip to Disneyland, with a room at the Holiday Inn and an extravaganza of rides for me and my brothers. I wrote it all down for Nigel's benefit and for mine. For his gift, I chose a white hourglass-shaped plastic bottle of cough syrup that had come in the care package and painstakingly converted it into a little doll. I drew a smiling face on the top part and took one of my black socks and fashioned it into a tiny tailored sweater, complete with sleeves. I sliced up a Q-tip stick to serve as my needle and unwound strands of dental floss for thread. I used Nigel's beard trimmers—which he'd left at my request on the window ledge in the bathroom—to do the cutting. I embroidered three words—"My Little Buddy"—on the front of the doll's sweater. I then made Nigel a Christmas card containing a pumped-up advertisement for his new toy. "Never feel alone again: Little Buddy is here!" Finally, I took out a blank sheet of paper and drew striped candy canes all over it, tucking Nigel's gift inside as if it were wrapping paper, securing the whole thing with more dental floss. I made him a stocking, using more paper, stitched together with more floss, and stuck my three toffees inside.

On Christmas morning, somewhat brazenly, I walked down the hallway with a bulge under my dress and left it all on the high ledge in our bathroom—the gift, the stocking, even the full notebook containing my story. I knocked on the wall to tell Nigel to go get it. A while later, he knocked again, instructing me to retrieve some things he'd left for me, a wrapped gift and a decorated paper stocking with his toffees in it.

We spent the morning singing carols—"Hark the Herald Angels Sing," "Joy to the World," things like that. We sucked our toffees down slowly, one after the other, until each became a grain on the tongue. Nigel's story was about the Christmas when he and his siblings bought airplane tickets for their parents to go to Ireland. At our windows, we asked each other follow-up questions to drag the stories out. I loved him in that moment, on that day, more than I'd ever loved anyone, in a way that reached past the standard boy-girl love and hit some sort of deeper bedrock. I loved him as a human, with no complication.

Blessedly, our captors left us alone. We sang "Little Drummer Boy" and, each of us throaty with emotion, we sang "Silent Night." Finally, standing at his sill, Nigel opened his little buddy with an amused gasp, and then I was allowed to open my gift. For the stocking, he'd used red ballpoint ink to color two full notebook pages. He'd torn them into matching sock-shaped sides and then sewn them together with dental floss, adding a dried strip of a Wet Ones to the top, as a stand-in for white fur trim. Inside it was a small box—the cardboard insert from a package of cologne Donald had brought Nigel months earlier—wrapped in hand-decorated paper. Inside the box was a delicate-looking bracelet he'd made for me, a chain of saved-up pop-tops from his old tuna cans, carefully and intricately strung together with threads and accessorized by colorful little tassels he'd pulled from the edges of his sarong, tying one to each link in the chain. It was clear he'd spent days putting it all together, using his fingertips to make knots the size of poppy seeds. It was done with care, made with exactly what he had. It was better than anything you'd find at Tiffany's. It was better, in that moment, than anything I'd ever received.

30

Escape

Was there some way out? There had to be. In January, we
started talking about trying to escape. It began one day when
Nigel announced he'd been studying the window in the bathroom and
thought we could climb through it.

I, too, had looked at that window, plenty of times. I saw no possibilities there. The window was about eight feet off the bathroom
floor, recessed far back in the thick wall up near the ceiling, with a
ledge maybe two feet deep, almost like an alcove or a cubbyhole.
What was at the end of that alcove hardly counted as a window. It was,
rather, a screen made of bricks with a few decorative gaps in between
them, serving as ventilation holes for the bathroom. The bricks were
cemented together. And then, as if that weren't enough, laid horizon-
tally in front of the bricks was a series of five metal bars anchored into
the window frame.

"Are you crazy?" I said to Nigel. "It's impossible. How would we
get out?"

"You should crawl up there," he said. "I've been looking at the
bricks. The mortar is crumbling. We could dig it out."

"Yeah, but the bars . . ."

"I think I could pull them loose. They're not that secure. I don't
know," he said, sounding not entirely confident, "but I think it could
work."

I was doubtful. The idea was crazy for other reasons, the most obvious one being that if we were caught trying to escape, I felt sure our captors would either kill us or punish us in ways we didn't want to imagine. Besides that, having been driven into the desert, I'd seen the outside world—our immediate surroundings—a landscape of big bonfires and young men wandering around with guns. If we were to run, it wasn't as if we were running toward any certain safety. Finally, too, there was the matter of the three Somali men being held captive with us—Abdi, Marwali, and Mahad—and what might happen to them if we got out. If we ran, I was convinced they'd be killed. And I could see no way that five of us would manage to escape together.

I hardly knew the three Somalis, but I felt a sense of kinship with them and a responsibility for having gotten them captured in the first place. Whenever I was in the hallway, I found myself glancing in the direction of their door, where their shoes—two sets of sandals and a pair of Western-style hiking boots that belonged to Abdi—were always arranged in a neat line, presumably so they could slip into them when it was time to visit their bathroom outside. Every so often, I'd catch sight of one of them sitting there in the light, reading the Koran or sometimes stitching a piece of clothing. What I knew of them came only from these narrow glimpses and sounds that carried through the hallway and from what little we'd learned before being kidnapped. Abdi struck me as an earnest family man. Marwali, the driver from the Shamo Hotel, seemed more boisterous. I appreciated the sound of his laughter in the house. He seemed to chuckle easily and often, despite the circumstances. Mahad, who'd come from the medical clinic we'd been planning to visit on the day we were kidnapped, appeared to be extremely religious, loudly reciting verses from the Koran through much of the day.

As we moved toward our fifth month of captivity, Jamal remained the best source of information on what was going on with our captors and our families back at home.

"Any news?" I asked one day as he carried in the morning bag of food.

"There is no news," he said, shaking his head, adding with a sigh, "*Inshallah*, this is done soon."

When I asked when the leaders would next visit, he pursed his lips, wearing an expression of slight distress. He said, "I don't know." They hadn't come in nearly a month.

It was only through Jamal and his penchant to speak English, to linger and gossip in our rooms, that we knew the boys, to some degree, also felt like hostages, living as they were under the thumb of the captain and the group's increasingly invisible leaders. They were eating poorly, Jamal said. The guard named Yahya, who was no more than eighteen or nineteen, had missed the birth of his first child earlier in the month, though Skids had granted him a few days' leave to go home for a visit. Jamal had appealed to take time off and marry Hamdi, but Skids had denied him, saying he had to wait until the ransom money came in and the Program—all of them referred to our captivity as "the Program"—was finished.

We all wanted it to be soon, every last soul in that house. I fell asleep at night thinking, *soon,* and I woke up in the morning and called the word back. *Soon, soon.* I believed it enough to think we shouldn't try to dig bricks out of the bathroom window, that we should trust *soon* was coming.

Until one day I stepped out into the hallway, headed toward the shower, and noticed a new quiet. It was January 14, a Wednesday. The shoes outside Abdi, Marwali, and Mahad's door were gone, all three pairs. It appeared they'd been moved. My hope was that they'd been released, though I knew it was unlikely. Our captors wouldn't want three witnesses roaming free.

A while later, I was able to ask Abdullah what had happened to our Somali colleagues. He didn't hesitate. Seeming pleased with himself, he lifted a finger to his throat and drew it in a straight line across. My mind flashed to the desert, to the lonely acacia tree under the moon. Had the leaders come in the middle of the night and taken them? How had I not heard anything? Was Abdullah telling the truth? When Nigel and I met up at the window, he said that he, too, had asked about the men's whereabouts. While Jamal had given a vague answer, suggesting that maybe they had been let go, Abdullah had made the same emphatic throat-slitting gesture. My stomach started to churn. The worst case seemed the most likely: The Somali guys had been killed. And it was our fault. Before we were captured, Abdi had proudly shown me pictures of his children—two boys and a girl, smiling little kids in school uniforms, who now, thanks to me, had no father.

Every part of me felt weak. The disappearance of Abdi and the others told us something important about our captors. Money to feed and house our group seemed to be running out. Desperation was setting in. That they could kill their fellow Somalis, Muslim brothers all three, didn't bode well for me and Nigel. There was no question in my mind: We had to get out.

*

It took some effort to pull myself up to the window in the bathroom, to check the possibilities. I had to stand with one foot planted on either side of the toilet seat, reaching up past my shoulders to get my hands on the ledge, and from there, to boost myself up, as if levering my way out of a swimming pool. The alcove leading to the window was too shallow to hold all of me, so I leaned forward, holding my weight with my elbows, stomach balanced on the ledge, legs dangling heavily back toward the ground.

With my chest pressed against the ledge and my face up close to the window, I could see instantly that Nigel was right. The bricks covering the opening were only loosely cemented. The mortar between them crumbled at my touch, coming away in small cascades of white dust. From my room, I'd brought my pair of nail clippers, and using the little knifelike apparatus meant to dig dirt from beneath the fingernails, I was able to reach between the metal bars blocking the window and poke into some of the deeper, rubbly spaces between the bricks, where I felt a promising bit of movement, the suggestion of bigger fault lines. With some diligent chipping, it seemed possible we could remove a few rows of bricks, creating an opening just big enough to fit through.

The bars over the bricks were another matter. They were about three feet long and appeared to be sunk deep into the walls on either side of the window, though I could see that Nigel had already managed to loosen one of them from its anchor points. He'd sworn to me that he could muscle at least one more out of its hold. Feeling elated, I dropped back to the bathroom floor, covered in grit and cobwebs. I hurried back to my room, for the first time in months not thinking about danger or hunger or worry, consumed instead by the idea that we could make a hole to the outside, a body-sized hole, and slip through it.

Standing at our windows, we began to work on a plan. What time of day would we go? What would we bring? Which direction would we run? Who would we seek out and what would we say? The considerations were enormous. We debated whether it would be best to escape at night, while most of the guards were asleep and we were less likely to cause a ruckus running down the street. Recalling the bonfires, I assumed night was a more dangerous time to be out. And maybe, too, we wanted to cause a ruckus. Maybe we needed to be loud and visible, forcing someone to call the authorities, whoever the authorities in these parts might be. Or did we find a sympathetic person and beg to use a cell phone, hoping he or she had enough calling credit to sustain a one-minute call to Canada or Australia? Or a cheaper call to Ajoos, whose number I had written on a hidden-away scrap of paper. Or to the Somali director of the World Food Programme office in Mogadishu, whose number I'd also been carrying when we were first taken.

Nigel and I agreed that we needed to put distance between us and our captors as quickly as possible and that we'd be well served by trying to blend in. For me, in an abaya and hijab, looking like any other woman on the street wouldn't be so hard. But there was no hiding Nigel's white skin. We considered whether I should loan him one of my Somali outfits and he could pose as a very tall woman, fully covered, but even my longest abaya would reach only halfway down his calves. We knew, too, that dressing Nigel in drag was the kind of thing that could backfire on us in the end. Every option we explored felt like a blind corner. Every idea seemed like a gamble, with myriad ways it could go awry.

We spent many hours discussing the plan. All the while, we traded shifts in the bathroom, hauling ourselves onto the ledge with fingernail clippers in hand, chiseling at the window mortar in hurried five- and ten-minute bursts. The work was gratifying, like surgery or digging for gold. Sometimes I'd grind and get dust; other times, with some careful prying, I'd manage to extract a nice little slab of fully intact cement.

Because my door was in easy sight of the veranda, I had to be more cautious—knocking for permission to leave my room, never staying too long in the bathroom, carefully brushing off all signs of white mortar dust before stepping back into the hallway. I also realized how frail I'd become, despite all the deliberate hours spent walking. Although my legs were strong, the muscles in my arms were wasted and wobbly. Midway through the second day, my elbows started to buckle every time I tried to pull myself up to the window ledge, and I had to give up.

Nigel continued to work diligently. He was in a better position than I to make undetected trips to the bathroom. I kept watch through my keyhole, ready to create a distraction if any of the boys started heading his way. Using my medical phrase sheets, I cobbled together a little message and wrote the Somali words on a piece of paper to carry with me when we escaped, tucked in the front pocket of my jeans, which I'd wear beneath my black abaya. "Please help. I am Muslim. Don't be frightened." I rehearsed the Somali syllables over and over, not 100 percent sure of what I was saying: *Fadlan i caawi. Waa islaan. Ha baqin.* On a separate tiny scrap of paper, I copied the few Somali phone numbers I had in my reporter's notebook, putting that in my pocket as well.

Each time I visited the bathroom, I looked up at the window to track Nigel's progress. Though he was careful to cover his work, sliding each brick he'd removed back into place, tucking it in with stray nuggets of cement, you could see the disturbance, the skewed bricks and mounds of loose mortar sitting on the sill. I tried to take solace in the knowledge that the boys walked into our bathroom only once or twice a week—mainly to take the oversized bucket we used for water and refill it. But still, the risk we were taking felt suddenly huge. Since Abdi and the others had disappeared, I'd felt too stressed to eat much, and now my stomach went into a full clench.

*

On the start of the third day, Nigel declared that he'd carved out the final brick. He now had to contend with the metal bars, but he already had that first one loose and thought it would take only one more to create enough space to pass through. Before that, though, we had to recommit ourselves to escaping. Once he yanked out the two bars, the side walls would likely collapse. There would be no masking the debris in the bathroom. We'd really have no choice but to run.

We decided that we should make our break that same night, slipping out the window at about eight P.M., just after the evening's final prayer. We had hardly slept in three days, hopped up on the perpetual buzz of adrenaline. It seemed pointless to wait any longer. I was worried that if we did, our nerves would give us away.

We hoped that the darkness would serve as a sort of camouflage. We'd try to disguise Nigel as a sick person, an old man, draping a sheet over his head to cover his skin, wrapping his shoulders in a blanket that would hide his hands. I'd pretend to be guiding him, burying my hands in the folds of the same blanket. Both of us would hunch deliberately, with our faces cast down, as if hurrying to a doctor. We'd carry a Koran in my little backpack to prove we were Muslim, that we weren't enemies. We'd look for a door to knock on, a house that somehow seemed like a friendly house, a place with women and children living inside. I was focused on finding a woman. I hadn't come into contact with one in five months. A woman, I thought, wouldn't turn us away.

We were banking on that night being like every other night in the house, governed by the mind-numbing clockwork routine—prayer followed by dinner, followed by prayer, followed by bedtime for everyone but the two boys on guard duty, who would sit outside, talking idly in the darkness.

I was startled, then, when Jamal arrived in my room with dinner a full hour ahead of when the meal usually came.

"*Asalaamu Alikum,*" he said with a slow smile.

My thoughts spun. Did they suspect something? What was happening? I'd spent the last week so anxious, I felt like I was releasing some sort of new scent, a giveaway to our plans.

I returned Jamal's greeting, sick with worry.

He gestured for me to pull out my tin plate and lay it on the floor. He then opened a plastic bag and slid something onto it—a slender piece of deep-fried fish, golden brown and glistening with oil. From his pocket, he pulled out two small limes and set them next to the fish. Finally, he produced two hard-boiled eggs and placed them on the plate as well.

It was protein. He'd been worried about my appetite. This was a gift, and Jamal was proud of it. "You like?" he said, pointing at the fish. "I can get for you every day at the market, but only at night. They don't make in the morning."

We stood for a few seconds, regarding each other. I gave myself an internal kick. *Snap out of it.* "Oh, Jamal," I said, lifting the plate, "this is so nice of you." I smiled at him gratefully, feeling a touch of guilt. I hoped the leaders wouldn't punish him too badly after I was gone.

Alone again, I sat on the floor and forced myself to eat the food, not just because it was fuel but also so I didn't arouse suspicion. I then went through the motions of the day's last prayer. When it was over, as I'd planned with Nigel, I rapped on my door and pushed it open slightly to see who responded. It was Abdullah who peered down the hallway, which meant that he was on nighttime guard duty. My heart dropped a little. Abdullah was less lazy than some of the others. He liked to roam.

"*Mukuusha*," I said in Somali, pointing at my stomach. *Bathroom.* "I am feeling sick. Very sick."

Without hesitating, Abdullah snapped his fingers to indicate that I could go. Normally, I didn't make a bathroom trip after the last prayers, but stomach problems were something they never argued with. It also bought me extra time once I was there. In this case, Jamal's slab of fried fish only bolstered the viability of my cause.

Slowly and coolly, I left my room and walked down the hallway in the direction of the bathroom. Earlier in the evening, I'd smuggled my backpack under my dress and left it on the window ledge. Nigel stood waiting for me at the doorway to his room. Out of Abdullah's sight, we accelerated. I figured we had ten minutes, fifteen tops, before he'd figure out that I hadn't returned from the bathroom and would come walking down to check on me.

Inside the bathroom, I drew the curtain and quickly pulled the black abaya from my backpack, putting it on over the red dress. Nigel climbed onto the toilet and reached up to start removing the window bars. He'd sneaked into the bathroom earlier and done some advance work, wrenching the bars out of the walls, then putting them back in place, propped up precariously by chunks of loose cement. Despite his efforts to conceal it, the walls on either side of the window at this point looked fully torn up, with gashes in the plaster where the bars once were set. The goal now was to move everything out of the way while staying perfectly quiet.

Within a minute, Nigel had wriggled the first bar free and handed it down to me. Then came the second bar, its weight cool in my hands. I laid both bars on the floor next to the sink, my nerves making me dizzy. Swiftly, Nigel heaved himself up from the toilet onto the alcove, and lying on his belly with his legs pointed back to the floor, he began gingerly unstacking the bricks from the window frame, moving them to the outer part of the sill. I could hear him panting. One brick came away, then two, then three, then four. When they were all out, he jumped back down and motioned that we were ready. It was time to go. Nigel interlaced his fingers into a stirrup for me to step into and then boosted me toward the window and the eighteen-inch gap that was now there.

I looked through that hole for no longer than two seconds, but it was enough to see everything. I could see the alleyway beneath, and the darkness of a village with no lights and everything uncertain beyond. We'd calculated about a twelve-foot drop to the ground, given that the house sat on a concrete foundation. We'd worried about breaking our ankles. We'd worried about so many things, and as I stared at the gap in the window, every one of those things felt there, right on the other side, along with our freedom. As we'd planned, I turned around and started to back my way through the remaining window bars, sliding both feet through the gap—with two bars above me and one bar beneath—lowering myself slowly into the air outside. The night was cool and moist. I could feel a breeze on my ankles. It worked until it didn't: I pushed myself back and felt my rear end jam up against one of the bars still in the window. I pushed again but went nowhere. The gap was too small. If I couldn't fit, Nigel never would.

From below, he was getting anxious. "Go, go, come on," he whispered.

"I can't. It's not working." I thrust again at the bar to show him my predicament. His face looked stricken, his forehead slick with sweat. I said, "Can you take out another bar?"

"Not now," he said, almost hissing. "It makes too much noise."

The window ledge was a mess of bricks and broken mortar. Abdullah was probably starting to wonder why I wasn't back in my room. We were stuck—not just stuck but screwed.

Nigel waved a hand, telling me to climb down. "Get back to your room," he said. "Quickly. I'll try to fix this up."

"What about my backpack?"

"Leave it," he said. "I'll bring it with me. Just go, hurry."

I stripped off the black abaya and stuffed it in my backpack. Then I walked back to my room as casually as I could and closed the door noisily, to let Abdullah know I'd returned. I lay on my mattress in the dark, trying to muster one calm thought. I listened for Nigel in the bathroom. It sounded as if he was vomiting in the toilet, his own nerves having betrayed him. There was a shuffling in the hallway, a flashlight. Through my keyhole, I saw Abdullah making his way down the hall. Nigel, too, must have noticed the light coming, because within seconds he was out of the bathroom and in the hallway, mumbling something about being sick and needing more water to flush the toilet. There was quiet discussion, the light disappeared and then came back after a few minutes, and soon Nigel was back in the bathroom, alone.

I knew it was only a matter of hours before our plan was discovered—before one of our captors spotted the jerry-rigged pile of bricks and bent bars that comprised the bathroom window or just read the whole stupid plotline in my eyes.

When dawn broke and Hassam came to open our window shutters before prayer, Nigel and I talked, agreeing that we had to leave immediately. Quickly, we redrew the outline of our plan. We knew from the calls of the muezzin that there was a mosque somewhere close by. We decided we'd run there. It seemed like the one good option, a place to find a crowd. I accepted the morning bag of food from Jamal, trying hard not to make eye contact. We waited for the midday prayer, for the heat to arrive and the boys to start nodding off afterward. I knocked for the bathroom, and Nigel met me there, holding my backpack and abaya. Early that morning, he'd pulled out a third window bar. The mess of it was staggering. I waited while he quickly unstacked the bricks again. This time, my pulse throbbing, I didn't hesitate. I got one leg out the window and then the second. I slid a few inches on my stomach to lessen the distance to the ground, holding on to one of the remaining window bars for support, and then I let myself drop.

We hit the ground one right after the other, me and then Nigel, two soft thumps in the sand. My heart lifted and crashed with the impact.

Things were bad. I knew it the instant I touched the soil. Nothing looked like I thought it was going to look. Nothing appeared the way I'd planned it in my mind. I'd built a scene, a stage set for us to run through, based on the sliced-up view I'd had through my window. I remembered bits and pieces from the car ride that had brought us to the house. I remembered seeing camels, people walking on the street, rows of bushes, and a shabby little village with twists and turns and places to hide. I'd figured all of that would be waiting for us outside the window. But now, looking toward the ends of the alleyway, I understood with absolute dismay that I'd been wrong. To the left was a sideways-leaning fence made of patchwork pieces of colored tin and old oilcans that had been hammered flat. To the right was a row of shanties, built from more tin and pieces of loose burlap and other refuse. There wasn't a bit of vegetation in sight, beyond a few brambly thornbushes, low and leafless in the sand. More alarming was the sudden appearance of an emaciated child, a boy of maybe seven, standing only a few feet away from me, naked but for a pair of shorts, swaybacked and wide-eyed, staring at me in a shocked way, as if just about to let out a mighty scream.

I fixed my gaze on the boy, trying to smile and appear kindly. I lifted a finger to my lips. The child looked at me and then Nigel, his eyes getting bigger. Without a sound, he took off at a sprint—heading, I was sure, toward the first adult he could find.

It was as if a starting gun had been shot, as if a seismic disturbance had unsettled the air, rippling over the rooftops to the patio where our captors lay in repose. Everything became instinctual then. The colors went flat and the world went insane. Nigel and I didn't even look at each other. We just started, madly, to run.

31

My Sister

The boy had charged to the right; Nigel and I dashed left, down the narrow alleyway, along the side of the house and toward where it opened onto a street, about ten meters away. Our feet flailed in the deep sand. Both of us wore flip-flops, which slowed every step. Now that we were running, there was no keeping Nigel's head covered with the sheet we'd brought, no pretending that he was a sick Somali man and I his gentle caretaker. There was no pretending anything. Every strategy we'd plotted at our windowsills had flown out of our heads. Every bit of reason had lifted away. Our bodies floundered in the free air as if our bones had gone to rubber during those months in the house.

At the end of the alley was a rutted sand road, and on the road there were shacks and some market stalls and the land beyond was a flat brown.

Nigel was yelling—another diversion from the plan—at nobody and everyone, screaming *I caawin, I caawin,* the Somali words for "help me."

I saw it all in a high-speed panic, which is to say I barely saw it, or caught it only in flashes—a half-collapsed wall, a few nervous goats, a man standing in an arched doorway, a donkey lashed to a cart by two thin poles. We ran through it and past it, this landscape we'd spent hours conjuring in our minds, this place to which we were colossally mismatched, me behind Nigel, Nigel shouting, the heat warping the air around us, all of it with the unreality of a bad dream. Up ahead, several women walked together in the sunlight, their hijabs flowing behind them in waves of hot pink and yellow. We shouted and moved faster, heading toward them—some women, *thank God*—only now the women were looking over their shoulders at us, murmuring and pointing, their faces floating inside their robes. Seeing we were headed toward them, they started to run.

More people spotted us and fled. The street emptied, everyone scattering ahead of us. Later, I would look back on it and realize that if you are running in a place like Somalia, everyone understands that you are running from danger. Which means that they also should run.

At the corner, we instinctively turned left, racing out onto a wider road. I looked for the mosque but couldn't see it. We'd deliberately timed our escape for the midday prayer, knowing we'd find a roomful of people at the mosque, banking on the hope that we'd encounter some sympathy there. Finally, Nigel looked back and spotted a minaret, a knitting needle in the blue sky over my shoulder. We reversed direction and bolted toward it. The mosque was a hundred meters in front of us, then fifty, then ten.

Ahead, I saw a young man standing in place, watching us with interest. I recognized him at once. He was the neighbor I'd seen through my window months earlier, the man who'd locked eyes with me across the yard.

I charged right up to him, adjusting my head scarf so it was tighter around my face, the words tumbling out. "Help, help, please, do you speak English?"

Appearing unsurprised, he nodded.

"You have seen me," I said. "Do you remember? The window?"

He again showed that he understood. Nigel had stopped running and come to join us.

I continued, speaking a careful English while trying to catch my breath. "We are Muslims. We have been kidnapped. They have kept us five months. Can you go with us inside the mosque?"

The man paused a second, as if weighing his options. Something told me that he felt guilt for having lived next door to us all these months and done nothing to help.

"Come with me," he said.

Flanking him on either side, Nigel and I race-walked toward the mosque, each keeping a hand hooked under one of the man's arms, almost dragging him, or at least preventing him from changing his mind.

The mosque building was tall and wide, painted green and white with a crescent moon on top and a short set of steps leading to a wooden platform and an entrance. The platform was heaped with shoes, signaling that the place was full of people. Moving up the stairs behind the neighbor and Nigel, I felt the first trickle of relief, a feeling so unfamiliar that I almost couldn't identify it.

Just then, a lone person came skidding around the street corner and halted maybe thirty feet away. It was Hassam—market boy and master of my Koran lessons—now just a thin dark figure against a canvas of sand. He wore a white tank top that hung from his bony frame, plus a sarong and no pants, a sign that he'd run from the house in a rush. His expression was one of disbelief and fury and selfish terror.

Then another of our captors rounded the corner—Abdullah, unmasked and carrying his gun.

I bolted forward into the mosque, forgetting to remove my shoes. What I saw first was a field of men—kneeling, sitting, milling about in small groups. There were prayer mats spread in lines across a concrete floor. Heads turned. A few people stood up. The interior of the mosque was vast, a single room with a vaulted ceiling, about the size of a gymnasium. I heard myself calling out Somali words and English words and also some Arabic, my brain blurry with distress. I shouted *Help!* and *May the blessings of Allah be upon you!* and *I am Muslim!* and *Please help me!* and *Help me!* and *Please help!* Nigel, too, was yelling.

A crowd magnetized around us, men with puzzled faces, some

showing alarm. I saw our neighbor talking to a few of them, gesturing and pointing, as if explaining what he knew. And then Abdullah was upon me, having blasted through the door with Jamal just behind him, both wearing sarongs.

Abdullah lunged and I dodged, feeling his grasp slip off my shoulder. I ran to a far corner of the room, where another group of men sat on the floor. I said every Arabic word I could think of as they lifted their bearded faces toward me, appearing dumbstruck. Off to the side, Jamal had corralled Nigel against a wall and was hitting him repeatedly in the head, pounding on him with a closed fist, beating him with every ounce of strength he had. Nigel, I could see, was trying to hit him back, all the while shouting, "Jamal! Jamal!" as if to remind him that, in a weird way, they'd once been friends.

Just as Abdullah was about to reach me again, I ducked through a doorway leading out into the air, not thinking whether it was good or bad to exit the mosque, making a move that was desperate and frenzied.

My fear organized itself into speed. With Abdullah two paces behind me, I leaped over the three stairs that descended from the side door of the mosque, landing in heavy sand beneath the white glare of afternoon sun. I ran and he chased, but now I was fast and light, shedding my flip-flops as I moved. There were thickets of bushes surrounding this side of the mosque, and I passed through them like a deer, the urgency of the moment eclipsing the sensation of the thorns—two inches long and straight as pins—slicing into my ankles and bare feet, one of them driving itself like a torpedo into the soft skin beneath the toenail of my left big toe. A gunshot ripped overhead, hollowing out the air. I looked back to see Abdullah, who had stopped running long enough to fire at me. His gun blasted again. My mind looped back toward the mosque. Nigel was inside. Inside was safer than outside. Keeping my shoulders low, I did a high-speed twenty-meter end run around Abdullah, who was running toward me but slowed by the weight and bulk of his gun. I made another pass through the thornbushes, throwing myself back up the stairs and into the mosque.

The scene inside was oddly calm. Nigel had managed to shed Jamal and was sitting, not quite placidly but pretend-placidly, at the front of the mosque, in the semicircular area that served as the imam's pulpit, surrounded by a loose cluster of maybe fifteen bearded men, most of them standing. Rushing to join Nigel, I saw Jamal and young Mohammed on the outskirts of the group, pacing and anxious, hands on guns. Whatever had happened, the power dynamic had reversed itself. Somebody had put the boys in their place. I dropped to my knees next to Nigel, who was speaking English with some of the men, sounding like he was answering to some skepticism that he was Muslim.

I remembered the backpack on my back, which held my Koran and two English-language books that our captors had given me early on, a small palm-sized purple paperback called *Hijab,* which was printed in Saudi Arabia and advocated the full veiling of a woman's body, and another one, based on the *hadith,* also addressing the customs of Islamic womanhood.

I fumbled with the books, putting them into the hands of the men around us. "See? See?" I said. "We are good Muslims. Please help us." I was begging. I reminded them that Muslims help Muslims. It was their duty.

Several of the men began to page carefully through my books, examining them with interest, passing them on for others to see. There was a large, low window to one side of the pulpit, and I could see a woman, sheathed entirely in black, peeking through it, until one of the men strode to the window and slammed its metal shutters closed.

Abdullah had reentered the mosque. I saw him creeping his way into the group of bystanders, his gun canted loosely in my direction, sweat gliding through his hair and shining his cheeks. In five months, this was the first time I'd had a clear look at him without a scarf covering his face. I was accustomed to his widely spaced eyes, but now they had a context, set beneath the broad half-dome of his forehead. He had a head of curly close-cropped hair and a sparse beard that made him look more like a kid.

Catching my eye through the sea of other people's shoulders, he sneered. I looked away quickly.

Nigel, meanwhile, was loudly reciting a *surah* like a schoolboy before the assembled onlookers. Dozens of new people were pouring into the room, some of them in face scarves and carrying weapons. Who knew who they were? What surprised me was how many of the men around us seemed to speak some English.

One of the men explained to us that someone was phoning the local imam, who was in a different neighborhood but would come to hear our story and give his judgment. *"Inshallah,* everything will be fine," he said, indicating that we should remain seated on the floor. *"Inshallah,* maybe fifteen minutes."

I felt relieved by this. An imam, I figured, would want to help us. I could hear Abdullah and Jamal arguing—politely—with some of the men.

Abruptly, a woman parted the crowd, elbowing her way past the men with the guns, through the chaos and the quarrelling. I recognized her. It was the woman who'd been looking through the window. She wore a black abaya and full hijab, including a niqab draped over her nose and mouth, covering everything but her eyes. Every man in the place was staring at her. The woman noticed no one. She came right over to me, kneeling down at my side without a word. Automatically, I reached for her hand. Her fingers wrapped around mine. I felt, for a second, safer than I'd felt in ages.

Her eyes were brown and somehow so familiar that it was as if I knew them from somewhere. The tops of her hands had been painted with delicate, tendriling patterns of rust-colored henna, the sort of ornament that one woman draws painstakingly on another. She was speaking in Somali to the men around us. I watched her, my nerves firing. I couldn't understand what she was saying. I knew she was helping me somehow. I heard distress in her voice. When she looked at me, her eyes swam with emotion.

Without thinking, I reached out and brushed my fingers over her face, feeling the warmth of her cheek beneath the fabric. Amid the confused din in the mosque, I pulled her toward me.

I said, "Do you speak English?"

"A little," she said, moving closer. "You are a Muslim?"

"Yes, from Canada."

"You are my sister then," she said. "From Canada."

She reached out both arms, and I let myself fall. I sank my face into the pillows of her heavyset body, which was lilacy with perfume. Her arms fit snugly around me. I felt the edges of my vigilance soften, the domino fall of my defenses, and began to cry. As men jabbered around us, the woman tightened her hold on me. It was the most comfort I'd known in half a year, more if you counted back through the lonely months in Iraq. I wanted to stay there forever. I wanted to tell her everything. Lifting my head to find her eyes again, I told the woman I'd been a prisoner, that I wanted to go home. My voice rose and fell unevenly. Uttering the word "home" caused me to sob. I pointed toward where Abdullah stood scowling at us, about ten feet away. "He is abusing me," I said, suddenly desperate. "He is raping me." To be sure she understood, I used my fingers to mimic the mechanics of sex.

I watched the woman's eyes get wide. She looked from me to Nigel, who nodded as if to confirm what I'd said.

"Oh, *haram*," the woman said, "*haram, haram*." She looked up to the crowd, her expression ferocious, holding my head against her chest, stroking my hair. She shouted a few agitated Somali words. A hush came over those around us. The woman was talking shrilly, in a blitz. She raised a finger and shook it at the men, delivering some sort of tongue-lashing. I felt a shudder pass through her body and realized that her eyes, too, ran with tears. Next to us, Nigel sat silently with his head bent, staring at the floor.

The dynamic in the room changed suddenly. Ahmed and Donald Trump had marched into the mosque, disheveled and furious, with Captain Skids right next to them, waving a pistol like a flag. Though they'd been absent for a month, they seemed able to materialize almost instantly in a crisis.

Ahmed located me and pointed a finger. "You!" he shouted. "YOU HAVE MADE A BIG PROBLEM!" People continued to flood into the room, all of them men. Clearly, the news of foreigners in the mosque was making its way through the village, the gossip at a high pitch. The air became stuffy and uncertain, filled with noise. Then came a loud, concussive crack, a gun going off somewhere inside the room.

The sound of it broke the spell, the holding pattern. People began to stampede, running in all directions. Another shot rang out. I saw Abdullah pushing through the crowd in my direction, his head lowered like a bull's. I screamed as he dove at me. I tried kicking, but he was strong. He had my feet in his hands. His gun was looped over one shoulder, swinging and hitting my legs as I thrashed. I felt myself sliding out of the Somali woman's arms. Abdullah was now dragging me in the direction of the side door. I clawed at the ground as he pulled. I don't remember any of the onlookers trying to stop him as he did.

It was only the woman who tried.

She clamped on to one of my wrists and pulled me back, using her weight for leverage, letting loose a torrent of Somali. For a few minutes, my body was strung between them, with Abdullah yanking my legs while the Somali woman, with both hands wrapped around my left arm, proved herself a stubborn anchor. When another man, someone I'd never seen, helped Abdullah by seizing my left leg and lurching us forward a few feet, I saw the woman, my protector, topple face-first. Undaunted, she used the break in contact to throw herself almost on top of me, repositioning her hands so that they were locked on to the flesh above my elbows. We were being dragged along—the two of us, linked like train cars—inch by inch across the floor of the mosque. My shoulder sockets ached to the point where I thought they'd pop.

Finally, she could hang on no longer. I felt the momentum shift as her hands fell away and Abdullah and the other man picked up speed. My abaya swept over the floor as we moved. As we reached the door, I managed to lift my head and look back. The woman was sprawled on the floor and weeping openly. Her head scarf and niqab had been torn off in the struggle, leaving her exposed. I could see that she was my mother's age, in her early fifties, with a gentle, plump face and high forehead. Her hair had been braided in tiny cornrows over her head. She still had one arm outstretched in my direction. Three men with guns now surrounded her.

Completing my ejection from the mosque, someone lifted my shoulders, maneuvering me roughly over the stairs outside the building and into a walled courtyard. I was kicking, twisting, flinging myself wildly, my elbows knocking the sandy ground. Once we were outside, the man who'd been holding my shoulders let me drop.

My abaya and the dress beneath it had ridden up over my waist. My jeans, which were already baggy because I'd lost so much weight, were slipping toward my ankles as Abdullah jerked me forward, holding my legs on either side of his chest as if he were pulling a cart. As we moved over the courtyard, my body skimming the dirt, I felt my frayed underwear sliding off as well. I was naked, basically, stomach to knees.

I craned my neck to look for some form of help or escape, but there was nothing—only about twenty men looking down at me. I was a spectacle on full display. I felt something wet hit my stomach and realized I'd been spat on. I heard murmuring but couldn't tell what was being said. We were moving past a metal gatepost marking the edge of the courtyard and the entry to the road, where there seemed to be an even larger crowd of people gathered. I reached out and caught the gatepost, latching on to it with both hands.

Abdullah turned to see what had stopped his progress. Beyond him and through the gate, I could see a blue truck waiting with its engine running. I was overcome by another rush of animal strength. I'd do anything not to reach that truck. Another gunshot echoed from inside the mosque. *Nigel*, I thought. *They've killed Nigel.* The thought was like a suck hole, a thing that could kill me. Abdullah pulled and I clung to the post, trying to kick my legs free. I spotted a woman's narrow face looking down at me. She was part of the crowd outside the gate, her expression unreadable. I screamed at her in English: "WHY WON'T YOU HELP ME?"

She looked stricken. "I don't speak English," she said in perfect English.

Suddenly, the knuckles on one of my hands exploded in pain. Someone had kicked my hand to loosen my grip on the pole. I howled and let go. Then I was being pushed to my feet and toward the truck, which had a double cab and four doors. Abdullah shoved me into the rear seat, but as he did, I saw one last opportunity: I rammed my foot into his crotch, hard, and watched him fall over backward.

I opened the door on the opposite side of the truck and ran, this time directly into the crowd, arms waving, ears ringing, pulling up my pants as I moved. I started reciting loudly the Arabic prayer that all Muslims say, the first *surah* of the Koran. I tried to make eye contact with everyone watching me. *Bismillahi ar-rahman ar-raheem. Al hamdu lillahi rabbi al-alamin. Ar rahman ar-raheem. Maliki yami d-di.n Iyaka na'budu wa iyyaka nasta in. Ihdina s-sirat al-mustaqim* . . . What it meant was "In the name of God, the compassionate, the merciful. Praise be to God, Lord of the Worlds. The compassionate, the merciful. Master of Judgement Day. You alone we worship, and to you alone we pray for help. Guide us to the straight path . . ."

I was saying it badly and rapidly and at the top of my lungs, but I was saying it to them—screaming it, really—to dozens of bystanders, trying to prove something—if not perfect faith, then affinity, and if not affinity, then the simple fact that, despite being wild-haired and dirty and utterly foreign, I was also human.

Nobody budged. Nobody seemed to know how to respond. They watched me, appearing more afraid than anything as I shouted my Arabic into a void. I yelled the words until I was hoarse, even as I felt someone's hands take hold of me from behind and start lifting me back toward the truck, even as I saw two other men hauling Nigel through the door of the mosque and in our direction. The sight of him brought a wash of solace and a hammer blow of anxiety. It had been all of forty-five minutes since we'd slipped through the window. We'd made it out but not truly out. We'd crossed the river only halfway.

He'd lived, I'd lived, but now for sure we were dead.

32

Tacky House

Stuffed into the backseat of the truck with Young Mohammed, Nigel and I held hands. I watched, dumbfounded, as two of the men from the mosque—unsmiling guys who, twenty minutes earlier, appeared to have been thoughtfully advocating for our freedom with the larger group—piled in with our captors, apparently having switched sides and joined the squad. One slid into the driver's seat next to Skids and Abdullah; the other sat himself wordlessly next to Nigel in the back. Jamal climbed into the truck bed. Doors slammed shut. The engine fired. Several people from the crowd waved goodbye.

Wherever we were going, it wouldn't be the same as what we'd left. I started to shake, and then I started to talk, delivering a last-ditch attempt at shame, directing my speech toward Young Mohammed next to me but, more generally, the rest of them, especially the new guys.

"How could you do this to us?" I said, watching the side of Mohammed's face as he stared straight ahead. "You say you're believers, but we're believers, too. You're holding us captive, and it's not right."

He had punched me several times before loading me into the car. My jawbone was sore. I waited for him to hit me now, but he didn't. He kept his gaze ahead as the truck boosted forward in the sand. Nobody in the vehicle said a thing. Nigel squeezed my hand. Through the windshield, I could see Ahmed and Donald driving in a station wagon ahead of us, half-enveloped in a cloud of yellow dust.

After about ten minutes of ripping over potholes, the truck blew a tire and careened to a stop. As it happened, we'd broken down right in front of a pink building bearing a sign that read MOGADISHU UNI-VERSITY, confirming for me that the houses they'd kept us in were close to—if not inside—the main city. The building's walls were pockmarked with bullet and mortar holes, making clear that student life was no walk in the park. With their guns, the boys directed us out and in the direction of Ahmed's station wagon, which had pulled up alongside. Ahmed stepped out. Over his shoulder, I caught glimpses of palm trees and low buildings. The urge to run again was like a tickle in my throat, a chance weighed against another chance, a rocket shot at nothing.

Suddenly, I felt more tired than I'd ever been in my life. I had no fight left.

We got into the new car with Donald, while Ahmed stayed behind with the broken-down truck. Skids, sitting on the passenger side, turned around and pointed at me and Nigel, then coolly put the finger to his own temple and motioned as if firing a gun.

"They're going to kill us," I said to Nigel, pointlessly. The message had been clear enough.

I noticed that one of Nigel's shirtsleeves had been ripped nearly off. His skin looked waxy, drained of color. Just then Mohammed, riding on the seat beside him, punched him in the face, hard. Nigel ducked his head and covered his eyes. I could tell he was trying not to cry.

He was saved from another blow by the ringing of Mohammed's cell phone, its ringtone the sound of croaking frogs. Without another glance at Nigel, Mohammed removed his phone from his pocket and answered it.

Talking just above a whisper, I started telling Nigel what I wanted him to say to my family if he should happen to live and I didn't. There was the obvious fact that I loved them, that I was sorry for the trouble I'd caused, for their grief. I told him to tell my mother she should go to India, since I thought she'd understand me better if she went there. "And tell my dad and Perry to go visit Thailand," I said, "because it would make them so happy."

Nigel said things back to me, messages for his parents, his siblings, his girlfriend—loving and sorry and hopeless, all of them, just like mine.

Mohammed crooned lovingly into his phone in Somali. I thought I could hear a child's voice prattling on the other end, laughing at whatever Mohammed was saying.

We drove through the streets, passing eucalyptus trees and lumbering minibuses and rubber tires strewn alongside the road. We passed buildings that were whitewashed and sun-weathered, like old bones. I saw men pushing wheelbarrows, women carrying pails, kids staring at traffic as it passed by. To me, everything now looked like a closed door, a reminder of how impervious Somalia was to our presence.

After a time, we stopped for gas, pulling up in front of a skinny old woman standing on a street corner next to several jerry cans. Skids handed some bills out the window, and she used a can to fill our tank. Nigel and I, in the backseat, were in plain sight. I looked at the woman imploringly, watching her eyes pass over us before she turned away.

We drove on. It seemed we were riding in circles with nowhere to go. I was convinced they'd wait till nighttime to kill us. Which meant we had hours to pass.

Donald, who'd shown us some empathy over the months, was sitting behind us in the hatchback. Taking a risk, I turned around and grabbed at his shirtsleeve. "You have to help us," I said. He pretended to be looking out the window. I added, "Please, please, please."

This caused Donald to snap. "You think you are the only ones?" he said, his voice edged with fury. "There are people from German, from Italian. They all go home easy." He was speaking about other hostages, probably people he'd read about in the news. He continued, "No one wants to pay for you, and now you have made trouble." He wrenched his sleeve from my grasp.

I sank into the seat of the car, feeling the aches start to override my adrenaline. My back and butt had been scraped raw by being dragged across the mosque. My feet were swollen and covered in dried blood from the thornbushes. Had they not been vaguely throbbing, I might have thought they belonged to someone else.

We turned from one road onto another before finally reaching some sort of destination—a house behind a wall, a house that, unlike the others we'd stayed in thus far, was clearly occupied. Children's shoes were strewn outside the doorway. Women's clothing hung on a line. Donald and Skids whisked us down a low hallway, past a number of closed doors, to a back room. They left us there, guarded by Abdullah and Mohammed. I could smell food cooking.

Immediately, I guessed that we were in the captain's home. The room we were standing in was a bedroom, and not just a bedroom but a full-blown frilly boudoir, with chintz curtains hung over the windows, a pink-flowered coverlet spread over a queen-sized bed, and a wooden dresser holding bottles of skin cream, perfume, and hair gels, all in a neat row.

We were in the interior of someone's life, someone's marriage, someone's sweet-smelling nest of pink. I could hear a woman talking loudly and furiously in Somali at the front of the house, likely protesting the sudden arrival of two foreigners and a mini-militia of unwashed teenagers with guns.

Donald returned. "Sit," he said, pointing at the floor.

Nigel and I sat against the wall opposite the bed while Donald began an interrogation. Mohammed and Abdullah stood over us, as if awaiting orders. Captain Skids posed questions in Somali. Donald translated with a blistering rage that held up across languages.

"Why did you run away?"

"How did you get out?"

"Who helped you?"

"Do you want to die?"

We answered every query more than once, with Donald berating us for being stupid and bad Muslims, with Nigel and me apologizing, swearing that nobody had helped us, saying that we didn't want to die, that we only wanted to go home.

Skids was pointing at me, his finger shaking with emotion.

Donald repeated the words in English. "It was *you*," he said. "This was your plan." In their minds, it was all my doing. I was, as I'd always been to them, the evil and untrustworthy woman.

They hit us both repeatedly. When I hunched over in pain, Moham-med slammed the butt of his gun into the space between my shoul-ders.

Donald finally boomed what seemed to be the culminating ques-tion: "Why," he sputtered, "did you say that we are fucking you?"

The words made me quake. Donald continued, "Do you know what fucking is? We could have done that, *subhanallah,* but we did not. You are a liar!"

The accusation hung in the air. I felt Abdullah blazing a warning with his eyes. All of them were looking hard at me.

My thoughts raced. This was my moment to expose Abdullah. Yet something in me couldn't do it. I was afraid. I was sure, without a doubt, that he'd deny what he'd done, and either way, it would again all be blamed on me.

I said to Donald, "The woman did not speak English! She did not understand. I told her I was afraid of the boys, I was worried they'd hurt me. I didn't use that word. It's not a good word. It's not good to say that. And I'm a Muslim." I turned to Nigel. "Tell them I didn't say that word. Tell them!"

Nigel said nothing.

Skids and Donald were conferring. Abdullah and Mohammed landed blows on my head and shoulders. I felt woozy, as if the ground had fallen away beneath me. When Donald walked from one side of the room to the other, I reached out and grabbed his pant leg, trying to make him look at me. "Help me, please. *Please.*"

"They're blaming you already," Nigel whispered to me. "I think you should just take this one."

These were words that would stay with me a long time. A long, long time. Through everything that was to come, through the many hours I'd have to think about it, I'd turn his words over in my mind like a rock in the hand, looking for some seam that wasn't there.

I think you should just take this one.

"I can't do that," I whispered back to Nigel.

Donald and Skids pressed on with their questioning. The boys kept on with their blows. All the while, Nigel offered nothing about how it had been his idea to climb out the window in the first place, or how we'd worked together to plot the whole endeavor. He owned no part of it.

The closest he came was saying to Donald at one point, his voice cracking with fear, "I'm sorry. I don't know why I did it. I shouldn't have listened." As in, he shouldn't have listened to me. Because I was just taking this one.

*

What did I feel toward Nigel? Hate, love, confusion, dependence, all of it bound up in a knot. In the moment, I couldn't unravel it in order to examine any individual strand. He was Nigel and I was Amanda, and we were stuck together in the most profound way. When I thought about it, it was not all that different from how I'd felt as a kid, caught inside the lurching, logrolling existence of my family. It's hard to be mad when you need someone so fundamentally.

I can't say for sure how long the questioning continued, whether it was another seven minutes or fifteen or fifty. All I could feel was my mind spiraling through a gap, into an empty, dark space with no walls and no floor, no connection to the world beyond.

What I thought was, *Now we are dying. They will hit us until we can't answer. They'll leave us only when we're dead.*

Eventually, Donald announced that he had to go. He shook his head as if he were fed up and exhausted by us. He was sitting on the edge of the mattress with the floral spread.

I didn't want him to go. I trusted Skids less than I trusted Donald. "Please don't leave," I said weakly. "Don't go."

Donald looked at me almost paternally. He patted a hand on the bed, indicating that I should come and sit next to him. Mohammed seemed to object, but Donald waved him off. Unsteadily, I rose to my feet and seated myself not far from Donald on the bed, my ribs aching with the motion.

He reached out and touched a hand lightly to my swollen cheek, causing a flare of pain. "Your face looks very bad," he said. He added that he had to leave and he was sorry for what would happen. "I don't know what it is," he said, "but it will not be good."

His cell phone rang, and he answered it with a brisk *Salaam*. Looking at me, he held the phone away from his ear. I could hear a woman's voice on the other end, speaking rapid-fire. "You see?" Donald said to me, rising to his feet, offering a quick smile. "I am late. I must go now."

After he'd departed, Hassam, who until now had been absent, arrived carrying a brown paper bag. He handed it to Captain Skids, who dumped the contents on the floor—two long chains and four padlocks, presumably bought at a nearby market, clinking in a pile. The chains were thick and heavy-looking, a dark steely silver—the kind of thing you might use to lock together two big doors. I watched Hassam's eyes flick over me, taking in the new bruises, assessing what had gone on. I thought I caught some small wave of alarm or compassion passing across his face and then vanishing, like a rabbit into the woods.

Skids lifted the chains, appearing pleased by their heft. He passed them to Mohammed, who knelt in front of me. He wrapped my two ankles with the ends of the chain and clicked a padlock into place on either side, so that each one was held snugly, each leg cuffed by a circle of cold smooth links, my left foot connected to my right by about six inches of loose chain. He then did the same to Nigel.

When it was over, both of us were hobbled. I avoided looking at Nigel, too confused by my feelings to view him as an ally or even a fellow victim. I was alone, more than before—my self caught inside my body caught inside my life. I could walk, but only with a clumsy slowness, the chain metal digging into my skin. Running was a clear impossibility. We were entirely theirs. Whatever game we'd tried to play, we'd lost.

33

Documents

As evening came, our captors moved us out of the house with the chintz curtains. My guess is that the woman who lived there—the one who'd been angry when we arrived—had ordered them to take their mess elsewhere. Before we left, she sent back a dinner for us, delivered by Jamal, a platter of spaghetti and a pitcher of fresh-squeezed orange juice served on a tray with two plastic cups. More elegant than anything we'd had in months. My jaw was so sore that I could hardly chew, but the food—the taste of the noodles, the normalcy of sipping from a cup—was dimly comforting.

Abdullah watched us eat, looking pleased with himself. Out of the blue, he said, "You fuck many men?" He sounded almost casual, but he was clearly trying out a new verb. I knew it was a question he'd never dare ask with any of the others around. "What number? What number men you fuck?"

I said nothing.

Abdullah looked at Nigel. "You," he said. "What number girls you fuck?"

Nigel swallowed his food. His face was puffed up from the beating. "Four?" he said, as if guessing at a correct answer.

Abdullah's smile grew wide. "Ah, four!" he said. "Many!" Appearing content, he leaned back against the wall.

Nigel and I finished our meal in silence.

*

Surprisingly, when they moved us that evening, they took us back to the Escape House, the house whose window we'd climbed through only hours earlier. Returning seemed risky on their part. The whole neighborhood likely knew about me and Nigel—our spectacle, after all, had been fully witnessed—but our captors were either unthreatened or desperate enough to bring us back. It occurred to me that they had nowhere else to go.

My room was just as I'd left it—my books, clothes, moisturizer, and medicine packs all lined up next to the foam mattress. The blue floral sheet sat folded on the bed. The window shutters had been closed.

I lay down, the chains sliding uncomfortably between my ankles, my body damp from a day of heavy sweating, my limbs thrumming with a dull bone-marrow ache. In the escape, I'd lost my shoes, my backpack, my eyeglasses, my Koran, and the two little instructional booklets on being an Islamic woman. I fought off dread. I couldn't stop thinking about the woman in the mosque—how brave she'd been, how surely she'd suffer some consequence for trying to help. I prayed that she would be okay.

Later, when Jamal showed up at my door, I asked to use the bathroom. He walked behind me down the hallway, his gun pointed between my shoulders. When I pushed back the bathroom curtain, my breath caught in my throat, seeing the mess Nigel and I had made. The room was littered with pieces of crumbled mortar and brick. The hole we'd made in the window at the back of the alcove looked enormous and violently rendered, like a wound, a jagged portal opening to the darkness beyond. I imagined the shock of whichever of our guards had discovered it.

As I used the toilet, Jamal hovered on the other side of the curtain. I could hear him breathing. I felt embarrassed, knowing he was listening to me pee.

Back in my room, I waited all night for them to take me away, my mind roosting uneasily on that empty patch of desert with the twisted acacia tree, the memory of a knife held at my throat.

Then, improbably, the muezzin was warbling. Sun sliced through a crack in the window shutter, lighting the gaudy green of my walls. At some point, I'd fallen asleep. And now I was awake, alive. Sounds floated overhead as if everyone in the house were up, washing and praying, same as always. I heard some sort of conversation going on out on the veranda.

I felt a flood of warm relief.

Maybe, I thought, we'd be okay.

*

It would be nice if bad things happened only in the shadows, if life split easily into camps of darkness and light. How I would have liked it if the stream of sun pouring over our house that morning, over the neighborhood and the neighbors and the whole city of Mogadishu, had some sort of diverting, uplifting effect.

It seemed to be one of those moments when nobody knew what was going to happen next, how anything should go from here. I could hear the murmur of our captors, huddled in a group conference on the porch, presumably discussing what to do. Yesterday had been a bad day, indeed. Their two treasure chests had grown legs and sprinted away.

A short while later, Captain Skids and Abdullah brought me food. Skids never concerned himself with day-to-day matters, and it was never Abdullah who carried in my meals. But they were standing in my room, looking almost kindly, placing in front of me what amounted to a bonanza of a breakfast—a ripe yellowish mango, a hot-dog bun, a cup of warm tea.

"Eat the food," Abdullah said without a trace of his usual fury. "We will wait."

With this, my heart began to tick faster. Wait for what? I looked at the food in my hands, the cup of tea on the floor. The sight of it made me light-headed. I was ravenous. The exertion of the escape had drained me completely.

Skids gave a curt nod and left the room. Abdullah turned to follow him, again looking at me in a way I couldn't read.

When they were gone, I tore a little piece off the hot-dog bun and ate it. I took a sip of the tea. I wondered if Nigel had been given the same food and whether they were waiting for him, too.

I peeled the fruit with my fingers, sucking the stray bits of flesh from each piece of skin. Inside, the mango was a vibrant orange, paler around the edges, deeper toward the core. Its sweetness was gratifying, though it would do nothing to fill the howling void in my belly. I'd learned enough about hunger to understand that the impulse to gobble down food was an animal thing, useless if you weren't in a pack. When you were alone, it was better for both soul and body to make a small meal last.

I chewed the hot-dog bun piece by piece, alternating it with nibbles of fruit. Through the wall, I heard a sound—a pained yelp. They were in Nigel's room, I realized.

After about ten minutes, Abdullah surfaced again at my door, appearing unrushed. "It is good?" he said. He sounded like he actually wanted to know.

I nodded, gesturing to show that the meal was only half-eaten. He walked away again, leaving my door open.

I ate what was left of the bun, continuing to tear it into tiny pinches, each bite the size of a little pearl. When I was done with that, I cleaned the pit of the mango with my teeth and tongue, all the way down to its woody center. I drained the last dregs of tea.

It was Abdullah and Skids who came back for me. Abdullah was holding his AK-47. Skids carried a pistol.

Abdullah said, "You are finished now?" He indicated that I should stand and follow them into the hallway. Skids said something to him in Somali. Abdullah pointed at my mattress and then at his *macawii*—the cotton sarong he wore tied around his waist—and then again at my mattress. They were telling me to pick up the blue-flowered sheet from my bed. It was about the same size and weight of a *macawii*. They wanted me to bring it with me, wherever we were going.

We walked out into the hallway, toward the veranda, past the room where Abdi and the other Somali hostages once stayed. The chains on my legs hampered every step, giving me a wobbly equilibrium at best.

I led with one foot and dragged the other, doing a kind of labored shuffle step. I was barefoot, wearing the clothes I'd escaped in, all but the heavy black abaya, which I'd taken off the night before. I wore the red polyester dress, a green tank top beneath it, the loose-fitting pair of jeans, and a black hijab over my head—all of it dirt-stained after my humiliating and involuntary exit from the mosque.

Midway down the hall, I lost my balance and fell, landing hard on one hip. Skids watched as I tried a few times to right myself, the narrow span of my chained feet keeping me from shifting my weight. I thought I saw a glimmer of pride in his eyes, seeing how difficult it was for me to move.

*

They led me through the double doorway of a wide, empty room. I'd been here once before, on the December day of Eid, when Nigel and I were invited to join our captors for prayer and we'd celebrated what Eid was about—the willingness of Abraham to sacrifice his own son to God. The room was bright with sunshine. Its walls were painted yellow. I'd stood behind my captors on the holiday morning, looking at their backs. I'd knelt on the concrete floor, watching daylight drift through two windows on the left-hand wall, fascinated by the sight of the single stunted tree in the wide yard beyond—what they saw and I usually didn't.

This time Abdullah pushed me to the front of the room. Skids was talking again in Somali, saying words that Abdullah translated for my benefit. "You are bad woman," he said, his voice rising. "You run away. Do you have documents?"

I said, "Documents? No, I don't have any documents."

"You lie," Abdullah said.

I realized that they must have searched Nigel's room and found the paper on which he'd written some Somali phrases, asking for help. It was hardly a document, but our captors had always been obsessed by what they called documents—any paper with words on it. The written word held a strange power for them.

Skids drew close, the first time in five months that he'd come within spitting distance of me. I didn't like what I saw in his eyes. Instinctively,

I shot out a hand to push him away, but it seemed to make his motions swifter. With his left hand, he seized the neckline of my red dress and, in the same instant, used his opposite hand to crack the butt end of his pistol over my skull. I felt the pain in my teeth, my eyeballs, my fingertips. My first thought was that he'd damaged my brain.

I fell sideways, but Skids still had a hold on my dress. He yanked me up and then pulled the dress over my head, his fingers finding my sweat-stained tank top. When I fought him, he hit me again.

"Please, please don't do this," I said.

Skids barked an order at Abdullah, and I began to understand why they'd had me bring the sheet from my bed. With Skids holding my arms, Abdullah took my piece of flowered cotton and hooded me with it, covering my head and tying it tightly at the back of my neck. Now I saw nothing but blue light. I felt hands on my body. My tank top was torn away. I twisted and squirmed, trying to dodge the hands, but they only came from new angles. Someone landed another blow on my head. I was dizzy, vomit rising in my throat. I felt myself sag. There were new voices in the room. More people. Speaking Somali. I heard Mohammed and Yusuf. The room seemed crowded suddenly, dense with male energy. I heard the voice of Hassam, the sweet young market boy, and that, more than anything, made my spirits plummet. I thought, *Not him, too.*

Someone was tugging on my jeans, sliding them down to just above where the chains lay yoked around my ankles. The air in the room was hot, and I was naked but for the hood over my head and the jeans at my feet. My skin prickled. I pressed my arms over my breasts and hips, trying to cover myself. Down by my feet, I could feel a set of hands moving around my ankles. I heard a murmuring and then a collective gasp. Someone pronounced the name of Ajoos, the fixer at the Shamo.

My heart sank at the sound. They'd been searching through the pockets, I knew, and had come upon my one bit of contraband. It was the two tiny scraps of paper onto which, prior to the escape, I'd copied my Somali phrases and phone numbers. I'd rolled the papers up until they were about the size of two sunflower seeds and tucked them into the narrow triangular front pocket of my jeans.

My captors were talking loudly, excitedly, almost triumphantly, as if they had permission now to continue.

And they did. They continued. They called it a search, what they went on to do to me that morning, in that room. But what they did was drag us all into new territory. All of the boys were there. I understood later how much this mattered, how it kept any one of them from judging the others in the months to come. Together, they crossed into a darker place, where there was no retrievable dignity for anybody. They became guilty, one the same as another. I bled not for hours or days but for weeks afterward.

34

New Rules

rom here, I went into darkness. By this I mean real physical darkness, a bleak black void with four walls around it, in the form of a new room in a new house—this one seeming to be far outside of Mogadishu, deeper in the country, somewhere in the catacombs of another whitewashed village. Just hours after what had happened in the prayer room, under cover of night, they brought us—me and Nigel both—to the new location. Shrouded in my black abaya and head scarf, I was strangely numb during the ride. My body had been shredded. So much of me was raw and hurt that I couldn't shift my weight without triggering a new pain. All the while, my mind felt caught in a net, rigged high above what was going on.

Next to me, Nigel was panting so loudly that I feared they'd hit him for it. He was shirtless, for reasons I didn't want to imagine.

In the back of the car, where several of the boys sat jammed beneath the hatchback with their guns, I could hear the rattling of cooking pots and plastic bags at their feet, a sign that they'd packed us up for a full move.

*

I saw almost nothing of the next house. I was hurried from the car through a doorway and then down a long hall.

Before we were pulled inside, I turned to Nigel and said one thing. "Stay strong," I said. "We'll get out of here, Nige. But we might not see each other for a while." My eyes welled at the thought. He, too, teared up. Despite everything, I wanted to crawl into his arms.

They put me in a room that was windowless and black, tossing in my foam mattress, several bags of my belongings, and the brown square of linoleum that appeared to travel with me now as well. The room was big. My mat lay in one corner, with the other walls far away. The air smelled sour, a stew of rot and urine. The room felt sealed off, like a cave, like a storage room, removed from light and the busier parts of the house. There was a bathroom inside the room, in an alcove near the doorway, smelling dank and unused.

Over twenty-two weeks of captivity, I'd nursed many thoughts that somehow Nigel and I would be found, that some cell phone signal could be traced and mapped, that maybe Canada or Australia would find a way to send soldiers or mercenaries to pluck us out or that some-one—one of our captors' wives or cousins or mothers—would blow the whistle on the whole operation and it would force an ending. My hopes had been dimming, but in the airless jar of the new room, they felt fully snuffed.

I'd lost a lot of blood and was burning with fever; my head ached viciously. I was certain I was dying and that it would happen slowly. As I lay on the mattress, my mind clung to the faintest of sounds: the scrabble of a rat in the far corner of the room, someone hammering something—a mosquito net, likely—into a wall. I heard something else, a light hacking coming from the hallway, a human cough that I didn't recognize. The sound was distinctly female, but that seemed impossible. I wondered if I was hallucinating.

Eventually, I slept, figuring that morning would relieve some of the pain and also the darkness. When I awoke, though, I was dry-mouthed and soaked in sweat, with chills running through my body, the bruises tender beneath the surface of my skin. From my mattress, I could see only a thin line of daylight running along the bottom of the door to the room, illuminating nothing.

★

This was the Dark House. There were new rules here. My captors made them clear right away. I was not allowed to speak; nor was I allowed to sit up on my mat, not even for a minute. I was permitted to eat and drink only by propping myself on one elbow. Any infraction brought a beating. My prison was no longer the size of a room. It had shrunk to the size of that mat, three feet wide by seven feet long. Gone, too, was the practice of bringing me plastic bottles of filtered water from the market. I was now given the same two-liter bottle every morning, refilled from what must have been an outdoor tap with water that tasted like iron and left grit on my tongue.

On the second afternoon, Abdullah came into the room with a flashlight and found me lying on my back. He gave me a furious kick. "Over," he said, using his toe to lever me to my side. "Like this only. No exercise."

He kicked me again, to drive home whatever point he was making.

I realized later that they'd seen me go through my hours of daily pacing back at the last house, in the weeks leading up to our attempt at escape. I remembered the look of frantic rage on Abdullah's face as he'd chased me through the mosque, the force of my legs thrashing as he'd dragged me across the courtyard. He wouldn't risk a repeat. They were going to do all they could to keep me weak. I was banned from lying on my back, for fear that somehow it would make me strong. I guess they thought I'd start doing leg lifts or crunches and find another way out.

Five times a day, I was allowed to totter the short distance to the toilet, lassoed by the chains, with a boy and gun poised nearby. The bathroom had a small ventilation grate high in the wall that, during the day, let in a feeble mosaic of light, enough to reveal a Western toilet that didn't flush, a sink without running water, and a rusted showerhead in the corner. The water came from a jug left inside the door.

After washing, I was expected to pray. I was now happy to pray, as it constituted the only bit of variety in my movement, the only moments I was allowed to remain upright aside from bathroom trips. Most of the time, one or two of my captors stood behind me as I prayed, using a flashlight or the silvery screen of a cell phone to provide light, watching as I went through the motions, murmuring the words, using my square of linoleum as a prayer mat. The leg shackles bit into my ankles as I moved from standing to kneeling. I could no longer sit back on my heels to finish each cycle of prayer.

The boys mocked my Arabic. They mimicked the pitch of my voice, my poor pronunciation.

"You are a bad Muslim, Amina," Abdullah said to me, his laughter like a horsewhip traveling the darkness. "You are liar woman."

By the fourth day, I was ill from the dirty water, my stomach scorched, my intestines gurgling. I used the plastic bottle to knock on the floor, signaling that I needed extra trips to the bathroom. Sometimes the boys obliged me, and sometimes they didn't. They'd taken to leaving the wooden door to my room slightly ajar, which gave them the ability to sneak in noiselessly, to surprise me while I was sleeping. I woke a few times to find Abdullah and Young Mohammed throwing my belongings against the wall, demanding to know if I had "documents," the beams of their flashlights raking over me. With the move to the Dark House, they'd taken away my books and medicine. I still had the Q-tips and the body lotion. I had a single change of clothes, the bottle of perfume, and the king-sized toothpaste. But that was about it.

The one new item I had, which had somehow ended up in my things, was a shirt belonging to Nigel. It was the shirt he'd worn during our escape—a purple button-up shirt that was torn in several places and missing a sleeve. I kept it in bed with me, sleeping with it pulled close.

I dozed in a fevered haze, my brain drifting, my body on fire. In the darkness, I felt myself shrinking toward nothing. Once I awoke in a panic to the feeling of someone kicking me repeatedly in the side. It was Mohammed, his foot jammed beneath my rib cage. It took me a few seconds to understand what he was doing. I'd accidentally rolled onto my back while sleeping, breaking the "no exercise" rule. He kicked me until I rolled back to my side.

A few times, I heard the faint sound of Nigel, his chains clinking in the hallway outside. I also heard, again and again, that unfamiliar cough coming from somewhere inside the house. It was jarring, barky, and decidedly female. I heard it at night and I heard it by day, which seemed to suggest she was living there. Whoever she was, she sounded quite sick. It confused my sense of things. Why would a woman be so near? Was she another captive? A wife? A servant? My mind reeled at her presence, though I was well past thinking that any woman, in any circumstance, would be able to save me. Whoever she was, I guessed she was just as stuck as I was.

*

When you are in darkness, time folds in on itself, surreal and elastic. It bellows like an accordion, stretching and then collapsing. An hour becomes indistinguishable from a night or a day.

My mattress floated like a raft in the middle of a black ocean. The darkness surrounding me had substance. It had weight. It was thick like tar, catching in my throat and gumming up my lungs. I had to coach myself on how to breathe it. There were moments when the darkness seemed aggressive, like it was trying to swallow me. I'd hold a hand in front of my face and see nothing. I fanned my arms, attempting to create wind, to exert some power over the dark. Sometimes I pressed the hollow at the base of my neck, just to remind myself that I was solid.

Eight days passed and then a ninth. I tried not to obsess about time, but without the rhythm of day and night, it was almost impossible not to. My thoughts were simple. *Don't panic. Don't go crazy.* I pushed my brain around like a miniature train on a track, traveling the same small circles. *Stay calm,* I told myself. *This has to be temporary. They're going to move us out of here soon.* I marked the days by following the summonses to prayer. It sounded like there was a mosque next door, literally just beyond my walls. The muezzin's singing voice was old and unpleasant.

My eyes strained against the blackness, causing a nearly constant headache. I began to keep them closed all the time, which was an effort, a disruption of the brain. I focused instead on my hearing, which I could feel was getting sharper. In the afternoons, I heard a tinny-sounding radio tuned to the BBC Somali Service, its announcer speaking in Somali. I listened for words I could recognize. I knew very few, most of my vocabulary accrued during the first several days in Mogadishu with Abdi, and in the early weeks of captivity, when our captors were eager to converse. I knew that *bariis* was rice and *basal* was onion. I knew *biyo* was water. I knew the words Somalis used for hotel, journalist, bathroom, mosque. I knew "How are you?" and "I am good" and "Help" and "We are doing everything we can to save lives." But little of this surfaced on the radio. The words I caught most often were the names of places and famous people. Over days of listening, I thought I heard the Somali newsman mention Mogadishu and Ethiopia, Germany and George Bush. The words, in their familiarity, were almost like food.

Occasionally I heard the clatter of a cooking pot somewhere in the house, along with the *etch, etch, etch* of the woman's cough as she moved about. I began to think she was likely a cook, hired to fix meals for the boys and clean up after them. I heard them delivering bags from the market to what must have been a kitchen at the end of my hallway. Every so often I caught the smell of onions frying in a pan. I decided she must be a widow, desperate for a job. No Somali woman of standing—unmarried or married, young or old—would be allowed to live with a group of young men as she was doing. And Somalia, I knew, had no shortage of widows.

From the words, from the sounds, I sometimes slipped into dreams. Once, with my eyes closed, I thought I heard the sound of Nigel laughing, but I didn't fully trust my own brain. It was wishful thinking, I realized. I was wretchedly, unsparingly lonely. I pictured Nigel in a dark room somewhere on the other side of the house. I sent him mental messages, imploring him to hang on, to stay strong. I couldn't stay angry with him for having tried to pin the escape on me. He was just so scared. I understood. None of it mattered, anyway. I tried to imagine him sending messages back to me.

In my lowest moments, I curled myself around his ripped shirt and cried. I lay with the fabric under my cheek, smelling the swampish scent of his body. We had a history now that added up to years. We had a catalog of shared experiences, though all I could recall for the moment, with my nose pressed into his shirt, was the sweaty paranoia of our escape, our frantic dash into the mosque. It was not a good memory, but it carried an electrical charge, a feeling I desperately needed. We'd been hopeful for how long that day? Ten minutes? Twelve? I wished for even three seconds of that hopefulness now. I craved just one hit of lung-clearing, odds-stacked-against-us, totally-fucked-up-but-still-not-impossible possibility. In the darkness, left with no other option, I tried to inhale it out of the fibers of that shirt.

35

A House in the Sky

T wo weeks passed, then a third. And then something closer to a month.

I lay in nothingness, drifting deeper into a state of half-being, the stale darkness eating away all boundaries. I saw skeins of blue thread, little plumelike spinnakers that floated in front of me, whether my eyes were open or shut. Sometimes I wondered if I'd gone blind. Other times I wondered if I was alive at all.

Was this hell?

It was not an unreasonable thought.

Gradually, I found my way into a sense of routine, curbed on all sides by the dark and the rules. But still, there was comfort in anything I could do for myself. I arranged my small collection of toiletries in a line along the top end of my mat. I used the body lotion in the mornings, after my bathroom trip, massaging the cream into my hands and forearms and over my face. My captors had given me a razor, a small straight-edged blade, kept in a paper sheath. With it, I was supposed to shave my pubic area daily, in keeping with conservative Islam's mandates on body hair. I did this in the dim light of the bathroom, testing the blade's sharpness against my skin, knowing that if I wanted to, I could probably slash my wrists with it. It was a thought, an idea waiting to be activated, but nothing more.

Each morning, between visiting the bathroom and lying down again, I stole fifteen critical seconds to make up the bed, tucking the bottom sheet tightly beneath the sides of the mattress, using a hand to smooth any wrinkles. I folded my blue floral top sheet into a neat flat rectangle and set it at the foot. This, for me, marked the beginning of a new day.

To pass the time, I reminded myself of what I knew, of things that tied me to the world beyond: It was February, almost March. Back at home, the Rocky Mountains would be covered in layers of deep white snow. My mother would be wearing a scarf. My father's gardens would be crushed and brown. The sidewalks in Calgary were being scoured by snaking winter winds. Wool, wind, dead flowers. I tried to feel them on my skin. I'd spent so many of my winters away from Canada, in far-off countries where it rarely got cold. Now, more than anything, I wanted the feel of a season, the coziness of a warm, safe house with the cold world outside.

In my room, the rats grew bolder. I sometimes woke to the hairy brush of a body scuttling over my legs in the dark. I looked for any pinprick of light, any movement inside the vacuum of blackness, but there was none. My legs ached from the enforced stillness. I rolled from my right side to my left and then back. I felt woozy and ill. I tried to drink as little as possible of the water they brought me. I ate what they carried in each morning—dry bread, pieces of camel fat over rice, bananas—with the same hesitancy.

All outside sounds seemed to come from a different world. Only the crotchety voice of the muezzin next door was clear, and the foot-steps—the *shhh-shhh-shhh* of a pair of sandals approaching my door. Hearing them, I'd feel my heart start to pound. I don't think I experienced something as simple as fear anymore. What I felt, when someone came near me, was a hot explosion of terror. With the footsteps, I never knew who was coming or why.

Most often it was Abdullah. The others paid visits to my room, too, sometimes under the pretense that they were inspecting me to see if I'd kept up with shaving my body hair, but often to abuse me. If, before the escape, I had been a curiosity to those boys—a foreigner with whom they could practice their English while earning points with Allah for indoctrinating me into Islam—all that was gone. They now treated me as a spoil of war. Some were worse than others. A few, like Hassam and Jamal, left me alone. But as a group, they seemed to believe that I'd shamed them by making a false accusation in the mosque, and that justified ditching whatever sense of dignity or communal restraint once held them back.

Abdullah sometimes came several times in a single day. He'd open the door and blind me with the beam of his flashlight. Then he'd drop to his knees on my mat, usually without a word. He didn't so much touch me as grab handfuls of my flesh. He'd find one of my breasts in the darkness and squeeze it like something he hoped would burst. Sometimes he'd tell me in a jeering voice that I was "dirty" and "open," since, unlike those of virtually all Somali women, my genitals had not been cut—my labia and clitoris had not been sliced off and my vagina stitched shut in some draconian bid to protect my honor.

Sometimes Abdullah tied my hands behind my back with the blue-flowered sheet from my mattress so that I wouldn't push at him as he choked me. I blocked out the sounds he made.

Death began to look welcoming. Whatever death was, it had to be better. I wasn't sure how I would die—even with the razor, I had no urge to end my own life—but I could feel death close by, waiting for me. Death would require no effort, just the letting go.

In my chest, I could feel pressure building every day, even every hour, as if a tree bough were bending inside me. I felt like I was approaching the point where I could no longer bear the strain, as if my mind were about to snap. The thought completely unnerved me. What would come with the snap? What lay on the other side? Death? Or madness? I didn't know.

I lay still as Abdullah did what he did, but my mind never stopped clambering to get away. I fought not to cross over. I fought to undo some of the pressure. He usually set his flashlight down on the floor. As he moved over me, exerting himself, his tongue poked slightly out of his mouth, the beam of his light shone up and away from us, illuminating things I otherwise never saw—the dark wooden beams of the ceiling and the dust particles that hung suspended in the air like little diamonds. I focused on these. I tried to climb away from the shock of what my life had become.

In my mind, I built stairways. At the end of the stairways, I imagined rooms. These were high, airy places with big windows and a cool breeze moving through. I imagined one room opening brightly onto another room until I'd built a house, a place with hallways and more staircases. I built many houses, one after another, and those gave rise to a city—a calm, sparkling city near the ocean, a place like Vancouver. I put myself there, and that's where I lived, in the wide-open sky of my mind. I made friends and read books and went running on a footpath in a jewel-green park along the harbor. I ate pancakes drizzled in syrup and took baths and watched sunlight pour through trees. This wasn't longing, and it wasn't insanity. It was relief. It got me through.

After he'd gone, my other emotions came streaming back. I cried every time, unsettled by the rushes of fury and despair. I felt like I was standing next to an ocean slicked with hate, my toes wet with it.

Day by day, though, I collected up old sweetnesses and fed on them. I remembered the happier moments in my life, unfolding them with languorous slowness, time being the one currency I had to spend. I revisited my early love for Jamie, with his mop of hair and his thrift-store outfits and his guitar.

Where do you want to go? he'd asked one afternoon in a park by the river in Calgary, back before we'd been to a single place or seen a single thing.

Anywhere, I'd said. *Anywhere is good.*

It had been the right answer.

In exacting detail, I could recall the rub of a heavy backpack on my shoulders, the petrol blur of Pakistani jingle trucks, the train stations and lamb kebabs, the flame-colored tent I'd slept in on the riverbank in Khartoum. I took myself back through the week I'd spent trekking to Everest base camp in Nepal one year with Kelly, the first nights I'd slept in Amanuddin's house in Kabul. I recalled what it was like to scoop handfuls of sugared pistachios into my mouth in Calcutta and to dip triangles of soft pita bread into a bowl of creamy hummus served with mint sprigs in Beirut. I remembered the boy—that quiet, carefully dressed

British stranger named Dan Hanmer—who'd sat by the green-black lake in Guatemala so many years ago, holding Kelly's hand. I remembered diving into swimming pools, cold bottles of orange Fanta at the end of long bus trips, the fresh start of every conversation launched in the breakfast room of a two-star hostel, out there in the world.

I conjured my father's laugh and my mother's cooking, the stars in the sky over Sylvan Lake. I made peace with anyone who might ever have been an enemy. I asked forgiveness for every vain or selfish thing I'd done in my life. Inside the house in the sky, all the people I loved sat down for a big holiday meal. I was safe and protected. It was where the voices that normally tore through my head expressing fear and wishing for death went silent, until there was only one left speaking. It was a calmer, stronger voice, one that to me felt divine.

It said, *See? You are okay, Amanda. It's only your body that's suffering, and you are not your body. The rest of you is fine.*

*

Things became more bearable then—not easier, just more endurable. Though I was hungry, bruised, and had a fever I couldn't shake, the rest of me was fine. I was alone and shackled, but the rest of me was okay. The rest of me knew not to panic. It had a place to go. It was as if that voice had come and quietly rearranged a few key things. As if, inside the stifling darkness, I'd been given more space, a cool pocket of air. I reminded myself again to breathe. I put a hand on my chest to be sure each exhale was really happening. I moved from one breath to the next.

I followed my breathing from moment into hour, day into week, as the boys came and went from my room, as my hatred for them swelled and receded, each time feeling as if I were climbing hand over hand out of a dark hole—this endlessly cascading place they threw me into every time they raped me, or beat me, or said something horrible to me. It was easier, I decided, for them to think of me a certain way, to not acknowledge that I was a human like them, because if they did—if any one of them stopped to think about what they were doing—they, too, might snap.

With this breath, I choose peace. With this breath, I choose freedom. It didn't matter whether it was the tenth time or the thousandth; enduring their cruelties never became any easier. It always had the same effect, consuming me, putting me in a knotted and unhopeful rage. I'd spent my life believing that people were, at heart, kind and good. This was what the world had shown me. But I couldn't find anything good about these boys, about any of my captors. If humans could be this monstrous, maybe I'd had everything wrong. If this was the world, I didn't want to live in it. That was the scariest and most disabling thought of all.

*

One day sometime into the second month in the Dark House, Yusuf— the oversized boy who sometimes led the others in calisthenics in the yard—came into my room with a flashlight and handed me a softball-sized half of a papaya, cut crosswise with a knife, its seeds making a dark star in the center. I stared at the fruit and then at Yusuf, who was dressed in a sarong and a white shirt with thin black stripes. Nobody had smiled at me in many weeks, but he was smiling. I waited for him to lash out at me or take the fruit away, but he didn't. I knew from earlier attempts to talk to him that he spoke almost no English. He patted his own chest to make sure I understood that the fruit was a gift from him alone, then he sat a few feet away as I bit into it.

Very softly, I said, "Thank you." The sound of my voice surprised me. I'd barely said a word in weeks.

Yusuf smiled again. As I continued to eat, he leaned in my direction and reached his arm out, lining it up with mine so that our forearms were side by side in the beam of his flashlight. "Black," he said, pointing at his arm. He then gestured at mine. "White," he said. Looking directly into my eyes, he said, "No problem."

I was pretty sure he was telling me that our skin color didn't matter.

When he left, I got teary. The whole thing had been so odd. Yusuf was no less guilty than the other boys. But the small kindness stayed with me.

The strong and calm voice stayed also. It told me to look for good, because good was always there. On days when I was really struggling, when I felt the pressure in my mind moving again toward a snapping point, the voice posed questions. It said, *In this exact moment, are you okay?*

The answer, in that exact moment, was steadying: *Yes, right now I am still okay.*

I ran through the things I had to be thankful for—my family at home, the oxygen in my lungs. I started a ritual for myself. Each evening after the six o'clock prayer session, I settled back on my mat and went through my own silent appeals, naming every person in my family, taking time to picture each face, asking that they all be protected. I did the same for Nigel and his family and for each one of my friends. I went through the people I'd worked with in Baghdad, the Somalis I'd met in my first few days in Mogadishu. I prayed for the neighbor who'd tried to help me and Nigel during our escape and especially for the woman who'd clung to me in the mosque. I prayed that she was alive and unhurt. I pushed out the guilt that followed my hopes.

I tried to locate what had been good about the day that had just passed. I looked for any moments when my captors had shown their humanity: *I am thankful that today Jamal set my food down on the floor instead of throwing it at me. I am grateful that Abdullah offered the greeting Asalaamu Alikum when he came into my room. I am happy that I heard a few seconds of the boys laughing and horsing around in the hallway today, because it reminded me, if only for a minute, that somewhere inside each of them is a teenager who wants to be carefree.*

In the context of the life I once lived, these were small things, ridiculous things really, but in this place and under these circumstances, they meant everything. By concentrating on what I was grateful for, I managed to stave off despair. Each time my captors threw me into that hole, I found another way to climb out. It wasn't easy—not ever, not once—but this way of thinking became my ladder, my doorway.

Anywhere, anywhere, I reminded myself. I could go anywhere.

36

Danger Is Coming

In Alberta, it was early spring. My mother continued to live in the government-rented house in Sylvan Lake, not far from my dad and Perry's home. On the wall, she kept a calendar with each of the 210 days I'd been held hostage marked with an X. RCMP negotiators stayed on duty with her twenty-four hours a day. She was, however, no longer negotiating. After the last time my mother and I had spoken—in December, when the kidnappers threatened to behead me in the desert before handing me the phone—the investigators shifted their strategy, instructing her not to answer the phone any time a Somali number popped up on the caller ID. The idea was that if she stopped picking up, Adam would be forced to deal with a team of Canadian intelligence agents based in Nairobi instead. This, people seemed to believe, would lessen the emotional manipulation and yield more progress.

Adam's frustration with the new phone situation was evident. He sometimes called my mother's number more than ten times in a day, hanging up without leaving a voicemail. Denied phone access, he sent angry e-mails filled with misspellings to the Hotmail address my mother had used when arranging to send our care package in the fall. One message, sent back in January, around the time of our escape attempt, summed up his ongoing point in its subject line: "Danger is coming soon to Amanda and Nigel if you don't pay the ranson we want!!!!!"

Seven months into the kidnapping, the hostage-takers had barely budged in their ransom demands. They were insisting on $2 million for both of us, down from the initial request for $3 million. Adam had rejected a onetime offer of $250,000 made early on in exchange for me and Nigel, an amount that had been put together by the Canadian and Australian governments and was technically categorized as "expense" money so that each country could maintain its official policy of not paying ransoms. They would offer nothing more than that. Any other solutions would have to come through diplomacy.

My parents were given only vague pictures of what that diplomacy looked like. Sometimes, they were told, a government might offer to fund a hospital in a place like Mogadishu, say, as a way of helping to enlist the local government. They were informed that Canadian officials had been trying to put pressure on clan elders and other Somali leaders to compel our release. But with the Somali government in a constant state of peril, and amid reports that the group holding us had no strong affiliation with any one clan, again and again the efforts yielded nothing.

The stalemate continued. Adam kept phoning my mother to no avail. Other calls came in from Somalia, and various strangers left voice messages, claiming to have news or a way to get us free. My mother never understood how people got her number, nor what they were after—whether they were connected to the kidnappers or just honest people trying to help. She usually wept, watching the ringing phone.

Expectancy, sustained over many months, becomes its own agony. In the late afternoons, after it was nighttime in Somalia, when there'd likely be no news coming, my mother would leave the house for a sanity break. She'd go to the grocery store or for a solitary walk in the snowy woods nearby, trying to settle her thoughts. The negotiator on duty stayed back at the house, keeping vigil, though it was hard to say what anybody was waiting for.

What my parents lived on, what they built their faith on, was the idea that others seemed hopeful. The government officers who called with daily briefings from Ottawa gave them opaque but reassuring intelligence reports. Nigel and I were being fed, they'd been told. We were being allowed to exercise. When, early on, my mother had fretted aloud about her worries for my safety as a woman, the investigators had been quick to soothe her: Among devout Muslims, rape was considered a crime worse than murder, they'd said. Chances were, I was not being abused.

The agents hinted that they had plenty going on behind the scenes that could not be shared. According to my mother, the message from Ottawa, almost daily, was that our case was "very, very close" to being resolved. She lived on those words—"very close"—never once knowing what they meant.

Tension built between my family and Nigel's over how to proceed. Our two families rarely spoke directly, having been instructed to rely on the respective government intermediaries. Disillusioned with the lack of progress, Nigel's older brother, Hamilton, had begun talking with a man in Australia named Michael Fox. He was allegedly some sort of security-expert bounty-hunter type who announced that he had a network of contacts in Somalia and believed that if the Brennan family could come up with five hundred thousand dollars, he could get at least Nigel out. It would mean stepping away from the Australian Federal Police's agenda, but the Brennans were increasingly questioning how effective any government could be in this situation. They also had resources, as Nigel had told me: money banked from the sale of their family farm. Other members of the family had property they could use as collateral for a loan. There was dissent among the Brennans over how to handle my family's lack of funds. If this Fox character was correct, they might be able to come up with the kind of money needed to free Nigel. Why, his brother was wondering, were they being saddled with the responsibility of getting me out, too?

In early March, my mother had learned that Hamilton had struck some sort of private deal with Michael Fox, okaying him to go into Somalia and use their family money to negotiate for Nigel. She was devastated. She had angry phone conversations with both Hamilton and Nigel's mother, insisting that the kidnappers would surely take the money, release Nigel, and promptly kill me.

Late that month, our two families reached an uneasy truce. The Brennans agreed to call off Fox's efforts and to sink their faith once again in the government agents working the case, hoping for some sort of breakthrough.

*

But then a blog post surfaced on the Internet, sending my parents into a dizzying tailspin. An American blogger reported that I was pregnant. His post—on a site that covered war and intelligence issues—was short, containing no specifics. He noted that the information came from Mogadishu, from a source he trusted, but at the same time, he warned his readers that it was little more than a rumor.

The RCMP negotiators in the house with my mother insisted that it was likely just gossip, one of dozens of unconfirmed stories that had floated out of Somalia since we'd been captured. Quite possibly, they said, it had been planted by the disgruntled Adam or someone close to him in order to boost the urgency of the negotiations.

Somalia seemed to be a factory for rumors, with a handful of news websites and uncredentialed bloggers pumping out what passed for information, largely for the benefit of the million or so Somalis who had fled the country and scattered across the globe. And also, it turned out, for the benefit of my mother, who scrolled every morning through poorly translated reports on the shifting curtain of the country's civil war, its clan politics and pirates, and the growing bond between Al-Shabaab and Al Qaeda. The media in Somalia was mostly underground and unofficial. Somali journalists attempting to do honest work were routinely threatened, detained, and sometimes assassinated. A number of radio stations had been attacked and forced to close. Some news sites were reportedly controlled by certain clans and accordingly biased in what they reported. It was impossible to know what was truth and what was not.

Any news about me and Nigel arrived in unfocused glimpses, either via a blogger or passed on to the Canadian or Australian intelligence agents through a mysterious network of informants. The two of us had been spotted in the back of a car. There were other, more dubious reports, like the one that said I was happily teaching English to Somali children. It would astound me later to learn how accurate some pieces of information had been, how droplets of truth managed to leak out of our otherwise sealed-off existence. My parents had been told, for example, that I'd sprained my ankle early on in Escape House, during my weeks of pacing in circles, which was true. They had been told that my captors took it upon themselves to bring me ice, a rare commodity in Somalia, which was also true.

It was the specificity of these fragments that both alarmed and reassured my mother. Despite the broken English with which it was delivered, the news was often worded in a chillingly sure-footed way. Most of the time, she took it as proof that I was alive and at least partially visible in Somalia, though it also could seem as if I'd been swept away and brainwashed, the phantom woman described in the news bearing little resemblance to the daughter she once knew. One of the more extensive reports, published on a Somali news website after we'd been held for nearly a year, read like this:

> The journalist Amanda Lindhout is no longer a Christian she has avert her believe of trinity to the worshiping of one God and that is Allah the most high she is now performing her 5 times of prayers and she is very contented with her marriage relationship with one of her captors you can't imagine how they exchange laughter and smiles through gesture since the couples don't understand each other in terms of languages, said Hashi one of the captors of Amanda Lindhout speaking to Waagacusub Website on Friday.
>
> A reporter for Waagacusub Website who lives in a house which is some few meters away from the house where Amanda lives has been closing following the situation of the two journalists has confirmed that Amanda is gleefully at a certain house at Suuq Holaha in the north of Mogadishu and is regularly performing her feminine work such as washing, cooking and cleaning the house at which she is residing.
>
> The reporter also added that he has no enough report about the Australian Freelance journalists but is sure that he is also living in the same vicinity with Amanda. Amanda wears a big black veil, and it is hardly to see part of her body and is now learning the Holy Quran.

*

We were, I can say with certainty, nowhere near Mogadishu when this particular item was published. It is also worth noting that I was not pregnant, married, nor anything close to gleeful. I did no cooking or cleaning, either, except just one time, on an afternoon nearly two months into our stay in the Dark House, when Jamal and Abdullah ordered me to scrub the bathroom that was mine. I think they believed they were humiliating me, but after weeks of being confined to my mat in the thick darkness, it was the best ten minutes I'd spent all winter. In the spidery light of the ventilation slats, I sloshed water from a brown bucket and an all-purpose powdered detergent around the filthy room, gratified by the freedom of movement, the idea that I was making the bathroom nicer for myself and no one else. With deliberate slowness, I pushed a rag over the sink and around the seat of the pink plastic toilet, dumping extra soap into the bowl, watching it streak into the vortex of dark stains.

Just outside my room, Abdullah and Jamal had seated themselves against a wall in the dim hallway. They were deep in conversation, speaking Somali in tones I hadn't heard in a long time, like two friends shooting the breeze. They seemed lighthearted, as if they'd forgotten to go through some routine to work up their normal hostility toward me.

I took a chance, sticking my head partway into the hall, holding up the box of detergent. "Please," I said, "could I wash my clothes in the bucket here?"

I hadn't been permitted to take a shower or change my clothes since the escape. When I cleaned my body, I did it while crouched next to the toilet, scooping water from a repurposed cooking-oil jug made from yellow plastic with its top cut off and its handle intact. I always washed in a hurry and with an eye toward conserving water, never using more than two cupfuls at a time, knowing that if the jug went down to empty, it could be days before the boys bothered to refill it. I smelled bad enough that my captors sometimes came into my room carrying a bottle of cologne, spritzing the air ahead as if clearing a sweeter path for themselves through the fetid dark.

That day, sitting in the hallway outside my door, Abdullah and Jamal conferred a moment about me and my clothes. As they did, I caught sight of a moving shadow, a thin figure riffling a light-colored sheet that hung across a doorway directly across the hall from my room. Someone had paused there, perhaps to eavesdrop, but then had stepped away. It was the woman—it had to be—the ghostlike other female in the house. I realized it was her bedroom that lay behind the curtain. Her proximity explained why I so often heard her coughing.

"Five minutes," Abdullah said, interrupting my thoughts. "You hurry."

It was impossible to remove my jeans with the leg shackles, but back in my room, I stripped off the red dress, plus my tank top and bra, and put on the heavy black abaya I'd worn during our escape. Returning to the bathroom, working quickly, I dumped the clothing into what was left of the water in the brown cleaning bucket, sprinkling it liberally with soap, and kneading each piece carefully with my fingers, feeling the detergent burning the tops of my hands, thrilled by what that said about its potency. The idea of having anything clean against my skin felt like a tremendous gift.

When I was finished, I hung the bra on a bar near the sink. I stepped back into the doorway and held up the dripping dress and tank top for the boys to see, gesturing that they needed to be hung somewhere to dry. I made a move to hand them to Jamal, but he recoiled. The two boys started arguing in Somali. Neither one wanted to touch my things.

After some debate, I was told I could hang the clothing myself. This was not a small decision. A few more of the boys were summoned, arriving with their guns. I was allowed, for the first time in two months, to step all the way outside my room. I stumbled in my chains, carrying the clothes. As the boys corralled me forward, pushing me down the long hallway, the light intensified, coming through an open doorway ahead. My eyes felt as if they were exploding. I saw flares—a hot, exter-

minating white swirled with strains of blue and orange. I could make
out shapes against the wall, people lining my pathway.

Someone shouted in my ear, "Fast, fast, fast."

I had spent so many hours imagining the layout of the Dark House.
Now my brain flooded with actual information. There were doorways,
windows, corners. I'd lived here, but I'd never seen the place. I was outside suddenly, having stepped onto a sun-drenched concrete veranda,
in front of a whitewashed wall. The light made me unsteady. The heat
of the cement burned the soles of my bare feet. I felt tears streaming
down my cheeks. I couldn't process the blue enormity of the sky above
me. Someone gave me a push.

"Now, now, fast. Hang here."

Ahead of me was a drooping, empty clothesline. I tossed the red
dress and the tank top over it and was hustled back inside.

The air changed again, to clammy and then stifling. I was traveling the hallway, my feet too slow for my body, my eyes floating with
sunspots, my mind trying to make sense of what I was seeing. We
passed, on the left, a large room where it looked like the boys kept
their belongings, then another open doorway on the right. The room
was small but with a window—filled with enough light to make my
sore eyes throb—and a person inside. It was Nigel, bathed in sunlight,
sitting on a mattress with his blue mosquito netting draped like a king's
robe around him. He was reading a book. He did not look up as I shuffled past in my chains. I could tell from the rigid way he held himself
that he knew I was going by, but probably felt too scared to look up.

They returned me to my mat, shining a flashlight so I could find it
inside the black maw of my room. I felt disoriented, my heart pounding. The room seemed even darker than it had before. My eyes struggled to adjust. Later on, someone—I didn't see who—would toss my
dried dress and tank top through the doorway. They were practically
weightless, absent the dirt I'd scrubbed out of them, smelling like soap
and still warm from the sun.

For hours afterward, I lay on the mat, my mind running high after
the half-minute spent in the outdoor air, and also stunned by my sight-
ing of Nigel. I tried not to hate him for what I'd seen. He had books, a

window, a net to keep the mosquitos away. I wondered if he had food, if our captors spoke kindly to him, if he worried about me or knew how different our two situations had become. I wondered what would have happened if he'd looked up and caught my eye, whether it would have given me solace or a window into his mind.

I didn't know, I couldn't know.

I thought about Nigel relentlessly for days to come, settling ultimately on the idea that I had no choice but to be glad for him, even if I felt whacked simultaneously by a bitter envy. For myself, I was grateful that I'd seen anything outside my room that day. It was a reminder of air, of oceans and continents, even. I carefully redrew the map of where we were, putting Nigel and his books toward the front of the house, where the boys slept, locating the kitchen and the woman with the cough closer to me at the back, sliding one room next to another like pieces in a puzzle, taking some satisfaction in the power of clicking things into place.

37

The Snap

One day in the Dark House, Skids turned up at my door holding a cell phone. On the other end was a man, speaking a heavily accented English, who said he worked at the Somali embassy in Nairobi. He posed a proof-of-life question, the first in many months, his voice crackling over the speakerphone. I hadn't heard a voice belonging to anyone but one of my captors since the day after we'd tried to escape.

"Tell me," the man said, "where did your mother take you for vacation when you were nine years old?"

The answer was Disneyland. California. Away on a plane.

After Skids had carried the phone away, I sobbed for a day and a half straight, unable to stuff my emotions back inside.

Still, that call delivered hope. The voice had come from an embassy. An embassy implied order. Even as I wept, my mind seized on the one thread of potential meaning, the single strand of substance in that query, and used it as a towrope. I convinced myself that the question had been a carefully scripted signal that Nigel and I were going home. My mother had asked it; I had answered. She was reminding me, deliberately, of a trip we had taken. It had to be a clue, a way of letting me know that I was soon to embark on the trip I most longed for. They— our families, our governments—had to be in the final stages of getting us out. We were about to be sprung. I knew it.

For the next several days, I waited in the dark, letting those feelings percolate, certain that I was enduring my last hours as a hostage, that the door soon would swing open.

It took about a week for my hopes to fully vacate. In my heart, an airplane tilted and took off without me. I felt my mind pooling, gushing almost, into the blackness around me. I'd fooled myself. I was alone, truly. The psychic link I'd felt with my mother was a delusion. I understood that now. A ravaging despair set in.

My thoughts veered toward the irrational. Emotions hit like flash floods, tipping me when I didn't expect it. Thoughts of Nigel came without warning and dismantled my defenses. I'd feel a wave of affection and worry for him—*How is he getting through? What does he tell himself?*—but it was almost always chased by a dose of paralyzing bile. *He let them think the escape was my idea. He's sitting there, in sunlight, reading books.*

When I was angry, I spared almost no one. I had way too much time to flay people in my mind, especially my captors. I fostered a vivid fantasy in which I became invisible. I pictured myself moving through the house unseen, tying up my captors one by one. Sometimes I imagined grabbing a gun and shooting them all, every last one. The only person I'd pass over, aside from Nigel, of course, was the other woman in the house, the cook.

I now had a sharp pain in my left side that kept me curled up, knees tight against my ribs. The tension inside me was growing unbearable, like a wire pulled tight. Nothing I did seemed to relieve it. I was aware of the pressure every waking moment.

One afternoon, I heard sandals slapping the hallway floor outside my room. I steeled myself, waiting to see who was coming.

It was Abdullah. He came directly to my mat. "How are you?" he said. Then, "I want. Pull it up."

He wanted the red dress pulled toward my waist so he could undo my jeans. I rolled onto my back, turned my head to the side, and squeezed my eyes shut.

Then he was on top of me, and I was hating him with every molecule in my body. I wanted him to die. I put my hands against his chest to create a sort of barrier between us. Something in me howled. I could feel what was happening—the bough of my mind had reached its snapping point. I couldn't lift myself away from it, couldn't lessen the tension. I couldn't stand another second of this life. I was collapsing into insanity. I felt it. My head pounded as it arrived.

Bracing myself, I pushed my hands harder against Abdullah's chest, and something happened. A searing blast of heat hit my palms, a delivery of some sort, a quick shock followed by a strange, spreading calm. I wasn't in my body anymore. I was somewhere else, my mind dissipating into a vast canopy, a thing hung over this place, stretched like a collection of tiny lights. Images ran past me, scenes from stories Abdullah had told me months earlier. His life was abruptly, seamlessly on display. I saw him as a young boy, running toward an explosion, realizing that his beloved aunt had been standing at its center. I saw him collecting and carrying home what was left of her—a piece of one leg—not knowing what else to do. I saw him a few years later, hiding behind a truck as a group of gunmen went from house to house, massacring his neighbors.

For one split second, I knew his suffering. It had assembled itself and looped through me in a rush. Its absolute clarity made me gasp. It was anguish, accrued over the brief span of his life. It was rage and helplessness. It was a little kid hiding behind a truck.

This was the person who was hurting me. His sadness trenched beneath mine.

When he was gone, I lay on the mat, my body hurting the same way it always did. I felt completely confused. What had just passed? I had no idea. Whatever it was, it unsettled me. In the moment, it had felt perfectly rational and even profound, like the lifting of some great curtain, the flash of a hidden truth. But now my mind started to analyze, attempting to hammer what had happened into words and structure, and the thing itself resisted. I couldn't shape it or explain it. I could only live with it, this new feeling, complicated as it was.

In the end, though, it helped me. Because with it, I began to nurture something I'd never expected to feel in captivity—a seedling of compassion for those boys.

38

Omar

The war around us was getting worse. Somalia, in 2009, was in political flux. The president of the shaky transitional government had resigned abruptly late in 2008, leaving a power vacuum in Mogadishu. Neighboring Ethiopia, which had spent two years trying to prop up the fledgling Somali government, had all but given up, calling its troops back home. Battles raged across the country as Al-Shabaab and other Islamist groups competed for authority, letting loose on one another in block-by-block street fights, while a few thousand African Union peacekeepers—mostly from Uganda and Burundi—tried to protect what was left of the functioning government in Mogadishu.

All I knew was that the fighting appeared to follow us. The neighborhood surrounding the Dark House at first was quiet, but after a month or so, I began to hear bomb blasts and ricocheting gunfire almost daily—the blam and zing of a rising turf war.

Its closeness must have worried our captors, because they moved us, this time to a house that looked more like a mansion. I rode in the car next to Nigel. He stared wanly ahead, his shoulders hunched, his whole body seeming deflated. When I turned toward him and said, "Are you okay?" Young Yahya hit me on the side of the head. "No talk!" he screamed. I didn't speak again.

The new house was shaped like a giant L, its yard enclosed by high walls. It was bigger and grander than anything I'd seen in Somalia, with an ornate front door made of wood and a boxlike outbuilding in one corner of the scruffy yard. Positive House, I would come to call it.

Abdullah and Yahya led me down a tiled hallway. I moved awkwardly in my chains, my ribs aching, my posture stooped. During my time in the dark, I'd been kicked in the mouth so hard that two of my back teeth had come loose. One had fallen out, but the other now had abscessed, leaving the gums swollen, my jaw shooting with pain that worsened as I moved. But entering the new house, I was also wildly alert, my senses assaulted by the change of scenery.

We were in a family home, it was clear—a place that, unlike the other places we'd stayed, felt only recently vacated. The air bore a certain freshness; the floor tiles were white and clean. I could almost feel the energy, the prosperity, of the people who'd left it behind. We passed rooms filled with furniture. I saw a couch and a lamp. I saw a plush-looking mattress with a wooden headboard behind it. At the end of the long hallway, we turned right onto a shorter hall, and I was pushed through the very last door on the left-hand side.

It was a small room with a window covered by a set of heavy shutters. In one corner was a straight-backed metal chair with a missing leg and a ripped seat cushion, its yellow stuffing spilling outward. A rolled-up Persian-style carpet lay like a long cigar against the wall.

Tacked to the right of the window was a brightly colored poster, laminated in plastic, depicting a suspension bridge. I'd seen posters like this many times before, hung in the cheap restaurants and guesthouses of the backpacker ghettos I once frequented, showing landmarks and nature scenes whose hues had been Photoshopped to a bursting Technicolor unreality. I'd always found them mockable for their artificiality. But here this was, pinned to the wall before me, a giant bridge spanning a giant river with flamboyantly green headlands rising toward an orchid-colored sky at sunset. I was starved for every color it held, transfixed by the geometry of cables and girders.

I studied the bridge, the chair, the carpet, the window leaking light along the edges of the shutters. All of it was beautiful. All of it carried something loosely hopeful.

The boys had tossed my foam mat into the room, along with two plastic bags containing my belongings and sheets, and departed. It seemed this would be my new home. As I set about making the bed, I noticed something sticking out from beneath the rolled-up carpet—a bit of paper, what looked to be the corner of an envelope. My heart fluttered at the sight.

I don't know what I thought would be in that envelope. A message for me? A map? It didn't matter. The paper, whatever it was, didn't come from my captors. It was left by other people, leading other lives. It carried with it a residue of normalcy. With shaking fingers, I pulled the thing toward me. It was indeed an envelope, a slim one with a fold-down top, the kind you got when picking up prints at a photo store. Inside was a single color photo—a passport picture of a boy, bordered in white—and a slip of paper with some Somali words written on it, including what must have been the boy's name: Omar.

He looked about nine years old. He wore a collared shirt and a sober expression. He had short brambly hair and dark circles under his big brown eyes. His neck was long, like a flower stem. Beneath the seriousness, he seemed sweet and eager, as if trying to appear older than his age, worthy of whatever journey might have prompted the photo session.

I stared at Omar's picture for ten seconds, then put it back in the envelope and left it on the floor, as if it were radioactive. Which it kind of was. Almost certainly, my captors would see it as a document, and documents were a problem.

After I finished putting the sheet over the foam mat, I lay down. Then I reached for the envelope again. It was irresistible. The boy was irresistible. I held the little photo out in front of my face, so I could better see Omar and he, I imagined, could better see me. We examined each other solemnly, and then, worried that someone would surface at my door, I put him back in his envelope and stashed it beneath my mat. My pulse raced. I knew if the boys found me with it, I'd be beaten. Some part of me couldn't let go of the photo, though. I felt like Omar was mine to protect. I thought of us as allies. He'd left his house and now, in the twisted logic of his country, I was here, in his

place. It was possible that his daddy was a militia leader and he himself was already bent on jihad. But something, maybe desperation,
told me otherwise.

Every few minutes, unable to stop myself, I took Omar's picture
out from beneath my mat and looked at it again, trying to memorize
the details of his boyish face, his narrow chin, the clamshell bend of his
mouth, all the while paying attention to the doorway.

I had just slipped the envelope back into its hiding place when
Abdullah and Yahya returned. Abdullah stared at me fiercely, seeming
to read guilt on my face, and ordered me to my feet. I was sure he was
about to do one of his document searches, but instead he gestured that
I should gather my things. They'd decided to move me to a new room
in a different part of the house.

The next room would have no furniture in it, only a cardboard box
filled with white porcelain dishes and a bouquet of plastic blue flowers set on top of it. Its doorway looked out onto a patch of hallway
wall. There I'd find, nailed into the concrete, a different oversaturated,
cheesy-in-another-lifetime poster, this one showing a pile of fruit—
a pineapple, red apples, bright bananas, and a dewy pyramid of bul-
bous green grapes—all of it luridly bright, heaped against a sky-blue
backdrop. The sight would be punishing. I'd stare at it from my mat.
It would sharpen my already vicious hunger for days to come, until
finally, either sensing the lust it pulled out of me or worried that the
image offended Allah, one of the boys would take the poster down.

But before that, as I was ordered to gather my things and move from
the first room, I had to figure out what to do with my contraband. I
spent my last thirty seconds in Omar's room caught in a heart-thudding,
should-I-or-shouldn't-I crisis as, under the gaze of Abdullah and Yahya,
I slowly pulled the sheet from my mat, trying to buy some time. The
envelope with the picture lay beneath the mat. Using the sheet for a
screen, I thought I could reach down and snatch it up, attempting to
toss it into one of my plastic bags before either of the boys noticed.
I could take Omar with me, which would make me happy and also
might be safer than exposing the envelope where it lay on the floor, a
sure give-away that I'd been hiding it.

There was no time to ponder. In one quick swoop, I picked up the bags and the foam mat while making, in my chains, what passed for a fast and obedient bolt toward the door. This left Omar where he was, somewhere between the broken chair and the carpet, under the gaze of the Technicolor bridge, faceup in his paper envelope, abandoned a second time. Leaving the room, I didn't look back, and thankfully, neither did my captors.

39

Positive House

We stayed in Positive House for about two months, and there, too, the fighting crept closer. I could hear gun battles outside my window. The boys seemed wound up by the war. A new president had been appointed to run the transitional government in Mogadishu—a former high school geography teacher named Sheik Sharif Sheik Ahmed, who, a few years earlier, had helped build an alliance of Islamist groups in Mogadishu and managed briefly to keep the city's warlords in line. The boys had been thrilled with their new president. The week Sheik Sharif was elected by the Somali Parliament, back in the Dark House, Abdullah had broken from routine and spent a few minutes talking to me about how excited they were to have the Ethiopian troops gone and a strong Muslim leader in office. The struggle was over, he said. Thousands of people who'd fled Mogadishu were moving back home. Sheik Sharif would unite all the Islamic factions using *sharia* law.

"The fighting will stop," Abdullah had predicted, sounding confident. The prospect of peace seemed to please him. I trusted that the new political order meant something hopeful for me and Nigel as well.

But all I'd been able to hear through the walls of the Dark House was more fighting.

What I learned when we got to Positive House was that not only had the boys lost faith in the new president quickly, they now saw him as an enemy. Their optimism had flipped into something darker. In

Sheik Sharif's first weeks in office, he'd established himself as a moderate and—more horrifyingly to my captors—a coalition builder, open to seeking support from foreign governments, saying he wanted to make peace with Ethiopia, a predominantly Christian nation. In Positive House, the boys docked themselves in front of the radio in the afternoons, listening to the news on the BBC Somali World Service. The war was escalating rather than dwindling, the hard-line Islamists pitted against the new president and his ideas about peace. Al-Shabaab and Hizbul Islam, another insurgent group, were launching fresh attacks against the African Union peacekeeping troops protecting the government in the capital. The peacekeepers were fighting back. After a roadside bomb hit one of their trucks, African Union soldiers were said to have opened fire on a crowd, killing more than a dozen bystanders.

With this, the boys declared the new president a *kafir*—an unbeliever—and the jihad fully back on.

They were talking to me again, more than they had since the escape attempt. All the rules held—I was not allowed to sit up on my mat without permission; I was expected to only lie on my side—but the boys' hatred had realigned itself somewhat; they seemed more focused on politics, less bent on making me suffer. They kept the windows of my room shut against the daylight, even stuffing the cracks with plastic bags to blot out any stray lines of sun. None of it worked, though. I could see and hear more than ever. Darkness, for me, was now relative.

Romeo began to make long visits to the house, staying for three or four days at a time and bringing with him a different energy. As a leader, he granted new freedoms to the boys and to Captain Skids. All of them now got full days and nights off, going home to see their families. They'd come back with new haircuts, in fresh shirts and good spirits. Sometimes they arrived with a bag of fruit or pieces of fried fish to share with everyone. Every so often, as a treat, they'd bring me something—a toffee or a ripe purple passion fruit sliced open at the middle.

From my mat, I could see out my door and down the hallway, catching a glimpse of the room on the opposite side where Nigel was kept. It looked big, like a living room, and was furnished. I could see a brown couch against one wall. The boys regularly spent time in there, talking with Nigel. I could overhear snippets of the conversation. Nigel told them about how he liked to build houses, saying he wanted to build houses in Somalia, even. I heard him ask if he could sleep on the couch, and I heard them answer no. They did, however, let him remove the cushions and make a bed for himself on the floor.

They seemed frequently to discuss girls and Islam. "We call it *masturbation*," I heard Nigel say loudly one day. The boys were tittering. They were teasing one another about who did it, making jokes about the extra bathing required by Islam after ejaculation. One of them made exaggerated sounds of orgasm, causing more laughter.

With Romeo in the house and the war in full swing around us, Abdullah was permitted to take on daytime soldiering jobs, going out once or twice a week and joining militias fighting the African Union troops. It was part of his jihad. Among the boys in the house, he seemed the only one keen on street fighting. He'd get a call in the evening from some commander and spend hours readying himself for the following day. He'd fiddle with his gear, sometimes lugging it into my room to show off. These were the rare moments when I could converse with Abdullah, when he'd allow me to ask a question or comment on what he said. He'd stand in my doorway and clean his AK-47 with an oily rag, talking all the while about how, God willing, he would kill a lot of enemies the next day.

"*Inshallah*," he said on one of the first nights we had this exchange, "tomorrow I am dead."

I reacted automatically, with an objection—not because I didn't want him to die but because it seemed the only decent response. "Don't say that!" I said. "You don't want to die. Think of your mother. She'd be so sad."

Abdullah shook his head at me. "No, it is best way." He added one of his favorite comments, "You are a bad Muslim." He took his gun and walked out the door. A few minutes later, he reappeared, carrying Nigel's blue leather copy of the Koran. Setting the gun down and seating himself near my mat, he paged through the book, finally alighting on the right passage. He pointed to the relevant line on the English side of the page. *Let those fight in the cause of Allah, who sell the life of this world for the hereafter.*

I'd read it before. I knew the boys believed that paradise would be their reward, that in a straight-up trade, there was no arguing that any sacrifice made in their hot, hungry country wasn't worth an eternal seat on a jeweled couch in *Jannah*. This, for them, was the creed. Abdullah was reminding me that I was supposed to believe it, too.

*

At twenty-four, Romeo was not only older than the boys but seemed to come from a different world altogether. He was sophisticated, speaking English without effort, in a clipped bookish accent that resembled the way I'd heard English spoken in India. He wore jeans and a nice-looking scarf and cologne that smelled expensive. He claimed to have a university degree in engineering and spoke of his travels to Kenya.

In the afternoons, he visited me, sitting cross-legged against the wall opposite my mat. He looked me directly in the eye and punctuated his speech with well-worn Western phrases. "You know what I mean?" he'd say after telling me something. "You get my point?"

He did not strike me as friendly, but talking to me seemed to feed his ego. He told me he was the twenty-eighth child in his family. His father had married four women. After his father died, everyone except Romeo had fled Mogadishu for the northern city of Hargeisa. He said that he himself was unmarried, focused on his education. He was taking correspondence courses through the University of Yemen. He wanted to get another degree, in information technology, and work with computers. He was applying to graduate schools.

"You look very nice," he said one day. "Very healthy." He leaned in closer. "You see, before we took you, you did not look good. You were looking very bad." He pointed to his forehead and then toward mine, mimicking the motion of eyebrow plucking, which I knew was an act of vanity forbidden by the *hadith*. In my previous life, I'd been an assiduous, even zealous, eyebrow plucker. After eight months in captivity, I knew that my brows were thick and straight as caterpillars.

Romeo was voicing his approval. "Allah makes you very beautiful," he said. "When you leave here, a man will be very lucky to have you as his wife."

I would have given anything, then more than ever, to go at my eyebrows with a pair of tweezers. I was vain. I was *still* vain, stubbornly vain. I'd rot in the hellfires for an arch in my brow.

The truth was, I was an unsightly wreck. My body was deteriorating. I had broken teeth from some of the beatings. My ribs never stopped aching before they were kicked again, and making it worse, I'd developed a bad cough. My hair was falling away in clumps. The dirty water cramped my stomach. The itchy skin fungus had spread along the left side of my face, down my neck and chest. My skin oozed with pus.

But I was past feeling sorry for myself. I began to make declarations, piggybacking them on to my regular silent talks with myself in the evenings. I'd made it out of the Dark House, I reminded myself, and I'd get out of this place. I summoned all my confidence and directed it at my body. Rather than thinking, as I often had, *I hope my stomach stops cramping and maybe tomorrow my diarrhea will go away,* I got bold. I stated everything like a truth, a proclamation. *My digestive system is healthy. I get nourishment from the food I'm eating. My skin is healthy, smooth, and healed.* I went through it daily, a point-by-point scan of my body—an incantation, a resurrection. *My eyesight is good. My teeth are solid. My hair is full. My mind is strong.* I focused a lot on my reproductive system, the part of me I worried about most. I hadn't had a period since being captured. I felt pains in places I couldn't identify. I tried not to think about them. *My organs are protected,* I told myself. *My ovaries still work. I am okay.*

One morning Skids came to my room and dropped a small plastic bag on the floor. Inside was a blister pack of capsule pills, sheathed in a narrow box that bore a picture of bananas and oranges on the front. Its information panel appeared to be written in Chinese. Half the pills were gone. At the bottom of the bag I found a square of paper, a form from a pharmacy, printed in English and filled out in pen. It read:

Name: Sahro

Age: 34

There was a check next to the word "Female."

It was a gift. The medicine was a gift, but to know her name meant even more. Sahro, Age 34. It had to be her, the woman whose retching cough had penetrated my nights in the Dark House, the otherwise silent cook for my captors. She'd heard me coughing. She wanted to help. She had pressed those tablets into the captain's hands, I was sure of it, telling him that I should have them. He might have balked at first, but she'd insisted, and he'd relented. I saw the whole story in my mind. She cared, and that mattered. I took Sahro's pills, one every morning. They didn't seem to help, but at least she and I had a bond.

*

The bathroom I used at Positive House was outdoors. Getting there involved a long walk down the main hallway, a turn to the right, and a trip down the shorter hall, past Omar's room—now being used as a kitchen—and then through a door to a bathroom stall in the yard. The boys had given me a pair of shoes—a set of oversized yellow flip-flops with the words "HAPPY 2008" and a bunch of balloons printed on the sole though half worn away with age.

As I moved, I kept my eyes on the ground, followed closely each time by one of the boys. My gaze was supposed to be always lowered. A few times, passing Omar's room, I'd seen a set of feet belonging to the cook—Sahro, Age 34—as she paused in the doorway, evidently watching me. She was close enough to touch. I could see the flowered hemline of her dress, long enough to graze the floor and hide her feet, in keeping with Islamic custom.

One day, overcome by a burst of courage and a deeper longing to know the woman who'd shown me such kindness, I glanced up at her face.

She was beautiful, strikingly so. Her body was willowy and tall, her features finely sculpted. Her eyes were dark, her cheeks sloping, her chin a slender point. She had the same angular face and elegant carriage as the Somali fashion model Iman. She wore a light brown scarf wrapped tightly over her head.

When our eyes met, Sahro let out a gasp. Her hand flew up to cover her mouth. We'd lived under the same roof for several months, but this was to be our first and only contact. Her eyes widening in alarm, she looked toward Yahya, who had been trailing me to the bathroom with his gun, and uttered a Somali word that seemed to indicate her state of surprise, something akin to "Oh!"

It wasn't a betrayal, but it certainly wasn't an act of allegiance. If anything, it told me that she was as afraid of the boys as I was, that despite being willing to share her medicine, she wouldn't, even for an instant, be caught conspiring with me. She didn't dare.

Without hesitation, Yahya hit me from behind, landing a punch on my back and another on my head. My gaze fell again to Sahro's hemline against the floor.

Later that day, Jamal and Abdullah would come to my room and hit me repeatedly as I lay curled in a ball, making me promise never to look up. I wouldn't dare try it again, but I was glad, at least, to have seen her face.

40

Wife Lessons

This might be difficult for you," Romeo said to me one afternoon in June, "but this life, it's like this." He snapped his fingers to show no time at all. "And the rewards of paradise are forever."

It was meant as encouragement. The idea was that we should hold steady because better things were coming. For my captors, God's plan was unfolding. For me, captivity was a moment—a long moment—that would pass. We all waited on an afterlife. Only I planned to be alive for mine.

We had moved again. We were staying a long way from Mogadishu, somewhere near the port city of Kismayo, in the south of Somalia, not far from the border with Kenya. I wasn't supposed to know where we were, but I did. On the drive there, about twelve hours in an SUV piloted by Ahmed, we fishtailed over desert tracks, slamming through ditches and climbing the sides of steep ravines, avoiding the north-south highway altogether. As the boys sat in the two forward seats, their gunmetal clinking in the dark, Nigel and I, too afraid to say even one word to each other, lay jammed in the hatch of the car, stuck between Romeo, who for some reason had volunteered to sit there, and a sloshing fifty-gallon drum of fuel. I'd listened to the boys murmuring with excitement at the promise of the unknown. It was as if they were on a school field trip. It seemed as far away from home as they'd ever been. With the moon coasting alongside us, they craned their necks to see out the window.

Kismayo, they were saying quietly, betraying the secret without realizing it, *Kismayo, Kismayo.*

In Kismayo, I could taste the Indian Ocean on my tongue. Its humidity coated my skin, causing the shackles on my legs to rust, leaving florid streaks on my ankles. It was never in my sight, the ocean, but I could tell it was nearby, reaching east toward Australia, sprinkled, as I imagined it, with yachts and tanker ships and islands full of people going about their business. At night, storms swept overhead, dousing the place with rain.

For weeks, Romeo and Ahmed had been threatening to sell me and Nigel to Al-Shabaab. I was sure they'd brought us here to complete the deal. Kismayo was known to be a Shabaab stronghold. The thought of having to live under new captors and new rules—among the most extreme extremists in the country—filled me with anxiety.

After a few days, though, I realized that we'd moved to Kismayo only to get away from the fighting. We'd spent two nights in a second-floor apartment in the heart of the city and were now living in an empty office building, a place with five small rooms, located away from the downtown bustle—a place we would later refer to as the Beach House. My captors were likely paying protection money to Al-Shabaab in order to stay. Several times on our trip through the desert, we'd had to stop so that Skids could hand cash to the various warlords who controlled the road.

Nigel had been put in a room across from mine. It was hot enough that the boys didn't loiter outdoors. Instead, they camped out in the reception area just beyond my door, closer than they'd ever been. They kept their Korans stacked on a battered-looking receptionist's desk in one corner. All of us shared a bathroom with a squat toilet, spattered and rank from its previous tenants. The water supply was a waist-high cistern, its surface wriggling with mosquito larvae.

Romeo, it seemed, had moved in with us for good. Over ten months, the faces had changed, with different men on duty at different times. A few of our captors disappeared altogether, vanishing like wisps of smoke. Ali, the man who'd been our main guard in the first days of captivity, the one who'd taken credit for our conversion to Islam, had left after only a few weeks. Ismael, the youngest soldier of all, who said he was fourteen but looked closer to eleven, who appeared terrified any time he came near us, also had slipped away during the first month. As winter passed into spring, we'd seen less and less of Donald Trump. Young Yahya, whose wife had a new baby at home, stayed a few weeks in Kismayo and then departed, never to return. Sahro, Age 34, my silent female ally, had not made the trip south at all.

I had only the vaguest of understandings of what knit our captors together. Ismael had no immediate family to return to. I knew that because very early on, when Nigel and I were kept in the same room, Abdullah had made Ismael pull up his pant leg one day, showing us how his entire calf muscle had been stripped off in an explosion, his lower leg shaped like a mostly eaten drumstick. The boy then lifted his shirt, exposing flamelike scars that wrapped around his torso, the skin puckered and tawny and hard to even look at. Abdullah had explained that Ismael had survived a mortar attack that killed the rest of his family. He was an orphan, and as happened with a lot of orphaned boys in Mogadishu, he'd been pulled into the group—promised shelter, food, and community.

After Ismael disappeared, I'd asked Romeo what had happened to him, and he'd had to think about it a minute, not recollecting the boy's name. Ultimately, he'd shrugged, saying that probably Ismael had been passed on to a new militia—shuffled, as it were, into a different deck of cards.

*

It was difficult to understand how our group functioned—who was pulling the strings, who recruited the boys and paid for food, who had made the decision to move us to Kismayo. Who, I wondered, would profit most if our ransom was paid? And if it wasn't, who then made the decision on when to give up, when to either kill us or set us free?

Much later, I would read about the rogue and rough-seeming Somali pirate operations in the Gulf of Aden, in many cases run with the acumen and polish of mini-corporations, complete with investors, accountants, and structured payrolls based on the net ransom. One journalist studied a successful seventy-five-day ship hijacking with a ransom of $1.8 million and determined that about half went to the financiers, while middlemen (presumably men like Adam, Donald Trump, and Romeo) made more like $60,000, and guards got something closer to $12,000. In a country with an average per capita income of $266 per year, it was very good money, but only if everything went the right way.

One afternoon, Romeo turned up in my doorway to announce some big news: He'd applied and been accepted to a university in New York City, to study information technology. He'd be leaving for America in a matter of months. He had many questions for me. Had I been to New York? How cold would it be there? Did I think people in America would be able to understand his accent? He planned to live with relatives who were already there. My ransom, he said, would fund his tuition. "*Inshallah,*" he added. "If Allah permits it."

He'd taken new interest in my education as a Muslim, carrying Nigel's English-language Koran into my room and delivering long sermons about devotion and destiny. Happy to have access to a book, any book, I was again inhabiting the role of eager student. When Romeo was present, I was allowed to sit up and talk. I felt human. His presence was also protective, keeping Abdullah and the others away. Once or twice, he opened the Koran and showed me the lines covering "those whom your right hand possesses," which, to his way of thinking, was a category that included me. He and the other leaders knew I was being abused by some of the boys in the house, but even while viewing themselves as too dignified to participate in such behavior, they believed I was not to question what the boys did. It was my lot as a captive. As it was with every person on earth, my fate had been written into my soul when I was in my mother's womb. "Allah will decide when it is over for you," he said. In the meantime, he was convinced that Allah was going to come through on his college plan.

"Why," I asked him, "would you want to study in the country of infidels?" I'd heard him refer to the United States this way many times before.

The question seemed to make Romeo momentarily uncomfortable, as if he recognized the hypocrisy, but he bounced back, his tone
languid and even. "Allah says that we can go to these countries if there
is a purpose," he said. "If we can take something from that country
and we can then give it to the Islamic community, then it is good."

Sometimes he would venture into a coyer sort of conversation. "Do
you think Somali men are handsome?" he asked one day. "Are they
better than men in your country?" Outside, a rare breeze blew, thrush-
ing over the tin roof. Romeo sat across from my mat with his knees
splayed and the Koran perched on his lap. When I didn't answer, he
tried a different tack. "Are there any of the soldiers you would like to
marry?"

By "soldiers," he meant the boys. I told him no, I never wanted to
marry any of those soldiers.

He smiled, raising his eyebrows. His voice was sonorous, wheedling. "If I asked you to marry me, would you be happy?"

I noted that he didn't ask whether I'd say yes. I'd sensed this sort of
proposition coming, but hearing him say it made me quake with fear.
If I were forced into some sort of formal marriage, I might never get
away.

"I am not in a position to make a decision about marriage," I said,
shaking my head to emphasize that there was no possibility whatsoever. "I'm a prisoner."

"Ah yes," Romeo said, "but this is where Allah has decided you
should be." He folded his hands in his lap and looked at me matter-of-
factly. "Do not fight it, Amina."

For Romeo, the ongoing conversation about marriage seemed in
part an active fantasy, a way to pass the time. Even he, I suspected,
got tired of talking round-the-clock about the Koran. He described
a kind of win-win situation in which he collected a fat payoff and a
bride to boot. He said that if it were up to him, he'd marry me right
away, except that everybody in the group had too much riding on the
ransom, so "the Program," as he called it, would need to be resolved.
Once it was, I could live in his mother's house in Hargeisa, he said,
even while he was at school in New York. He added that because I was

white, I would probably have to stay hidden in a room—"a big room!"
he said, as if the idea might thrill me—so that I wouldn't be harassed
or kidnapped.

"If you were the mother of my children," he told me, "you would
teach my sons about jihad. You would encourage them to fight jihad in
Somalia or in another country. You would teach them the Koran, and
you would be very, very good with that."

His flattery was never comforting. One afternoon, he leaned in
close and pointed out a certain verse of the Koran. It was one of the
ones I'd read plenty of times before. *Your wives are a tilth for you, so go
into your tilth when you like* . . . A tilth, as I understood it, was a field to
be plowed.

Romeo smiled. "Do you know, when you are my wife, what this
will mean?"

My heart sank. "Yes, but I don't want to discuss these things," I told
him.

His term for sex was "making enjoyable." "*Inshallah,* when you are
my wife, we will be making enjoyable all the time," Romeo told me
that day. "Because I am wanting enjoyable all the time."

I kept my eyes on the floor and said nothing until he stood up and
left the room.

★

In the Beach House, when Romeo wasn't around, all I could do was
listen. In the reception area just past my door, I could hear the boys
coughing and spitting. I listened to them wash and pray. I knew when
they were cleaning their teeth with fibrous acacia sticks, or telling
jokes, or sunk into a collective state of dull misery. I could hear when
one of the boys snapped his fingers, summoning Nigel to get up and
do his ablutions.

Much of the noise in the house came from their cell phones. Everyone had one. A couple of the boys owned two. These were high-end
phones, some with touch screens, bought with money they'd earned
fighting prior to our kidnapping. Because we had no electricity, someone would carry the phones to the marketplace late in the day to be

charged at a kiosk, left overnight in exchange for a few coins. Rarely were the phones used for actual conversation. Jamal occasionally had short, awkward dialogues with Hamdi. Only the captain and Romeo received regular calls, presumably from the leaders who had stayed behind in Mogadishu.

The boys fiddled endlessly with their phones, changing their ring-tones, which, given that *sharia* law prohibited music, were never musical. They used birds chirping, bells ringing, and children laugh-ing, all of which drove me crazy. Away from the house, they loaded their phones with *nasheeds*—Arabic chants that extolled the glory of Allah or the virtues of Muhammad. Sometimes the boys would come into my room and show me videos downloaded from Saudi Arabian websites. The videos seemed designed expressly to incite and enrage, showing dead Palestinians and dead Afghans and lots of dead chil-dren. There were explosions in Iraq, intercut with video of the World Trade Center buildings collapsing into a haze of yellow dust. There were masked mujahideen soldiers performing military drills and fir-ing mantislike grenade launchers against a backdrop of jagged moun-tain peaks. With Arabic subtitles running along the bottom, one video repeatedly showed George W. Bush announcing, "This crusade, this war on terrorism, is going to take a while." All around the world, Islam was under siege.

I was soon able to distinguish between the voices of the individual imams who narrated them against a backdrop of tinny gun blasts and people screaming. I could tell which jihad video was most in vogue at any given time. New videos cycled in and out of our household rou-tine. *My God, I remember thinking, these guys spend something like ten hours a day watching people die on their phones.*

★

Through the bars over the window in the Beach House bathroom, I could see past the walls of our compound to a green neon light that shone in the distance at night, marking what I guessed was the entrance to a mosque. Every so often, I saw the headlights of a pass-ing car.

Feral cats sometimes wandered into the house, scavenging for food. The boys threw things at them—shoes, garbage—to shoo them away, but still the cats often found their way into my room—side-winding, rickety-backed creatures, most of them nearly bald. Stuck on my mat, unable to stand, I was in no position to defend myself as they advanced. They hovered while I ate a meal, erupting in violent hissing fights over the grease-slicked, deep-welled tin plate I'd ultimately leave on the floor.

The weeks blurred. My twenty-eighth birthday came and went, though I'd lost track of the individual days. I woke and slept, listening to the thumps of frigate birds landing on the roof. One day the voice of the Somali newscaster for the BBC threaded through my consciousness as the boys sat gathered around the radio in the next room. "Michael Jackson," he was saying. "Michael Jackson. Michael Jackson." The singer was dead, but it would be a long while before I knew it.

I was beginning to starve. Each morning, I was given three cubes of animal fat boiled in a weak, oily broth and a few small pieces of dense flatbread. Sometimes I got a cup of tea. Later in the day, after the evening prayer, I'd get the same thing again, often with a very ripe banana alongside it. At times, instead of three cubes of fat, there'd be only two. Once in a while, a day would pass with no food at all. My own body shocked me. My hip bones jutted like chicken wings. I could see each one of my ribs. My breasts had all but disappeared, my chest no more than a striation of bones.

Hunger feels like a rock in your belly, heavy and painful at the edges. Other times, my stomach felt like a balloon inflated to almost bursting, filled with a tight, dry emptiness. The ache took over my brain, to the point where I wanted to bash my head on something to make it stop.

Lying on my mat, I found relief in visiting my house in the sky. I went there and tried to stay as long as I could. Inside the shelter of my mind, I cooked and ate and took care of my body. I made soups, salmon, healthy things. I imagined picking fresh vegetables from a garden, or plucking oranges from the laden trees I'd seen long ago in Venezuela. This sustained me. It made all the difference.

Still, I needed to get more food. As I had done with other problems, I looked for solutions inside of my captors' religion. I had read in the footnotes of my Koran that the Prophet recommended his followers fast on Mondays and Thursdays. It was not obligatory—the way fasting over the month of Ramadan was obligatory—but several of the boys in the house routinely did it, saying it kept them pure. Hassam, one of the more diligent fasters, once explained to me that the Prophet called for his followers to break a fast with bread and dates, but in Somali tradition, they broke it with samosas, which counted as bread.

Knowing this, I decided to try something. "Hassam," I said one morning, a Thursday, when he arrived with my morning food, "Allah said it is good for the Muslims to fast. I want to fast, to be a better Muslim, like you."

He smiled broadly at this, knowing that he got credit with Allah for any uptick in my devotion. "Okay, Amina. It is very good." He left the room, and I could hear him relaying my announcement to the others outside.

Jamal and Yusef both stuck their heads in my door to congratulate me on my decision to fast. I could see they were surprised, but again, my growth as a Muslim gave them more points on Judgment Day.

My gamble paid off. I made it through the day, having declined the morning meal, and just before the muezzin called at six P.M., Jamal showed up, carrying a small plastic bag whose contents I could smell from across the room. Inside the bag were five little samosas, deep-fried triangles filled with spiced rice and what seemed to be cabbage. I fasted in order to eat. Sometimes the samosas were warm and delicious; other times they weren't fresh and would make me sick. But either way it didn't matter. They were nourishment.

*

I began to hear a new voice coming from the boys' phones. This voice was calmer than that of the fiery sermons they played, a man's Arabic alto that rang through the Beach House, sometimes broadcast from multiple phones at once. Outside, I heard the same voice being blasted from cars passing by.

One afternoon, Romeo came in holding his cell phone and a pad of paper. "Amina," he said almost genially, "I need help to improve my

English." Taking a seat on the floor, he handed me the paper and a pen. "You can write down the words for me. In English. And I will practice them. You get my point?"

He hit a button on his phone and then pivoted it so I could see the screen. A video began to play: A black screen with some Arabic writing on it faded into a map of Somalia, with a still photo of Osama bin Laden superimposed in one corner. He was dressed in a dark robe with a white cotton scarf draped over his head and shoulders. He held one long finger hoisted in the air. The audio began to play. It was the voice I'd been hearing. Bin Laden had released an audiotape addressing the mujahideen fighters in Somalia and, for the first time, linking the country's struggle to Al Qaeda's larger aims. Over the course of several months, the message had gone viral. Everyone around me, I realized, was electrified.

"Please," said Romeo, "write the English." I squinted to see the tiny subtitles running across the bottom of his screen and began to write. *To my patient . . . persevering . . . Muslim brothers . . .* The video was eleven minutes long. It would take me almost three days to transcribe the whole thing, with Romeo coming and going, sitting by me holding his phone for an hour or so at a time. It had been months since I'd written more than a few words. My hand ached from the effort. Bin Laden was calling for the Islamic soldiers to overthrow Sheik Sharif, the new president, who was barely hanging on as it was. He praised the Somali fighters and made clear that he saw them as being on the front line of a battleground, protecting their brothers in Palestine, Iraq, and Afghanistan. In an even, paternal tone, he railed against the Americans, urging everyone to dig in, to show no tolerance of alliances with the West.

Bin Laden spoke. Romeo watched. I wrote, my head bent low over the paper in the dim light of the room. The video played then paused, played then paused, as the words filled pages of the notepad. Bin Laden was warning his Somali brothers against falling prey to peace deals or diplomacy, all the trappings of compromise: *How can intelligent people believe that yesterday's enemies, on the basis of religion, can become today's friends?*

In other words, a war, once begun, must be seen through to the end.

41

Everything Is Changed

R omeo's application for a student visa to the United States had been approved. He was in high spirits, asking more questions than ever. How long would the plane ride be? Was it true that girls in New York wore shirts that displayed their bellies? When he came now to give me lessons in Islam, he asked me to help him correct any pronunciation errors in his English, to smooth out the edges of his accent. He bought a special notebook—a thin, cheaply made book with pink and purple cartoon hearts across the cover—asking me to write down the most difficult English words I could think up, terms that would be useful for an eager student wishing to sound intelligent in a new country.

It was August. He was supposed to leave in September to begin school. I hoped that would put new pressures on whatever negotiations were happening with my family and Nigel's.

In over three months at the Beach House, though his door was about eight feet from mine, I'd caught sight of Nigel only a handful of times. Every so often, when he heard the boys snapping to tell me I could go to the bathroom ahead of the noon prayer, he would crawl forward from his mat and crane his head to see across the narrow hall. The sight of him was a shock, his face thin and haggard, his beard a bushy mess. He wore a *macawii* and a tank top that hung off his bony shoulders. We peered at each other, mutually heartbroken and helpless.

Taking an extra risk one day, Nigel pointed to himself and then to me, making the shape of a heart with his hands. *I love you.* We'd been prisoners for close to a year.

Through the window in the bathroom, I watched the season change again, the daily rains slowly lightening to nothing, replaced by the hard-bitten burn of late summer, what Somali people call *hagaa* season. At the mosque in the distance, someone had switched out the entrance light from neon green to a garish, mesmerizing pink.

Along with the heat, tension was rising in the house among the boys, frustration laced with futility. Hassam had spent a couple of weeks stricken by malaria. Jamal's wedding to Hamdi had been put on hold indefinitely. Now that Yahya, one of my primary guards, was gone, Young Mohammed—among the more violent members of the group—watched over me with renewed intensity. Money seemed to be running low. The boys complained constantly of their own hunger.

I took hope from the fact that Romeo was still talking about New York, as if money for his plane ticket—the money from our ransom— would be coming through any day. As an act of faith, I jotted down words for him to study.

Sectarian, I wrote. *Parsimonious. Autonomous.*

*

I could see that the boys were desperate to be done with our kidnapping, but I couldn't begin to guess what was happening with the leaders of the group or at home. When I asked about progress, Romeo feigned helplessness, blaming my mother for not paying the ransom. Having invested twelve months of time and expense, and having conjured some idea that all Westerners swam in rivers of cash, my captors weren't interested in compromising on money. They were convinced that my mother was the gatekeeper to their fortune. They just needed to find a way to break her down. Only later would I understand how calculating they were, what kind of chess match was being played across continents.

At home, my family had given up on the Canadian government, joining with the Brennans to hire an outside kidnap-and-ransom specialist named John Chase to get us out of Somalia. Attempts at diplomacy and intelligence gathering had yielded no visible progress. The families would need to raise money and strike a deal directly with our captors. At the start of August, they committed to a contract with Chase's company, a British-based "risk mitigation" outfit called AKE. The two families agreed to split the costs—the ransom and AKE's fee of about two thousand dollars per day—even if my family needed to rely on funds raised by the Brennans up front and repay them later. Quickly, they began pooling whatever money they had.

After months of not answering her cell phone when Adam called, my mother was back on the job as negotiator—this time with the guidance of Chase and his associates in England and regular phone input from Nigel's family in Australia. Nigel's sister, Nicky, was also communicating with Adam. The RCMP operational center in Sylvan Lake had been shut down: My mother rented a basement apartment for herself a few hours away in Canmore. She recorded phone calls with Adam on her own, transmitting them to Chase through encrypted e-mail.

On the phone, Adam sounded more bellicose than ever. The group, he said, was angry. They would take $2 million and no less. My mother, on behalf of the two families, made a series of counteroffers, rising in small increments, closely following AKE's advice. Every move was meant to slowly fold our captors into a deal. Chase thought the matter could be settled for about half a million dollars. On August 2, my mother told Adam they could pay $281,000. By the end of the month, she was offering $434,000.

None of it was good enough. Adam dug in. The phone calls grew heated. He suggested that I must not be my mother's biological child, since she cared so little about me. Fed up with his unwillingness to drop the ransom demand even slightly, my mother at one point accused him of "playing games."

This ratcheted up Adam's temper even higher. And led to a threat. "I am playing a game?" he said with blistering scorn. "You should see my game."

*

With the start of another Ramadan late in August, I had let my defenses down. It was the holy month, a time of restraint. Sexual activity was forbidden during daylight hours, which helped me feel safer. Through my windows, I could hear *nasheeds* playing over the mosque loudspeaker.

Romeo had left for a while, not saying where he was going. The boys' moods seemed to lighten a little. Skids had received some money and bought everyone new sandals. We were eating better—abstaining from food from dawn until sunset but then rewarded with fresh, sweet dates to break the fast. A couple of the boys would go to the market late in the afternoon and buy a sticky mound of them, delivering a few to me at dusk, wrapped in a piece of an English-language paper printed in Dubai called the *Khaleej Times*. Back when I'd been trying to freelance as a journalist, I'd pitched stories to an editor there. Now I read whatever small scrap lay beneath my dates, looking for any piece of news I could find. I saw stock market listings and, at one point, a short item from Canada—a story about how rabbits were overpopulating on the University of Victoria campus.

With the extra money, Jamal and Hassam had the supplies to prepare an evening meal, usually a dish of red beans and rice that they called *ambola*. They'd cook it all afternoon and serve it after the sunset prayer, topped with heaps of white sugar and salt for extra taste.

"You like?" Jamal would say, watching me eat, hoping for a compliment. "Is good?"

At night, the boys were busy running through extra sets of prayers, called *taraweeh*, or "rest prayers." I'd read about them in the *hadith*. Nighttime prayers during Ramadan helped Allah forgive a person his or her sins.

One day things shifted abruptly. Three of the boys—Abdullah, Mohammed, Jamal—came into my room, looking grave. Abdullah barked an order, telling me to stand up. They were all business, avoiding eye contact with me.

They had me walk to the middle of the room and lie facedown, my forehead pressed against the concrete floor. Abdullah lifted the blue-flowered sheet from my mat. Standing over me, he used the sheet to tie my wrists behind my back. A minute later, he adjusted it, loosening and sliding the sheet so that it sat at my elbows, then yanked it tight again. My shoulders pulled painfully off the floor. My pulse raced, my mind careening toward panic. What was happening?

I could hear the boys conferring above me in Somali, sounding as if they were debating something. After a minute, they untied me and waved me back toward my mat, continuing their discussion all the while, as if I weren't present. Sweating, I lay back down. Mohammed was pointing at a couple of pieces of rebar that protruded from a high spot on the wall, as if maybe they could hang something from them. Jamal twisted and tugged at my blue sheet, testing its strength. The three of them inspected everything in the room carefully, methodically. Without another glance in my direction, they left.

I lay on my mat, knowing that something terrible was coming.

I waited all day and the next.

The following evening, they came back after sunset, after the fast was broken and dinner served. It was Mohammed and Abdullah this time. They closed the door behind them. Mohammed carried a bedsheet, a pale shade of yellow. It had been twisted up like a rope. He dropped it on the floor.

I sat up on my mat. "Is everything okay?" I said. All I could see was that twisted sheet.

Abdullah said, "Stand up."

I got to my feet very slowly, the chains clicking between my ankles. I looked at their faces and saw nothing there, just blankness. My mind started leaping along with my heart, ferreting for an escape. "I haven't prayed yet," I heard myself say. "I need to wash."

The boys looked at each other. They could never argue with Islam. "Quickly," Abdullah said.

Shuffling to the bathroom, I noticed that they'd closed the door to Nigel's room.

Once inside, I stood at the open window, watching the buzzy pink light of the mosque in the distance, trying to steel myself against whatever was coming. The night was inky, starless. I could feel a low breeze. The dread I felt was primitive, animals racing for the hills, an ancient bell tolling loudly for the village to evacuate. They were going to hurt me, I knew. *Gather your strength,* I told myself. *You need to be strong.*

Abdullah and Mohammed waited outside the bathroom. They followed me back to my room, closed the door, and then sat against the wall as I prayed. I ran through the cycles of prayer as slowly and precisely as I could, hoping to lodge some reminder that I was like them. Finishing the last *raka'ah*, I commenced the silent prayer, one of the add-ons to regular prayers, in which you praised Allah a hundred times in your head. I was sliding a different set of words through my mind, as slowly as I possibly could. *Be strong, be strong, be strong, be strong.* I repeated it a hundred times over.

When I was done, when all my options for stalling had been used up, I stood and turned to face the boys. Abdullah told me to lie on the floor, on my stomach, as I had two days earlier. With the yellow sheet, he bound my arms together just above the elbows and below my biceps. My shoulders and chest pulled up awkwardly, and I felt them jerk back even more. My whole torso arched. My feet were being pulled upward, too, behind my back, in the direction of my bound arms. I felt cloth winding around my ankles and, suddenly, a connected tension. I understood then what they had done: My hands and feet were roped together, pulling in opposite directions. I was immobilized. My body had been drawn into a taut bow. My muscles immediately started to scream. Mohammed tugged off my head scarf and refitted it as a blindfold over my eyes, yanking it tight. My eyeballs instantly throbbed, the nerves behind them stabbed with pain. I saw white light. My head felt like it would pop.

I was trussed like an animal. My panic was immediate. I couldn't last a minute this way. I couldn't last even a second. I couldn't form a thought beyond the pain of that position, my back straining from neck to tailbone. The twisted sheet dug into my arms and ankles, cutting off circulation. My lungs felt compressed. I struggled to breathe, gagging as if someone were pouring sand down my throat. "It's too tight," I shouted, my voice raspy and alien. "It's too tight!"

At some point, the boys left the room. Neither had uttered a word the whole time.

*

What did they think about, the whole group of them, sitting outside my door during those first minutes, those first hours? Did they talk? Did they laugh? I'd never know.

I was lost to everyone, drilled down into some underground place, trying to lift imaginary boulders, trying to pull up enough energy to get me through. Pain tore through my shoulders and back, searing the length of my spine. My neck bent toward the floor, my head unable to reach it and take away some of the strain. My thoughts warred: *I can't bear this. You have to hang on.*

At one point, in the dark of night, I heard the door open, some footsteps.

I tried to form words, but they came out a strangled moan. I begged at the darkness, at whoever was there, to untie me.

Something landed roughly on the small of my back, causing my muscles to seize up further. It was a foot. Whoever it was, he was tugging at the sheet, using his bare foot for leverage. I felt a new tension in my shoulders, my thighs lifting higher off the ground. He'd only come in to tighten the knots.

By morning, I'd peed myself, having tried to hold it back as long as I could. I heard voices in the room. I knew they could smell the urine. Maybe they could see a puddle of it seeping from beneath my dress. I couldn't tell what they were saying, but at first they sounded offended. Then somebody was laughing. I felt sure they were making jokes about who would have to clean it up.

More hours passed. I lay awake and fully alert, my body stuck with hot pins. I tracked the calls of the muezzin, intoning in his minor key. Units of time had unfastened themselves from wherever they normally lived and were floating around me, big and small. I'd undergone another adjustment with the bindings: Someone had entered the room and wrapped what seemed to be a scarf around my neck, tying its ends into the sheet that kept my arms and legs in place, so that any time my head started to sag, the tension on the scarf caused me to choke. *They've studied this,* I thought. *They've consulted some manual on how to make a person suffer.*

I'd coached myself through a full year of captivity by breaking time into survivable pieces, telling myself to try to make it to the next day. When a day felt too big, I told myself to make it to the next prayer session or the next hour. Now, lost in the cacophony of my mind, I worked only to get myself to the next breath.

The pain in my body had begun to blend, engulfing me like a swirling, pulsating star. Elbows, back, neck, knees—they'd lost all their distinction. I felt the pain every second. I was never unaware of it.

But something else was happening, too. Some little compartment had hinged open in my mind, like a perch. If I steadied myself enough, I could rest there. I could observe the pain more calmly. I still felt it, but I could feel it without needing to thrash, without feeling like I was drowning in it. When I didn't thrash, the time floated by a little more easily. Though I'd figured out how to balance on that perch, it was only for a few minutes at a time. The hurt in my body always wrenched me back, setting my brain screaming again.

Every so often a voice cut into my thoughts—the same calming voice that always seemed to offer counsel, telling me I would be okay. This time, though I heard it, I couldn't believe it. I was wishing my captors would kill me so the pain would leave.

Jamal came in at one point and removed my blindfold and the scarf that had been holding my neck. The light flooded my eyes. I begged him to help me, but he only looked at me coldly.

"I am sorry," he said finally, his voice sounding flat. It seemed clear that he was not apologizing for himself. He was sorry I'd ended up in this situation, and that was it.

*

They came and went. They fussed with the ropes. They put the blindfold on and then took it off. When I screamed for help, they shoved a sock in my mouth, forcing me to breathe through my nose. I must have lost consciousness, because I woke to find Skids, on his hands and knees before me, peering intently at my face—checking to see if I was alive. Twice on that second day, they rolled me over onto my back, on top of my tied arms and legs, which caused my blood to flow into all the parts of me that had gone dead. The sensation was excruciating, a blast of stippling circulation, but it gave my limbs moments of relief. Each time, though, when they returned me to the stomach-down position, the pain felt worse than ever.

The calm voice tried to say things, but I argued with it now.

Breathe, it said.

I can't.

You're going to be okay.

I'm not. I'm going to die.

You won't die. Keep breathing.

I'm dying.

No, you're not.

It was afternoon again. Or that was my best guess. Mohammed and Abdullah came in and kicked at my ribs as I yowled into the sock. I floundered in the riptide of my own panic, my mind going limp with exhaustion. I knew I would die in that room. The pain was vivid to the point of being electric, electric to the point of being like lightning on water. I couldn't get away from it.

Then I felt a force whip through me like a strong gust of wind. It was like being seized by something, snatched, pulled upward. The pain was gone. I felt a bizarre, disembodied relief. Nothing at all hurt. I'd become unhitched, like a blown bit of dandelion drifting on a pillar of air. I was an observer, purely an observer, a self without a body. Maybe I'd died. I wasn't sure. I was high up in one corner, looking down at what was below.

From above, I could see two men and a woman on the ground. The woman was tied up like an animal, and the men were hurting her, landing blows on her body. I knew all of them, but I also didn't. I recognized myself down there, but I felt no more connected to the woman than to the men in the room. I'd slipped across some threshold I would never understand. The feeling was both deeply peaceful and deeply sad.

What I saw was three people suffering, the tortured and the torturers alike.

*

Late on the third day, about forty-eight hours after it began, they untied me. I don't know who undid the knots or whether anything was said. I slumped forward onto the floor. The blindfold was pulled off. The gag came out of my mouth. Someone rolled me over. They picked me up by my arms and legs and tossed me heavily onto my mat. The sun had set and the house had gone dark. I could see Mohammed kicking me again and again, but I couldn't feel it. They were yelling things at me. I squinted at them through bleary eyes. The words seemed to pour from their mouths in slow motion. I could feel myself drenched in sweat. My arms lay like dead things on either side of me.

Jamal loomed overhead. He was holding a bottle. I opened my mouth, and a curve of clear water arced toward it. Jamal poured half the bottle down my throat, the stream causing me to sputter and choke and to lift myself into a sitting position. Jamal was thrusting something new at me—a paper and pen. "Take, take," he was saying. They wanted me to write something down. My fingers couldn't grasp the pen. My hands were useless. I could see in the light of the boys' flashlights that they were a sickening shade of gray.

Abdullah was dictating notes for a phone call. "Today everything is changed. You tell your mum. Everything is changed." I couldn't take in what they wanted me to say. I was in too much pain.

I could hear the squawking of a phone on speaker being carried into the room. Skids held it to my face. Mohammed kicked one of my dead legs. The line crackled and spat, but my mother was on the other end.

"Amanda? Hello? Hello? Hello?" she said.

"Mummy."

"Amanda . . ."

"Mummy," I said, my head too drained to muster anything else, my need for her keener than it had ever been. "Mummy, Mummy, Mummy . . . Mummy . . . Mummy . . . Mummy . . . please."

42

The Bird

In the end, I said most of what they wanted me to say to my mother, though it was an effort just to form words. I said, as they had told me to, "Everything has changed," and I meant it. I told her I had been tied up and tortured. I told her I couldn't handle even one more day.

She told me they'd offered Adam half a million dollars, but he wouldn't take it.

Both of us wept the whole time on the phone. It felt like a farewell.

When the call was over, Skids and the boys filed out of my room, leaving me alone on the mat with a half-empty bottle of water. Just before exiting, Abdullah looked back at me. "Tomorrow we do to you again," he said. "Every day until your mother pay money, we do to you."

He left the room. The words fell like concrete blocks. This wasn't the end of the torture. It was just a reprieve.

They were going to come back and do it all over again.

A blackness edged over me. I understood then what it means to feel hopeless. To despair. To feel no trace of faith in anything. They were going to tie me up again.

I lay rigid on the mat as the blood flowed back into my joints with a rotoring intensity. My mind stayed stuck on one thing: It was going to happen again. They would keep going. They would push and push at this impossible idea that our families had millions of dollars to pay.

They would push for an eternity, because to them, time didn't matter. Time on earth was just time spent waiting for a chance at paradise.

They had figured out how to destroy me without totally extinguishing me. They'd keep me alive till they got their cash.

I heard a sound rise out of my lungs, a long keening sob, more animal than human.

Was this my life? It was.

I was done.

It would be better to die.

This was the calmest thought I'd had in a long time.

*

My razor, the straightedge my captors had given me months earlier to shave my pubic hair, had gone rusty in the humidity, its blade spittled with orange. But it could cut. I knew that because I still used it. I kept the blade tucked in its paper sheath among my toiletries, the little fortress of bottles I'd lined up next to my mat. With some pressure on the razor, I was sure I could slice open my wrists.

In the dark, I lay waiting for the sensation to come back to my hands. I curled and uncurled my fingers, feeling their function slowly return. I planned how it would go. I figured all I needed to do was jab myself hard and then rip the blade through the vein, right side first and then left. I guessed it wouldn't take more than twenty minutes, beginning to end. With some satisfaction, I imagined the boys coming in and finding me half alive, but not being able to save me. It gave me pleasure to think I could watch them lose their fortune as I died.

I decided I'd wait until the early morning to do it.

I had spent hours, many hours, in the last year being hard on myself. I'd chastised myself for the life I'd led, for all the self-indulgent things I'd done. I'd berated myself for having run stupidly into Somalia, for having empty ambitions, for believing I was invincible. I'd been mad at myself for never telling my mother that I forgave her for the ugliness of my childhood. I'd regretted the years I'd spent hating my body, starving it to stay thin. I'd wanted another chance to do all of it better, but now I accepted that it wouldn't come.

With that acceptance, I felt something different, soothing. A peace, a receding of my regrets, a low tide sliding back to leave a skirt of glittering beach.

Had I lived a life? I had. Had I seen the world? I had. I'd done things. I'd loved people. I'd seen beauty. I'd been fortunate. I was grateful.

By the time the first thin light slipped through the cracks in my shutters, I had thought, person by person, through my family and my friends, through everyone I would miss when I was dead. I felt saddest about Nigel, for leaving him alone there in Somalia. In my mind, I'd asked forgiveness, his and everyone's, for not trying to live longer. I'd sent love and hoped that somehow it would translate from my place on the mat, up over oceans and continents, to where each of them was. I'd cried a little, but I also felt ready. It was time.

What I wanted was to die quickly. I could hear, beyond my doorway, the sound of the boys sleeping out in the reception area—the occasional unconscious snort or sigh. The muezzin, I knew, was probably lifting himself from bed now, trundling through the dark toward the mosque with its pink neon to make his first call of the morning. Mornings, for me, had always been the most difficult, the drowsy moment when dream sorted itself from fact, when I woke just enough to realize the chains around my ankles. Sometimes I touched them to confirm that they were real.

I reached for the razor, and once it was in my hand, I lay back down, waiting another minute to make the first cut.

This is it, I thought.

But before I made a move, I felt a curious warm sensation spreading from the top of my head down through my body, like a liquid being poured into me. It relaxed me completely, making me feel as if I were melting into the mat. I didn't feel any pain. I felt like I was pooling into something larger, connecting to a new source of strength. Images flashed through my mind—beaches, mountaintops, the street I lived on with my mom and dad for the first six years of my life—almost as if I were being taken on a rapid-fire trip. Its clarity was piercing. I longed to see it all again, to be a part of it.

Something moved in the doorway. The early sun at a window in the reception area had washed a pale square of daylight onto the floor of my otherwise dark room. In the middle of it was a small brown bird, something like a sparrow, hopping back and forth on the dirty floor, cocking its head and pecking at the ground. The bird looked up, seeming to study the room and me in it. A moment later, it lifted off the ground and, in a flurry of feathers, was gone—flying through the door, back into the reception area, out toward the sky.

I hadn't seen a bird in nearly a year. I'd always believed in signs—in charms and talismans, in messengers and omens and angels—and now, when it most mattered, I'd had one.

I would live and go home. It didn't matter what came next or what I had to endure. I would make it through. I believed it with a sureness I hadn't felt since the beginning.

43

A Notebook and a Promise

R amadan finished. Our captors slaughtered a goat, ate it, and moved us again, to a house far out in the country, away from Kismayo and the coastline, somewhere back toward Mogadishu. Bush House, I called it. The house had a big sandy yard with two broken trucks rusting in one corner and a high stone wall that surrounded the whole place. A row of ragged trees grew on the other side.

Skids and the boys had not come back to tie me up the next day. The abrasions around my elbows and ankles slowly began to heal. A few days after I'd been untied, Skids had tossed a plastic bag into my room. Inside the bag were two new dresses, folded neatly, made of thin cotton, in bright floral prints. They were a gift, an acknowledgment that I'd suffered.

I sensed a lingering guilt among my captors over what had happened. Hassam and Jamal avoided me completely for several days. The others focused on the new dresses—asking me to try them on, complimenting me when I did, telling me I looked like a Somali woman. In truth, the fabric was too thin to feel comfortable. I felt exposed in the dresses and never wore them for long, sticking instead to the heavy red dress I'd worn for so long. Abdullah showed up in my room one day and gave me a small plastic tub of perfumed body lotion, telling me proudly that he'd paid for it himself. "From Germany," he said. It seemed his way of appeasing his own guilt. I opened the tub and sniffed it but never once put it on my body.

Romeo had not been present in the house during the days I was tied up. When I told him what had happened, he pretended to be surprised, but I could tell from his expression that he was fully aware. It was possible, even, that he'd been the one to issue the order. As the weeks passed, he'd grown increasingly morose. Allah, it turned out, had not wanted him to go to graduate school in New York after all. His departure date came and went with no money surfacing for a plane ticket. His fate was to stay with me and Nigel and the boys and Skids, to keep waiting.

We spent about six weeks in the Bush House, long enough that, through the bathroom window, I watched a sea of green wheat sprout and grow tall in the backyard, swallowing up the two trucks. It was raining again, the start of another season.

Romeo threw himself into teaching me to recite the Koran. He brought me Nigel's copy to study, leaving it with me overnight. Beginning from the back of the book, where the chapters were shorter, I learned the verses, usually five or six lines at a stretch, slowly working my way into longer passages, until I could chant thirty lines at a time in halting Arabic. I followed along with the English, trying to make sense of what I recited. *Allah is the light of the heavens and the earth. The parable of his light is as if there were a niche and within it a lamp: the lamp enclosed in glass: the glass as it were a brilliant star . . .*

Sometimes Romeo laughed at my pronunciation. Every so often, he'd slap me if I got something wrong. But once in a while I'd hit some benchmark and make him proud.

He'd summon the boys into my room so that I could chant for them, not unlike a prize canary. "You see?" Romeo would say to the boys, as if proving a point. "Amina is a good Muslim woman."

This always seemed to be the debate.

The Koran was traveling regularly from Nigel's room to mine and back, along with a hardcover book of *hadith*. I was allowed to sit up on my mat while reading them. When Romeo wasn't around, Hassam came and gave me my lessons. He seemed contrite over what had happened and went out of his way to check on me, bringing me tablets of ibuprofen and stealing back to my room once in a while with an extra cup of tea. He also allowed me to have a couple of the books that had come months earlier in the care package, sneaking them to me for a few hours at a time. To help with my Koranic studies, he brought me a pen, a pencil, and a thin unlined notebook with mint-green covers, the UNICEF logo emblazoned on the front.

Catching sight of the notebook one afternoon, Abdullah tore it out of my hands and waved it in my face. "Do you know what this is?" he said in a seething voice. He was pointing at the logo—a mother in profile, holding a young child against the backdrop of a globe.

I said, "UNICEF?"

His finger moved from mother to child. He looked at me emphatically. "Very bad."

He carried the notebook off, leaving me despondent. So far, I'd used it only to write down a few questions I wanted to ask Romeo or Hassam about the Koran, but it had mattered to me—the milk white of those pages, the freedom of making even a simple query visible in ink. About twenty minutes later, Abdullah returned, throwing the notebook onto the floor with disdain. He'd taken a marker and scribbled big black slashes over mother and child, abiding by the Prophet's rule that living beings were not to be displayed in artwork. Now it was okay to use.

I spent hours staring at that notebook, daring myself to record a real thought in it, worried that Romeo—the only one who could read English—would ask to see it.

In the meantime, I noticed that Nigel had used a pencil to underline some of the English verses in his Koran. On a blank page at the end of the book, he kept notes—a simple list of page numbers, marking verses I assumed he wanted to revisit. What he'd underlined concerned captives and laws about behavior. It seemed that Nigel, like me, had been using the Koran to argue for better treatment.

I decided to try something. I paged through the book, skimming the English, looking for individual words with which to make a message. When I found one, I'd underline the whole passage surrounding it lightly in pencil, but under the word I wanted him to notice, I'd make a firmer, more distinct line, almost as if drawing an arrow to it. I picked one word, then another, then another, and then, at the back

of the book, next to Nigel's notes, I wrote down an ordered list of the
page numbers on which they could be found. Later that afternoon, I
told Hassam I was finished studying the Koran for the day. I watched
him scuttle out the door with the book, trusting that he would bring
it to Nigel.

The message I'd sent went like this: I / love / you / my / mother / says
/ they / have / half / million.

The next day, when the Koran came back to me, I waited until I was
alone and then flipped to the end of the book. Nigel had jotted down a
new string of page numbers. My heart leaping, I whipped through the
corresponding pages, hunting for the references.

He'd understood the code and responded: I / want / home / I /
despise / men.

*

During the weeks we spent in the Bush House, we were getting mixed
signals about what was going on at home, whether any progress was
being made. Nigel and I had been allowed a few quick, scripted phone
calls. I'd overheard parts of one conversation Nigel had with his sister
Nicky on speakerphone, in which she told him the family had sold two
houses and a couple of cars.

One day Romeo came into my room, trailed by all the boys. He
said, "There is one chance. Your mother has five hundred thousand
dollars, and if she pays tomorrow, we accept that." He added, "She can
pay for you only, not Nigel. His family has money, and she is poor. But
she decides today if she will save you."

Moments later, his phone rang—a call being patched in from
Adam, with my mother on the line. "Make her understand you have
only this chance," Romeo said. He gestured toward the boys, standing
tall with their guns, and shrugged. "After this, I cannot say what they
will do to you."

With Romeo holding the phone in front of my face, I repeated
his message. I begged my mother to get me out, even if it meant me
alone. It crushed me to say the words. I knew Nigel would be able
to hear some of the conversation. I hoped he'd understand that this

was just another manipulation: Romeo was trying to assess how much money my family had. But my mother was resolute. The families were working together, she said. They had five hundred thousand dollars for both of us. There was nothing more they could offer.

Romeo then left the house, replaced for a few days by Ahmed, who arrived in his car, clean-shaven and in city clothes, a polo shirt and pressed pants. He brought a new proof-of-life question for me— *What is your father's favorite color?*—and did not hide his disgust at the squalor in which we were all living. Seeing that my feet were swollen and scabbed from mosquito bites, he ordered the boys to hang my mosquito net over my mat. I'd had it in my belongings all along but hadn't been allowed to use it since the time we'd escaped, nine months earlier.

It was less an act of goodwill on Ahmed's part and more, I figured, added insurance that I wouldn't get sick and die on him: Skids had fallen ill with malaria and spent his days curled in a ball on the floor. In order to reach the bathroom, I had to pass by where he lay, writhing in fever on the floor in the main room of the house. He looked hunched and craven, his bald head gleaming with sweat. I hoped he would die.

"Hunter green," I said to Ahmed. My father's favorite color.

I asked if he could give me an update on the negotiations, whether we would go home soon. Ahmed shook his head vigorously and delivered some chilling news. The group, he said, had given up on reaching an agreement with our families and was working instead to strike a deal to sell us to Al-Shabaab. Shabaab would then sell us back to our families.

He passed me a few pages of paper and a pen and ordered me to write out a statement for him, something he referred to as "the Promise." In it, I was to declare that wherever I ended up, I would adhere to the tenets of Islam and promote the faith. If I were freed, I needed to find a way to send him half a million dollars for jihad. He wanted me to put into writing exactly how I'd raise the money. I thought about it a minute and then wrote down that I'd start a jihadi website for profit and write a book that promoted Islam for women. Knowing how he loved documents, I used as much official-sounding language as I could, dropping in words like "hereby" and "herewith," in case that would help tip the balance toward our release.

At the bottom, I put a signature: Amina Lindhout.

Ahmed looked the whole thing over and told me it was good. Before leaving, he said, "*Inshallah,* your situation will be better soon."

I didn't believe him for a second. If they struck a deal with Shabaab, it would not be better. I felt sure, in fact, that things were about to get worse.

*

I took a chance, finally, and wrote something personal in the UNICEF notebook. I'd lived with the notebook for about a month. It had become a temptation I could no longer resist. Having the tools to write and not using them was like sitting in front of a meal and not eating it even though I was starving.

So one day I did it. I sat on my mat with the notebook flipped open in front of me, ready to slide it out of sight if anyone came into the room. I drew the blue mosquito netting around me like a curtain. Then I wrote a sentence, taking care to keep my writing so small that if any of my captors looked at it, they wouldn't be able to read it. My words, as they accumulated, looked like the writing of a lunatic, like strings of tiny pearls packed onto the page.

I phrased what I wrote as a letter to my mother, a one-way conversation. I told her about my days. I described how I passed the time by escaping in my mind, how, if I needed to use the bathroom, I had to bang an empty water bottle on the floor to get my captors' permission. I wrote about being hungry and lonely, and about the regrets that gathered at the edges of my mind each day, asking to be reviewed. The two things I deliberately didn't mention were religion and the abuse I'd suffered at the hands of my captors, knowing that those, more than anything, would get me punished if the journal were found.

Writing felt like defiance, an outlet, a vein opened up. I kept the notebook hidden under my mat and wrote in it almost daily, usually when the boys lazed around in their midafternoon torpor, always with the Koran or the book of *hadith* open on my lap so I could pretend to be studying. The guilt streamed out of me, old memories firing at close range. I wrote about how, years earlier in Afghanistan, during my first attempts at being a journalist, I'd visited a big prison outside of Kabul and, in the women's wing, had met a Sudanese woman who'd been arrested and sentenced to eight years in prison for attempting to smuggle heroin. She shared a cell with five other women. I'd taken note that the room was clean, that they had their own small bathroom. I remembered thinking, *Well, this isn't so bad.*

The Sudanese woman was heavyset and wore a flowered dress. She had corn-rowed hair and her eyes struck me as sad and empty. She had been the only prisoner in the cell who spoke English. She'd talked to me urgently, desperately, as if telling me her story would help get her out. "I'm sorry for what I did," she told me. "I want to go home."

My reply was something I now regretted deeply, the words of a young woman who knew nothing, understood nothing. I'd said something like "Yes, but you have to pay the consequence of your crime."

I'd given her no consolation. I'd only shamed her. The memory of it burned painfully in my mind.

To my mother, in the journal, I wrote, "I wonder sometimes if this has happened to me because I have been such a thoughtless person." I also made what was the very beginning of a larger vow. "I wonder, when I am free again, how I can help oppressed people. I owe it to everyone to make my life into something."

*

Our next move was to a ramshackle village. I could understand enough of the boys' chatter to know that we were now just outside of Mogadishu. Skids, the boys, and Nigel stayed in a grubby concrete house, while I was put in a windowless, attached storage room, which, judging from the droppings that littered the floor, recently held goats.

The fact that we'd moved nearer to the city might have made me feel hopeful—closer, even just a little bit, to a world I could recognize. In a different state of mind, I might have imagined the Mogadishu airport—the place Nigel and I had flown into two summers ago, feeling thrilled by the first canted glimpse we'd had of Somalia's golden coastline, the low-lying, unexplored city beyond. I might have listened for the sound of planes flying overhead and tried to calculate the distance between me and that tarmac, as Nigel and I had done so carefully before we'd escaped. But I didn't. I'd had my hopes raised and then dashed so many times now. I couldn't dream myself out of the leg shackles and over the wall surrounding the property and into a car driven by someone—anyone—who didn't fear or hate me, who would take me to a waiting plane.

To my chagrin, Skids had made a full recovery from his malaria, though the toll on his body was evident. He no longer looked like a militia captain but rather like a stooping dowager. The whole group seemed to wear the time more heavily. Hassam, who had always been small-framed, looked emaciated, swallowed up by his clothing. Romeo no longer lived with us. He'd come for a last visit while we were at Bush House, having abandoned all discussions about school or marriage. He'd talked only about the impending deal with Al-Shabaab. If it worked, the transaction would allow his group to pay off debts and turn a small profit. There were new men, he said, who couldn't wait to own us.

According to Romeo, Al-Shabaab had enough money to keep us alive and wait for the full ransom amount. They could hold out ten years or longer, he said.

"We cannot do this anymore, Amina," Romeo had told me, shrugging. "I am sorry about your luck."

★

One evening shortly after the six P.M. prayer, the door to the shed hinged open, revealing Skids, Abdullah, and Mohammed. All three of them had their faces wrapped in scarves. They were holding guns. My heart whirred. I knew it was time. A day or so earlier, as if signaling an end, Hassam had passed me a scrap of paper with his e-mail address written on it. "Hassam123" was his handle. "Maybe one day, *Inshallah*, you write me," he'd said.

Skids had me hobble inside the house, where I was given a new abaya—a thick gray satin thing—to wear over my jeans and then he waved me back outside, toward an SUV parked in the driveway. When I reached the car, he gestured for me to sit on the pavement. Abdullah produced a small bow saw and began to hack at the two padlocks that bound the chains to my ankles. He sawed wordlessly, switching from one leg to the other, the sweat dripping from his face onto my feet, the links twisting into my flesh with a bruising force. It seemed they'd lost the keys.

The saw blade grazed my ankle as Abdullah worked. Everyone around us was tense. I heard cell phones ringing. My captors came and went from the house, propelled by an urgency I didn't understand. Skids peered down impatiently at my legs, tracking Abdullah's progress with the saw. Eventually, Jamal came out, also wrapped in scarves, and took a turn, having me sit in the backseat of the car with the door open so he'd have better leverage. One padlock fell away. My ankle was so numb, I felt no difference.

As Jamal started work on the groove Abdullah had put in the second padlock, Nigel emerged from the house, limping in my direction. His chains had been removed. He was wearing a clean shirt and new jeans, and moving clumsily. His gaze stayed fixed on the ground. Just as my other foot was freed, he was pushed into the other side of the car.

I figured the new clothing and removed chains represented an attempt to spruce up the merchandise before they passed us on to Al-Shabaab, to show that we were worth the money paid for us. Nearly every one of the boys piled into the vehicle, while Skids took the wheel. Ahmed, I could see, was leading in a car up ahead. We commenced another swerving ride through the desert. Nigel and I said nothing to each other. Quietly, I began to cry. The sun was setting, and I remember how purple the land looked. I remember my stomach heaving with fear.

At some unnamable place, some characterless sandy path, we pulled over. Nigel and I were pushed hurriedly into another car, this one holding two Somali men we'd never seen. Ahmed tapped a finger on my window three times, indicating that I should roll it down. When I did, he bent to look at me.

"Don't forget the Promise," he said.

Romeo also appeared, holding Nigel's Koran, passing it to him through the window.

And then the new car took off—me, Nigel, and the two silent strangers—rocketing into the darkness before anyone could say a word. Nigel and I held hands, hiding our touch beneath the folds of my billowy new abaya. He kept his other hand resting on the Koran in his lap.

We'd been passed to Al-Shabaab, I was certain of it. I felt as if I were falling through space, as if I'd stepped off the top of a skyscraper and was plummeting with nothing to reach out for, my mind unable to catch on to one thought. I fell and fell and fell, so fast I was tingling, so fast it was all blackness, until the car lurched to a halt and we were tugged out into the night. Forty or more gunmen surrounded us in the darkness, shouting and waving, many of them hidden behind scarves. I felt shock, exhaustion. It was happening all over again. I clung to the open door of the car as some of the men pulled at my legs, trying to tear me away. It had been ten months since I'd taken a single full step without shackles on my legs. I stumbled and fell as they pushed me toward yet another car, an SUV parked with its headlights on by the side of the road. Men yelled and clamored and pointed guns at us. I was sobbing, screaming words I didn't recognize, batting at whoever's hands were near me. I was shoved into the backseat of the SUV. Nigel, who'd also put up a fight, had been thrust in ahead of me.

"I can't believe this is happening," I was saying. "I can't believe this is happening." Next to me, Nigel looked terrified.

The car doors slammed shut. We were surrounded by a new set of men—two sitting in the front seat, one in the back. I caught the faintest whiff of a long-forgotten scent—cigarette smoke. Someone in the car was a smoker. A realization bubbled from the recesses of my rational mind: A fundamentalist wouldn't smoke. The men in the car didn't belong to Al-Shabaab.

A gray-haired Somali man appeared at the window, a cell phone pressed to his ear. He leaned in and inspected us. He had a close-cropped beard and wide brown eyes and was the spitting image of the actor Morgan Freeman, as if he'd stepped right out of some movie set and was now standing alongside a car parked in the Somali desert, watching me sob. His expression was impassive, confused. "Why are you crying?" he said. He passed me his phone. "Here, talk to your mother."

And there was her voice, closer than it had ever sounded, my lifeline back to the world.

"Hello, hello?" she said. "Amanda, you're free."

44

Beginning to Understand

What came next felt both unreal and yet utterly vivid. Our captors, it turned out, had handed us over to a group of intermediaries, who then passed us on to the man standing at the side of our car, the man we began referring to as Morgan Freeman. He was a member of the Somali Parliament and was being paid by AKE, the security firm our families had hired. Working by phone over several weeks with John Chase, AKE's director, Morgan Freeman had helped arrange for the delivery of ransom—six hundred thousand dollars—transferred from Nairobi to a banking kiosk in Mogadishu earlier that day. Our families had been assured that a receipt for the money would be handed to some group of tribal elders, which, in a country lacking police, organized military, or a well-functioning government, constituted the only authority available. Once it was confirmed that Nigel and I were safe, the elders would withdraw the money and pass it on to the kidnappers, minus whatever debts were owed to other militia groups and presumably keeping some for themselves. Nobody here worked for free.

The plan that night was for me and Nigel to go directly to the airport in Mogadishu, where the same chartered plane and two men working for AKE—both of them former Special Forces soldiers, one from South Africa, one from New Zealand—waited to take us to safety in Kenya. But Morgan Freeman had made a critical mistake, failing to alert African Union peacekeeping forces that we'd be driving through the darkness to the airport, which was normally closed at that hour. When we turned down the road, the troops guarding the airport opened fire on our vehicle. We were forced to reverse direction and drive back toward the city.

It didn't matter that I'd spoken with my mother. It didn't matter that our captors appeared to be long gone. We were still in a car, hurtling at a panicky high speed. We were still in Somalia, still surrounded by armed strangers. No part of me trusted that we were free. After a while, the car skidded to a halt in front of a tall gate, and we were ushered into the open air. "Come, come," Morgan Freeman was saying, waving us through a door inside the gate.

My legs felt like stumps beneath me, unaccustomed to motion, let alone moving quickly. I fell twice trying to reach that door. Nigel stumbled, too. The two of us held on to each other, our arms intertwined. Through the door was a garden filled with manicured shrubs and a patio restaurant where Somali businessmen sat at plastic tables, eating dinner under the stars. We were at a hotel, a place to spend the night, waiting for morning, when it would be safer to reattempt the airport drive. The businessmen on the patio gaped as we wobbled past.

Nigel and I were rushed through the hotel reception area and into a ballroom filled with couches. Framed paintings of Mecca and ornate renderings of Islamic text hung on the walls.

"Please, please, here," Morgan Freeman was saying, directing us toward a red love seat in the center of the room. The room began to fill, men drifting in and surrounding us. Some wanted to shake our hands. A number of them spoke English, saying they'd heard bits of gossip about us over the months—the hostages who'd tried to escape. Several introduced themselves as officials with the transitional government. Many jumped on their phones, appearing to be spreading the news. "You are safe," the hotel manager kept saying. "You are safe." He told me I could take off my head scarf, but I didn't dare. A uniformed waiter materialized before us, offering two dewy bottles of Coca-Cola on a tray. Nigel and I stared, not quite bold enough to reach for them. When you have spent fifteen months having every move monitored and controlled, the first glimmers of independence can leave you stunned.

Both Nigel and I were too afraid to behave in any way like Western-ers. *"Allahu Akbar,"* we said to the men in the hotel ballroom when they congratulated us on our freedom. *"Inshallah,* we will soon go home."

Eventually, the hotel manager led us to two rooms on the same hall-way. He read the anxiety on our faces and kept repeating, as if it would mitigate it, that he had relatives in the United States. He gave us each clean towels and soap, toothbrushes and toothpaste. He handed me a fresh-smelling flowered dress that belonged to his wife.

Alone in the room, I felt like an alien landed on a new planet. A ceil-ing fan rotated overhead. The double bed held two pillows and faced a small television. Curtains were drawn over the windows. I locked the door and pushed the bedside table in front of it for good measure. In the bathroom, I turned the knobs on the sink to confirm there was run-ning water. I then peeled off the gray dress my captors had given me only hours earlier. Standing naked in front of the full-length mirror, I looked at myself for the first time in many months and was aghast at what I saw. My body was all bones. My skin looked waxy, so pale it had a bluish tint. My hair dangled in thin strands past my breasts, longer than it had ever been and dark after months hidden away from the sun. My ankles were ringed with purple bruises where the shackles had been. It was like looking at a stranger.

In the shower, I put the water on as hot as it would go, scrubbing myself all over. I did everything hurriedly, believing that the luxury of washing was something I'd lose at any moment. I clutched the bar of soap, feeling a little war going on in my mind.

Slow down, you're safe.

No, I'm not.

Yes, really, you are.

*

Afterward, Nigel and I sat together on the bed in my room. I'd tried to comb the knots from my hair but it fell out in clumps, so I'd given up. He, too, had showered and donned fresh clothes. His beard remained an untrimmed monstrosity. The officious hotel manager delivered us a couple of chicken sandwiches. Like the Cokes, they looked almost too strange to touch. Nigel and I held hands and talked, which in itself felt like a miracle. We were shy around each other, steeped in our individual uncertainties, hit by the night's surrealism. Were we really going home? Were our captors truly gone? When we heard a muezzin call for the final prayer and other hotel guests rustling down the hallway, we debated whether we should join the men in the ballroom and make a show of praying. In the end, we opted to stay in the room.

That we'd made a choice and we weren't punished for it felt like a second miracle.

Nigel and I talked through much of the night, neither of us interested in sleep. He asked questions about what had happened to me, about the extent to which I'd been abused, but I wasn't ready to discuss any of it with him. Everything felt too raw. We joked lightly about how we'd never eat bananas again, or canned tuna. We shared bits and pieces of information about the months after we'd been separated. Nigel had been allowed books and writing materials during his months of isolation. He'd been shackled for the duration, but never tied up and tortured as I had been. We reconciled ourselves to the fact that as a man, he'd received better treatment right through. We flipped on the television in the room and were startled to see a news story about our release playing on Press TV, the network I'd worked for in Baghdad.

*

The next morning, we flew out of Somalia, 463 days after we arrived, lifting away from the glittering coastline that at first glance had struck me as gorgeous, away from the city I'd once mistaken for calm. Landing in Nairobi, we were met on the tarmac by representatives from the Canadian and Australian embassies. I was put into a vehicle with little Canadian flags flapping from the side mirrors, and Nigel was loaded into an official-looking car of his own. Sirens blaring, we were driven to the Aga Khan University Hospital nearby.

The first person I spotted was my mother, waiting for me in the sunshine on the curb. She looked a little thin but beautiful. I was struck by how beautiful she was, in fact. It was as if time had folded in half, putting us back together as if nothing had ever happened. When she embraced me, we both wept hard. I rested my head in the crook of her neck. She rubbed my shoulders with one hand and kept the other pressed firmly against the back of my head. It felt like shelter. It felt like home.

She said the same thing over and over. "You made it. You made it. You made it."

At the hospital, Nigel and I were given rooms in a private wing, where we stayed for a week. His family—his mother and sister—had come to be with him. My father, too, flew to Nairobi, along with my old friend and traveling companion Kelly Barker, whose hair I had cut on the lakefront dock in Guatemala all those years earlier. Kelly, it turned out, had been a huge source of strength and a confidante for my mom while I was in captivity, driving from Calgary to visit, bringing her meals. After AKE was hired, Kelly had become part of the official "crisis management team," joining weekly Skype calls with John Chase and our families to discuss the case.

In my hospital room, I was tended by nurses, doctors, and a female psychologist who specialized in trauma and had been flown in from Canada. I was treated for dehydration and malnourishment, put on an IV, and given a battery of tests. A dentist examined my broken and abscessed teeth. One of the first things I requested was to have my hair cut short, ridding myself of the inches acquired in captivity.

I'd spent so many months fantasizing about food, imagining the day when I could choose what to eat, and then eat until I was full. And now it had arrived: The nurses brought me a menu before each meal. The first few days, I wanted everything all at once. Even as the doctors told me to take it easy, they didn't try to stop me from indulging, recognizing that I needed in that moment to exercise this most visceral form of freedom. I ordered chicken, pasta, vegetables, french fries, fruit, cake, and pie with ice cream. My heart boiled over with desire, but my body wasn't ready for any of it. My stomach cramped viciously after eating. I couldn't keep much down.

One afternoon, Kelly showed up, bearing a bag of food she'd bought in a fancy Nairobi supermarket—an extravaganza of gourmet cheeses and Cadbury chocolate. I'd always been an insatiable cheese-

and-chocolate eater. She'd teased me about it as we traveled together through so many humid, rice-eating countries, where such rich foods were scarce. Now, in the hospital room, we both laughed at the memories. But within moments, I was in tears. I knew that eating any of what she'd brought would only make me sick.

The frustration I felt echoed something larger I was only just beginning to understand. I was caught in a lag time: I was free, but I wasn't yet well.

That first week was something of a blur, not unlike the gradual waking from a nightmare. From the cloud of a soft bed, I'd open my eyes in the morning and feel a rush of disbelief. The pillow under my head, my mother sleeping on the couch nearby, a hairbrush set on the table, the vases full of flowers sent by well-wishers, the stretch of morning sky outside my window. All of it seemed illusory, capable of vanishing. Nigel and I huddled with our respective families, both of us just starting to really consider and process what we'd been through.

Slowly, I learned more about the work that had brought about our release—the stress and sacrifice and round-the-clock effort put in by Nigel's friends and family in Australia and mine at home in Canada, not to mention that of investigators, negotiators, and consular employees. The total cost of our freedom, including the bill from AKE, amounted to just over $1 million, shared equally by our two families. Old friends, distant relatives, and total strangers had stepped up to help. My dad and Perry had remortgaged their house. Restaurant-business friends in Calgary had held fund-raisers on our behalf. Robert Draper, the *National Geographic* writer, had flown to Canada to speak at one of them. People I'd never met on two continents had donated to our ransom fund, many in amounts of ten and twenty dollars, several contributing tens of thousands. Learning of it, I was humbled.

Early on, Nigel and I were given some surprising, happy news: After months spent believing that our captors had killed Abdi and the other two Somali men who'd been kidnapped with us, we learned that all three men were alive. In mid-January, roughly five months after we'd been captured, they'd been blindfolded in the middle of the night and driven into the heart of Mogadishu, where they were set free, unharmed, in a deserted marketplace.

I didn't learn what happened to Mahad and Marwali, but it turned out that Abdi, the cameraman, had relocated to Nairobi, having been granted refugee status after his ordeal in captivity. He'd felt unsafe returning to life as usual in Mogadishu. He couldn't afford to bring his wife and children with him, so they had remained behind. After I was released from the hospital, I spent another couple of weeks recuperating in Nairobi, staying with my parents at the home of the Canadian ambassador. One morning, I was able to arrange a meeting with Abdi at a local hotel.

He was the same as I remembered him—thin, handsome, soft-spoken. We hugged for a long time. He was trying to find freelance work as a videographer in Nairobi, but so far, wasn't having much luck. He showed me photos of his children at home, saying he missed them. Life as a refugee in a city that already teemed with refugees was difficult. Our kidnapping had left him rattled, unable to sleep at night, tormented by memories of being hungry and beaten and kept in the dark. Abdi had questions about my experience as a hostage. We compared notes on what we'd observed about the boys and the leaders. He and Marwali and Mahad had suffered greatly over five months. He couldn't fathom that Nigel and I had endured another ten. He gently asked if I'd been raped, and when I confirmed it, he began to cry.

Abdi called me his sister. I called him my brother. We were united, I could see, by what we'd both been through but also what we still yearned for. We wanted the same thing—not just to be free, but to *feel* free.

*

Nigel and I said our final goodbye at the Canadian ambassador's house in Nairobi late in 2009. We'd been free for two weeks. He'd left the hospital and stayed on at a hotel with his family, building up strength to make the trip home. We were pale and thin and haunted, but at least on the outside, we were beginning, slowly, to resemble normal people again.

I always assumed that we'd be friends forever, that we'd simultaneously move on while continuing to share—as we had over so many months—the minute intimacies of our inner lives. I figured that Nigel and I would always, in some way, be standing at our respective windows, swapping stories and finding ways to get each other through. On that first night of freedom in the hotel in Mogadishu, we made earnest promises to make visits and stay close. We wondered what it would be like to step into our former lives, full of people who couldn't possibly understand what we'd experienced. We said "I love you" again and again.

As soon as we reached Nairobi, though, our circumstances quickly began to tug us apart. There was lingering tension between our families over the stress and financial burdens they'd been forced to share. Nigel and I would go back to our respective countries and sink into our individual efforts to make sense of what had happened and to start new lives. I think it's safe to say that neither of us knew how challenging it would be.

For the first couple of months, we tried to Skype and e-mail, but our conversations were disjointed, sometimes tense. We are not the same people we were when we were taken. We've found it hard to connect, and this has been painful. Nigel wrote a book recounting his experience in Somalia and resumed his work as a photographer. I will always wish him well and be thankful for his strength and friendship during those fifteen months.

Returning to Canada just before Christmas, I was reunited with my brothers and Perry, with my grandparents, aunts and uncles, cousins and friends. I felt like a foreigner in my own life, half-caught in the world I'd left, sorrowful for the trouble I'd caused at home, yet surrounded again by people I loved, I also felt a pure and absolute joy.

Epilogue

For a while, I kept careful track of my freedom. I counted each hour, and day, and week that separated me from the 460 days I spent as a hostage. It seemed like a natural thing to do, to work some internal abacus, sliding and clicking the days until one part felt like the past and the greater sum became the present. Being free is something I will never take for granted. I'm grateful for even the smallest pleasures—a piece of fruit, a walk in the woods, the chance to hug my mom. I wake up every day feeling thankful for all that people have given me, from working to get me and Nigel out of Somalia to helping me adjust to life after captivity.

I have tried to make good on the promises I made to myself. I finally got the chance to attend university, completing a six-month diploma course in international development leadership at the Coady International Institute at St. Francis Xavier University in Nova Scotia in 2010. My course of study was chosen in service to another vow, one made from the depths of the Dark House—that somehow I'd find a way to honor the woman who charged into the mosque to help me after Nigel and I tried to escape, who literally threw her body over mine and fought until I was dragged out of her arms.

When I think about Somalia, I think about her. I can picture her face, her head scarf ripped away, her eyes wet with tears. I never knew her name. I don't know whether she lived or died.

It was for her, really, that six months after my return to Canada, I founded a nonprofit organization called the Global Enrichment Foundation, to help support education in Somalia. I'd spent so much time in captivity wondering about the boys who guarded me, specifically, whether they'd have been different—less entrenched in religious extremism and war—if they'd had more opportunities to go to school, and maybe more meaningfully, if they'd been raised in homes where their mothers and sisters had been able to attend school. The Global Enrichment Foundation partners with other organizations to help bring about change in Somalia—from providing food aid to supporting girls' basketball teams and funding full, four-year scholarships to thirty-six bright, ambitious Somali women attending university. Several of the GEF's projects, including funding a primary school and the construction of a community library, are happening inside Dr. Hawa Abdi's camp, the same place Nigel and I had set off to visit on the day we were kidnapped.

*

About a year after Nigel and I were released, I received a phone call from Ottawa. A National Security officer informed me that in a shed somewhere outside of Mogadishu, a notebook had been discovered. It had the UNICEF insignia on its cover, though the image had been blacked out with a marker. Inside were pages of cramped writing. Somehow, through a network I'll never know or understand, the notebook had been passed on to the Canadian authorities. I was given a scanned set of those pages. My whole body shook when I first dared to look at them. Even today, I see that writing and feel the stream of desperation running beneath the words.

There are days when my memories of Somalia loom and oppress, and other days when they take up less space in my mind. I suspect it will always be this way. In the nearly four years since I was freed, I've learned a lot about trauma—about what it does to both the brain and the body. One morning when I was attending a lecture at school in Nova Scotia, a classmate sitting next to me ate a banana, leaving the peel on the table near my notebook. The smell ambushed me, triggering instant panic, unlocking a memory I'd kept out of reach in some far corner of my mind—of a day in the Dark House when I discovered a rotten banana peel on my floor and was so hungry and desperate that I ate it. Suddenly, all the old sensations were back—pain, hunger, terror—and I ran from the classroom, locking myself in a bathroom stall, feeling like I couldn't tell what was real and what wasn't, wondering whether my freedom was only a dream.

I've realized that the world is, in essence, full of banana peels—loaded with things that may unwittingly trip an internal wire in my mind, opening a floodgate of fears without warning. I continue to be afraid of the dark, to have nightmares that jolt me awake at night. In confined spaces, such as elevators, I sometimes feel like I can't breathe. Often when a man gets close to me, my mind screams, *Run!* My body too carries the memories. My ankles sometimes ache as if they were shackled; my shoulder sockets get sore as if my arms were still tied.

Dealing with the aftermath of trauma is not something anybody can do alone. I went through a specialized treatment program to help me cope with symptoms of Post Traumatic Stress Disorder. I've also worked regularly with therapists, psychologists, psychiatrists, acupuncturists, nutritionists, and meditation experts. All have helped me in different ways. I've also found comfort in talking with other women who've survived rape. Yet even so, there are times when I feel deeply alone with what happened to me, mismatched to my surroundings—to regular everyday life. There is still plenty I long for—for education, new adventures, and opportunities to be of service to others, and also for love and a life that someday includes children.

I remain focused on healing. I've sought out quiet places to reflect, continuing to travel, to find sustenance, as I always did, out in the world—in the mountains of India, in the jungles of South America, and in Africa, where my work for the foundation sometimes takes me.

*

It's hard, of course, to feel comfortable with the fact that my captors profited from our kidnapping. Since my release, I've followed stories of other hostages—in Somalia, in Mali, in Afghanistan, Nigeria, Pakistan and elsewhere—and felt anxiety and empathy for everyone involved. Some governments quietly pay ransoms. Others strike diplomatic deals or send in armed commandos. Many, including the Canadian and U.S. governments, try to provide family support while also maintaining a hard line about further fueling terrorism and hostage-taking through ransom payments. As one U.S. State Department official put it in an interview with the *New York Times Magazine*, "If you're out there feeding the bears, the bears are going to keep coming into the camp."

Still, try telling that to a mother, or a father, or a husband or wife caught in the powerless agony of standing by.

I think often about the boys who held me hostage. How could I not? My feelings about them can't be easily measured or fixed, especially as time goes by. That's another set of sliding abacus beads. For my own good, I strive toward forgiveness and compassion above all the other feelings—anger, hatred, confusion, self-pity—that surface in me. I understand that those boys and even the leaders of the group were products of their environment—a violent, seemingly unending war that has orphaned thousands of children and reaches back over twenty years now.

I choose to forgive the people who took my freedom from me and abused me, despite the fact that what they were doing was absolutely wrong. I choose also to forgive myself for the impact that my decision to go to Somalia had on family and friends at home. Forgiving is not an easy thing to do. Some days it's no more than a distant spot on the horizon. I look toward it. I point my feet in its direction. Some days I get there and other days I don't. More than anything else, though, it's what has helped me move forward with my life.

One of the Global Enrichment Foundation's programs has been to help create a school for Somali women living as refugees in Eastleigh, Kenya—a run-down section of Nairobi known as Little Mogadishu. In the winter of 2012, I spent several weeks there, arranging for computers and supplies, meeting with teachers and some of the seventy-five women who had signed on as students, listening as they described the sorts of skills they hoped to acquire. The school was set up to offer computer and literacy classes, job skills training, medical workshops, and information sessions on the legal rights of refugees. One afternoon, I attended a meeting with Nellius and Farhiya, the school's two teachers. Joined by the GEF's program director, we sat in a small classroom at the community center where we'd rented our initial space. Pinned to the walls were colorful posters of vegetables, animals, and numbers, each labeled with the corresponding English word. The four of us were there that day to brainstorm ideas for the new school's name, writing various options on a big black chalkboard.

A single possibility stood out among the others, and one of the women drew a thick circle around it with white chalk. *Rajo* was the name we picked for the school. It's the Somali word for *hope*. And hope, we all agreed, is the best thing in the world.

Acknowledgments

T here were so many people who supported us as we worked on this book. Thanking them is the most joyful part of all.

We are grateful for the incredibly smart and compassionate team at Scribner and Simon & Schuster: Daniel Burgess, Kara Watson, Brian Belfiglio, Lauren Lavelle, Leah Sikora, Greg Mortimer, Mia Crowley-Hald, Beth Thomas, Colin Harrison, Paul Whitlatch, Tal Goretsky, Kevin Hanson, David Millar, Rita Silva, Elisa Rivlin, Elisa Shokoff, Roz Lippel, and Susan Moldow. And finally, to the incomparable Nan Graham, who is wise, passionate, and so very gifted with her editorial pencil: Thank you, Nan, for caring so much.

At ICM Partners, we had a humbling amount of help from Kristyn Keene, Heather Karpas, Liz Farrell, and John DeLaney, and most especially from Sloan Harris, who understood early on what we wanted to do and with unwavering grace and marvelous ferocity helped us get there.

To our friends and early readers, who offered editorial insight, pep talks, and courage, we are so very thankful: Caitlin Guthiel, Debra Spark, Lily King, Susan Conley, Anja Hanson, Peggy Orenstein, Beth Rashbaum, Susan Casey, and Elizabeth Weil. Anouar Majid and Dina Ibrahim loaned their eyes to the Arabic in the book; Hassan Alto checked the Somali. Anne Connell offered early copy editing support.

And Tom Colligan poured his heart into fact-checking the manuscript, becoming a friend and ally along the way.

This book emerged from innumerable hours of recorded conversation between the two of us and long interviews with others: Thank you to Kimberly Wasco, Emily Umhoeffer, Caitlin Allen, and Annie Sutton for helping with transcription.

We are grateful for the work of a number of journalists who have focused on Somalia and on the global epidemic of hostage-taking. Special thanks to Jeffrey Gettleman and Mohamed Ibrahim of the *New York Times*, who have covered Somali war, politics, and culture with exceptional intelligence; their reporting provided consistently helpful background. The reference to the payroll and accounting of Somali hostage-takers on pages 321 and 322 comes from Jay Badahur's excellent book, *The Pirates of Somalia: Inside Their Hidden World*. Robert Draper, who initially introduced us and has written insightfully on Somalia, forever has our friendship and gratitude.

Ilena Silverman belongs in a category all her own. A steady friend and incisive editor, she asked all the right questions at all the right times. Our debt to and respect for her is enormous.

And to Dr. Katherine Porterfield of the Bellevue/NYU Program for Survivors of Torture, who gave selflessly and expertly to this process in so many ways. From the bottom of our hearts, thank you.

*

From Sara:

A MANDA'S FAMILY IN Canada opened its doors to me with uncommon warmth and generosity. I'm grateful to Lorinda Stewart, Jon Lindhout, and Perry Neitz for their excellent record-keeping and unending willingness to answer questions. Thanks to Pascal Maître for his time and beautiful images of Somalia, to Ajoos Sanura and Abdifatah Elmi for the hours spent with me in Nairobi, and to Sasha Chanoff and everyone at RefugePoint for the humbling introduction to the people of Eastleigh.

I am sincerely thankful for the friends, writers, teachers, and neighbors who support, inspire, and indulge me—the always-bright stars in my sky, so numerous they can't all be named here. Specific gratitude goes to my family: to Dick and Marianne Paterniti; Manny Morgan; Lorraine Martin and Diane Bennekamper; my brothers and their families; the extended Simmons, Corbett, and Paterniti clans; and above all, to my amazing father, Chris Corbett, who gives me shelter in so many ways. I am grateful to others who've also kindly provided quiet places to work: Emily and Steve Ward, Melanie and Eliot Cutler, Patty and Cyrus Hagge, Aimee and Mark Bessire. Thanks to those who've kept me merry, fed, and generally together during this time: Andy Ward, Jenny Rosenstrach, Joel Lovell, Liz and Pierre Meahl, Lynn Sullivan, Derek Pierce, Andrea Hanson-Carr, Mark Bryant, Alan Liska, Kim Wasco, Ned Flint, Benjamin Busch (the Marine in my basement), Linda Murray, Lane and Brock Clarke, Joe Appel, Carlos Gomez, Angela Weymouth, Michael Seymour, Chris Bowe, and Stuart Gerson, not to mention the ever-vibrant crew of kids and adults at The Telling Room, who again and again remind me that the world is very much okay. And extra-deep thanks to Clare Hertel, Anja Hanson, Hallie Gilman, Susan Calder, Susan Conley, Lily King, Katie Redford, Peggy Orenstein, Sara Needleman, and Melissa McStay—my dear, everyday, lodestar friends.

To my husband, Mike Paterniti, who has shown me that life is much more fun when you dive headfirst and heart-first into everything: Thank you for all of it, big and small. And to our incredible children, exuberant divers-in, all three. I love you very much.

And finally, I'd like to express my love and gratitude to Amanda—for our three-year mind meld, for all you've taught me about being strong, for the many psychic miles we have traveled together, for the absolutely tireless way you worked on every line of this book, for staying open, for being a friend. I treasure all of it. I'm proud of what we've made together.

★

From Amanda:

I AM GRATEFUL, FIRST and foremost, to my mom Lorinda Stewart, and my two dads, Jon Lindhout and Perry Neitz, for their

Herculean efforts to rescue me. I am humbled by their courage and love and have the deepest appreciation for what they have endured, the sacrifices made. My brothers, Mark Culp and Nathaniel Lindhout, my grandparents, and the entire Lindhout and Stewart clans were anchors of strength throughout; and following, they have ensconced me in the warm embrace of family, tucking me into their hearts. Aunt Alison—an extra special thank-you. To my godparents, Wendell and Beryl Lund, for the many ways they have cared for me.

To those who have nurtured me, loved me, and encouraged me to play: Zoe, Brenna, Nicola, Zahra.

My dearest friend Kelly—for your generous spirit, your determination, and for giving me a beautiful, smiling goddaughter who delights in the wonders of the world.

In Calgary, Sarah Geddes, David Singleton, Michael Going, and Steve Allan took a stand for me, and because they did, I lived to write this book.

I am reminded, again and again, of the prevalence of generosity and goodness. In Red Deer, Calgary, Sylvan Lake, Rocky Mountain House, Ponoka, Nelson, and across Canada and Australia, people gave generously to bring Nigel and me home. These many kindnesses have shored me up. There are too many people to name, and I wouldn't want to leave anyone out, but you know who you are. Allan Markin, Gord Scott, Dick Smith, and Bob Brown stand out for special recognition.

To the entire Brennan family for their perseverance and many contributions.

I recognize efforts made by the Government of Canada, RCMP, DFAIT, and CSIS on my behalf. In particular, I'd like to thank Ross Hynes and his lovely wife, Vanessa, for their steadfast devotion to my case. I am forever indebted to Richard, Jonathan, Chris, Matt, Evelyn, and their families.

A successful release would not have been possible without the assistance of AKE, and I am indebted to JC, Ed, Shaun, Alto, and Derek for swooping in to save the day.

I am earnestly learning about trauma recovery and feel gratitude for the education I received at Sierra Tucson on Post-Traumatic Stress Disorder. The serenity of the facility and gifted therapists gently helped me move forward, mindfully, into the sunshine. I am especially thankful to Dr. Mark Pirtle, Joanne Sorenson, and Dr. Judy Gianni.

To Katherine Porterfield, again, for understanding all the parts of this journey. I am so fortunate you held out your hand to help me along. I love you.

Many top-notch professionals have supported my recovery process: the doctors and nurses at The Aga Khan University Hospital in Nairobi, Karen Barker, Dr. Charl de Wet, Patti Mayer, Dr. Tim Kearns, Dr. Lizette Lourens, Dr. Rick Balharry, and the wonderful teachers at the Hoffman Institute Foundation in Canada.

Eckhart Tolle, your teachings, gentle guidance, friendship, and thoughtful insights encourage me and have shaped my perspective in more ways than you could possibly know.

Heather Cummings and João Teixeira de Faria have shown me that anything is possible. Thank you to the generous patrons of the St. Ignatius Fund.

The entire team at the Global Enrichment Foundation, past and present, in Canada, Kenya, and Somalia, for working so very hard with open minds and hearts. I am proud of what we have done together and excited about what the future holds.

To Nigel: As our old friend Thierry once told us at the Baro Hotel, "Many good things." Wishing you, Nigel, many good things.

And here at the end, to Sara, my coauthor, confidante, and friend, who saw the promise in this project from the very beginning. I am immeasurably grateful. Three years ago we took a leap of faith and began a long journey. Much more then merely writing, we lived this story a thousand different ways together. Without your meticulous intelligence, infinite patience, and precision, I doubt it could have been told. I have the deepest appreciation for your wisdom, your commitment, and your faith in me. My life is infinitely richer because you are in it.

A SCRIBNER READING GROUP GUIDE

A House in the Sky

Topics & Questions for Discussion

1. Above all else, Amanda identifies herself as a traveler, an identity born out of her childhood obsession with *National Geographic*. Why do you think *National Geographic* had such a large impact on her? What led Amanda to make the leap from the legions of armchair travelers into someone whose life revolved around her journeys?

2. On page 14, Amanda discusses sneaking into an amusement park after dark, with a childhood friend. She writes, ". . . we allowed ourselves to relax and feel giddy, forgetting that it was dark and we were trespassing, forgetting everything that scared or haunted us . . ." How does this childhood memory reflect Amanda's experience traveling to foreign countries and unknown places? Is part of the thrill of travel related to risk?

3. Amanda's first trip, to South America, initially disappoints her because Caracas doesn't feel foreign. What does this demonstrate about the different ways people travel? As she leaves Caracas and ventures into the kind of journey she'll come to crave, what changes for her?

4. During this trip to South America, Amanda confronts the experience of venturing off the beaten path, and defines the feeling of the frontier as "a knifepoint between elation and terror" (p. 34). How will this balance come to define her travels?

5. The memory of cutting her friend Kelly's hair will become one of the things that sustains Amanda throughout her captivity. Why do you think this memory sticks with her?

6. In Dhaka, Amanda experiences what she sees as the "beautiful" side of Islam, but also confronts the dangers inherent in being a solo female traveler in that particular place. How does this dichotomy influence her experiences in captivity?

7. On page 67, Amanda quotes Paul Theroux's *Dark Star Safari*, "All news out of Africa is bad. It made me want to go there . . ." Both Nigel and Amanda understand this sentiment, and it's partially what draws them to Somalia. What do you make of the idea that bad news would bring someone to a place?

8. Amanda's time in captivity is spent trying to negotiate the best way to stay alive—she vacillates between trying to understand and connect with her captors; through things like converting to Islam, and resistance like trying to escape. Why do you think Amanda and Nigel have such different takes on how to best manage their captivity? What do you think are some of the advantages and disadvantages of each method?

9. When Amanda overhears a report of their capture on the radio, she writes of the feeling as "crushing. It was confirmation that our troubles were both real and deep" (p. 146). Why do you think this affects her so powerfully?

10. When Amanda is given an English-language Koran, it is the beginning of her "conversion" to Islam. How does Amanda's relationship with Islam change throughout her time in captivity? As she reads the Koran and begins to understand it, and thus her captors, better, how does her awareness of her situation change?

11. Amanda reflects throughout the book on the strangeness of the relationships with her captors—even though they were imprison-

ing her, she attempted to feel compassion and understanding for them. Were you surprised that this was possible? Discuss Amanda's relationships with Jamal, Ali, Adam, and the rest.

12. Nigel and Amanda's relationship as fellow captives is at times extremely difficult. Discuss their different ways of coping. How did you feel when Nigel told Amanda "I think you should just take this one"? Did you blame Nigel?

13. Throughout the book, and in particular during her captivity, Amanda uses mantras to calm herself. What does she find so effective about repeating simple words and phrases? Why do you think this kind of practice can be soothing?

14. On page 220, Amanda writes about what being alone does to her mind, and refers to a kind of psychic energy that seemed insane before her captivity, but became more believable. What did you make of her account in your reading? Have you ever experienced this kind of psychic energy?

15. Discuss Amanda's "house in the sky" (p. 292). How does this dream help her maintain hope, and survive?

16. Of writing notes to Nigel, Amanda says ". . . writing it helped me to believe it. It staked some claim on the truth (p. 226)." How does this idea relate to Amanda's decision to write a book about her experience? How does Amanda's relationship with writing evolve over her time in captivity?

17. How did reading *A House in the Sky* change your understanding of the role fundamentalist religion can play in a war-torn society? How did it change your perception of Somalia? What surprised you most in your reading?

Enhance Your Book Club

1. Since her release, Amanda has dedicated herself to humanitarian efforts, including some that have brought her to Africa, and back to Somalia. Visit her website: AmandaLindhout.com and learn about the Global Enrichment Foundation, globalenrichment foundation.org. How does the knowledge of Amanda's work after her captivity alter your understanding of the book?

2. Amanda is active on social media. Connect with her on:

   Facebook (https://www.facebook.com/AmandaLindhoutPage)
   Twitter (https://twitter.com/AmandaLindhout)
   YouTube (http://www.youtube.com/user/globalenrichment)
   Instagram (http://instagram.com/amandalindhout#)
   Twitter (https://twitter.com/AmandaLindhout)